CONFLICTED

CONFLICTED

**MAKING NEWS
FROM GLOBAL WAR**

ISAAC BLACKSIN

STANFORD UNIVERSITY PRESS
Stanford, California

Stanford University Press
Stanford, California

© 2024 by Isaac Blacksin. All rights reserved.

No part of this book may be reproduced or transmitted in any form or by any means, electronic or mechanical, including photocopying and recording, or in any information storage or retrieval system, without the prior written permission of Stanford University Press.

Printed in the United States of America on acid-free, archival-quality paper

Library of Congress Cataloging-in-Publication Data
Names: Blacksin, Isaac, author.
Title: Conflicted : making news from global war / Isaac Blacksin.
Description: Stanford, California : Stanford University Press, 2024. | Includes bibliographical references and index.
Identifiers: LCCN 2024003579 (print) | LCCN 2024003580 (ebook) | ISBN 9781503638242 (cloth) | ISBN 9781503639447 (paperback) | ISBN 9781503639454 (ebook)
Subjects: LCSH: War—Press coverage. | War correspondents. | Reporters and reporting. | Journalism—Objectivity. | Newspapers—Language.
Classification: LCC PN4784.W37 B63 2024 (print) | LCC PN4784.W37 (ebook) | DDC 070.4/333—dc23/eng/20240205
LC record available at https://lccn.loc.gov/2024003579
LC ebook record available at https://lccn.loc.gov/2024003580

Cover design: Daniel Benneworth-Gray
Cover art: Report on the details of the Charge of the Light Brigade at the Battle of Balaklava of the Crimean War, *The Times* (London), November 13, 1854; sourced from the British Newspaper Archive

For Judy. I miss you.

CONTENTS

Preface   ix

INTRODUCTION
War's Lobby: The Displacements of Journalism in Wartime   1

        INTERLUDE   CHEAPENING EXPERIENCE   24

PART I
The Language of War Reportage and Its Conditions

ONE
Folklore of the Future: The Certainty of Journalistic Expression   29

TWO
Visible System and Invisible Rules: 60
Commodifying Common Sense

        INTERLUDE   AVAILABLE STORIES   90

PART II
The Meaning of War Reportage and Its Exclusions

THREE
Extermination as Protection: Depoliticizing War,   93
Remoralizing Violence

FOUR
Power Speaking to Truth: Struggles with the Problem of War   120

                     INTERLUDE   WHAT TO MAKE OF IT   153

PART III
The Practice of War Reportage and Its Contradictions

FIVE
Writing Conflicts: The Tension Between Experience and Expression   157

SIX
Agitation at the Margins: Return of the Journalistically Repressed   184

                     INTERLUDE   LEAVING MOSUL   215

CONCLUSION
War's Exit: Entangled Possibility in the Age of Endless Conflict   219

EPILOGUE
From Mosul to Mariupol   233

Acknowledgments   241
Notes   245
Bibliography   283
Index   307

PREFACE

> Birds flying home together—
> There is meaning in this to know but not to say.
> —TAO YUANMING

I stood at the bay window at the end of the terminal watching Blackhawk helicopters return from the Nineveh plains. In the airport, big men with clipboards appeared busy, dark suits rushed past, a C-130 transport plane lumbered to the apron. War was underway.

What can we know of the recent wars in the Middle East, what can be said, and how might we account for the difference? Arriving to Erbil as conflict in Syria deepened and conflict in Iraq intensified, I wanted to understand war's journalistic representation and what is experienced in the process of representing war. Journalists were then flocking to Erbil, and as I hurried through customs and into the gathering dusk, I wondered if they'd find the war for which they came.

There is no "arrival scene" in war reportage. This conventional ethnographic device, deployed to authenticate the ethnography and to authorize its author, is journalistically nonsensical. The omniscience of war reportage forecloses the self-reflexivity—however performative—the arrival scene demands, while the omnipresence of war reportage confers the position of the already-arrived. The journalistic gaze, narratively imparted, is ever fixed on the war underway.

Because the news, it would seem, never stops, and never does it quite begin; in the endless stream of events, journalism must merely keep pace. In this sense, any scene of arrival would undermine rather than augment the authenticity of journalism as an always-renewing "first draft of history." War can be self-evident in its journalistic representation, and journalism objective and true, in part because war and war reportage do appear concurrently. The apparent synchronicity of violence and its documentation are what the discourse and its market demand.

And yet journalists do, of course, arrive. In the late summer of 2016, as *Wired* magazine declared the Islamic State conflict "the world's most important beat" (Roper 2016), journalists were converging in Erbil in anticipation of what would become the largest military operation since the 2003 US invasion of Iraq, and the worst urban combat since the Second World War. Many of these journalists had been covering Iraq and Syria from regular posts in Baghdad, Beirut, and other regional cities. Also arriving were freelancers from around the region and indeed around the world, some of whom had been reporting most recently from the war in Syria. That conflict's growing dangers, and the global attention on Iraq, prompted many freelancers to shift focus. Then there were the "parachuters": magazine writers, special correspondents, those on short-term assignment. Many of this group were well known from previous wars, recognizable by book jackets and TV talking-head spots. Some were once based in the Middle East full-time; others had roved through a dozen wars around the world. Together, these journalists—staff and freelance, green and grizzled, from near and far—are the subjects of this book, observed and interviewed between 2014 and 2018 across Iraq, Lebanon, Syria, and beyond.

When I began my research, the war in Syria was still metastasizing. Homs was back under Syrian state control; Hama and Aleppo were in contention as the opposition fragmented; neither the Russian nor US militaries had yet intervened directly. Some prominent journalists had died. The Islamic State controlled Raqqa and, in Iraq, had recently taken Mosul, the country's second-largest city. The United States would soon conduct airstrikes against the group, joining Iran, and videos of the executions of foreign journalists would soon circulate. Erbil and even Baghdad seemed threatened. In Lebanon, refugees streamed in and tensions rose. The wars in Syria and Iraq intertwined and internationalized.

By the conclusion of my research, the world's attention on the region had largely waned. The war in Syria seethed onward, but the Islamic State was no longer a primary global threat militarily or rhetorically. Many of the journalists in my study—those whose words and experiences are related here—had moved on. The news must be *new*, after all.

In the middling years of the so-called Global War on Terror, many journalists were eager for the kind of war expected of the name, and the kind that allowed for war reportage as generically understood through the twentieth century.[1] With a few exceptions, the era of major military battles—with frontlines to visit and pitched offensives to observe—seemed bygone. Left was the automated drone strike and the counterinsurgency night raid, the scattered air war and the far-flung special operation, the asymmetric siege and the routine occupation, the black sites and the IEDs and the blast walls everywhere. From the perspective of news producers, a degree of nostalgia loomed. Past, journalists assumed, was the sustained, cinematic combat that can be consistently accessed, easily witnessed, and most dramatically told—the sort of war formative to war reportage as a practice and a discourse.

I had my own expectations, not unrelated. After interviewing and observing journalists in Baghdad and Beirut—and, before that, in Kabul—the mass concentration of war reporters in a single site, and the ethnographic opportunities that might result, seemed unlikely. With wars endless and pervasive, journalistic coverage tended to be episodic and defuse. The economic pressures roiling the news industry, the wide availability of the technologies of mass mediation, and the lack of news-consumer interest in atomized and complex conflicts made the enduring wartime presence of a global journalistic community improbable. I'd assumed that war would no longer receive the daily, focused coverage that necessitated consistent and concentrated journalistic resources. I considered such wartime media circumstances similarly bygone.

Yet there we all were in Erbil, with notepads open and helicopter gunships in the sky. This would be a war as war is imagined to be, one with the access and the interest to drive significant journalistic engagement. Some journalists were about to experience their first war; others would try to relive that experience. All hoped to get good stories, and a few would not survive the attempt. Around the flophouses and cafés of Erbil, I could feel the gaze of the international press fixed on northern Iraq. And on the horizon, the awful news of suffering and death, of violence cruel and lawless, of soldiers amassed to intervene.

As this book goes to press, the war against the Islamic State is no longer of much media concern.[2] The War on Terror broadly, in its journalistic representation, is again largely scattershot and obscured. As an overarching military paradigm, as a cypher for societal fears and desires, and as a rationale for bloated defense budgets, the War on Terror may even be losing its grip. The US withdrawal from Afghanistan signals a turn in military priorities; the war in Syria is mostly ignored; other conflicts—in Yemen, Somalia, Sudan—flash in the international press before fading to the background. The war in Ukraine overwhelmed the news cycle and diverted global news resources, though that conflict too, lurching toward a stalemate, dims in popular awareness. But on October 7, 2023—just a few days after US National Security Advisor Jake Sullivan declared the Middle East "quieter today than it has been in two decades"—intensifying violence returned media attention to the Middle East. After a mass killing in Israel, more bombs were dropped on Gaza in a week than in the worst year of the US war in Afghanistan. The rate of casualties—some ten thousand killed in a month, 40 percent of them children—was higher than in any war of recent memory. Journalists too were dying at record levels in Gaza, and news coverage was wall-to-wall. Counterinsurgency had resumed its bloody mandate. So too did journalism.

This book tracks journalism's path to a conflicted present. Reportage from the War on Terror often justified mass killing on the basis of intentions that could not be proven. Disseminating official claims to self-defense and security management and humanitarian rescue, journalists represented civilian death as an incidental necessity of war rather than a strategic feature. In Gaza, such rationalizations have foundered.[3] Given the representational tensions assessed in the chapters to follow, the increasing bankruptcy of dominant justifications for human suffering might have been predicted. Predictable too is a growing disidentification with the war reporter's steadfast position of address: the witness to suffering who remains above the fray. As the War on Terror mutates, if not quite fades away, journalists reckon with an audience less inclined to grant the benefit of the doubt to war makers *or* news makers. Recent wars, and recent war reportage, anticipate these shifts in the politics of journalistic representation.[4]

After arriving in Erbil, I rented a room and opened my laptop. I considered what was being said about the war and what journalists would say to me. As I scrolled through the reportage, a gap between war and its representation was already becoming apparent, but to what ends I could not yet grasp. I read the news and listened to the gunships fly by.

CONFLICTED

INTRODUCTION

War's Lobby

The Displacements of Journalism in Wartime

> Thus I stood there, safe and sound, and let the furious tumult pass by me.
> —JOHANN VON GOETHE

At the Classy

At the Classy Hotel in Erbil, in northern Iraq, journalists fill the bar and spill through the open-air café into a neon-lit lobby. Old hands murmur with colleagues from wars past; young freelancers compare notes on frontline access; camera equipment and battered notebooks lounge about. War is underway, and there is work to be done.

A long table sprawls through the lobby with chairs akimbo as journalists come and go. Plates are emptied and stacked and empty bottles of Almaza beer clank against errant silverware. Diane is laughing at Rami's bad puns; Robert is gesticulating wildly over Liam's incredulous smirk; Max and Behcet lean in close for furtive whispers. Peter quickly drains his beer before leaving to file against his deadline in Paris. Amy receives a call from her editor in New York and backs away to a quieter corner of the bar. Phones ping with messages from an aid worker in Dahook and a Czech diplomat in the know and a young engineer trapped in Mosul and tweeting wildly.[1]

I take a seat next to Mazar, a gruff local fixer who walks and talks at rough angles. Journalists remark among themselves, a bit too casually, that Mazar probably killed people during the bad Kurdish wars and that he would commit war crimes again if asked. It makes him good company for checkpoints, less so for dinner parties. Liam and Mazar are discussing the day's events, the rules of luck and fate, the best approach to the story of two brothers trapped on either side of a vicious frontline. "There are many ways to die," Mazar remarks, and then begins to list them: suicide bomber, car-borne suicide bomber, sniper round, mortar round, airstrike, IED, grenade from a drone, missile from a drone. Over at the bar, a journalist with long velvet hair becomes the vision of a corpse decayed.

The Classy Hotel is a space that appears through wars past while remaining unique in each iteration, a site of sociality and production poised on the edge of violence. Here one can observe the practices of journalistic meaning making: the testing of language, the trading of narratives, the processing of experience. The Classy Hotel plays the role in the recent war with the Islamic State that the Caravelle Hotel played in the war in Vietnam, that the Commodore played in the Lebanese Civil War, and the Holiday Inn in the Kosovo War, and the Hotel Palestine in the US invasion of Iraq, and the Gandamack Lodge in the war in Afghanistan. These spaces sustain war reportage as a situated and social activity, where a relationship between language, meaning, and practice is formed and reformed, and from which a certain culture emanates. At the Classy Hotel, war reportage can be observed not merely as a profession or a craft, but as a social world unto itself, a world engaged with the uneasy transposition of knowing war into telling war. As a central site of journalistic life in Iraq, the Classy Hotel stands for all those war-zone hotels looming behind the scenes of wars past. It is a place where journalism becomes journalism and journalists become journalists.[2]

If, as Jean Baudrillard (1995) insists, a war in Iraq, like the one he examined some thirty year ago, "did not take place"—if global audiences access war only through the mediations of news media, necessarily partial and interested and self-referential—then the Classy Hotel is one place where this war disappears behind its mediation. It is a place where ideas are exchanged among journalists, resources pooled, logistics plotted, networks enhanced, fears related, values compared, fantasies indulged, limitations realized. It is a place where journalists negotiate how the recent war with the Islamic State—the primary concern of the journalism examined in this book—"takes place" representationally or ceases to do so. Fieldwork in war zones complicates Baudrillard's approach, and related arguments from Paul Virilio (2002) and others, by revealing the transfiguration of war into news of war—into a war that "did not take place"—and the realities effaced in the process.[3]

As endless war has become a global condition in the post–9/11 era, those producing the most prominent representations of war—the daily news—should know war well. But what journalists know of war is always transformed through the representations they produce, and through the erasures inherent to this transformation. In the chapters that follow, I attend to these erasures in journalistic production, looking at what war reportage displaces—those words not expressed, those meanings not made, those experiences not reported—in order to capture the particularity of war as rendered in the news today. The displacements inherent to war reportage throw into relief both the authority of journalism for ordering what war *is*, as well as the surplus to journalism agitating at the margins of war's authoritative representation. For the boundaries of war's reality, as policed by journalism, always produce an outside. War reportage can then be approached as a process of selection and appropriation and determination, a mastering of war that must excise what remains unsuited to an established discursive domain. While only particular meanings are constituted in war reportage, particular routines of production undertaken, particular names and numbers expressed, this process of delineation creates, as well, an excess to war reportage, an Other that both contrasts and contests a journalistic Self. What is reported of war, what is left out, and what, thereby, does war reportage allow its consumers to think?

In the Classy Hotel, knowing war transmutes into telling war. It is, thereby, a site crystalizing the three concerns treated in the chapters to come: the language, the meaning, and the practice of war reportage. The order imposed by journalistic language is affirmed in the discussions among journalists in the hotel lobby. How the events of war are named and classified, how authorship is apportioned, how bodies are counted, what makes a "good story"—such matters, subject to the constraints of linguistic convention, are negotiated among journalists in the places they live and socialize. And the contingencies of war's representation, hidden by the standardization of journalistic language, become evident in what remains journalistically unexpressed.

The relations of power implicit to the meaning of journalism are also apparent at the Classy Hotel, where political and military officials converse with journalists over imported liquors while other subjects of war, and other participants in journalistic production, never appear. Who counts as a victim, whose violence is justified, which sources determine war's truth: These elements of journalistic meaning are reflected in presence and absence at a hotel bar.

The experiences of war that challenge journalism's normative narratives are often shared around the tables in the Classy Hotel lobby, where reflection on a day's events reveals what cannot be reported. The practice of war reportage demands an encounter with war's ambiguities, absurdities, and confusions, yet it is precisely these elements of war that are excised by the generic demands of war reportage. The hotel itself—a critical site of news production—is just another element of journalistic practice obscured in the news produced.

In examining the language, meaning, and practice of war reportage, this study reckons with what war reportage excludes: Those experiences erased from journalistic narrative, those meanings unsanctioned by journalistic authority, those things of war left undefined, unclassified, uncounted. The transformations of war through its reportage entail a series of displacements— displacements consequential to how war is represented and thereby understood. For war, as this book demonstrates, has a way of exceeding those boundaries that war reportage attempts to secure, and the task of what follows is to recover this remainder. *Conflicted* maps the restrictions imposed on reportage of war and the possibilities entangled in war reportage for knowing war anew.

The Content of War, the Form of Reportage

What is the relationship between practice, meaning, and text under conditions of combat? How does this relationship respond to consumer demand for war's reality? How is authenticity calibrated, truthfulness enforced, and authority claimed in the production of news about conflict?

The value of war reportage is premised, at the most basic level, on its direct transmission of the reality of ongoing warfare. War reporters "bear witness" to war, delivering the suffering, the ruin, the devastation unfolding in faraway lands. Transparency, accuracy, objectivity, facticity, verifiability: These are the normative ideals that still shape the broadest conceptions of what war reportage is and does, and these ideals underwrite journalistic claims to truth. In providing truthful stories of war, war reportage informs news consumers about what is happening amidst conflict and who is harmed by whose violence—about what war *is*. Through a set of established forms, discursive and embodied, war reportage renders war's reality.

But what does this reality of war entail? A glance at the war reportage now being produced from places like Iraq and Syria, Sudan and Somalia, Yemen and Afghanistan, and in Ukraine and Gaza too, indicates a particular reality for contemporary warfare. It is a reality of victims and perpetrators, wherein the former are innocent sufferers of the latter's unjustified harm. It is a reality in which violence, immanent and bodily, plays the most significant role in wartime events. It is a reality that can be categorized, defined, plotted, and thereby understood. It is a self-evident reality, the encounter with which—by journalists sent to "cover" conflict—allows for the transparent representation of war.

These elements comprise one way to infer war's reality as delivered by contemporary war reportage. A point-by-point correspondence between the journalistic text and an extratextual occurrence offers us a means of assessing what war is like. But there remains another mode of account: that of a figural correspondence between the journalistic text and some domain of experience understood to be real. Thus, a victim of war reported in the news may correspond to Hawra, a girl pulled from the rubble of a collapsed building after an airstrike in Mosul. But this victim may also correspond to "Hawra": a figural representative of victimhood and, thereby, of the truth of human suffering amidst the cruelty of wartime violence. That we can confirm two realities in this journalistic representation—one empirically perceivable and one discursively composed—does not reveal a clash between two varieties of truth so much as a certain simultaneity of war reportage as a truth-telling, meaning-delivering enterprise. War may be perceivable by journalists—it may be encountered, experienced, and narrated—but war, in its journalistic representation, also adheres to a coherency, an orderliness, determined by the matter of journalism itself. War reportage manifests both mimesis and figuration, both verisimilitude and conviction, both self-evidence and regulation.[4]

Hayden White, in a study of historical narrative, cuts to the quick of this matter: "What is at issue here is not, What are the facts? but rather, How are the facts to be described in order to sanction one mode of explaining them rather than another?" (1978, 134). This book demonstrates how war reportage asks itself the first question while answering the second. What journalists do when they report from a war zone and how they make war intelligible through narrative is premised on coherence between the war encountered and the meanings journalistically produced. Yet in order for the facts of war to be adequate to normative understandings of war, those facts must indicate something beyond themselves. Hawra the fact must also be "Hawra" the figure. And thus, even as journalists may encounter a war where saving victims is indistinguishable from killing victims, where violence is less consequential than the nonviolent systems that perpetuate it, where conventional definitions and categories are inadequate to war's events, this encounter must yet establish only those realities for war already acceptable to news consumers. Even as journalists may encounter confusing, ambiguous, or absurd answers to the question *What are the facts?*, they must still describe those facts in a manner that responds to—and thereby sanctions—expected explanations for war. A concern of this book, then, is to track the simultaneity of war reportage as both a factual enterprise and a figural one. My aim is to show how the meanings given in war reportage can constrain understandings of the reality of warfare; how the practice of war reportage can result in experiences exceeding what journalism can represent; and how the language of war reportage can constitute, and thereby order, what war is narrated to be. In so doing, *Conflicted* seeks to track the metamorphosis war undergoes through its reportage and to recover what is mystified, occluded, effaced thereby.

A central premise of this act of recovery is that the forms of war reportage will determine its contents. What could be called the content of journalism's forms—the linguistic, ideological, and practical determinations of war reportage—becomes, I believe, the consequential matter in how war is made knowable within societies consuming news of war. My overarching site of inquiry is the relationship between content and form, between war's represented reality and the narrative conventions, interpretive worldviews, and professional routines with which journalists engage. Even as the specificity of its content can shift between wars and among journalists, the *form* of war reportage—standardized through professional, institutional, and social pressures—allows a connection between war and a news-consuming public to be maintained. This connection authorizes a very specific way of knowing war. And in constituting what war is supposed to be, journalism enhances and reproduces a particular social order. While journalism, as Stuart Hall (1982) notes, appears to "speak for itself," providing a natural reflection of war's reality, it simultaneously renders invisible those struggles, codifications, and interests foundational to how war's reality is rendered. Folding figuration into fact, the descriptive into the declarative, the social into the symbolic, journalism organizes war's reality in relation to considerations operating far from the war zone. The forms of war reportage become autonomous of their content as they discipline war's reality to suit a reigning common sense, at the same time displacing what that reality cannot accommodate.

To define war reportage as an institution or a narrative form or a set of practices does not itself answer the question of how war reportage shapes understandings of war—of what war, as reported, *is*. If, as Walter Benjamin (1968) suggests, the fate of a society is linked to the way stories are told, then how journalists tell stories of war becomes consequential beyond the content of representation and the specific event represented, and perhaps especially so regarding the wars perpetuated—militarily, economically, politically—by those societies consuming much of the news reported from recent war zones. For as war reporters produce news in relation to various linguistic, political, and practical dynamics, war reportage also produces symbols of an age. The innocent civilian, suffering corporeally and individually. The ruthless insurgent, employing a cruel violence illegitimate and unjustified. The hardened soldier, whose heroism is shadowed by his trauma. The determined journalist, bearing witness to atrocity. These narrative figures of contemporary war reportage shape, and are shaped by, broader social processes. Their significance is buried in their very self-evidence, in the way they seem to reflect rather than regulate the reality of war today.

This self-evidence, in which figuration and facticity merge, suggests how war reportage comes to moralize the reality of war for those societies within which it circulates. In fashioning a coherent war, a war capable of "representing itself"—of displaying itself in the form of the news—journalism establishes "that moral authority without which the notion of a specifically social reality would be unthinkable" (White 1980, 27). The reality of war, fashioned by journalistic representation—and displaying a seamlessness and significance that can *only* make sense as representation—establishes that moral authority to arbitrate what war *is*. As the narratives of twentieth-century conflicts, particularly the Holocaust, helped define both modernity and its violence, so is war reportage, produced in the age of anti-terror "forever war" (Filkins 2008), similarly implicated in a process of definitional power broader than the journalistic texts themselves. In moralizing war's reality, in granting war a narrative significance and interpretive shape, war reportage imposes an order reproductive of a dominant social consensus on war and of the authority that any consensus claims.

By this I do not mean to simply reassert Virilio's (2002) argument about the "fourth front" of informational warfare and the participation of mass media in things like "shock and awe" military operations. I mean to suggest, rather, that the relationship between war and war reportage, while not simply one of reflection, is not just fabrication either. War reportage is not merely "constructed," as many theories of popular narrative (and many dismissals of mass media) insist. Rather, war reportage is the satisfaction of a desire, a desire for war's reality already resonant within those societies consuming news of war. And as a very prominent mediation of contemporary warfare, war reportage enacts an authority upon the wars it claims to merely reflect. This authorial-authoritative enactment entails more than representational fashioning; it entails the fulfillment of a social process. To borrow the terminology of Edward Said (1978), war reportage *distributes* geopolitical awareness; it *elaborates* and *maintains* a series of interests; and it *is*—rather than merely expresses—a will to know and, thereby, often to control.

War reportage is not, then, merely a matter of ideas (ideas about war, or suffering, or violence), but a matter of ideas constituting, perpetuating, and naturalizing the material realities of the war zone.[5] The relationship between war reportage and war, I mean to argue—and, thereby, between journalism's social processes and its symbolic products, between its factual claims and its figural resonance, between its practical limits and its epistemic power—is more dynamic, and more consequential, than terms like "construction" suggest.

Logistics of a Study

This book is based on three years of ethnographic fieldwork in areas of conflict and in areas from which conflict is reported. While my first, limited fieldwork on war reportage took place in Afghanistan in 2012, the bulk of this research was conducted in Lebanon (2015–2018), in Iraq (2016–2018), and in Syria (2017). I did additional fieldwork in Ukraine in 2022.[6] Other interviews were conducted in New York, Los Angeles, and Paris in 2021 and 2022.[7]

The qualitative interviews and participant observation that constitutes this research included fifty-nine foreign journalists and eleven fixers (though more casual conversations occurred with a wider pool of individuals, perhaps a hundred). Subjects were granted anonymity throughout. Forty-three of my research subjects were men, and twenty-seven were women; thirty-nine held staff positions, while thirty-one worked as freelancers; forty-three were below the age of fifty and twenty-seven were over fifty; fifty-four worked for "legacy" media outlets (newspapers and wire services), and sixteen worked for "digital native" organizations (though many freelancers published in both). The journalists and fixers in this study worked primarily in print, though a few staff journalists worked in radio, and some of the fixers and freelancers worked occasionally in television and video.[8] That is, the journalists involved in this research are writers, producing their journalism through written narrative command.

All the fixers, and a majority of the journalists, lived and worked full-time in the Middle East, while a few journalists were "parachuters" on short-term assignment. The majority of those interviewed and observed worked for US- and UK-based news outlets—the dominant purveyors of reportage from conflict zones in the Middle East—though some worked for French- and Middle East–based outlets, and a few individuals worked for outlets based in India and elsewhere in Europe.[9] Journalists who participated in this research worked as staff or in a freelance capacity for the following news organizations: ABC News (US), Agence France-Presse, Al Arabiya, Al Jazeera, the Associated Press, the *Atlantic,* the BBC, Buzzfeed News, CNN, the *Daily Star* (Beirut), *Der Spiegel,* the *Economist,* the *Financial Times,* GlobalPost, the *Guardian, Harper's Magazine,* the *Hindu,* the *Independent, Le Monde,* the *Los Angeles Times,* the *National* (UAE), National Public Radio (US), the *New Yorker,* the *New York Times,* Reuters, Rudaw, the *Telegraph,* the *Times of London, La Vanguardia,* Vice News, the *Wall Street Journal,* and the *Washington Post.*[10]

Most of the journalists and fixers involved in this study were interviewed more than once over the span of many months. Those interviewed were self-selected; some journalists responded to emailed requests for interviews, while others were asked in person after chance meetings at bars, checkpoints, and social events in the region. I also operated through a process of referral, where those interviewed would assist in arranging interviews with their colleagues. In this manner, I was able to speak with almost every foreign journalist based in Lebanon and Iraq during the period under study (by 2016, no foreign journalists were based in Syria). Interview content ranged widely, with most interviews exceeding two hours in duration. More than a dozen of those interviewed were also observed in the field as they witnessed events, conducted interviews, and traveled around the region. Observation occurred for days or weeks at a time, over the span of many months.

The questions I asked journalists necessarily inform the answers they gave; the things I observed supplant those I did not. My position as an author—and as a representor of war—is in this way similar to that of the journalists I encountered, insofar as my frame is also constrained, my perspective also situated, my context also determinative. Some reflection on this condition is one way to set my representations apart from those I reckon with here. Another is my motivation: critical assessment of the work of representation, rather than a disappearance of that work behind the veil of self-evidence. Yet another distinction is style, wherein use of vignette, anecdote, and juxtaposed quotation is intended to capture the fragmentary and ambiguous experience of doing representation in and on war.

But my orientation remains circumscribed. Local news production receives little scrutiny (though local journalists' employment as fixers is treated in Chapter 2). News coverage of the Middle East from outside the region is similarly bypassed (though some comparisons to this coverage are considered, particularly on the issue of civilian casualties). The most contentious omission will be the Middle East itself, insofar as Said's orientalist problematic pertains: This book examines how war in the Middle East is fashioned in journalistic discourse, and what underlies, exceeds, and disrupts that process. Approached in this manner, journalism says more about the representors than it does about the object of representation, and an "actual" Middle East comes to exist only on the margins of the inquiries to follow.

Moreover, by embedding with journalists, their frame of reference often determined my own. While long-term fieldwork allows me to introduce the sights and sounds of wartime news production in the Middle East, less attention is given to the geopolitics of the region, to the cultural character of local communities and their responses to conflict and its effects, or to the experience of local individuals confronting the miseries of warfare. Many studies exist on these important topics. My intent is to contribute to a conversation about a dominant discourse of international (and especially US) militarism by examining those dynamics of representation that privilege a normative knowledge of war. To this end, I track the power of war reportage and the threshold at which it falters.

Critical Contexts

The cascading failures of the 2003–2011 US occupation of Iraq, the diminishing significance of Gulf oil to major global economies, American military retrenchment after the 2008 financial crisis, and the Obama administration's reconsideration of US military commitments all prompted a recalibration of active American hegemony in the Middle East, a process that influenced US and global media investment (Hinnebusch 2015; Phillips 2016; Thépaut 2022). By the 2010s, international media attention to the region was waning after a period of intense interest. Foreign journalistic resources in Iraq were dramatically slimmed after the drawdown of US forces in 2011, approaching the light footprint of foreign media in Syria, while Lebanon—relatively stable, and with historic claims to journalistic concern—persisted as a steady, if often marginal, site of news production.

The 2011 US military drawdown in Iraq left a vulnerable and sharply sectarian government ill-equipped to respond to the needs of neglected Kurdish and Sunni Arab communities. The same year, in neighboring Syria, an uprising against the entrenched ruling order quickly transitioned to a civil war and, as foreign support flooded in, became a widening sectarian conflict by 2014. Lebanon's proximity to the war in Syria affected it demographically, politically, and militarily. Sunni militants led by the Islamic State group—itself an effect of US interventionism and occupation—declared a caliphate in 2014 and expanded its presence across Iraq, Syria, and beyond. After concerted international attention to the Syrian conflict in its first few years, the rise of the Islamic State shifted the center of journalistic gravity in the region back to Iraq.[11]

The United States and Iran began air campaigns against the Islamic State in 2014, the same year the group seized Mosul, Iraq's second-largest city. Russia and the Syrian state began bombing Islamic State positions in 2015 (as well as other Islamist groups such as Jabhat al-Nusra and secular groups such as the Free Syrian Army). Along with Iraq, Syria, Iran, Russia, and the United States, forces from Australia, Belgium, Canada, Denmark, France, Germany, Italy, Jordan, Morocco, the Netherlands, New Zealand, Saudi Arabia, Spain, Turkey, the United Arab Emirates, and the United Kingdom engaged militarily in Iraq and Syria after 2016, with another twenty or so nations providing indirect military support.

This global dynamic spurred fervent journalistic attention. The war in Syria, the rise of the Islamic State in Iraq, and their spillover effects across the region once again elevated the Middle East in the priorities of international media organizations. The entwined conflicts became the biggest story in the world. The relatively limited coverage of the previous years' slow-burn anti-terror wars and regional political machinations became the wall-to-wall news of a historic conflagration. Journalists—freelance and staff, famous and fledgling—descended on Iraq, Syria, and Lebanon. The world was watching, and representations spilled forth.

At the same time, a number of interlocking crises affected the news industry broadly, though their implications for war reportage are specific and uneven. These crises include financial pressures leading to downsized foreign bureaus and increased reliance on local staff; the democratization of media technologies and the resulting competition, particularly by so-called citizen journalists, in coverage of wartime events; technological changes, especially in the realm of social media, triggering faster news cycles and an intensified struggle for audience engagement; and the undermining of journalistic authority amidst consumer trust deficits and the proliferation of misinformation and disinformation. These interlocking crises inform the institutional context for the war reportage I engage here.

Changes in technology both impact, and are impacted by, the linguistic, ideological, and practical dynamics of journalism. Tarrying with technological change in news production, journalists marshal an array of material and semiotic resources. Yet this active engagement with technological change does not make technology a determining force in war reportage. In my research, things like Twitter and satellite phones and trackers (in case of kidnapping) were rarely remarked upon in interviews and rarely proved consequential in the field. Twitter seemed to figure, for the journalists in this study, much like a flak jacket—one technology among others in the operation of reporting on war. Such technologies are less decisive for how the news is made from war than they are iterative of the programmatic routines already in place. Prior to or absent a flak jacket, the journalist still approaches the frontline; prior to or absent a Twitter account, the published story remains the abiding journalistic concern. While much scholarly attention has been given to the role of technology in news making (most prominently, perhaps, Downie and Schudson 2009), this attention tends to be more descriptive of technological transformation than it is analytical with respect to the impact of such transformations on journalism. My research finds technology rarely determinative of journalistic representations of war, except in the most general sense. Rather, the technologies of news making, as Raymond Williams (1974) suggests, are activated by the social practices within which they are embedded.

The crisis of competition in news making, born of expanded access to the tools of mass mediation, is less prominent in war reportage than in other facets of the journalism industry. News other than that produced by corporate and state media is relatively rare in the case of international conflict, where the barriers to entry—especially in the case of frontline coverage—remain high. The costs and risks of reporting from war, and the stature often required to access sites of military activity, diminish outside competition in war reportage generally. Activist media, citizen journalism, and remote investigative media from organizations like Bellingcat do present alternatives to "mainstream" mediations of conflict, though the threat these alternatives pose to corporate supremacy and narrative normativity in war reportage is relative. Where journalists are forced to report remotely (as for many areas of Syria), citizen journalism can both challenge and enhance the dominance of corporate news, and investigative teams adept at the use of digital sources can fill gaps in-the-ground reportage.[12] However, and as Barbie Zelizer (1990) notes, the value attached to journalistic proximity to wartime events will exert its pressure. Despite costs and risks, war reporters will do what they can to access war, and news organizations will publish the results.

Economic pressure on news production has led to the downsizing and closure of foreign bureaus and increasing reliance on stringers, freelancers, and local staff (Otto and Meyer 2012). According to the most recent survey from the *American Journalism Review*, twenty US news organizations, including erstwhile foreign news stalwarts such as the *Boston Globe* and the *Chicago Tribune*, closed all foreign bureaus between 2003 and 2011, while the number of foreign correspondents (staff and contract) working for US news outlets fell by 25 percent during the same period (Enda 2011). The Pew Research Center, in a 2014 report, indicates that US coverage of international news fell by more than 50 percent since the 1980s and that foreign news desks suffer steep cutbacks on a year-to-year basis (Jurkowitz 2014). The Nieman Journalism Lab notes that the *Los Angeles Times*, a representative large-size US newspaper, cut its foreign bureaus from twenty-two in 2004 to ten in 2014 (Hammer 2014). The trend is international, and it has worsened since this data—proprietary, and thereby difficult to acquire—was compiled.

Considering its costs and relatively uneven consumption rates, foreign news coverage has become a prestige endeavor.[13] The expense of war reportage can be especially onerous; outlays for security management, translators, drivers, and the maintenance of far-flung bureaus have been impacted amidst an altogether dismal economic environment for the global news industry. According to a rare study, news organizations budget over $250,000 per year to support a single foreign correspondent, a cost that increases with coverage of conflict (Hamilton and Jenner 2004). Yet the social capital accrued from war reportage remains high, and thus the return on investment may be best measured indirectly, by the prizes and prestige that increase news organization profiles and, thereby, subscription and advertising revenue.[14]

Such returns are tenuous; it is no coincidence that so many of the journalists in this study are freelancers. As many news organizations still see war coverage as part of their institutional profile, declining revenue has led to increased reliance on contract labor. And because the professional prestige of covering war remains coveted, and thus competition for publication fierce, the dependence on freelance reportage has perpetuated a race to the bottom. There is no standardized fee for a news article produced by a freelancer in the Middle East, and there is little labor organization among the community of freelancers operating in this competitive professional environment. The result is a circumstance in which freelancers may be spending the entirety of their presumed payment for a given story on a fixer, driver, and other necessary outlays in advance. The financial precarity of freelancers is often acute, and borne only by those successful enough, thrifty enough, or privileged enough to sustain this difficult professional position.

The most broadly consequential crisis affecting the news industry today, and the one to which the journalists in my study most often referred, concerns mass media's trust deficit and associated "fake news" machinations.[15] The "constructedness" of journalism has become something of a truism, taken as obvious in a poststructuralist world and as problematic in a "post-truth" one. In the former instance, the partiality and interests of journalistic truth have long been inherent to anthropological, sociological, and political-theoretical understandings of what mass media is and does; among readers of a book such as this, discursive contingency may seem hardly worthy of remark. In the latter instance, that of a post-truth social landscape, the increasing trust deficit among news consumers—a circumstance tied to the exponential proliferation of news narratives, the loss of local newspapers, information siloing through algorithmic preference reinforcement, and related dynamics—leads to much handwringing among those concerned with collective understandings of things like war, and results in much nostalgia for the stability of an elite knowledge and the consensus it authorized. And yet, spotted on the coffee tables of our most illustrious theorists, the daily newspaper remains. And yet, among those who disavow the "lamestream media," the *New York Times* remains the record to which competing truths are compared. Despite our discursive circumstances, the news keeps getting read for information on war and on many other things too.[16]

Not enough surprise has been registered by this circumstance. How do we live this way, consuming journalism for worldly information while guarding an awareness of journalism's discursive contingency? Few peddlers of disinformation report from the scene of war's events, and war reportage tends to maintain a trusted status, albeit relatively, amidst the current climate of media skepticism. Yet the question remains as to how the essential partiality and historicity of journalism is at the same time understood and overlooked in the consumption of news. As Niklas Luhmann puts this question, "It is not: *what* is the case, what surrounds us as world and as society? It is rather: *how* is it possible to accept information about the world and about society as information about reality when one knows *how* it is produced" (2000, 122). Knowing *how* journalism is produced—with its interests, elisions, authorial impositions—does not seem to undermine an acceptance of journalism as the delivery of reality. Even those who dismiss journalism as fake do not generally deny the truth-producing abilities of journalism as such. So again: How do we live like this, consuming news amidst the comforts of doubt?

One answer to this question relates to the way we do not necessarily consume news for truth but for confirmation of what we already believe to be true. This is, of course, a basic function of ideology, as understood by Antonio Gramsci (1971), Louis Althusser (1971), and Stuart Hall (1985), among others. The problem with war is the suffering it causes, and this suffering is experienced corporeally and individually. Civilians in war are innocent, and harming the innocent is illegitimate and cruel. Violence may be justified if intended to stop human suffering. Bearing witness to war delivers war's reality. These are common assumptions about war, specific to a particular time, place, and social formation, and war reportage responds to and reproduces these assumptions. Journalism may be less about truth and falsity, in this case, than it is about a rhetoric of truth registered through the kinds of stories journalists tell.

The challenge of accounting for this discursive circumstance is to do so without ceding ground to the dismissal of all journalistic representation as "fake." When I began fieldwork for this study, many journalists I interviewed accepted the discursive contingency of journalism as understood in a poststructuralist intellectual era. War reportage, these journalists agreed, is subject to authorial interests, and to the determinants of social, cultural, and historical context. In the wake of the US elections of 2016, and amidst the increasing weaponization of "fake news" allegations, some of my interviews assumed a sort of rearguard positivism, with journalists defending the mimetic capacity of journalism against perceived charges of relativism. How to affirm, then, both the contingency of journalistic truth and its usefulness as a window onto war? How to confront journalism's representational authority in both its partiality and its potential? How to read journalism for truthful experiences of war while conceding that some truths remain better than others?

The relationship between journalism and its consumer reception is difficult to track, and doing so is not an aim of this study.[17] For my purposes, it is enough to assume of this relationship a shifting and abundant complexity. This ethnography intends, instead, to map the relationship between journalism—with its commitment to consumer expectations for war's truth—and journalists themselves, as they live, work, and represent in wartime. Here the presumed opposition between truth and falsity cedes to messier circumstances in which journalistic performance is predicated on the need to tell affectively truthful stories about war, even as war's truths can exceed journalism's generic mandate. Under such circumstances, the relationship of journalist to journalism, and of war reporter to war, can trouble easy distinctions between relativism and positivism, manufacture and mimesis. In the process of reporting war, journalists are constantly navigating the interstices of fact–fiction, objective–subjective, known–unknown, meaningful–meaningless, certain–ambiguous, form–figure, real–surreal, truth–falsity—a liminal space that *is* the experience of war and its representation. This condition—in which journalists are simultaneously storytelling professionals and experiencing individuals, and journalism is a transmission of reality that also orders that reality—exposes both the power of war reportage and its insurgent frontier. At this cusp, attention to truth and disinformation shifts to matters of production, figuration, subjectification, and to the relationship between representor and representation.

Grappling with this relationship in the Middle East means placing war reportage within a fraught history of foreign imposition in the region and the contributions of popular media to the imperial imagination. For as Melani McAlister (2005) observes, the news media has historically aided in the establishment of those ideas, sentiments, and relations enabling (though sometimes also contesting) the enforcement of US and European power in the Middle East. Journalism, through the force of its representations, facilitates the naturalization of dynamics that help to validate a basis for domination: the vulnerable innocent, the compassionate savior, the circumstances chaotic and in need of control.

It is a basic premise of this book that war reportage actively produces the meaning of war rather than reflecting a preexisting reality of war. This premise does not position wartime journalism as merely a functionalist process in the service of power. Instead, I approach wartime journalism as the result various interests, events, and ideas converging toward a common (if contingent) enterprise. This convergence suggests the role of the Middle East in war reportage as a "mobile sign" (McAlister 2005, 42) amenable to various projects—military, humanitarian, aesthetic—in keeping with a longer history of orientalist depiction. The sign's mobility accommodates numerous rationales for foreign intervention in the region, rationales that are culturally embedded rather than self-evidently factual. In deploying this sign, war reportage produces for its audiences not only the foreign Other—whether that be the catastrophe of warfare itself, or those suffering such catastrophe—but it produces, as well, the self-image of its audiences. In the case of recent Middle East conflicts, as for past colonial adventures, as Edward Said (1978) shows, it is the self-image of a citizenry of a benevolent world power, where benevolence must, at times, assume a violent form.

These contexts—geopolitical, economic, epistemic, historical—suggest how journalistic representation of war in the Middle East, and beyond, is a process unfolding *within* war rather than a matter of observational remove from the war represented. War reportage is a part of the conflict it seeks to capture, and the dynamics of this reportage (linguistic, ideological, practical) necessarily affect, for many people around the world, what war comes to be.

The Form and Contents to Follow

The succeeding chapters pursue this entanglement of war and its reportage. Examination of the language of war news, the meanings war reportage makes, and the practices of journalism in war zones elaborate the specificity of conflict journalism as an enterprise authoritative, contestable, and ensnared.

The first and second chapters of this book attend to the language of war reportage. Examining news industry "style manuals" and the reportage of my interlocuters, these chapters lean on discourse analysis to specify how language structures journalistic truth telling and thereby shapes popular knowledge of war. Chapter 1, "Folklore of the Future," examines journalism's narrative realism and designations common to journalism from the Middle East, and it uses case studies to illustrate these two primary conventions. On narrative realism, I examine a news story disruptive of the way allies and enemies, heroism and villainy, are normatively accounted for in Iraq, and I track the fallout from this reportage. I demonstrate how "journalistic realism" organizes a prevailing legibility for war and thereby reproduces a hegemonic common sense. On journalistic designation, I assess the term "Hezbollah stronghold"—a name often used by journalists for an area of southern Beirut—to indicate the way such designations maintain a consensus about the reality of conflict in the Middle East. Disassembling these formal elements of journalism reveals how language regulates what war reportage is professed to be: an authoritative account of war coterminous with reality itself. War reportage, this chapter suggests, is less a record of war than a result of linguistic conditions determining how war can be recorded.

Chapter 2, "Visible System and Invisible Rules," continues my analysis of how language asserts semantic preconditions on journalism, and how formal conventions function as a set of rules determining the way war's reality is journalistically coded. This chapter examines casualty counting and the byline (the mark of news authorship) and again uses case studies to illustrate these two conventions. On casualty counting, I consider efforts to determine the total death toll for the war in Syria and examine the contingencies inherent to this process. I argue that the importance of casualty counts for journalism may be less the statistical reality of war such numbers purport to deliver than it is the symbolic truth these numbers provide. Concerning the byline, I examine the role of the fixer in war reportage, contending that the local, "situated" knowledge of fixers is both structural to, and ultimately suppressed by, the global, "professional" knowledge of international news. By excluding fixer authorship and thereby devaluing local knowledge, the byline authenticates only particular representations of war. The chapter emphasizes how linguistic conventions underwrite journalism's claim to the accurate transmission of war's reality, substantiating journalism's social function and perpetuating its mediational power.

The third and fourth chapters address the meaning for war currently ascendent in contemporary war reportage and in popular understandings of war. Utilizing the 2016–17 battle for Mosul as a case study, these chapters lean on political analysis to examine how journalists made meaning for a central confrontation of the War on Terror era. Chapter 3, "Extermination as Protection," assesses the prominent and much-lauded journalism that revealed official underestimates of US-caused civilian harm in anti–Islamic State operations. I argue that, in questioning official death tallies, journalists failed to challenge the rationale offered for this harm: an accidental exception or necessary excess to justified violence. Focusing on individuated victimhood and corporeal suffering, categorizing violence as lawful or extreme, and attending to immanent violence—rather than the structures perpetuating violence—as the central problem of war, journalists emphasized the morality of militarism while mystifying its political logic. This chapter demonstrates that war reportage, in its contemporary humanitarian mode, transforms war from the effects of policy on populations to the effects of violence on the innocent.

Chapter 4, "Power Speaking to Truth," continues my examination of the meaning made for war by staging a historical and political analysis of a "humanitarian turn" in wartime journalism. This turn indicates why news coverage of US-caused civilian death in Iraq and Syria, widely presumed to function as a critique of US intervention, instead served to sanction the official rationales for war. Assessing the historical formation of a humanitarian militarism, US airstrike targeting protocols, and the politics of journalistic objectivity, I demonstrate that "speaking truth to power" can indeed legitimate power and show why war reportage tends to reproduce only those meanings for war already sanctified by a reigning order. By mapping journalism's ideological circumstances, and the humanitarian frame now hegemonic in coverage of conflict, the chapter specifies how some meanings for war gain prominence over others. Protection rather than extermination, liberation rather than siege, intervention rather than civil war: Such selections clarify the relationship of war reportage to the conflicts it represents and to the powers driving these conflicts.

The fifth and sixth chapters are the most ethnographic of the book. They turn to the practice of war reportage, leaning on psychoanalysis to assess the persistence of what is repressed in the news. The confusions, absurdities, and distress of war are common to the experience of journalists reporting on war, yet the generic conventions of journalism erase these essential experiences from the news journalists produce. Journalists are left struggling with a twinned burden: the violence that saturates journalistic life and the demands of an authoritative narrative genre. Chapter 5, "Writing Conflicts," examines journalists' dreams, fears, traumas, and jokes as an archive for those experiences of war that transgress the reality represented in journalism. My aim is to illuminate both the tension between the experience of war and the content of war reportage as well as their hidden intimacy in propelling the practice of journalism. Contrary to media scholarship emphasizing the separation of experience from output, which theorizes journalism as merely a rhetorical performance, I argue that the production of war news is precipitated by what is occluded from that news. Experience and output form a relationship essential to the practice of war reportage and to the production of a social fantasy of war.

Chapter 6, "Agitation at the Margins," continues my focus on the practice of war reportage to consider how a social fantasy of war can be maintained through journalism despite the return of the journalistically repressed. Here I examine journalistic practices of interviewing sources, accessing and witnessing combat, choosing what stories to cover, and representing a violence that can challenge representational norms. These practices indicate where, precisely, experiences of war transgressive of journalistic conventions can be glimpsed, and how journalists manage those dynamics that trouble audience expectations for war's legibility. By observing a violence that breaches both journalistic norms and popular understandings of war, I argue for rethinking the viability of both. This chapter then offers a close reading of the marginalia found in journalists' notebooks, the tropes journalists employ to describe atrocity, and the ambiguities of "bearing witness" as a journalistic ideal. These sites reveal how journalists struggle with the misalignment between the practice of reporting war and the desires of news consumers. In recovering an excess to war reportage—an excess frequently confronted by war reporters—this chapter exposes the fragility of journalism's attempt to control what war *is*.

The conclusion, "War's Exit," explores possibilities inherent to war reportage for understanding war otherwise. By considering the language, meaning, and practice of war reportage for what they conceal as well as what they sanction, opportunities for contesting hegemonic conceptions of war can emerge. Turning from critique to possibility, then, this chapter seeks capacities embedded in war reportage for differently representing contemporary warfare. Rather than asserting the limits of war reportage as something to overcome, I address these limits as evocative of potentials for representational transgression. By looking back at the activities and narratives examined in the preceding chapters, certain opportunities already entangled in war reportage can be ascertained. I excavate these entangled possibilities as they become available both *through* and *despite* the linguistic, ideological, and practical constraints regulating news production in wartime. Returning to the post-truth crisis in media authority, I argue that achieving new ways of knowing war entails not only a deconstruction of the discourse through which war is constituted, but an examination of the social order that constitutes war reportage as a discourse.

Finally, the epilogue, "From Mosul to Mariupol," draws comparisons to a new war in Ukraine, which many of the journalists I interviewed and observed in the Middle East began covering in 2022. How are the language, meaning, and practice of war reportage transformed in the transition from one international war zone to another? As the war in Ukraine grinds on, I find journalists once again struggling in the wake. After covering war in Iraq, Syria, and across the greater Middle East, war reporters in Ukraine confront familiar—if transposed—frictions.

Dances with War

There is commotion at the far end of the long table in the lobby of the Classy Hotel, where journalists are discussing another day on the Mosul frontline. Liam is telling his colleagues about something he saw out in the Mosul rubble, something other journalists have seen too, but which no one can quite categorize: lean figures in white, swaying amidst the ruin. Liam, a staff reporter for a British news outlet, was traveling with Iraqi soldiers through the waste of western Mosul, where building upon building had collapsed into a labyrinth of shattered grays. Rounding a corner in an armored Humvee, his group encountered six teenagers in bleached robes engaged in what appeared to be a modernist dance beneath a canopy of exposed rebar. Dipping and swaying, the young men contorted their bodies toward the earth before collapsing, one against the other. Artillery rumbled in the near distance as the Humvee slowed to assess the scene. The men on the ground began to twitch, as if exposed to a chemical agent, and then jerkingly resurrected their ashen frames. Then the movements repeated, dipping and swaying, dipping and swaying as a city lay collapsed all around. Strewn concrete, pocked with recent sniper fire, became a disconcerting stage for a dance performed for no apparent audience. The Humvee lingered a moment before moving on toward the frontline. Liam had news to report.

After recounting the scene, some of the journalists around the table nod in recognition. Diane has seen the dancers. So too Peter. Others have heard mention from a fixer or a driver. Dancers in a war zone—who would believe such a thing? Some quick texting indicates the apparent destruction, by US–Coalition airstrike, of a dance academy near the scene. But was this news? There was no straightforward story with which to feel empathy or disgust, no victims suffering as they should. It was mostly illegible as war reportage, signifying nothing of the extremity or horror of war, nothing of war's violence as it is represented to be. Here was a fact lacking proper figuration, an event too ambivalent to be truthful. The dancers were meaningless as journalism but meaningful indeed for the assembled journalists, who mentioned the scene for weeks. The story became a collector's item, exchanged and admired among war reporters. It was something that could capture—for journalists, though not for journalism—the dark ambiguity, the humor and absurdity, the erratic beauty of life amidst war.

In offering the story of the Mosul dancers to the table at the Classy Hotel, Liam confirmed his understanding of journalism as a process of reification and refusal, wherein a journalistic economy of truth includes only certain stories and thereby renounces others. The appreciation for this strange scene—this collector's item—throws into relief journalism's mandate and its limits, revealing war reportage as both storytelling profession and lived experience. The journalistic insignificance of the dance, and its simultaneous significance for journalists, marks the liminality within which journalists live and work. The threshold from meaninglessness to meaning, from facts to their figuration, from the strange and ambiguous to the legible and certain: This is the space of journalistic production examined in the chapters to come.

The Classy Hotel, like other sites discussed in this study, delivers this liminality between practice and product, where the discursive and the lived interact and transmogrify. The Classy is one space for observing the interdependence of facts and fictions, their mutuality in the language, meaning, and practice of war reportage. In such spaces we can examine war reportage not in order to discover what war *is* as opposed to what journalism *says* it is. Rather, the sites where war reportage can be captured in action—cafés, military checkpoints, refugee camps, burned-out city blocks—allow us to ask how journalists come to say the things they do about war, and to what effect.[18]

For an analysis of journalism's power over war is insufficient, I believe, without an exploration of this power's limits and, thereby, of the possibilities for representing war otherwise. To observe and analyze the limits of reportage in wartime—to track the frontier beyond which journalistic sense falters, the meaning that journalism cannot make, the experiences journalists bear but do not narrate—is to recognize that there is indeed an outside to journalism's economy of truth, and to the self-evidence it claims. One of the essential tasks of this book, then, is to map the contours of journalism's facts and figurations in order to seek their boundaries, boundaries that allow us to question journalism's assertation of totality in the representation of war. An attempt to realize an outside to the reality war reportage delivers—an outside that war reporters regularly confront—becomes a means to divest from the universality professed by hegemonic conceptions of global conflict. To contest the realities of war sanctioned by journalism, and to discern what is displaced in the process of reality-delivery, opens opportunities for rethinking what war and its reportage can be.

By excavating the fantasies buried within the facts, by engaging the ambiguities stalking the authoritative, we find ourselves confronting both the dominance of journalistic representation in wartime and the fragility of the legibility that war reportage provides. Our desires for war's reality, satisfied by war reportage, are shown to be what they always are: an attempt to master a reality up for grabs. This book demonstrates how contingent war's represented reality can be, and how authority over war is constituted through the erasure of this contingency. By examining the language, meaning, and practice of war reportage from the Middle East, we can grapple with both the limits of conflict journalism and the possibilities waiting at this bleeding edge.

INTERLUDE

Cheapening Experience

Journalist: I could try to write a book. But what's the profound thing you're going to say about war? It's a topic people have wrestled with forever, since Homer. It's hard to say anything new about war. I read [Sebastian] Junger's *War* recently, and I've heard that stuff before. War is something you want to see for yourself, but when it comes to describing it, you fall back on others, and on all the old tropes. In journalism too. All the more remarkable when you read something not trite and cliché.

Ethnographer: Why do people keep reporting war, then, as opposed to topics where there may be more room for innovation or novelty?

Journalist: People cover war because it's easy. It's not just because they're adrenaline junkies, but because there's a drama to war, there's a plotline, its fill-in-the-blank. There's no real need to chase sources all the time; all the pieces of the story are already there. And because war stories are easy to sell.

Ethnographer: Reportage still requires context though. You have to have some knowledge of things.

Journalist: Maybe. People disparage parachute journalists, but in a way that's the purest journalism. People who can know nothing and touch down and bang it out. That's what the industry seems to reward, anyway. Otherwise, you're an academic.

Ethnographer: Do you see yourself covering more conflicts in the future?

Cheapening Experience

Journalist: I don't know. This transition between young, hungry journalists getting up at 4 a.m. to interview all day around the frontline, and older guys who have contacts, contacts who've moved from the street to positions of power, these older guys who don't want to get up at 4 a.m. and would rather call someone who calls someone to find out what's going on—this is the career trajectory. That's why established journalists didn't see the Arab Spring coming; their contacts were establishment people. You have to know what you don't know. I'm not sure that I want to fall into all that.

Ethnographer: But you've been out there in Mosul; you've been reporting from the street, as they say. Do you feel good about that approach?

Journalist: It's about doing work. If you're not doing that, you're not helping anyone. I couldn't afford a fixer at first, so I read for the holes in the Mosul coverage and tried to fill those. But it was hard. In *Scoop* [by Evelyn Waugh], one attribute of the journalist is "rat-like cunning." Then, when I got some contracts and could afford a fixer, I could do the stuff I wanted to do—I could see stuff, I could experience the dynamic events of war. I wrote some heavy stuff, but when I went back, the stories read as tabloidy. Describing a dead body doesn't turn anyone off war; it reads like war porn. You get a lot of that from on-the-ground coverage. It's like telling war stories. What a fifteen-year-old looks like when he's hit by an airstrike and takes a dump when it impacts. It's not cool or necessary or productive.

Ethnographer: No one is making you write stories like that, though.

Journalist: Aren't they? [Redacted] wanted a story about freelancing in Mosul. I wrote a story: What it's like when a suicide bomber explodes in a small place, shit splattered against the wall, and the head popped off like a cork. The editor wanted to know. But then he said to revise it because it was too gory, and that seems dishonest. It's not an adventure. It's bigger and more serious, and it would be disingenuous to say otherwise. Editors want what it's like but then want to delete the parts about dead kids. I can't unsee them, so why should I delete them from a story so there's a better product? It makes you look oblivious to write adventure and leave out the dead kids.

Ethnographer: So the negotiation is how to write a reality that's not too real?

Journalist: Editors, the news audience, they don't really want to know what it's actually like. Maybe some people do, and I'm uncomfortable with that as well. How real do you want it? Real, but not too real—yes. And it can't just be a performance, like storytelling over a beer. That's the ultimate way of cheapening an experience: telling a war story about it.

PART I

The Language of War Reportage and Its Conditions

ONE

Folklore of the Future

The Certainty of Journalistic Expression

> In fact, we were never allowed to call it war. But it was, of course.
> —GEN. WESLEY CLARK

Rules of the Game

The *New York Times*'s *Manual of Style and Usage*, a 385-page reference guide for *Times* journalists and editors, includes entries on proper abbreviations, acceptable use of popular clichés, and the difference between Islam and Islamism. In the preface, the editors of the manual urge a thoughtful application of all the guidelines to follow, and they note a piece of wisdom included in earlier editions of the regularly updated volume. "A single rule might suffice: 'The rule of common sense will prevail at all times'" (Siegal and Connolly 2015, 15).

How does common sense and its rule prevail over war reportage and the reality it represents? How is sense made common, and what other senses are subsumed in the process? What conditions does common sense impose? In directing journalists to the "rule of common sense" as a sufficient "single rule" for their journalism, the *New York Times* style manual echoes theorists such as Michel Foucault (1982), Antonio Gramsci (1971), and Stuart Hall (1982), who understood common sense as a set of rules governing how people speak about the world, rules so powerful and so pervasive as to become invisible within the sites of their emergence. "Every social stratum has its own 'common sense'" writes Gramsci, "which are basically the most widespread conception of life and of men." Gramsci observes how common sense creates "the folklore of the future": "a relatively rigid phase of popular knowledge at a given place and time" (1971, 326).

War reportage can be assessed for the common sense it precipitates and, thereby, its effectiveness in adjudicating the "conception" of war in our time and place.[1] And by inspecting the formal strategies through which a sense of war is made common in the news, the self-evidence of both war and its reportage can be called into question. This chapter and the next parse the discursive tropes, rhetorical protocols, and linguistic standards of war reportage in order to map the conditions they impose on the journalistic representation of war. In scrutinizing the obviousness of war's represented reality—in excavating the particularity of the conventions through which war becomes real—the ideological character of war reportage can be glimpsed. Journalistic common sense is revealed as folklore.

Here I assess news of war not for how it is practiced or received but for how it says what it says and, thereby, what messages journalism's particular discursive design communicates. Rather than interpreting the topical content of the news, then, I examine rules—like those codified in the *Times* style manual—through which journalism assembles a realistic war. These rules predetermine what it is possible for journalism to disclose of war and in what manner. Journalism's generic conventions indicate a field of conditions, a space of organization, in which war achieves a discursive regularity. Here, precisely, is where war reportage perpetuates and reproduces a sense for war called common.

Analysis of the generic conventions of war reportage demonstrates how standardization in language exerts semantic preconditions on the work of individual journalists.[2] Such conventions, institutionally imposed, function as a set of rules determining how reality is coded by journalists irrespective of their personal experiences or individual views on a given topic. Journalism's rules allow for only certain messages in the process of journalistic communication, and here journalism becomes autonomous in relation to the intention of any singular journalist. Journalists can only *be* journalists, we might say, if they report within the boundaries of the sense deemed common. The regulatory force of generic convention assures that this is so.

The turn to generic convention is also, then, a turn toward the political economy of journalism, where trade in particular designations, descriptions, characters, and plots substantiate reports of war as a commodity in the information marketplace, a commodity designed to meet consumer demand. Journalism's forms of language, which produce specific realities for war, sustain its market value. Once again, it is journalism's discursive protocols, and not the inner worlds of journalists—their beliefs, understandings, convictions—through which the determinative power of war reportage becomes most apparent. For if, as Foucault asserts, a site of enunciation is a site of ideological inscription, then it is protocols of enunciation and not the beliefs of the enunciator in which ideology can be best tracked. As far as representations are bearers of ideology—as far as the news adheres an ideology in its very *form*—so does it becomes possible to explore journalism's formal dynamics for an understanding of how a particular knowledge of war is authorized and legitimated in and through journalism. These formal dynamics dictate what of war can be included in war reportage, and how war is to be addressed, while the dynamics themselves are concealed. As Evelyn Cobley argues, "The author's motivation for adopting certain formal strategies is far less important than the reader's often blind or unacknowledged absorption of the ideological inscriptions these modes of representation continue to carry" (1993, 16). Presumptively value-neutral formalities of the news—linguistic elements seemingly obvious, even banal—are often the most redolent of ideological force. The power of war reportage to control war's reality is not only a matter of the content it delivers but of the system it institutes for coding that content.

The two chapters of this section approach war reportage not as the expression of a journalist's individual consciousness, then, but as a product of the conditions under which individual journalists can express war *as* war reportage. War reportage is here recognized not as a record of war—that "first draft of history" lauded by media professionals—but as a result of discursive determinants that structure how war can be recorded. Taking up formal elements of news language—narrative realism, naming and classification, counting and enumeration, authorship and authorial presence—I aim to show how these conventions determine what war reportage is professed to be: the authoritative account of faraway conflict, an account coterminous with reality itself.

In what follows, I address several journalistic conventions in turn, and pair each with an example that elaborates relevant concerns. This chapter assesses narrative realism and examines a news story disruptive of the way protagonism and antagonism, allies and enemies, are normatively accounted for in wartime Iraq. It then turns to naming, where I look to the designation of southern Beirut as a "stronghold" and what this name reveals about journalism's narrative preconditions. The next chapter assesses numbering, looking at the death toll reported for the war in Syria, as well as authorship, to discuss the collective efforts of producing the news. In selecting conventions to examine, my aim is to assess narrative style broadly (through what I am calling *journalistic realism*); foundational elements of journalistic narrative (naming and numbering); and proof of professional authority (constituted by the byline). Together, these selections illustrate the discursive protocols and semantic preconditions that determine how war reportage represents war.

Journalism's Narrative Realism

What are the conditions allowing for journalistic communication of war, and what order do these conditions sustain? Of course, and as Foucault observes, a long list of factors is involved in any discursive formation. In the case of war reportage, such factors range from the "criteria of competence" (Foucault 1982, 50) for those journalists representing war, to networks of professional relationships and institutional hierarchies in news making, to the historical establishment of the role of the journalist as a truth teller within society broadly. At the level of language, perhaps the primary condition of journalism is legibility. That journalism must *make sense*—and how it does so—is a critical factor in war reportage, where the "spectacle of the Other" (Hall 1997) that *is* war and violence demands the imposition of narrative organization and epistemic order. A wartime reality suitably intelligible wins legitimacy through war reportage, and it assumes a self-evidence as other realities are ignored, dismissed, displaced.

The mandate for legibility was frequently expressed by the journalists I interviewed, who understood war and violence as a topic unfamiliar to faraway news consumers. "War, for my audience, is foreign," a journalist remarked to me in Beirut. "It's what the people I report for don't really know and have trouble understanding." A journalist in Baghdad explained, "The foreign is the bang-bang, the violence, and it's what everyone wants." This foreign topic, journalists told me, requires transformation in order to be made intelligible as news. A journalist in Saida, Lebanon, asserted, "We're explicit about explaining things. We say what things mean. We play things straight: What this means, period. You have to make clear. As a foreign correspondent, you make the foreign legible."

Legibility is the overarching strategic claim of war reportage, and its political-economic center. The success of war reportage as a commodity and as a social institution depends upon the discursive management of war as that which can be categorized, defined, and understood by news consumers. The designation of war reporters as "foreign correspondents" is appropriate: Their task is to establish correspondence—accordance, connection, affinity—between the foreign (conflict, suffering) and a "home audience" experientially unfamiliar with the topic at hand.

As a narrative style, realism is ideally suited to the task of legibility production, its formal properties suggesting a transparent rendering of reality and the consequent disavowal of the inexplicable or disorderly. According to Leo Bersani, realism serves society "by providing it with strategies for containing (and repressing) its disorder within significantly structured stories about itself" (1984, 63). War reportage is tasked to represent war's reality in a manner realistic to news consumers in coincidence with consumers' *own* conceptions of what war's reality entails. The "significantly structured stories" that war reportage delivers (stories that rely on particular figures, plots, tropes, and categories) are stories "about itself" insofar as such stories reflect the demands on reality made by the society to which journalists report. The war-reality produced as war reportage (the allies and enemies, victims and perpetrators, destruction and suffering that are the stuff of reported war) is never far from ideas about peace, law, security, otherness, death, and related matters already hegemonic in those societies consuming this reportage.

What counts as an intelligible reality for war is thus established by various semantic preconditions, preconditions never themselves accounted for in the narratives war reportage delivers. Rather, in telling realistic stories of war, war reportage must elide the fortuity of what qualifies as realistic and demote what fails to meet accepted standards thereof. Historical context is narratively downgraded while the trauma of suffering is prioritized. The profit from international weapons sales is narratively inferior to the damage those weapons do. Such meanings for war are assessed in Chapters 3 and 4. Yet the choice of story and the precise manner of its delivery appear natural, obvious, given. The semantic conditions of war reportage, which organize war in particular ways, must be hidden away in order to achieve the seamless legibility demanded of the news commodity. Realism, as a formal commitment, is suited to this task.

A *New York Times* column (Rudoren 2016), written by an international news editor and former Middle East reporter, usefully summarizes journalism's narrative concerns when reporting on "terrorist" violence:

> There is something of a journalistic routine each time terror erupts. Cover the news, of course, and put it into geopolitical context. Capture the drama of the scene. Pursue every tidbit about the attackers. And, perhaps most wrenchingly, try to showcase the human suffering.

Journalistic focus on the "drama" of immanent violence and individualized suffering suits a narrative preference for what can be seen and described, for vivid characters and compelling plot, for an immediately understandable event. These narrative preferences legitimate a particular reality for war by downgrading other matters—of policy, history, economics—that might conflict with ideas preconditional to the narrative produced. What I call a journalistic realism both orients itself to this representational consensus and at the same time authorizes and legitimizes this consensus, positioning war within the delimited meanings that this consensus demands. Journalistic realism delivers not knowledge of war but a recognition of what is already thought to be true of war.

The realism of war reportage coheres with a history of narrative style that Erich Auerbach, in *Mimesis* ([1946] 2013), theorizes as the fulfillment of a promise to represent reality realistically. Rather than an effort to produce a verbal mirror image of war's extra-verbal reality, war reportage is better understood as the fulfilled form of a prefigured cultural notion of war's reality. In its figural capacity, war reportage can be placed in a tradition of realism that "arose in the West and infused the dominant stream not only of modern Western literature but also of Western (Baconian) science and (bourgeois) historiography" (White 1999, 96). Neither a stream of data nor a transcendentalized account of the world (as found in religious and philosophical texts), the narrative style of war reportage is heir to the nineteenth-century literary realism that, according to Auerbach, best consummated a prefigured notion of social reality. Like a promise kept to a promise made, war reportage confirms its audiences' antecedental notions of war.

Realism, as a narrative form, presents certain ideal types in order to foreground features of reality that competing genres (tragedy, comedy, epic, myth, romance) cannot readily accommodate (Jameson 2013, 4). Journalistic realism offers specific wartime subjects, types of violence, and meanings for war symptomatic of those experiences and events that conform to certain normative understandings of what war is and does. The traumatized victim, the steely soldier, the empathetic aid worker, the crafty insurgent. The siege and the liberation, the ambush and the last stand. The refugee camp and the migrant trail and the morgue. "Iraq at a crossroads" and "Syria on the brink." These ideal types do the work of legibility-production, containing the reality of war within explicable and expected scenes, characters, and plots. A journalistic realism expresses—and thereby reproduces—what the real is already supposed to be. The work of war reportage is to recreate what counts as factual, accurate, objective renderings of faraway conflict.

War reporters are aware of the power of narrative to structure and sanction a specific reality of war. A journalist in Erbil made this clear: "Telling a story, you select material. You are crafting—it's the nature of the work—so the audience engages with the story. You're highlighting what's important, beautiful, engaging, like a novelist or a playwright." "Journalists wouldn't exist if it wasn't for narrative," a journalist in Beirut explained. "A foreign audience is towed in by narrative." This "towing in" is precisely the work of realism, in which a narrated reality is designed to satisfy consumer desire for the real. Narrative, in this manner, "summons us from afar" (White 1987, 21).

Journalists often discuss narrative elements when speaking among themselves about reporting plans. "Are there any good characters there?" a journalist asks a colleague while preparing a reporting trip to a remote Lebanese village. "What's the plot?" a journalist inquires of other journalists about Iraq's regional political disputes. "But is it a story?" a journalist wonders aloud at the bar after an assassination in Syria. These were questions frequently asked in places like Erbil and Beirut as journalists gamed out the representational possibilities for a given event or circumstance. "The stories editors will want," noted a journalist in Qamishli, Syria, "are those with immediate relevancy, and good characters are a constant." A journalist in Baghdad told me, "You know what you want. You hear that quote, and you're done. It's hard to avoid these formulas." In assessing wartime situations for plot, character, and story, journalists are arranging the world into a preestablished narrative framework. "I know how to pitch a story, and that's unfortunate," a journalist in Erbil remarked. "It's not the best version of reality, and that shapes the news." Those realities that seem real in the way reality is supposed to be are those that become news and not the "best version of reality" by any other metric. For the "best version of reality" by another standard might undermine the premises of confirmation upon which journalism's realist account is based. But in presenting stories that meet consumer expectation, a presiding common sense about war is both authorized and perpetuated.

Journalistic realism, and the elements thereof—characters, numbers, descriptions—standardize what is represented in war reportage and reproduce reigning assumptions about war. War must be made appropriately realistic by war reportage, and generic conventions, by delimiting journalism's representational possibilities, become the means by which a "realistic" reality is secured. That war is a matter of individual suffering rather than political-economic systems. That violence can be categorized by its rationality and lawfulness, or its lack thereof. That allies and enemies, victims and perpetrators, are separate and distinguishable. These determinations follow from unstated premises that condition what reality *is* in the news and thus what a realist narrative of war can deliver. Todd Gitlin notes how news narratives function as "a gloss, a slick overlay, stretched over the unasked but necessary questions: How did this war happen? What sustains it? How did incidents stretch into a history beyond tragedy? Who sold the arms, and still sells them?" (2017). That such questions are *not* asked is what allows news the validity, transparency, and truthfulness of a representation that fulfills accepted standards for war's reality. Like all realisms, then, journalistic realism functions as what Fredric Jameson calls a "hybrid concept" (2013, 5), wherein journalism's aesthetic ideal doubles as an epistemological claim to truth. The way journalism represents war—its formal elements—is also an assertion about what war entails and what its reality *is*. Ideology is in this manner elaborated through generic convention, and war reportage becomes both *episteme* and *techne*, both a way of knowing war and a technique for producing that knowledge.

This ability to both arbitrate and authenticate the reality of war is expressed through journalism's formal qualities, qualities that establish both journalistic professionalism and journalism's social power. In the terminology of J. L. Austin (1962), war reportage is both performative and constative: Presented as the transparent observation of facts on the ground, war reportage also brings those facts into existence through the discursive conditions that codify journalistic observation. If victimhood or bodily suffering is the reality of violence observed and expressed by the war reporter, war reportage also brings victimhood and suffering into being through the types of stories it foregrounds, the kinds of details it presents, the choice of facts it offers, and the frames of understanding it legitimates.[3] This productive capacity is rendered invisible by the taken-for-granted quality of the reality journalism transmits. Journalistic realism disappears the partiality and contingency of the reality it delivers, and thereby disappears too those interests served by this act of narrative naturalization. When the reality of war is one of suffering rather than systems, a certain order is both maintained and mystified.

How, then, to "provincialize" (Chakrabarty 2000) war reportage so as not to leave invisible the preconditions that undergird its representations? How to render journalistic narration not as culturally or politically or historically given, but as premised upon particular and particularizing ideas about who is able to speak about war and in what manner? How to read journalism such that war's reality is understood as managed, and thereby regulated, through the processes of its depiction? Such a task involves interrogating those dynamics seemingly natural to war reportage, dynamics such as naming the things of war, counting the dead, and identifying an author. By assessing war reportage in its discursive anonymity and through its semiotic resources, the formal dynamics of news narrative begin to reveal their productive capacity. We can then understand the names, numbers, authors, and other formal features of war reportage as an apparatus controlling war's reality, an apparatus rendered invisible as the way war *is*.

Realist Disruption in the Arkady Report

The fixed and distinct figures of protagonist and antagonist, ally and enemy, good guy and bad guy, help to institute the reality of war normative to war reportage today. The stability of such figures is fundamental to war as conveyed in the news, where a contest of forces and a division of justified from unjustified violence is established through the narrative organization of those involved in a given conflict. The portrayal of protagonists and antagonists structures wartime reality in a manner expected by global news consumers while suppressing any ambiguity that might disrupt the common sense granted to war. A protagonist's support for an alleged antagonist (such as US supply of chemical weapons to Saddam Hussein), or the imbrication of the good with the bad (as when sanctions imposed over human rights violations cause mass death, or when a terrorist group exhibits an ability to successfully govern) is ideologically and thus discursively disruptive. Such disarrangements disturb the basis of legibility for faraway war and scramble journalism's realist frame. A subject's failure to suitably fulfil the prefiguration of protagonism or antagonism in war thus results, for journalism, in a "matter out of place" (Douglas 1966).

Journalistic realism manages such disorder by hiding the preconditions determinative of how protagonism and antagonism are narratively applied. For example, journalism might hide the foreign policy interests that underwrite the assignment of "goodness" to some dictators and not others, or the alignment of a chosen protagonist with popular conceptions about secularism, rationality, and law. For if war's protagonists are as cruel as its antagonists, or its antagonists as lawful as its protagonists—if these two figures cannot be meaningfully distinguished—then something of the semantic preconditions undergirding journalism's narrative design is revealed. Examining an instance of such figural disorder throws into relief the ideational stability that journalism is called upon to provide and, thereby, the contingency of the reality that journalism delivers.

In May 2017, Iraqi photojournalist Ali Arkady published images and video of an elite Iraqi state military unit—the Emergency Response Division (ERD) of Iraq's Interior Ministry—torturing and executing suspected members of the Islamic State in November and December of 2016. Arkady's footage depicted at least six distinct incidents in which the ERD conducted forced confessions, inflicted stress positions and other torture methods, used death threats and beatings, and committed murder. Arkady insisted that the unit tortured civilians in order to obtain false confessions as justification for further raids, arrests, and executions. Those soldiers featured in Arkady's reportage did not deny their actions or the authenticity of the footage. An ERD captain told ABC News that their tactics were justified because those tortured and killed were linked to the Islamic State. Regarding footage of an ERD execution of a handcuffed prisoner, the ERD captain insisted that the prisoner "is not human, he is a monster." After publication, Arkady and his family received death threats and were eventually forced into exile. Arkady has not returned to Iraq.[4]

The ERD received praise from the US military just months before Arkady revealed these abuses. According to the *New York Times*, US Army Col. Brett Sylvia, the commander of Task Force Strike in Baghdad, called the ERD "a very effective fighting force" that had recently been advised by American officers. "It has been really a fruitful partnership in all regards," Sylvia told reporters. After the release of Arkady's footage, the Pentagon denied having been involved in training the unit or supplying it with weapons, though US military equipment, including American-made Humvees and anti-tank armaments, can be seen in the ERD's possession in Arkady's photographs. One member of the unit, captured on film torturing a suspected Islamic State member, claimed to be a US citizen and to have worked as a US military contractor.

The ERD, along with other elite Iraqi military units, such as the Golden Division and the SWAT, received much positive press coverage throughout the Islamic State conflict. Freelancers and staff correspondents from several news organizations embedded with these units during the battle for Mosul, and many news stories attested to the bravery, professionalism, humor, and emotional hardship of the units and their personnel. Reporting tended to frame their fight against the Islamic State as legitimate and lawful, their intentions as just. In this reportage, journalists often emphasized the religious diversity of these units, allowing the conflict to be framed as a repudiation of sectarianism rather than the reestablishment of Shia rule over Sunni populations. These soldiers were journalism's protagonists in a conflict with an extremist enemy; they were a ragtag group of fighters whose compelling personal stories elaborated the sacrifice and courage of crucial US allies in the fight against terrorism.

Such reportage fits snuggly within a tradition of embedded journalism dating from at least the Vietnam era, wherein a journalist's commitment to a fighting unit results in descriptive stories of plucky and earnest grunts confronting adventure, sorrow, and insight (McLaughlin 2016). Such reporting is generically kindred to hero narratives, complete with challenge and temptation, transformation and atonement, revelation and return. A journalist for the *New York Times* wrote that members of the ERD "exemplify what it meant to be a soldier in Iraq" (Solomon 2017). The figure of the soldier-hero was realized through ERD personnel and narrated through stories of ERD warfare. Such military units, as commonly rendered in war reportage from Iraq, expressed a reality of war already substantiated in the societies within which war reportage circulates. The ERD fit a prevailing consensus regarding what a protagonist in war should be and, thus, what war is all about.[5]

Arkady's access to these units, as for most embedded journalists, was premised on fulfilling this narrative expectation and articulating the conventional figural design. Arkady told ABC News that he had intended to produce a "positive story" about the ERD, and his previous work with the ERD duly conformed to an established common sense. Arkady's first film about the ERD included the captain whose later denials of torture are quoted above. In this previous representation, the captain remarks, "We are liberators not destroyers. All of ISIS are criminals and psychopaths. Don't expect us to be cruel to you [Iraqis]. We are one of you and more merciful than those strangers and intruders." Another ERD captain, in the same video, adds, "We came to free you and to save you from ISIS." The roles of protagonist and antagonist, ally and enemy, victim and perpetrator, were previously rendered by Arkady in the manner normative to the news of war produced by the international press and expected by distant news-consuming publics.

When word of Arkady's photographs of ERD torture and execution began to percolate through the journalist community in Iraq prior to their publication, many were deeply affected. At bars and parties and over dinner, there was widespread acknowledgment among journalists of how their stories of Iraqi fighting units may have lacked critical awareness or deeper context; of how some journalists may have been taken in by the performance of professionalism, or post-sectarianism, or compassion exhibited by these units; of how conventional narratives of the war might require reexamination.

"Ali [Arkady] showed a different side of things," a journalist remarked to me in Erbil. "He was able to do that. And we realized that there's always the possibility of telling another version of the story of the battle for Mosul." But was such a possibility widely engaged? After the Arkady revelations, many journalists expected changes to how war was reported on the ground, and especially with respect to how allies and enemies, protagonists and antagonists, were framed in the war with the Islamic State. But discussion of Arkady's work soon ceased; less and less reference was made to his reportage among the journalists I interviewed and observed. The news cycle moved on, and the conversation among news producers did likewise. A certain ambivalence set in.

"Ali's story showed a commitment to truth and honesty," a journalist in Beirut told me:

> And it revealed how shallow my reporting was—*our* reporting. It made me look differently at our work. Since the start of the ISIS war, Ali's been embedded with everyone—the Peshmerga [the military forces of Iraqi Kurdistan], ISOF [the Iraqi Special Operations Forces], in Ramadi, in

Sinjar. But the people who will be remembered for their work won't be Ali. Maybe we're doing a bad job. I don't expect the audience to know about Ali's reporting because it doesn't fit into the narrative. The public's understanding is the reason why we've done the reporting we have. But I have a low opinion of public understanding. I've learned how difficult it is to do anything interesting or new. Before, I knew how to report, I had a drive to sell stories, to professionalize. But the nature of reporting war is such that good thinking tends not to emerge.

The ambivalence that many journalists came to feel about the Arkady revelations was not a reaction to the work itself, which was seen by most journalists as courageous and important. The ambivalence stemmed, rather, from widespread doubt that Arkady's reporting would change the ruling narrative of the war with the Islamic State. As this journalist notes, the inability of Arkady's story to "fit into the narrative" relegated its impact, since the "public's understanding"—the presiding consensus on war— underwrites that narrative.[6]

I spoke with a journalist in Beirut who worked for a German news organization that was one of the first to publish Arkady's images of abuse. I asked this journalist, some months after publication, whether he felt the revelations had had an impact. "None at all," he replied. He noted, too, that Arkady's images were supposed to be published simultaneously by a number of international news organizations in order to maximize their impact. ABC News, however—the US partner in the enterprise—kept delaying publication for American domestic news deemed more important. According to the journalist in Beirut, the domestic news in question amounted to Trump tweets, and their prioritization by ABC spoke to the relative unimportance of Arkady's story for the American public. In explaining why the Arkady images did not alter the conventional narrative of the war with the Islamic State, the journalist cited a lack of news-consumer interest in any narrative that conflicted with those already entrenched.

Journalists, however, are the ones producing the narratives of war that become conventional, so why did the Arkady images not alter the journalism of those who professed shock at what those images revealed? Why did those journalists who expressed a new awareness about the limitations of their narratives, limitations exposed by Arkady's reportage, not produce different narratives thereafter? Why did Arkady's reportage not change how the war with the Islamic State was covered by such journalists, and thus challenge the narrative then hegemonic?

"We were gung-ho in Mosul, but we knew bad things were happening," a journalist told me in Erbil after the battle for Mosul concluded. She continued,

> We hadn't thought about our moral entanglements or our moral delusions. We knew, from Ali and others, that torture and abuse was happening. But torture wasn't the primary revelation of Ali's reporting for journalists. The real revelation was how implicated Ali was in that. We didn't imagine that we ourselves as a body—as a profession, or as a people going into this—that we ourselves were tainted in a weird way by our involvement in the war. A lot of journalists felt tainted after that, like we were all being compelled to take part in conflict.

Here is an expression not only of the limitations of the conventional narrative of war, but of how the conventional narrative is already predetermined by the journalist's professional role. Rather than a choice made by a journalist among various possible narratives, the conventional narrative of war is a condition of war reportage as a narrative endeavor. Journalistic realism makes war real only in a particular way, and any competing reality is not simply a matter of a journalist's preference. Rather, the unstated premises that are the basis for journalistic realism must *themselves* be changed in order to affect a different reality for war. That the good guys are good and the bad guys bad is a matter determined not by what journalists believe but by national foreign policy interests, institutional economic concerns, societal understandings of law and violence, and other matters preconditional to journalistic production. In this sense, journalists are indeed "taking part in conflict" through their perpetuation of particular ideas about what that conflict *is*.

I asked this same journalist if she felt Arkady's reporting had changed the narrative of the war in Iraq. She shook her head.

> It didn't have the impact because journalists recoiled. Plus, it wasn't published right away, so the impact was blunted. But the obsession with civilian death that emerged toward the end of Mosul was one of the ways that journalists reckoned with Ali's reporting. So maybe there was a slow impact. For me, it made me want to write differently. It made me not want to write the news, to not want to write war journalism.

For this journalist, war reportage *itself* is the obstacle to a different narrative framework for war. Because war reportage must operate within the boundaries of the consensus that it both reflects and reproduces.

No change in the journalistic narrative of the war in Iraq is readily discernible in the period after Arkady's reportage was published. In fact, the *Times* journalist who wrote that the ERD "exemplify what it meant to be a soldier in Iraq" wrote this *after* the publication of Arkady's footage. "One reason the narrative didn't change" a journalist in Baghdad recalled, "is because people wanted to protect their access, and the access of journalists generally." Another journalist, on the phone from London, noted, "These soldiers were up against the boogeyman. There was little public appetite for space given over to ISIS being treated as humans deserving of human rights. Also, we still had the ISOF guys, so it didn't require a wholesale reappraisal of the good guys versus bad guys dynamic, and in a way it kind of reinforced the fact that the ISOF guys really are the good guys." The preconditions determining how protagonism and antagonism were applied in the reportage from Iraq could remain invisible as long as ERD violence was seen as an aberration rather than a feature of the protagonism represented. And with the antagonism consistent—with the Islamic State remaining murderous, sectarian, and extreme in its journalistic representation—the role of protagonist simply shifted to other Iraqi military units adequately free of concern. The preconditions of the normative narrative framework did not, then, require scrutiny.

As individuals, journalists were affected by the Arkady revelations, and many understood the failures of the established narrative order. Indeed, journalists "recoiled." But as professionals, the reality normative to war reportage required continuity. Popular disgust of the Islamic State; the ability of the conventional narrative to adjust to the disorder of a protagonist undermined; the need to safeguard the access upon which narrative production depends: These things preserved the common sense of the war in Iraq, and they protected the semantic underpinnings of this dominant sense. As the narrative realism of war reportage fulfills a certain prefiguration of war, so are protagonists narrated to fulfill a prefiguration of compassion, or of heroism, or of liberal post-sectarianism in the War on Terror. Arkady could puncture this fulfillment; he could report a protagonist that was other than what a protagonist is expected to be. But rather than alter the prefiguration, only the figure of its fulfillment—its fulfilled form—changed.

The legibility provided by a story of guilt and innocence, tolerance and extremism, compassion and brutality, fixes the reality of war in a manner stubbornly uncompromising. Meanwhile, the preconditional premises of that reality—regarding policy, violence, justice—are mystified beneath the self-evidence of the narrative in use. Journalistic realism consummates what we already know to be true while repelling the contingency, manufacture, and ideological basis of that truth. To examine that basis is to trouble more than the legibility that war reportage provides; it is to undermine the reality of war itself. If the protagonists in a war are as immoral as the antagonists, the reality of war as a contest between good and bad is shaken, and the determinations of what makes a good guy good are called into question. To complicate journalism's realist design, or to challenge it—to "do anything interesting or new," as the journalist above puts it—is to disrupt reality *itself* as it is widely expected to be, and to thereby threaten the very basis of the news commodity as a reality-imparting, truth-telling enterprise. The closures of realism guard against such challenge. Heroes who are criminals, enemies who are no worse than ourselves: The connotative force of journalistic realism disavows such narrative impurity.

One of the stories that accompanied the publication of Arkady's images declared, "As the battle for Mosul intensified, the Iraqis lost the plot, descending into torture and murder of civilians." Loss of plot is exactly what Arkady's revelations express. Murderous protagonists disrupt the plot of war as journalistically instituted; such figural contradictions distort journalism's realist narrative enterprise. A loss of plot is what accompanies any scrutiny of the preconditions that establish that plot as coterminous with reality itself. To question war's expected reality—to ask why a good guy is good or how the good is different from the bad—is to risk exposing the plot given to war in war reportage *as* a plot only, a plot necessarily partial, contingent, and interested.[7]

What's in a Name

Naming and classifying the things of war is perhaps the primary means by which the ambiguities of conflict are fixed. "Siege" or "liberation"? "Insurgent" or "rebel"? "Government" or "regime"? Naming and classifying exemplify the journalistic necessity to make sense of war, to make it legible in particular ways. It is through the application of definitional certainty that war gains its specific significance, and here war reportage enacts a particular understanding of what war *is*.

The names and classifications war reportage applies to war reflect a consensus mystified beneath the declarative assurance of journalistic naming and classifying. As Stuart Hall and coauthors note, "A pivotal element in the production of consent was how things were defined" (1978, 59), and here the work of designating, categorizing, and defining is also the work of structuring, shaping, and producing. "The media were signifying agents," they continue, confirming the inevitable order of reality (1978, 60). The seemingly natural and universal validity of the names war reportage employs, and thus of the reality of war as journalistically rendered, erases the productive capacity of war reportage as a discursive force. And in establishing the givenness of reality through the names and categories it applies, war reportage enacts the function of ideology—to make sense common—while hiding its role therein.

In organizing war's reality through the application of names and categories, war reportage can satisfy news-consumer desire for certainty, accuracy, truth—for a reality that is indeed fixed. "People want certainty about what's happening next," a journalist in Erbil told me. "Even if I qualify an Iraqi commander's quote that the Mosul offensive will end in a week, people love it—they want the knowable. It's like the octopus that chooses the Super Bowl winner. It's a currency." The value of certainty necessitates the definitive account of a given event, and naming is integral to this process. Since reality is fashioned through war reportage rather than naturally occurring, and since different kinds of realities could conceivably be expressed of the same event, the question remains as to how a particular reality of war wins credibility and marginalizes competing realities. The certainty invoked by naming suggests one answer, wherein a designation or classification, consistently deployed, can maintain a delimited range of meanings.[8] Naming is a practice through which a particular account of war becomes privileged.

The certainty that a name provides is critical to the process of journalistic meaning making because it obscures the particularity of the consensus undergirding the meanings given. The declarative style of journalism—in which designations, categories, and definitions are applied definitively and without hesitation—renders invisible the contingency of the reality named and the interests underpinning what seems self-evident. The names and categories applied in war reportage appear to "speak for themselves," as Hall would say; they are "proposition free—natural and spontaneous affirmations about 'reality'" (1982, 70).

When CNN calls Ebola "the ISIS of biological agents" (October 6, 2014), presupposed is the perniciousness of the Islamic State as a faceless threat comparable to a viral pandemic, and denied is the capacity of the

Islamic State as an entity responding to historical circumstances and political dynamics—Iraqi state policies, US military actions, global economic inequities, worsening environmental conditions. When violence is named as genocide, military intervention becomes both an international obligation and an opportunity for powerful states. When an identical violence is named as war or counterinsurgency or police action, these names "give expression to the *normal* violence of the state, the reason why states are said to have armies and armed forces" (Mamdani 2010, 59). Iran's foreign policy is regularly categorized in American news coverage as Iran's "behavior," and by journalists reporting "inside" Iran rather than *in* Iran. Military attacks on "infrastructure" abstract any reference to vital means of human survival. Naming thus presupposes certain commitments and positions regarding political responsibility, state sovereignty, and the force of law—things that perpetuate names while remaining hidden within the names given.

As Mahmood Mamdani notes, the act of naming or categorizing a violent event often "isolates and demonizes the perpetrators of one kind of mass violence . . . and at the same time confers impunity on perpetrators of other forms of mass violence" (2010, 59). Names, in this manner, are not so much signifieds for the signifiers of war as they are products of particular rules journalism enacts for signifying war. These rules remain invisible in the discourse they underwrite even as they determine what journalists can report and what of war remains unreported, unnarrated, unnamed. Names do not express war, then, so much as they express the social logic of war reportage: to reflect and reproduce a ruling consensus. A consensus, for example, regarding which violence is threatening to a social order and which violence is the normal functioning of that order.[9]

"Violence here in Lebanon becomes part of an essentialist cultural dynamic," a journalist in Beirut remarked, "revealing the precarity of the state, religious fanaticism, a danger of things getting worse." Journalism, in its categorization of violence in Lebanon, already aggregates particular presuppositions about Lebanon's reality. "There can't be a normal shooting in Lebanon," the journalist continued. "It has to be tied to geopolitics. It's already emplotted. A shooting in the US can be personal; it doesn't say anything about America's condition as a state." A shooting in Lebanon becomes a geopolitical event through its naming as "terrorism," or "political resistance," or "assassination." The act of violence is already contained, in its journalistic designation, within an order of understanding as to what violence in Lebanon *is*. A shooting in Lebanon, when named as an assassination or an act of terrorism, when named as "spillover from the Syrian war" or "Lebanon on the edge," indeed names an event. But the event named is already conditioned by the rules for its emergence in journalism. The rules of international journalism in the Middle East—to produce definitive accounts, often of conflict, in ways coincident with dominant consumer understandings of the Middle East—already determine the names assigned to events in the news.

Consider this recent job advertisement for a Middle East reporter for the *Los Angeles Times*:

> This correspondent will anchor our coverage of the ongoing conflicts in Iraq and Syria, as well as monitoring the turbulent progress of "democracy" in Egypt, North Africa and the Gulf. But more than that, we are looking for an accomplished writer who is capable of plunging into these ancient and dazzling cultures, capturing their mesmerizing variety, deep intellectual history, turbulent social upheaval and—from ISIS insurgents to entrenched dictators—their capability for brutish violence. The successful candidate will be the one who avoids the office and wanders the back roads; who will leave the others to tally the daily mayhem and bring us stories we will not have the power to forget.

The scare quotes around democracy, the "brutish" quality of regional violence, the cultures called dazzling, the self-evidence of a "daily mayhem": Such designations are deemed suitable for the Middle East even prior to any individual taking up the professional task of applying these designations. Or perhaps the advertisement should be read as an institutional insistence that a Middle East reporter be one who applies such designations, regardless of the circumstances actually encountered in the Middle East. In any case, the names already in journalistic circulation indicate those rules that condition how the things of the Middle East are to be named. As Allen Feldman argues, "We are today embroiled in archival wars of naming and unnaming, including what can be named as war, enemy, and violence" (2015, 186). The ability to name the things of war is an act rife with power, in which war reportage (among other discourses) plays a role in a struggle for ideational control.[10]

Even as the act of naming and classifying fixes reality, it also suggests the contingency that this act seeks to erase. For Zygmunt Bauman, "Ambivalence is a side-product of the labor of classification; and it calls for yet more classifying effort." He continues, "Though born of the naming/

classifying urge, ambivalence may be fought only with a naming that is yet more exact, and will set still tougher (counterfactual) demands on the discreteness and transparency of the world and thus give yet more occasion for ambiguity. The struggle against ambivalence is, therefore, both self-destructive and self-propelling" (1993, 3). As will be discussed in Chapters 4 and 5, the circumstance in which a "siege" in Aleppo can be a "liberation" in Mosul, despite the similarities between these events of conflict, speaks to the ambiguity lurking behind definitional certainty and to the function of names for disciplining the reality journalism represents. Bauman calls naming and classifying "a managerial problem" (1993, 3), and management of war's reality is indeed at stake in war reportage. Here we can see the tension that lies behind the power of naming, and in which the ratification of a consensus about war's reality requires the subjugation of competing realities. Insurgency *cannot* be revolution; counterinsurgency *cannot* be genocide. In the news and elsewhere, the distinction between these designations reflects crucial preconditions—political and social—that determine the name given. As Mamdani suggests, the naming of violence is contingent upon a political context already acting upon the discourse in which that name appears.

Because names are conditional in this way, there is always some excess to the act of naming, some unnamed remainder threatening to the order that naming institutes. Where a siege can be named a liberation, where counterinsurgency can be classified as genocide, there the work of order is revealed and the contingency it attempts to master apparent. A journalist in Baghdad explained to me, "I disagree with using the word 'insurgent' to describe events in Syria. When al-Qaeda is in the picture, we use 'insurgent,' and when they're not we use 'rebel.' But it's a false distinction. I think the words we use have too much power." Yet power is precisely the point of such naming. In 1984, the US State Department announced it would no longer use the word "killing" in reference to American acts of war, but rather "unlawful or arbitrary deprivation of life" (in Cohn 1987, 691). For Carol Cohn, such anodyne language works to "tame the world. . . . [It is] a way of gaining mastery over the unmasterable" (1987, 698). Language provides control over wartime violence, Cohn writes; it "shapes your categories of thought and defines the boundaries of imagination" (1987, 714). Yet this attempt at delimitation cannot quite close the gap between the name applied and the thing it purports to signify. The very fact that names are subject to preconditions suggests that other names are possible.

"Many don't think about the terminology that enters the ecosystem," a journalist in Kobani remarked. "There's little awareness or question. 'De-escalation zones,' 'local ceasefires'—the terms don't match the reality. A local ceasefire is really a surrender." "With the word 'militia,' it's politicized," a journalist in Beirut told me, adding,

> But what else can we call them? I still have to explain what the thing is to a reader. Names sweep up so much. And Syria—what kind of war is it? Civil? Proxy? We have to make the judgment calls quite a lot. It makes me uncomfortable. Are there terrorists in Aleppo, or just rebels? How do you define terrorist and terrorism?

Designating conflict as a siege rather than a liberation, categorizing fighters as rebels instead of insurgents, reporting on a ceasefire as opposed to a surrender—these choices obscure a lurking ambiguity in their insistence on definitional order. For as Bauman notes, order's Other is not the pure negativity of chaos but *uncertainty*. Chaos is less frightening to order, Bauman asserts, than "undefinability, incoherence, incongruity, incompatibility, illogicality, irrationality, ambiguity, confusion, undecidability, ambivalence" (1993, 7). This is because, and unlike uncertainty, chaos can still be identified and thereby fixed. The journalistic practice of naming is fundamental to this discursive function: providing legibility for, and thus mastery over, what cannot be finally controlled. Naming and classifying violence indicate a journalistic attempt to fix war's reality, yet the ambiguity that naming dispels always waits there at the borders of the certainty war reportage supplies.

We can glimpse the contingency that naming displaces, and the order naming authorizes, in any number of journalism's linguistic sites. During the recent wars in Iraq and Syria, US and Iraqi combatants were variously designated in international news as Coalition troops, ground forces, soldiers and allied soldiers, or they were named by division, regiment, or unit. Those fighting against the US-Coalition were named, most frequently, as insurgents, if not extremists or jihadists. The style manual for the *Independent*, the UK-based newspaper, includes the following entry:

> Please try to minimise calling people who go to fight for Isis (or any other such group) "militants" unless absolutely necessary for some specific reason. They may be fighters, terrorists, killers, Islamic extremists, jihadists, Isis supporters (if not fighting) . . . but "militants" makes them sound more like striking trades unionists.

This proscription suggests that "militant," as a designation, is either insufficiently negative or insufficiently alien to the *Independent*'s readership. The precondition for the name given to Islamic State members in the *Independent* seems to be an understanding that those who fight for such groups are beyond the pale of either recognition or reprieve.[11]

While the accuracy of these designations can be debated, more consequential is how they codify a normative understanding of who is subject to international law, the Geneva conventions, and associated judicial instruments; of who is worthy of particular affective dynamics, such as empathy or respect; of who is granted proper political subjectivity and justified use of force. Names like "enemy combatant"—the technical classification for US prisoners of the War on Terror—substantiate the foreclosure of Geneva convention protocols and the writ of *habeas corpus*. This name erases the juridical incongruity, political ambiguity, and societal ambivalence that accompany the torture and indefinite detention of those so named. The "so-called Islamic State," a frequently employed epithet in war reportage from the Middle East and beyond, serves to delegitimize the aims of the Islamic State *as* a state and to aggregate the rights of law and governance to those opposing the Islamic State, that is, to those societies for whom much war reportage is produced. The "so-called" modifier challenges Islamic State statehood, and war reportage here becomes party to a semantic conflict with the Islamic State.[12] In denying unsanctioned claims to statehood, the modifier also hides the ambiguity of statehood as a designation sanctifying the use of violence on grounds that may be contentious. A journalist in Baghdad wondered, "What *don't* we decide is 'so-called'?"

A name says less about war than it does the possibilities presented for how war can be understood. By naming and classifying war, war reportage performs certainty while mystifying both the consequential omissions of the name given as well as the basis by which a name becomes conventional. "Terrorism," of course, is Exhibit A in this process, such that, according to Banu Bargu, "discourse on terrorism has become an ideological battlefield in which even the deployment or avoidance of the term itself has been transformed into a signifier of a normative and political position." She continues, "The labeling of these acts as terrorist does the cryptonormative work that incorporates a judgment of the cause for which the . . . act is performed" (2014, 19). In naming terrorism, the judgment attendant to the name must remain cryptographic in order for war reportage to achieve the mimetic, transparent delivery of war's reality that is its social function.[13]

The War on Terror (so called) is in a fundamental way a conflict over naming, and it provides perhaps the sharpest example of the entwinement of classification and power. In this war, the application of a name makes available a spectrum of state capacities, including the ability to rendition and imprison individuals indefinitely and without trial; to invade sovereign states and occupy foreign land; and to summarily execute. As a classification, "terrorism" institutes and perpetuates violence in accordance with a consensus about what that name signifies. Conversely, the withholding of a name—the failure to apply the name of "terrorism" to particular individuals or groups—allows for a degree of latitude in the use of a violence named terroristic in similar contexts. The name "terrorism" is not bounded in any fixed way; its application allows for certain violences to be deployed or policed based upon the interests of those with the power to name. When asked whether the killing of a woman by a professed neo-Nazi constituted terrorism, then-President Donald Trump gave a revealing answer: "You can call it terrorism. You can call it murder. You can call it whatever you want. . . . Because there is a question. Is it murder? Is it terrorism? And then you get into legal semantics" (in Segarra 2017). Naming something "terrorism" is indeed arbitrary; it is a designation applied in response to demands other than clarification itself. The name "terrorism" allows for the furtherance of a specific plot, with specific characters and meanings, suitable to specific interests regarding the reality of the violence in question. In naming the terrorist, the reality of violence is managed in conjunction with a particular order, while the influence of that order on the name given is hidden away. The certainty displayed in a "war" on "terrorism" can then be taken at face value and proceed accordingly.[14]

In this way, naming essentializes its object, occluding the politics of this essentialization and holding at bay that which speaks back to its realist pretensions. This process reaffirms the celebrated empiricism of journalism, the materialism of its testimony, and its forensic capability to deduce and separate the victim from the perpetrator, the innocent from the guilty, the lawful from the extreme. The terrorist, the mass grave, the unexploded ordnance become data points in the definitive reconstruction of the life of violence. Scrutiny of naming, then, challenges the evidentiary premise of journalism as a mode of disenchantment, in which journalists seek to know the world, to classify it, and to thereby reveal reality in its self-evidence, rendering invisible any discursive imposition. Journalism's names become canonical in their ubiquity as the way to write about, and thus to understand, war and violence. Designations, definitions, and categories disgorge other ways of knowing war—the war crime that is policy as well as aberration, the protection of civilians that is at the same time their extermination, the terrorists that are also a state. The name, in its very givenness, disciplines wartime reality while validating those conditions under which a name achieves regularity.

"It's the 'sixth anniversary of the war in Syria,'" a journalist noted in Beirut. "This is what all the journalists are writing now. But is it? No, it's the anniversary of the uprising, it's the anniversary of the demonstrations. These things are now folded into 'war.'" For even "war"—a name exuding neutrality, certainty, and closure, and which provides stability in its affirmation of news-consumer expectations regarding the reality of mass violence— itself suggests what a name cannot fully contain. In an age when US military forces are involved in everything from healthcare and agricultural reform to disease control and microfinance—when the US military operates in almost every country on earth (including those not designated "areas of hostile activities") and when official national security threats now include climate change, financial collapse, cybercrime, viral pandemic, and human migration—the categorical fixity of war is at risk. Gen. Wesley Clark, who commanded the Kosovo War, suggests this lexical instability in the epigraph at the beginning of this chapter (2001, xxxvii).

Are sanctions—for instance, in Iraq after the Gulf War, and which killed more Iraqis than that war—*war*? Is the Biden administration's decision to freeze Afghanistan's central bank assets after the Taliban victory an act of war, as the subsequent economic catastrophe from that act may kill more Afghans—from starvation and exposure—than the war so named? Is a "war on drugs" *war* or is it merely a metaphor, despite the militarization attendant to this phenomenon? Are US drone strikes *war*, even if they occur in areas not considered war zones, and even as they remain unsanctioned by the governing body tasked with officializing state violence as *war*? *War* reveals the conceptions and assumptions, interests and vulnerabilities, fears and desires that determine whether "war" names the things that it does.[15] Insofar as war, when described in its complexity, may no longer *be* war as popularly understood, then "war" continues to bring war into being by naming it. Walter Benjamin argues as much: "The answer to the question '*What* does language communicate?' is therefore 'All language communicates itself'" (1978, 316).

A Stronghold of Certainty

A particularly contentious instance of naming occurred early in my fieldwork, when the *New York Times* Beirut bureau produced a story headlined, "Deadly Bombing in Beirut Suburb, a Hezbollah Stronghold, Raises Tensions" (Hubbard and Barnard 2014). The lead of the article describes a car bombing in a southern suburb of Beirut—in an area called Dahiyeh, but which is unnamed in the article—that is "home to top Hezbollah offices and heavily populated with the group's supporters." The article describes the scene of the blast, explains the "sectarian tensions" "aggravated" by the ongoing Syrian war, and lists other recent bombings in Beirut. It quotes residents of the area who expected an attack and details their experiences of the bombing. Hezbollah's "domination" of the area is narratively certified through reporting that posters of martyrs are common, that the group's media office and construction company are nearby, and that Hezbollah agents responded to the scene of the attack. Reaction to the bombing from various regional groups are related, and Hezbollah's involvement in the Syrian war discussed. The "kicker" (a journalistic convention in which the end of an article presents a narrative turn or emphasis) mentions both recent bombings in areas "where Hezbollah holds enormous influence" and the bombing of a Sunni mosque in the city of Tripoli, Lebanon. This conclusion establishes the bombing as a sectarian act raising "the specter of reprisal attacks."

During the same period, the *Times* also ran a similarly headlined article: "Deadly Blast Rocks a Hezbollah Stronghold in Lebanon" (Hubbard and Saad 2013). The lead was, again, a car bombing in a southern suburb of Beirut—Ruwais, also in Dahiyeh, unnamed until the seventh paragraph—"in the heart of a stronghold of Hezbollah, the militant Shiite movement that has the country's strongest military force." The bombing is identified as "spillover" from the war in Syria that targeted a "complex often used for Hezbollah rallies." Bystanders are quoted, torn bodies described, and local support for Hezbollah emphasized. "Hezbollah's control of the area" is narratively confirmed by reporting that "most residents are Shiites," that posters of martyrs are common, that Hezbollah party members responded to the scene of the attack, and that local residents listed "the group's enemies"—such as Israel, al-Qaeda, and the Persian Gulf states—as to blame for the bombing. The kicker mentions a recent bombing in a Christian neighborhood of Beirut that "many suspect" was planned by Hezbollah, again suggesting sectarian animosity as the meaning of the violence in question.

"Stronghold" implies fortification and militarization, or an area where a particular cause or belief is prominent. However, my casual strolls through Dahiyeh around the time of these bombings indicated mixed political affiliation in the area, with signage and flags promoting Amal, another Shia political party, as well as Hamas, the Palestinian Sunni party. Dahiyeh is home to Palestinians and Syrians as well as Lebanese, and both Christian and Muslim communities of various sects reside in the neighborhood. This pluralism is not proof against Hezbollah's power and influence in the area. Rather, it indicates that the relationship between the name "stronghold" and the area it names may be less obvious or natural than the use of the epithet suggests.

The *New York Times* is not the only news organization to designate the area a "stronghold." National Public Radio, the *Guardian*, France24, CBS News, *Haaretz*, the *National*, the *Wall Street Journal*, Vice News, ABC News, BuzzFeed News, and many other news organizations have used "Hezbollah stronghold" to name the area also known as Dahiyeh. This frequency indicates an established perception, authorized by and reproduced in journalistic discourse, of southern Beirut as politically and religiously homogeneous, as violent and militarized, and as sectarian and subject to attack. It is the very regularity of "stronghold" as a name in the news that suggests a larger context for such naming, some understanding of the area that has achieved legitimacy over other, marginalized understandings. The self-evidence of "stronghold" as a journalistic designation—its common sense in international news—points toward invisible rules determining when and where "stronghold" makes sense as a name. "Stronghold," that is, expresses a consensus about southern Beirut among (mostly Western) news producers and consumers, a consensus in which civilian death in the area can be expected and perhaps justified, and in which some political entities are terroristic and the neighborhoods under their presumed rule are thereby subject to violence. That the area has been a target of military action by both Israel and the Islamic State indicates even broader agreement regarding the "stronghold" designation, or at least regarding what that designation allows. The name "Hezbollah stronghold" essentializes the suburb in a way that seems to account for its inevitability as a target. By naming the area a stronghold, journalism corroborates a cause-and-effect dynamic, whereby Hezbollah's sectarian interests and its involvement in the conflict in Syria precipitate and account for the bombing of its "fortress."

However, use of "stronghold" does not itself reveal how the name comes into being nor how a social order guides this process. One cannot look internally at the stronghold named—that is, at Dahiyeh—to understand what a stronghold is and why it makes sense. Rather, one has to look at journalism as a discourse in which "stronghold" appears as a name for a place and then gives that place meaning. "Stronghold" does not exist prior to its emergence in a discourse, and the meaning that this name confers is less a matter of its reference to something outside itself than it is the conditions of the name's regular occurrence in the news, and the self-evidence achieved thereby. For the civilian character of Dahiyeh (literally, "southern suburb") is disappeared by the "stronghold" designation, and the naturalness of this erasure—as well as the consequential self-evidence of Dahiyeh as a militarized Hezbollah fortress—cannot be established in southern Beirut itself. It is journalism, not Dahiyeh, that conditions the emergence of "stronghold" as a name and that organizes the appearance and perseverance of those meanings associated with the southern Beirut thus named. The naming of a stronghold in the news brings a stronghold into existence for news consumers, satisfying a desire for what is expected of Beirut.[16]

I asked a journalist who grew up in Lebanon, and who reports for US and British news organizations, what he thought about the reportage on the bombings in Dahiyeh and the use of "stronghold" specifically. "Using the term 'Hezbollah stronghold' doesn't really add value," he told me. "The idea is that we should categorize them instead of treating them as people. We didn't report 9/11 as an attack on a 'neocolonial stronghold.' It changes civilians into combatants. We can justify 9/11 this way too. In a stronghold, everything becomes justifiable."

In the context of war and conflict, who counts as civilian is a matter arbitrated through the process of naming, and here designations like "stronghold" do powerful work. "This is more than damaging," the same journalist continued. "The license of throwing words around wouldn't be given to reporters in the US 'In this place, that happens'—there's an arrogance here that's far from justified."

I asked about the attention to "spillover" from the war in Syria, evident in the *New York Times* articles and in much of the news on Lebanon at that time. "It's the language of infection," he replied, and referenced a recent mass shooting in the United States.

This is a genre. "The violence of Orlando spills over into Miami"—you'd never read this. It's the same with "ancient hatreds" or sectarianism as an explanation for violence. You don't see mentions of slavery when you read about police shootings in the US. Everything in Lebanon happens for a reason: religion, fanaticism. Yet it would be racist to say, "That happens because of Black culture." Journalists say the equivalent all the time about Lebanon. It's a tidy narrative, and readers expect to be told this narrative.

Hezbollah is a recognized political party in Lebanon, with representation in parliament, and even as its military involvement in Syria is locally controversial, support for the party is not considered particularly radical. Hezbollah is involved in charity work, health care, education, and benign forms of political organizing. In much of the world, however, Hezbollah is understood more as a militia than as a political party. Hezbollah is classified as a Foreign Terrorist Organization by the US State Department and is thus considered, administratively and by the American political establishment, a threat to American persons and interests. Multiple classifications for Hezbollah can thus be considered accurate, but only some win legitimacy as commonsense labels journalistically applied to this group.

Naming Dahiyeh a Hezbollah stronghold, and thereby naturalizing the area as a military target, might then be expected of a discourse attempting to meet US or European news-consumer expectations, where a certain consensus about Hezbollah and Lebanon, and about war and violence, is already achieved. While the complexity of Hezbollah (and, for that matter, of Dahiyeh) is difficult to convey in a short news article focused on a specific incident of violence, the naming conventional to journalism does align, consistently, with a perception of the world that already authorizes a name's use. If the deployment of a name in the news demonstrates how journalism organizes the world, and what it makes possible to think and express about the world, this organization yet responds to and perpetuates an order already influencing the designations journalists deploy. The frequency of the name "stronghold" across international news organizations suggests how southern Beirut has been globally understood, and how it should be understood: It is a militarized space that can expect violence.

Even the name "Beirut" has acted as a byword for violence, where memories of Lebanon's fifteen-year civil war tend to overshadow an image of yacht clubs, cozy bars, refugee influx, family restaurants, financial mismanagement, global universities, and crowded slums more indicative of

Beirut today. The danger that the name "Beirut" can signify, even despite Beirut's relative safety, seems to be taken for granted within those international news organizations that cover Lebanon, and whose journalists live, raise children, and sometimes grow old in Beirut. An Iraq-based reporter for a British news organization explained to me how the anxiety of living in Baghdad—at that time, a city more dangerous than any in Lebanon by most metrics—prompted frequent vacations to Beirut, where she could dance at clubs, attend dinner parties, and sit on a beach. Yet, when her colleagues based in Europe for the same news organization want to visit Beirut, they must complete risk assessment forms before travel. The violence that "Beirut" might signify responds to existing—and contextually specific—expectations, fears, and vulnerabilities. "Beirut," if it acts as a byword for violence, indicates a particular field of discursive emergence, in which a city can be considered dangerous even despite a relative lack of discernible danger.

In Beirut, a staff journalist at an American newspaper told me about his wedding in Lebanon and the reactions of his American family invited to attend. "'Lebanon is so dangerous,' they told me after the invitations went out. But who do I have to blame but myself?" This journalist was asking his family to attend his wedding in a country he himself has represented, quite frequently, as dangerous. He continued,

> Before I went to cover Cast Lead [the 2008–09 conflict in Gaza], I tried to imagine how bad it would be. And when I went, it was really nasty, and I think the observers would say this war was worse than the last one. But being there didn't feel as bad as my imagination of Cast Lead. When reporting, you focus on the violence, and you'll never read about the fifteen people in a park having a picnic, laughing and playing. It won't be in the coverage. Baghdad too is not as bad as the image. So I don't know if we can give an accurate picture of what life is like in these places. Normal life is not what drives newsworthy events. I don't know if we can do it differently. And I do think, a lot of times, we are importing meaning that's not there.

This admission about the journalistic importation of meaning accounts for the work of naming, wherein a name already suggests the preconditions that allow for a name's appearance in the news. "Cast Lead," "Beirut," "Baghdad," "Hezbollah," "stronghold," "terrorism," "trauma"—these names become sites of contested inscription, where the denotative aspect of naming is overcome by its connotative potential. "Stronghold" already delimits what southern Beirut can be, and the ambiguous line between civilian and combatant, municipal and military, innocence and guilt is fixed by the certainty a name supplies. This is why, as the journalist quoted above notes, a shooting in Lebanon cannot be represented as random but is always tied to a geopolitical plot—spillover from Syria, sectarian hatred. An act of violence in Lebanon is always already political, and in this manner always already plotted, classified, explained. The designation of Dahiyeh as a "stronghold" does this work, explaining violence in the area as the natural consequence of an ongoing conflict. The name perpetuates an imagination for violence that has achieved consensus in the society for whom that name is produced, and this process determines both the objects named and the names given.

"Stronghold," as a name for an object represented in journalism, comes to resemble the "statement" theorized by Foucault. As for Foucault's "statement," a name in the news reflects the particular way that a discourse (here, journalism) organizes reality (here, of the Middle East). Widespread journalistic use of the name "stronghold," then, indicates how the social order underpinning journalism regards the world journalism represents. Less a reference to the reality of Lebanon, or of Hezbollah, or of the violence expended in the region, "stronghold" is the product of a set of rules governing how journalism represents reality. These rules include particular ways of categorizing (e.g., war as separate from peace), particular approaches to violence (e.g., as means or ends, as lawful or extreme), and a focus on particular figures (e.g., allies and enemies, victims and perpetrators). "The statement circulates," Foucault writes, "is used, disappears, allows or prevents the realization of a desire, serves or resists various interests, participates in challenge and struggle, and becomes a theme of appropriation or rivalry" (1982, 105). It is the apparent self-evidence of the name "stronghold"—its mystification of the desires, interests, appropriations determining its emergence in the news—that reveals the power of journalism as a discourse that orders the world.

The matter of naming is not whether "stronghold" is a true or false name for a place otherwise known as Dahiyeh. Rather, the matter is the organizational determinants, the field of emergence, that allows the label a taken-for-grantedness in the journalism that represents Lebanon. At issue, that is, are the rules governing an understanding of the world, and the forms of authority that institute those rules, that make "stronghold" possible as a name regularly appearing in news coverage of Beirut. While the international press professes neutrality and accuracy, the names appearing in the news suggest a convergence with only particular interests, desires, imaginations, and struggles: those of a reigning power, globally dispersed and naturalized as common sense. Which civilians are also combatants? What neighborhoods are also targets? When is peace also war? Answers to these questions, as determined within those societies consuming international news, establish the rules governing the names given in war reportage. The declarative character of the name "stronghold," applied to an area unfamiliar to most global news consumers, renders invisible the political logic in which that name is embedded. "Stronghold" speaks for itself; it is, again, a "spontaneous affirmation about reality" (Hall 1982, 70) rather than a name determined by underlying—and disappeared—considerations. This quality of self-evidence is also apparent in casualty counts, a critical feature of war reportage, and in the byline, the mark of authorship—and thus of authority—in news of war. It is to these formal properties of war reportage that the next chapter turns.

For journalists in Lebanon, both foreign and Lebanese, the sense they make in their journalism is very often assumed common. Speaking with journalists who use the term "stronghold" in reference to Dahiyeh, the ease and obviousness of the name was consistently evoked. Use of "stronghold" simply responded to a perceived news-consumer consensus around Dahiyeh, around Hezbollah, around Lebanon—a consensus that already accounts for the name given. "I use 'stronghold' reflexively," one journalist told me. "Sometimes you just want to name it and move on." Considering the deadlines, the stress, the churning news cycle, the complexity of the Middle East, one can hardly blame journalists for using the names already at hand. But by scrutinizing the names journalists apply to the world, we can watch journalism legitimating only particular meanings, only particular realities, only particular violences. And we can thereby assess the role of war reportage in the maintenance of a consensus about what war in the Middle East *is*.

TWO

Visible System and Invisible Rules

Commodifying Common Sense

> But it is not the case that the words are one thing and the rite another. The uttering of the words is itself a ritual.
> —EDMUND LEACH

Who Counts?

Counting—and, particularly, counting casualties—is a central means by which war reportage establishes the accuracy, truthfulness, and authority of its representations of war. Less the precision of the numbers themselves, it is journalism's ability to present a number that marks its credibility as a truth-telling, reality-imparting enterprise. Numbers do the symbolic work of authenticating journalism's ability to impart what war *is*. By signaling certainty and factuality, numbers enhance the effectiveness of the news (Lugo-Ocando and Nguyen 2017; Van Dijk 1988). Numbers, then, are a rhetoric of truth and casualty counts a rhetoric of the truth of war. "Subjectivity comes in with description, the words used, and the placement of a fact in the news hierarchy," a journalist in Beirut explained. "But you can't fudge casualty counts. And this is why they're important."

This chapter explores how the neutral and objective aura of numbers becomes suitable to the discourse of war reportage, and why these qualities are rhetorically coercive. I then turn to the byline—the mark of journalistic authorship—to examine how authorial power is constituted and what, precisely, it controls. Finally, I examine the commodity form of news, showing how journalism's formal dynamics mystify the conditions of their production in meeting consumer demand for war's truth.

Some of the earliest known examples of what can be recognized as journalism in the modern sense concern faraway war. According to Andrew Pettegree, the fall of Negroponte to the Ottomans in 1470 and, ten years later, the Ottoman siege of Rhodes were the first events to find significant resonance as news in print (2014, 59). Published reports of faraway violence, and the specter of the violent Other, attracted wide attention in Europe and eventually motivated a pan-European response.[1] And as early as the Thirty Years War, news circulating across Europe included casualty counts. That a number was offered in reports of war was not a mere matter of course, but something that could be leveraged as a major selling point. Death tallies conferred a market advantage. The illustrated title page of a news report from 1620 boasted, "News from Vienna and Prague, with the number of the principal gentlemen fallen in the battle" (in Pettegree 2014, 192). Numbers enhance the value of news as an authoritative account of war, while at the same time regulating how war is to be understood.

Numbers, particularly of death or injury, are a means for journalists to exert rhetorical control over the chaotic and often imprecise circumstances of war and violence. Numbers evoke precision, objectivity, neutrality, accuracy, certainty, verifiability—dynamics that cohere with the ideals of contemporary war reportage. In this manner, numbers enact journalism's authoritative claim to truth by their very appearance in a news text, irrespective of their relation to the reality that numbers are presented to explain. The correlation between a number and the thing it counts can be less important for journalists than the deployment of a number in their journalism. It is as if a number's occurrence itself testifies to that number's accuracy, and thereby to the accuracy of the news within which the number appears.

In post-invasion Iraq, as bombings proliferating amidst an intensifying insurgency, foreign journalists' movements were largely curtailed for security reasons. Daily casualty counts became both more important as the major news item from Iraq and, simultaneously, more difficult for journalists to obtain. "We needed the daily toll," a journalist in Baghdad told me. "But the toll was actually impossible to get." My interviews with those who reported during this period indicate that at least one major US news organization put an official at the Interior Ministry of Iraq on payroll in order to secure a regular death tally from a source that seemed rhetorically reliable. This was done despite an awareness among reporters in Iraq that the tally given by officials at the Interior Ministry was at best a loose estimation and likely an outright fabrication. It was further understood at the time that the Interior Ministry was itself operating a death squad that contributed to the daily casualty count. But the credibility of the number reported in the news was a concern secondary to that of having a number to report. As this circumstance suggests, numbers may be less an indication of war's reality then they are of the terms by which journalism organizes the reality of war.[2]

The discursive authority evoked by numbers is the critical matter of the casualty count and not, or not only, the correspondence of the number to the violent reality it purports to quantify. This doesn't make the number false; an accurate number of those harmed in war is difficult to ascertain in the best of reporting circumstances, and an inaccurate number can at least provide an impression of the scale of the violence in question. However, it is the conditions that underwrite a number's emergence as an authentic conveyance of war's reality, and thus as a mark of the authenticity of war reportage, that is often the abiding concern of enumeration in the news. Such concern is distinct from accuracy as such. It is the compression of violence into a casualty count, and the way this convention shapes conceptions of war, that is pivotal. For the essentialization provided by a number allows wars, and the events of war, to become quickly intelligible, seamlessly legible, to be compared and ranked—all while relegating to the background those matters not so easily quantified.

"News is led by body counts," a journalist in Erbil remarked, explaining:

> We get numbers from Congo, Yemen. But do you need to know how many people died somewhere, or what it means? Body count is the story, and you are left none the wiser about why it happens and where it's going. We should know why Africans are dying. Most of the stuff in your cellphone is from Congo. Is that why these people are killed? If so, we should say why.

In distilling war to the number killed in war, war reportage can reduce war to a conceptually and representationally manageable core. If violence is the most important thing about war, and if the effects of war's violence can be counted, then war is knowable by casualty counts. Journalism's delivery of that critical number becomes a direct and transparent means of accessing war's reality. However, and as discussed in Chapter 4, the turn to casualty counts in the representation of faraway conflict can neutralize interrogation of what makes casualties happen and naturalize corporeal suffering (and the immanent violence that is suffering's direct cause) as the central matter of war. The systems perpetuating war, and the interests served thereby, fall away as representational attention is drawn to a tally of harm. The journalist just quoted understood the limits of casualty counting, yet his reporting from Iraq (as well as his reporting on Darfur a decade before) nonetheless privileges death tallies as a primary news item. The convention can be questioned, but its influence is difficult to escape.

Numbers are not naturally given, of course; someone must count, and must decide what or whom to count. The death toll is subject to a complex of conditions that propel a number's regularity as a rhetorical element in the news. While civilian casualties during the NATO intervention in Kosovo, for example, were closely tracked in the news, the civilian impact of the US intervention in Afghanistan was largely overlooked. In the latter case, William Merrin argues, "The crisis was ignored . . . because here it undermined rather than supported Western military action. The West's narrative of the defeat of evil in the name of humanitarian values would have been undermined by exposure of the effects of the war" (2018, 83). A memo from CNN's chairman to its staff made explicit that news organization's position on counting casualties in Afghanistan: "It seems perverse to focus too much on the casualties or hardship in Afghanistan. . . . We must talk about how the Taliban are using civilian shields and how [they] have harbored the terrorists responsible for killing close to 5,000 innocent people" (in Kurtz 2001). Both the haphazard production of numbers, and their selectivity—decisions concerning who is counted, and thus who counts—are mystified beneath the symbolic truth that numbers provide and the representational authority of their provision.

"A high number will get attention," said a journalist in Baghdad. "A car bomb that kills three people here can be ignored. It has to have a higher death toll to pursue it. Unless it affects the West." Bigger events, where more are killed, tend to be perceived as more newsworthy by journalists and editors and thus receive more representational recognition. Major bombings are more likely to be noticed and thus counted. Deaths in urban areas of a county at war, where more journalists live and work, are likely to receive more attention—and thus produce more numbers—than deaths in rural areas. These distinctions are themselves geographically relative: Dozens killed in Iraq may not spur the focus, and thus the efforts to count, as would a few killed in France. On this matter, a journalist in Beirut was blunt: "Numbers are arbitrary, and they depend on what affects the rest of the world. We fetishize numbers at the expense of context."[3]

Such contingencies are a matter of institutional pragmatics (where journalists happen to live often depends on access to telecommunications) as well as generic demand (more death is more newsworthy than less death). Yet, broadly speaking, it is the meaning that violence must make in war reportage that remains the inexorable foundation for counting casualties. "It bleeds, it leads," an old refrain still repeated by journalists, is thus demonstrably false: Who is bleeding, and where, and how much, determine journalistic attention. When the dead assume greater value based on their cultural, social, racial, or national identity, or when killing is considered an issue of national security or societal concern, then death is more likely to be deemed newsworthy. Death, in this way, registers journalistically in response to invisible determinations about how certain individuals should and should not die, and which deaths are thus worthy of inclusion in the news. As for naming and classifying, examined in the previous chapter, the numbers given in the news depend on preconditions obscured by the certainty and precision that counting evokes. The occluded basis for casualty counting allows journalism to enumerate civilian harm as naturally important rather than selectively newsworthy. The attention to death that a numerical account crystallizes does not correspond, unilaterally, to an event's importance, but to how importance is selectively applied and the social and political determinations of this selection.

"Sometimes we say, 'Six deaths, that's not enough.' But who am I to decide how many deaths matter?" This is what a journalist told me in Qamishli. Amidst the grinding consistency of violent events in Syria—barrel bombings of apartment blocks, shifting frontlines in various contested cities—which violence to report to a global audience could seem almost arbitrary. How many were killed, and where—the scale of death and the novelty of its infliction—remain abiding factors in the negotiation of relevance. "Newsworthiness is calibrated in human death," the journalist continued. "Twenty-five people killed is worth a breaking news alert, twelve is worth a small story, six is not worth anything. But novelty matters too. If six people died in East Aleppo it didn't matter, in West Aleppo it did."

To count in journalism is an instance of performed factuality and of granting value—it is both *techne* and *episteme*, both a technique of knowledge production and a way of knowing. By counting suffering, that suffering is marked as newsworthy; it becomes a suffering deemed to matter. Enumerating injury or death gives that harm significance, and war reportage here comes to redeem, for its audience, an otherwise unseen and unknown victimhood. War reportage in this way functions as a theodicy in news-consuming society, making suffering matter by including it in the "first draft of history." Inclusion in war's tally becomes a proof of victimhood, and this authentication is one that war reportage is uniquely positioned to bestow. By counting and thus validating victimhood in war, war reportage recognizes these victims within the purview of what a news-consuming society deems important. Numbers give meaning to wartime suffering, and the lives that are counted are thereby made meaningful.

To count the injured and dead also satisfies a particular social desire: to conceptually manage atrocity through its enumeration. A casualty count testifies to extremity while controlling and sanctifying this very excess.[4] Such a tally, then, both attracts and repels; it gives closure while expressing brutality. Counting casualties becomes a means to produce knowledge of war while signaling how war is to be understood. To lack a number of casualties is to lack both managerial command over violence and the emotive significance of a classified devastation. The symbolism registered by a casualty count is today essential to how violence—from mass shootings to genocide—is popularly consumed, and journalism is critical to this process. Through the provisioning of a casualty count, war reportage satisfies a social desire for conceptual control over wartime violence and for the affective exhibition of its wreckage.[5]

As a rhetoric of accuracy, suggestion of scale, method of closure, signal for affect, granting of value, or means of comparison, the casualty count is determined by conditions mystified in the war reportage within which the casualty count appears. Individual journalists may quibble with this process; they may understand the contingencies of casualty counting for delivering war's reality, or the politics that dictate who is counted. But counting casualties remains conventional to contemporary war reportage and, thereby, it helps to constitute war reportage as a discourse representing war as it is widely expected to be.

At Least 400,000 Dead

In most news reports on war and violence, journalists rely on third-party monitoring organizations for the procurement of death tallies. The World Health Organization, the International Peace Research Institute, the International Crisis Group, the United Nations High Commissioner for Human Rights, and other organizations provide databases of worldwide conflict death, while organizations such as Iraq Body Count and the Syrian Network for Human Rights provide casualty numbers for specific regions and conflicts, and organizations like Airwars and the Committee to Protect Journalists supply data for particular categories of dead. Nations or groups involved in a given conflict (such as the United States and the Taliban, in the case of the recent war in Afghanistan) also provide—often selective—casualty statistics.

Estimating death is a highly contentious practice and has resulted in sharp and polarized debate (Bohannon 2008; Giles 2007; Sloboda et al. 2013). Controversy frequently stems from distinct methodologies for counting the dead, with their particular emphases, biases, and obfuscations. In reporting estimated casualty totals, journalists reproduce not only the number supplied by a given source but, as well, the problems associated with the production of that number and the preconditions upon which it rests.

The primary counting methods fall into two broad categories. The first is *incident reporting,* which collates media reports and other publicly accessible information on wartime events (known as event data) as well as eyewitness testimony often requiring third-party corroboration. The second method is *estimation,* which utilizes survey data on peacetime mortality rates or other epidemiological values, as well as retrospective large-scale interview data and other statistical techniques, and compares with wartime conditions in order to infer casualty numbers. Both methods have considerable limitations.

With respect to incident reporting, governments may restrict media coverage of war death, especially among their own forces. In conflicts with high death counts, such as the recent wars in Iraq and Syria, incidents resulting in relatively less death may be overlooked by news media and other monitoring organizations even as small-toll violence proliferates. Journalists may be banned from certain areas of conflict or deem the risk of reporting too great. Each of these factors results in undercounting by incident-reporting organizations, since many wartime deaths can go unreported by the media and other information-gathering institutions. With respect to estimation methods, there may simply be meager available data to allow for adequate comparative tallies (Landman and Gohdres 2013). Interview subjects' recall of the wartime deaths of friends and family may prove faulty, especially after long periods; peacetime surveys can remain incomplete due to official repression, distrust of survey collectors, or logistical and administrative obstacles; the slow pace of data collection makes survey-based tallies ineffective for real-time casualty estimations of ongoing conflicts. These factors can result in undercounts, overcounts, and counts that are an unreliable indicator of wartime casualty rates (Seybolt et al. 2013).

Journalistic citation of a monitoring organization's death tally rarely acknowledges these contingencies in its deliverance of numerical certainty. Comparing incident reporting with estimation-based casualty figures for a given conflict often reveals a wide discrepancy; even among tallies sharing a common methodology, the casualty total in a given conflict can vary considerably. The most debated death statistics in recent memory are from the 2003 US invasion of Iraq and its aftermath. A survey-based estimate for war deaths in Iraq between 2003 and 2006, published in the *Lancet* (Burnham et al. 2006) and relying on a comparison of epidemiological data from before and after the US invasion, produced a figure about four times higher than that reported by a major UN-funded survey-based estimation from the Iraq Family Health Survey study group in 2008, which applied similar methods and data (Spagat et al. 2009).

After questions arose about the *Lancet* study's methodology, many US media outlets, such as the Associated Press and the *Los Angeles Times*, began referring to the study as "controversial." The *Baltimore Sun* called it "politically motivated," the *Boston Herald* called it "discredited," and the *Washington Post* called it an "October surprise" ahead of the 2008 US elections (in Farsetta 2008). Moreover, the existence of the Iraq Family Health Survey effectively allowed news organizations to ignore the *Lancet* findings; rather than reporting the range of available estimates, journalists simply cited the lower death tally. The politics of death in Iraq—in which a high death rate reflected poorly on US management of that country after the invasion—may have influenced which number gained credibility and, thereby, which number was reported in the news. Here we can see how determinations other than those related to statistical accuracy might influence whether a number is granted legitimacy through its journalistic appearance.[6]

But third-party methodological complications are only one aspect of the trouble with casualty counts in the news. Historically, processes of quantification and estimate production—the statistical sciences broadly—are the pedigree of the modern bureaucratic state and entwined with the maintenance of state power (Desroisieres 1998; Merry 2016; Porter 1996; Scott 1998; Wiggins and Jones 2023). The tallies given in news of war are often downstream from this dynamic, and official numbers are often cited in the press without reference to how such numbers suit particular interests.[7] Where death tallies become the focus of journalistic representation, the preconditions that determine the importance of this number *as* news are obscured. As argued in Chapter 4, whether a death tally is accurate—and whether the meaning of this tally is death that is proportional to the force used or death that is excessive—are matters that implicitly accept the problem of killing as a problem of numbers. A focus on how many were killed can set the terms of a narrative by sidelining the context of the killing in question. Considering all of these issues of methodology and meaning, tallying war casualties seems less a matter of war and its enumeration than a matter of war reportage and the discursive utility of numbers. Here the ongoing war in Syria presents a particular case.

For the war in Syria, as for many major conflicts, a total tally of death is a regular feature of journalistic representation. The routines of journalists I observed, whether reporting on the ground in Syria or remotely from Lebanon and Iraq, included habitual study of the Syrian fatality data provided by monitoring organizations.[8] I regularly watched journalists consult the websites of such organizations, and I often heard journalists asking sources for a casualty count. In the first years of the conflict in Syria, the most widely cited source for fatality estimates was the United Nations High Commissioner for Human Rights (UNHCR), a trusted arbiter of such data. Until 2016, the UNHCR provided an estimation of those killed in Syria since 2011 (the beginning of the Syrian uprising) that collated figures from six different sources, including the Syrian government. That government stopped providing casualty data to the United Nations in 2012; in 2014, four of the other UN-reporting sources were unable to update their data. In 2016, the UNCHR gave its last estimate (relying in part on 2014 data) of 400,000 deaths in Syria. This figure continued to be cited by journalists well into 2017, 2018, and beyond, despite a likely increase in the number of dead as the conflict expanded.

Since the UNHCR last updated its death toll, entire neighborhoods—including areas of Aleppo, Syria's second-largest city—were attacked by Russian and Syrian state airpower; Britain, France, and the United States launched airstrikes in retaliation for suspected chemical attacks; Islamic State-controlled territory in eastern Syria was repeatedly bombed by the United States; and dozens of militias, many backed by foreign powers, clashed throughout the country. Yet journalists continued to cite the UN's unchanged and thus increasingly inaccurate number, attesting to its relevance through a simple rhetorical adjustment. Instead of reporting that, according to UN estimates, 400,000 people have died in the Syrian conflict, many journalists simply added "at least" or "more than" before the number given. In this manner, the authority of the United Nations could still be leveraged by journalists in the conveyance of certainty about war despite the uncertainty of the UN's data. The rhetorical authority of the number was more important than a correspondence between the number and some actually existing amount of death.

The symbolic truth of a death tally can in this manner supersede its statistical accuracy. As a journalist in Kobani explained,

> Journalists don't have the skills to tabulate the number themselves. We just want a number. We don't care about its precision so much as what it represents. 600,000 deaths may be worse than 500,000, but it makes no difference for how I assess the scale of a tragedy. We move in increments, orders of magnitude.

If it is assumed that the war in Syria is best represented through the amount of suffering it generates, then a casualty count becomes critical for meeting this expectation of war's truth. And insofar as casualty counts provide proof of war's horror, lacking an enumeration of harm undermines both the representation of the Syrian war as horrible and the authority of war's representors. An inaccurate number, in this case, is better than no number at all. And more: The inaccuracy of the number makes little difference with respect to the meaning the number is used to provide.

Another primary source for data on death in Syria is the Syrian Observatory for Human Rights (SOHR), a London-based organization that relies on a network of informants to gather information about the daily human toll of the war. Citation of SOHR in the international press, and among the journalists I interviewed and observed, became increasingly widespread in the years after the United Nations ceased updating their death data. In the beginning of the conflict, SOHR reported more Syrian military deaths than civilian or non-state combatant deaths—improbable data for a popular uprising and even more so for an asymmetrical war. As the conflict progressed, SOHR continually delivered death tolls far in excess of other monitoring groups, such as the Violations Documentation Center and the Syrian Human Rights Committee.[9] Why were SOHR numbers so often cited in the news? It may be that SOHR's higher casualty estimates raised its profile among the pack of monitors and drew journalistic attention.

My interviews indicate that one of the primary purposes of the casualty count is to suggest how bad a conflict is. As discussed, numbers testify to the enormity of atrocity, providing a symbolic or moral truth of violence in addition to a statistical truth. A higher death tally better indicates the meaning of war currently ascendent: its cruelty, its trauma, its inhumanity. We know from war reportage that the war in Syria is terrible; how terrible it *is* can be proven by an enumeration of harm, where a higher number seems to provide more proof. More death indicates a more horrible war. Additionally, as numbers register authority, a higher number seems more authoritative. The accuracy of journalism is indexed by a number, and a higher number of dead appears to be more comprehensive and thereby more accurate, since more death is counted. While SOHR's high numbers may be a result of a more comprehensive, and thus more accurate, counting methodology, comprehensiveness serves as much a symbolic as a technical purpose for journalists. A higher casualty count seems more accurate and thus more true, while also making war seem more violent and thus more newsworthy.[10]

"Narrative organizes pieces of information into a way that can be understood," a journalist told me in Baghdad, adding,

> The number acts as a mark of tangibility that operates in the same way as a narrative does. The number operates as an authoritative marker to point towards an otherwise incomprehensible loss. Mapping tangibility onto meaninglessness, senselessness. The news genre requires sense, and the casualty count is a formal, recognizable, simplified synecdoche, something to grasp onto, a mapped meaning where it's hard to gauge meaning.

For this journalist, the symbolism and authority evoked by casualty counts is clear. Yet the use of a casualty count as meaning-making technique—as a way to make sense of the insensible—does not preclude the use of an inaccurate number. Rather, the accuracy of a number is not, or not primarily, why a journalist might choose to report it. The number works, as this journalist puts it, "in the same way as a narrative does"—its function is figural, a signifying device for war's horror, deployed by those tasked to represent atrocity.

In Erbil I spoke with Victor, who was reporting on war in both Syria and Iraq. Victor has the lean but sturdy build of a runner, with deep-set blue eyes and a thick chestnut beard. After freelancing for American news organizations, he secured a staff position first at a French news outlet and then at a Middle Eastern one. Victor's knotty hands rested heavy on the table between us. I asked why so many journalists were employing numbers from SOHR as opposed to other casualty-estimating organizations.

"There's an efficiency to using one organization's number, which makes it easier to write the story," Victor told me. He continued,

> You can just grab the figure or the entire paragraph from another story. "The Syrian Observatory says this," and I'm not wrong even if the number is, because they *do* say it. It gives continuity between your pieces. And we, as journalists, are conferring authority upon ourselves by tacitly agreeing to use the same numbers, which gives that number more credibility. It's a legal fiction, things that are not true but assumed to be true. Within a publication and across publications, it makes the number seem more authoritative to a reader.

Regularity allows a number to win credibility over other numbers, regardless of its accuracy. It allows a number to achieve a common sense.

I asked Victor if he ever questioned the use of SOHR's data. "These things accrete over time and become part of the furniture," he replied. "Zombie paragraphs—things get used again and again without question. And when you do question it, someone will say, 'This is how we've been doing things, there was some meeting about it at the time.' They'll say to look at the hand-over note"—the note outlining why a decision was made—"from the Beirut bureau, or from some years ago, and no one can remember the reasons for it. It's like the transmission of the hadith."

I asked whether he believed that the casualty count provided by SOHR is accurate. "No one believes that this is the precise number," he said, adding,

I don't think anyone thinks its within ten thousand of that. But we can't imagine those figures anyway—it's too many bodies. So this is just shorthand for a really large number of people, with the authenticity to sound authoritative or credible. Too much of a round number—500,000—wouldn't sound credible; it sounds rounded.

My conversation with Victor took place in 2017. In 2020, I followed up with him by phone to ask how he was reporting the total death toll in Syria, three years later and with even less direct access to conditions on the ground. His news organization was still relying on SOHR estimates. "What we're using at the moment is 385,000 dead," he told me from his apartment in Beirut:

> And the conventional wording is, "Since the war began in 2011, more than 380,000 have been killed." The decision to use this, well, we can say that the number is true. But that figure then takes on a power of its own. A few months ago, we got an alert on the wire—meaning it's a priority story—that the Observatory had increased the toll from 380 to 385,000, and so we put that out as a news alert. But nothing had actually happened other than this increase in the tally. There hadn't been a battle that day.[11]

This interview reflects a broader trend in coverage of the war in Syria, wherein the use of casualty data reflects the discursive needs of war reportage more than it does the circumstances of a war. A number more likely to appear in war reportage is a number that responds, first, to representational exigencies as they are socially and discursively determined. For an American news-consuming public, and for the powers driving conflict, the intervention in Bosnia was thought to need more bodies and the occupation of Iraq less. A higher number, a number that better exemplifies the horror of war, while best attesting to accuracy and thus authority, is a number that meets the demands of journalists reporting on the war in Syria for a global audience. The number may be true, but it is its symbolic truth that counts.

How many have died in the war in Syria? The symbolic truth of the answer may be other than its statistical truth, and the unavailability of the latter does not dissuade journalists from providing the former. In war reportage on the Syrian conflict—reportage predetermined by ideas of that war as cruel, as horrible, as inhumane—consistent use of phrases such as "at least 400,000 dead" and "more than 380,000 have been killed" satisfy a discursive need. The inaccuracy of the number may be known, but the truth it evokes remains journalistically effective.

Authorial Authority

How are things like numbers, names, categories, and other narrative dynamics authorized as accurate journalism? One factor in this process concerns authorship, wherein the reality represented in the news is affirmed by the presence of the professional journalist. The byline is the textual manifestation of this presence.

The byline is the customary mark of authorship in a news story, usually located below the headline in a published article. But authorship in the news is less straightforward than the byline suggests. Both institutional dynamics (namely, the collective production of a news story) and formal dynamics (for example, the customary use of third-person narrative prose) make bylines a consequential site of inquiry into how journalism's conventions shape the meaning news makes. In its uniformity of authorial voice, and in its excision of both individual subjectivity and collective production, the byline constitutes the authority of journalistic representation in a very particular manner. By looking at who is allowed to speak in—and *as*—journalism, we can grasp the discursive context within which particular realities of war emerge as news.

For Foucault, *who* gets to speak is one of the "rules of formation" that allow certain kinds of statements to achieve regularity (1977; 1982). In naming an author—and thereby granting, discursively, the right to speak—the byline indexes the professionalism of the journalist and the legitimacy of their journalism. By presenting the name of a journalist, that is, the byline underwrites the authority of that journalist to represent reality, an authority on which the news—economically, institutionally, culturally—depends. For while the byline references the name of an author, it is more than simply a proper name. If part of what legitimates journalism as a discourse is the authority of the person producing the discourse, that authority must itself be discursively constituted, and the byline accomplishes this double move.

In signaling journalistic authorship, and thereby conferring narrative authority, the byline signals those things that make the journalist—and, consequently, the journalism—what it is supposed to be in the society within which it functions. As mark of authorship, the byline characterizes the existence of the discourse of journalism as a societally sanctioned purveyor of reality. Embedded in the byline, then, are those professional norms and values presumed of journalism as a reality-representing form.

Truthfulness, accuracy, verifiability, facticity, certainty, and similar ideals are certified by the byline, in concordance with societal expectation, in its confirmation of journalistic professionalism. In the case of war reportage, the byline guarantees a direct and transparent representation of faraway violence; an intimate witnessing of war that yet delivers objective truth; and a legible, verifiable, accurate account of conflict. Moreover, in substantiating the discourse of journalism, the byline expels what does not meet a normative standard of journalistic professionalism. Not everyone is granted authorship in the news; not everyone is allowed to speak for, and as, journalism.

The byline thus points to the status of journalism within society, and the function of the byline, "to characterize the existence, circulation, and operation" of journalism within a social order, is thereby revealed (Foucault 1977, 124). In this manner, and as Foucault argues of authorship generally, the byline is both a formal designation (of the individual filling the role of reality representor) and a description of a type (the journalist as a professional authorized to represent reality). As such, the byline embodies both industrial and epistemic dimensions; it signals the way journalism is produced and underwrites journalism as a way of knowing.

The byline constructs the rational entity called the journalist and mediates the contradiction (explored in Chapters 5 and 6) between the journalist as an individual experiencing war and the journalist as the producer of war news. And while it ratifies the figure of journalistic professionalism, the byline conceals the preconceptions about rationality, objectivity, and authority—preconceptions not natural, but situated and interested—that structure what a journalist *is*. The byline corroborates journalistic professionalism without indicating the social basis on which professionalism is constructed and judged. The byline both instantiates and disappears the social systems that "circumscribe, determine, and articulate" the position of journalism in the world (Foucault 1977, 130). In analyzing war reportage, then, one must look not only at journalism's expressive dynamics but also at its attribution, and thereby determine the *byline function* that communicates the complex of operations maintaining war reportage today.

What are the conditions that allow a journalist to appear in journalism? What is the position a journalist occupies, the purpose a journalist exhibits, and the rules a journalist follows, *within* the news narrative? Who appears to control journalistic narration and who fulfills the role of a subject within that narrative? These questions provoke an understanding of journalistic authorship as determined by a network of social structures and norms of expression hidden within the byline. Obscuring the rules of authorship (among other rules), the discourse emerges as if of its own will, "speaking for itself" in the representation of faraway war. As the rules of authorship are subsumed, ignored, displaced, so war reportage becomes less a response to societal expectations and predeterminations, less a commodity produced for a market, than a transparent delivery of war's reality.

The most striking aspect of journalistic authorship may be its absence. In most news texts, third-person prose works to understate the role of the author-narrator in the news. Normatively, and with the critical exception of the byline, there is a total excision of the journalist from the journalism she authors. This is a remarkable sleight of hand. Phrases like "The journalist was shown the bunker," or, "A journalist was offered to inspect the wreckage"—occurrences where subjectivity is necessary and, thereby, the presence of the author-narrator momentarily revealed—serve to deemphasize the presence of the journalist in journalism and naturalize the *ex nihilo* character of the news. Here the exception becomes the rule: The byline is often the singular indication of the journalist as a subject with involvement in—let alone influence over—the events reported.[12] However, and as Tuen Van Dijk (1988) argues, the byline does not signify personal expression or individual subjectivity so much as an institutional voice delegated to a professional spokesperson. By eliding individual experience even in the mark of individual authorship, the byline underwrites professional ideals such as neutrality and distance in the representation of reality. Situated, partial knowledge, accrued through the experience of events on the ground, is displaced by the universal, transcendent knowledge of professional journalism. The byline indicates authorship without quite personalizing its agent.[13]

Following Émile Benveniste's (1966) study of linguistic structures, we can notice how third-person narration liberates the journalist-narrator from the text and leaves only the residue of a journalist-reporter at the scene of events. The context of expression is severed from the context of the event, with the journalist's ghostly occupation of the latter and a byline marking their sole involvement in the former. The authenticity of proximity, the "having been there" so essential to journalistic authority (further assessed in Chapter 6) is preserved and indeed leveraged, while the event's existence as a *story* with an *author* is suppressed. The genericism of the byline, combined with normative third-person prose, obscures the situated dynamics of news production, such that an event must merely be witnessed and transmitted, rather than experienced and interpreted, to become news.

Of course, war reporters (in the case of print, and most of the time in radio and television too) narrate the events of war only after their encounter with those events, and the collapse of narration into event achieved through journalism's formal dynamics is consequential. By disembodying the news narrator, the accuracy of the news is folded into its authenticity; "being there" seems to bestow omniscience through third-person narrative command. A narrator assessing the significance of an event can only do so after the event is encountered, yet no interpretive or retrospective voice allows the news consumer to see that this is the case. The event becomes self-explanatory, its meaning inherent rather than granted. A retrospective narrative voice—a space of authorship transparently distinct from the occurrence of the event—would compromise the illusion that events are self-evident; that newsworthiness is natural rather than ascertained; that facts are there waiting to reveal themselves rather than fashioned, selected, organized. The mystification of authorial subjectivity—accomplished through third-person prose and the containment of authorship to the byline—has the effect of authenticating the events reported as "the way things are" irrespective of the presence, interpretation, or craft of a journalist.[14]

"I try to extract myself from the story," a journalist in Erbil told me. "We're storytellers, not the story. In inserting myself, I become the person telling, and the stories we try to tell become backdrops to our own stories." A journalist in Baghdad explained, "Sometimes there's a need to remind the reader you're there. But it requires a light touch. It can't get in the way of the story. At worst it's vainglorious and confusing." "We talk a lot about the *I*," a journalist in Beirut noted. "The *I*, it's so big, it casts such a big shadow across the page. When is the *I* necessary, and when is it a distraction? It's an open question. But there are other voices that need to be heard. My voice is the least interesting. I'm not on safari." The reluctance of journalists to insert themselves into the news they produce remains acute even as their presence can never be erased. War reporters "get" the story, they don't *tell* it, and the byline performs this rhetorical dodge.

It is useful to note here another textual indication of journalistic presence: the dateline. The dateline is a named location that appears just before the lead in a foreign news story and serves to indicate the place from which that story is reported. As journalistic legitimacy is established by "being there" at the scene of events, the dateline can be used to validate this claim, offering proof of proximity and thus of the accuracy of the news. I've been told of journalists traveling to remote or dangerous locations simply to achieve a particular dateline, even when presence at that location did not bear on the narrative produced. True or not, the rumor indicates the professional value of presence as guarantee of authenticity and, thereby, of authority. As Van Dijk explains, "The closeness of the reporter to the events is a rhetorical guarantee for the truthfulness of the description and, hence, the plausibility of the news" (1988, 86). Barbie Zelizer argues that news "begins with a sense of place, and it is up to each journalist to align him or herself in some way with the sense of place that has been communicated" (1990, 40). The dateline signifies this alignment between journalist and place, and thereby adheres to what Zelizer calls "presentational practices" that aid in the construction of journalistic proximity, authorship, and authority. For Zelizer, the dateline should be read as a "code" signifying journalists' adherence to the institutional value of proximity (1990, 46). It is the figural importance of proximity that the dateline instantiates, rather than the importance of the knowledge that proximity might bestow.

A *New York Times* column (Kahn and Mitchell 2015) explains the dateline:

> Datelines mean that The New York Times is on the scene. They catalog the reach of our journalists, who seek to witness what they write about, probe deeply into events and capture the most memorable images. In an age of instant posts and pundits, we believe more than ever that going there makes our journalism distinctive, richer, more personal and more reliable.

This column appeared at a time of declining trust in mass media, and it may have been intended to reassure news consumers about the authenticity of *New York Times* journalism. As Zelizer (2007) notes, "being there" is also a matter of journalistic branding and institutional relevance. It is clear from the column that the dateline functions as proof of journalistic presence and thereby certifies the witnessing that is the most "reliable" form of reality-delivery. But the power of the dateline to substantiate journalistic truth indicates how the value of being there supersedes the actual insight produced thereby. It is the formal commitment to presence, rather than the things presence reveals, that is of primary institutional concern. The dateline codifies this preference.[15]

"The dateline is the key," a journalist told me in Beirut. "It's proof of boots on the ground. But it's an illusion. No one has the infrastructure to maintain a full international presence, so that lack is mystified with stringers, parachuters, et cetera. The dateline almost always outdoes expertise." This journalist indicates the strategies a news organization might employ to achieve a dateline, and thus the dateline's importance for what journalism is expected to be. A journalist in Kobani said, "Proximity is everything. You have to be on the ground to know what's going on. That's authoritative." Indexing this proximity, the dateline textually enacts journalistic authority regardless of the content of the journalism.[16]

The byline (as formal mark of authorship) as well as the dateline (as proof of authorial presence) perform the textual appearance of the fact-gathering, event-encountering, witness-bearing journalist, but without the interpretive messiness that subjective presence might evoke. Professionalism, and all that this entails in journalism, is secured by these discursive conventions, while the production and preconditions of professionalism are erased. The violence and suffering witnessed by the journalist is left to speak for itself, a self-evident event of war, free of the imposition—and the ideology—of representation. In staging this performance, these conventions reveal their function: to constitute the authority of journalism as a truth-providing, reality-delivering, interpretation-free discourse.

Fixing the Discourse

The byline elides a fundamental aspect of news production: The journalist is not the only author. The idealization of the war reporter as the one who witnesses atrocity, gathering testimony for the public record, mystifies not only the dialogic, negotiated, and socially mediated basis of reporting. The byline, in its proof of journalistic authorship, mystifies others indispensable for producing the news.

A fixer is a local individual hired to assist foreign journalists. Fixers can take on a range of activities pertaining to news production, and the depth of their involvement depends on language skills, writing ability, news sense, range of contacts, and other factors. Fixers might suggest interview subjects and arrange logistics. They can be risk analysts, assessing where and when journalists should report from a given location. They might translate official statements, local media reports, and foreign journalists' interviews. Fixers often provide the connections necessary to pass checkpoints or obtain official permissions. These are the pragmatic, industrial dimensions of the fixer's role in news production, addressed in the scholarly literature through attention to the "hybridity" of international news (Waisbord 2013, 222), the "transnational and collaborative process" in foreign bureaus (Palmer 2018b, 317), and the "international space" of fixer-journalist coproduction (Murrell 2015, 7). Fixers offer company, comradery, and a local's eye for detail. In an email sent from Iraq, archived at the American University of Beirut, the late journalist Anthony Shadid defined his fixer as "a kind of assistant, and . . . my closest friend here."

Fixers often provide political, historical, and cultural information for foreign journalists reporting on conflict in the Middle East; as locals, fixers tend to know more about relevant contextual dynamics than visiting outsiders. "A fixer is a captive source for background and context," a journalist explained in Kobani. "One of the most important decisions we make as reporters is who to hire as the fixer." A journalist in Beirut told me, "Part of the institutional memory of journalism in this region are the longtime fixers. They are the source for deep knowledge of how journalism works here. We couldn't do it without them." Journalists I interviewed in Iraq, Lebanon, and Syria perceived fixers as local helpers whose knowledge of the region formed the bedrock from which professional news emerges. Besides their pragmatic, industrial contributions, then, the fixer is also a knowledge broker, supplying the contextual insight that allows for the representational operations of journalism.

But the contribution of fixers, pragmatic and discursive, is a matter of simmering professional dispute. Many foreign journalists consider fixer labor necessary but ultimately inferior to the work of journalists. Fixers, however, see their role as essential. "Journalism here wouldn't work without fixers," a fixer told me in Baghdad. "I understand the culture and the language here. I don't wear shorts while reporting because I know the context. Journalists don't know the context." Good fixers are familiar with local cultural dynamics and the political and linguistic nuance of the area being covered. A journalist in Erbil asserted, "The only reason journalists are able to work in conflict conditions is because of fixers. There have been times when my fixer has helped me so much that the story is essentially theirs. Journalists and fixers need each other."

A fixer's investment in the norms of journalistic professionalism can vary widely. Fixers are often local journalists, whose professional values cohere with the standards of the international news organizations for whom they "fix." Other fixers are ex-military, laid-off bureaucrats, or simply enterprising individuals seeking a paycheck, and all of these backgrounds can be useful for war reportage in different ways.[17] A fixer in Beirut told me, "I'm a street man. I lived on the street. I'm a wise guy when it comes to risky things." This fixer, though without any background in journalism, was renowned for his contacts and access to insular armed groups. Whether a fixer knows how to report the news for a global audience, or whether the fixer is invested in journalism's conventional ideals, may matter only in certain circumstances; the ability to pass through a checkpoint or land a particular interview can depend little on traditional journalistic skill. Unlike the institutional contribution of a fixer, then—wherein ability hinges on familiarity with journalism as a profession—the local knowledge of a fixer is an asset often independent of journalistic training. The usefulness of what a fixer *knows* as a local individual is a matter distinct from the usefulness of what she *does* as a news producer. Moreover, the local knowledge of a fixer is essential to news production even where industrial contributions are lacking.[18]

"A fixer, for me, is someone who can open a network—phone numbers, contacts," a journalist told me in Baghdad. "I usually do the interviews, and they provide local knowledge: Who is this guy, is he who he says he is, is he important? A lot of times it's the journalist doing the higher-level thought on why the story is relevant. The fixer doesn't have the perspective to see that or is too wrapped up in local conditions." This is a common view of fixers among foreign journalists in the Middle East. Fixers are seen by journalists as most necessary to news production because of their local knowledge and *not* because of their professional skills in journalism. But this local knowledge, while fundamental, must still be translated through the apparatus of journalistic professionalism, a "higher-level thought" (as this journalist puts it) that establishes the legibility essential to international news. What this journalist calls the "relevance" of a story both requires and relegates local knowledge.

An ongoing debate among both fixers and journalists, as well as editors and other media professionals, is whether fixers can operate as fully-fledged journalists. "I've tried to train fixers to be journalists unsuccessfully," a journalist noted in Beirut. "There are people who make the jump, but those people are few." As falling revenues necessitate downsized bureaus and incentivize the replacement of foreign journalists with cheaper local labor, many in the news industry, as well as many media scholars, anticipate a growing role for fixers (Hamilton and Jenner 2004; Murrell 2010; Otto and Meyer 2012). Increased danger to journalists amidst the proliferation of nonconventional warfare further encourages industry dependence on local news-producers (Myers 2011; Plaut and Klein 2019). If locals have the linguistic and logistical abilities, the contacts, the reporting skills, and other necessary attributes, then why should international news organizations employ a more expensive, and perhaps more vulnerable, foreign staff?

"This is one of these things that's always about to happen," a journalist at an American newspaper told me in Erbil. With a shock of stiff brown hair and a bare, boyish face, this journalist disavows the term "war reporter" and refers to himself as an Arabist. He expressed doubt as to whether a transition from foreign to local media labor would ever actually occur. First, he mentioned safety concerns, and the crucial ability of foreign journalists to leave a country in the event of threats or danger. "Foreign correspondents can leave, but locals can't. There's a certain amount of protection as a foreigner, so we can be more critical." I asked about the conditions of war specifically, and he conceded that "war is dangerous for foreigners too." He then mentioned sectarian, political, and class identities as an obstacle for locals, since such factors are disruptive of the neutral, distanced perspective customary to today's war reportage. "Locals are too tied to conditions on the ground. It damages the credibility of the news," he said. When I suggested that foreign journalists too harbor identity-based perspectives, he concurred. Finally, he emphasized familiarity with faraway news audiences as the most pronounced constraint on locals who might replace foreigners in news production. "Foreign correspondents have this expertise that fixers don't," he explained. "The foreign journalist can be an arbiter of sense. You need to know the audience, what makes sense to people far away, what the audience can understand and what they care about. What matters to Iraqis is different than what matters to Americans or Brits or Italians."

For this journalist and others, the expectations of faraway news consumers—and associated requirements regarding the legibility or sense of the news—marks the definitive difference between locals and foreigners in news production.[19] This difference may well be fundamental. For if journalism is understood as an enterprise concerned with access to events, or range of sources, or narrative nuance, then local fixers can certainly replace foreign journalists given adequate skills in writing and reporting, skills that can be learned, developed, and institutionally authorized. But if journalism is a matter of legibility creation, of producing meaning for war in coincidence with reigning news-consumer expectation, then familiarity with a discursive status quo remains primary. Those operating under distinct epistemic conditions—those whose knowledge is "only local"—cannot produce satisfactory war reportage, a task that must be left to those who recognize a dominant consumer worldview and, thereby, the meaning the news is expected to make.[20]

If epistemic conditions trump industrial ones, then the "localness" of fixers' knowledge is both their essential asset and their definitive constraint. Understanding of political, cultural, historical, and linguistic context; the long-term cultivation of regional contacts; grasp of logistical conditions and an awareness of security risks—these make the fixer indispensable for international news production. But this familiarity with local complexity can make fixers' knowledge incongruous with what global news consumers demand. As the journalist quoted above notes, what matters to fixers about a given event may be different from what "should" matter in the news of that event, and here the foreign journalist must become the "arbiter of sense." This is a matter of discursive fidelity rather than technical ability.

"Rarely do fixers bring me the story," a journalist told me in Kobani. "They don't get the narrative. The ideas they come up with are not appropriate. Fixers have trouble with the bigger picture that needs to be conveyed. In that quest for comprehensibility, they don't pass the test." Again, "comprehensibility"—legibility, intelligibility, the "bigger picture"—is cited by journalists as a primary obstacle for fixers in news production. Many journalists expressed something of this kind, wherein a fixer's ability to help produce international news does not amount to an understanding of what the news *is*. "Localness" may be critical for the former, industrial process but is often treated as disruptive of the latter, discursive process.

"Just because you live in a place doesn't mean you have the tools to convey what's important," a journalist in Beirut explained. In Baghdad, a journalist remarked, "Locals can be too involved in the place. It's good to have an outsider point of view, especially in a war zone. Locals can be too close." Such journalists see the perspective of a foreigner as necessary for translating local conditions for a global news audience. Yet the foreigner must still know something about local conditions, and here the fixer remains critical. "We should be guided by local knowledge. But some of the time their truth is not true." This is what a journalist told me in Baghdad, and her apprehension reveals the crux of the tension that fixers present to international news production. A local truth is necessary to "guide" journalistic truth telling even as it is dismissed as unauthorized, nonprofessional, insensible—even untrue.[21]

As both an essential foundation for journalism's authorized knowledge, and as a challenge or disruption to the authority thereof, fixer knowledge can be understood as what Donna Haraway names "situated knowledge." Whereas hegemonic knowledges such as war reportage strive for "translation, convertibility, mobility of meanings, and universality," situated knowledge is premised on partiality, specificity, and difference (1988, 580). Fixer knowledge, as a situated knowledge, is locatable and specific; it is intimate with, and in some ways accountable to, what it knows. Fixer knowledge is in this manner contestable—its truths may not be journalistically true—because it is not above human subjectivity but connected with the conditions of its emergence. Fixer knowledge is rooted in the specific local contexts that journalists must generalize for a faraway audience, and fixer knowledge must thereby be suppressed in the reification of globally legible, internationally marketable, institutionally authoritative meaning. As a prevailing common sense about war predetermines the reality war reportage delivers, so the situated knowledge of the fixer becomes a subjugated knowledge in the newsroom.

The displacement of the fixer, as coproducer of the news, is sanctified by the byline. As a mark of authorship, the byline establishes an authority claimed by journalists only, since fixers rarely receive byline credit.[22] In coordination with other generic conventions, then, the byline codifies a preference for some knowledges over others: of universal victimhood over specified struggle; of immanent violence over the systems that perpetuate it; of common sense over contextual complexity. In constituting the discourse of journalism as such, the byline can be read as a choice for what counts as journalism, and here the fixer's *institutional* position as a not-quite-professionalized journalist is less consequential for byline accrual than the fixer's *knowledge* as an unprofessional, unglobalized knowledge. It remains the "situatedness" of fixers that the byline rejects in its articulation of journalistic authority, since the discourse characterized by the byline is premised upon a distinction between local and global knowledge.[23] The status of war reportage is of a discourse that speaks to "here" from "there," to "us" about "them," where "there" and "them" may refer to faraway peoples, disparate sociocultural conditions, or simply to war itself as an alien and complicated thing (Said 1981). By marking journalistic authorship (an implicit extension of an "us"), the byline reinscribes a fundamental dimension of war reportage as a discourse delivering faraway war in a manner suitable to "our" understandings of what war *is*. To achieve a byline is to represent reality as "we" know it to be.[24] And here the localness of fixers—their primary resource for foreign journalists—must be formally disavowed in a journalism constituted on contextual transcendence.

"It seems like every article written by foreign reporters tries to 'encapsulate' the country. It's a quixotic pursuit." I was speaking with Farez, who worked for many years as a fixer for American and British newspapers, magazines, and television networks. Farez has cloudy gray eyes, dark hair neatly cropped, thick stubble on a prominent chin. His gaze is steady through wire-rim glasses. We met at an upscale bar in Beirut busy with stylish professionals. Farez is now a freelance journalist for local and international news outlets, a position better suited to his goals and values. But the job is not without tension. "When I pitch stories to the foreign press, they want a story about a big thing, a news peg. The specific isn't interesting to them, but only useful as an introduction to the general, what it says about 'the Lebanese' as 'a people.'" Farez sighed and worked his palms into his eye sockets. His livelihood now depends, in part, on translating local conditions for a global audience, a process that conflicts with what he feels the news should do. "I'm not a cultural taxonomist. I don't know how 'the Lebanese' do things, only how people do things. I don't believe in these stories, showing how 'they' are different from 'us.'"

For Farez, normative journalistic attempts at legibility are essentializing and reductionist, and make for worse journalism. But in rejecting a distinction between "us" and "them"—a distinction conventional to international news—Farez fails to represent reality in a way appropriate to the discourse. He sees "taxonomizing" reportage as a problem to overcome rather than the mark of international news as such. "Foreign journalists write *about* people here, not *for* them," Farez remarked into his beer. In war reportage, the local is to be employed, translated, essentialized, but not to be engaged on its own terms. "And *that*," Farez said, "*that* impacts how we represent the Middle East."

Only knowledge classed as general and global, rather than situated and local, can achieve the authenticity of international news, and only the purveyor of that knowledge is formally granted professional credit. For if war reportage is premised on delivering legibility, then relevant interview subjects, grasp of context, logistical capacity, or any of the other things fixers are institutionally called upon to supply remain secondary to a familiarity with what news consumers expect. The byline organizes this distinction, establishing who counts as a war reporter and, thereby, what counts as war reportage.

The Commodity Speaking

Realist narrative, naming and classifying, casualty counting, and proof of authorship are a few of the generic conventions of war reportage that determine how war is made legible for much of the world today. These conventions are the expression of unspoken rules regarding what it is possible to report of war, and their examination allows us to understand how war achieves a regularity in its representation. These conventions structure what war *is* in the news, mystifying the conditions of their production *as* conventions and smoothing the frictions between war as experienced by journalists and war as expressed in journalism (frictions explored in Chapters 5 and 6). These conventions underwrite journalism's claim to the accurate, transparent, truthful transmission of war's reality; they substantiate journalism's social function and perpetuate its mediational power.

As the formal elements determining what of war can be included in the news, and shaping how war is made meaningful, generic conventions can be assessed for their ideological significance. Examining the generic conventions of war reportage demonstrates how ideology flows through informative, objective journalism. For even as individual journalists may not know the rules dictating what they report, the rules instituted through formal conventions nonetheless function as a premise for the reportage individual journalists produce. In representing war as journalism, journalists are already negotiating a matrix of preconditions concerning the rational use of violence, the agency and identity of victims and perpetrators, the role of power in the world. As these preconditions become concealed in the news, we see an ideology functioning as common sense. War reportage, then, is not so much a record of something happening somewhere else—of a wound incurred in Mosul, of Raqqa reduced to rubble. Rather, war reportage is an autonomous realm of meaning making, a visible system of invisible rules.

Journalism's language, formal dynamics, and narrative strategy broadly determine how the news commodity expresses a dominant consensus regarding war's reality while mystifying the process of that commodity's production. As Althusser (1971) argues of ideology generally, war reportage offers not knowledge of war but recognition of war as news consumers already know it to be. War reportage does this by taking as true certain assertations very much open to question. That protagonist and antagonist, innocence and guilt, allies and enemies, are distinct and consistent. That a place is reducible to an essential characteristic dictating its fate. That the enumeration of death reveals something objectively true about the death enumerated. That authorship signals only the individual producer of a text. By asserting such matters as self-evident, the news commodity provides the position from which war "makes sense" as it should. War reportage in this way sustains what Hall calls "closures"—"systems of equivalence between what could be assumed about the world and what could be said to be true" (1982, 71)—which suture the fissures between what war *can* be and what it is *expected* to be. The news commodity universalizes its particularity, producing the nature of war itself, and the nature of war reportage, in order to legitimate the truthful reality it delivers.

The practice of war reportage, then, is a practice of signification, where "practice," as Althusser argues, is "any process of transformation effected by a determinate human labour, using determine means (of 'production')" (1969, 166). Journalists use their material and semiotic means of production to effect the transformation of war into a representation, and that representation is then sold on an information marketplace. This is a social accomplishment: It is determined by social processes negotiating the struggle over what "makes sense." Edmund Leach, in the epigraph to this chapter, describes the use of words as a social ritual with practical effects (1966, 407). However, the conventions of news narrative are designed to be invisible, and the contest over signification—a contest inherent to the transformation of war into representation—is intended to be erased. The *New York Times* style manual admits as much: "The only time [news consumers] should notice our writing at all is if, occasionally, they pause to admire it" (Siegal and Connolly 2015, 12). The writing of news—its assembly as a rhetorical apparatus, as a *representation*—should not be noticed. Rather, the news should merely be accepted as a window onto reality itself, as common sense deems reality to be. Struggles over which sense is deemed common—and how, and to what effect—is subsumed beneath a secured consensus. And as the news commodity displaces the social processes of its production, so it forecloses consideration of whether the reality it delivers may not be the only reality of war.

An inherent function of war reportage is its ability to turn a representation of war into an object of desire. News consumers want to know about war, and war reportage delivers what is expected. It does so, as Hayden White observes of history writing, "by its imposition, upon events that are represented as real, of the formal coherency that stories possess" (1987, 21). Unlike surrealist montage or a list of events, the reality given by journalism seems to be "speaking itself," as the *New York Times* style manual suggests, by cohering with consumer understandings of what war is like. Journalism's designations, descriptions, numbers, plots—the things journalism selects as signifieds for the signifiers of war—are thereby invested with fetishistic force. An enemy, a bombing, a tally of dead gather unto themselves, in their appearance in war reportage, the eagerness of news consumers for the transparent reality of conflict. And like a fetish, these elements become parts standing in for wholes: They offer a partial rendering of war as if it were a comprehensive one. A stronghold, a hero, a town's liberation—these deliver, in their figural resonance, the shape and character of a larger, and already established, narrative ideal. Such figures deliver—as if seamlessly—a reigning fantasy of war. Appearing in journalism's realist narrative, these figures become natural, given, self-evident; they absolve all the traces of their production and the interpretative, social experience of that production. They absolve the social struggle over a consensual common sense that preconditions the reality represented. They absolve their symbolism, their contingency, their rhetorical power. This does not make war's represented reality "fake." Rather, that reality simply does not disclose the conditions that make it appear real. The news commodity appears as a "thing in itself" while disguising the system of social relations that gives that commodity its significance.

As Foucault (1982) notes, the ability of a discourse to effectuate social fantasy is a factor neither hidden within the discourse nor external to it. Rather, fantasy is one of the formative and formational elements of discourse, shaping its specific structure. Who becomes a hero, which neighborhoods will be bombed, what counts as too many deaths, who can produce knowledge of war: Such considerations already determine the generic design of the news as it elicits and satisfies consumer desire for how those considerations are addressed. As a primary commodity form of the representation of wartime reality, war reportage enters a marketplace receptive to its particular configuration. The value of war reportage as a reality-delivering discourse meets a demand for war that displays the "coherence, integrity, fullness, and closure" of an idea of war that is, and can only be, imagined (White 1987, 24). Subscription models, advertising models, philanthropically supported news: All depend upon the value of journalism as an enterprise that can fulfill this social function.[25]

Mystified in the news is the creation of a social consensus around what war is and the interests that this consensus serves. This is the basis of the commodity structure, wherein social relations take on, as for György Lukács, "the character of a thing," acquiring "a 'phantom objectivity,' an autonomy that seems so strictly rational and all-embracing as to conceal every trace of its fundamental nature: the relation between people" (1971, 83). Whether the number of dead is more important than the policy that perpetuates death, whether allies are lauded for their virtue or for their violence, whether the merit of a narrative depends on its authority or its insight: These kinds of considerations, socially generated, are disappeared in the objective presence of the news commodity, even as that commodity both reflects and reproduces, both legitimates and authorizes, these very considerations.

In displacing the sociality embedded in the news commodity, war reportage appears autonomous and self-reliant, transmitting numbers and events, victims and suffering, as things waiting out there in the war zone, immutable and given. And the journalist becomes an instrument that must merely register and record the facts of war. This is what Lukács calls the reification of the commodity structure. Here is a world that is not social, that is not historical, but a world of autonomous objects, bound to their own rules, and delivered to us by intrepid professionals.

But the true significance of the news story, as a commodity form of wartime reality, is always elsewhere, in the social relations of production whose trail the story has obscured. The significance of war reportage is its dialogic nature, its polyvalence, its versatility, its hidden quality of struggle and transformation and exchange. This culture of production is smoothed in the story of war, which disappears all traces of the messiness of its making. The significance of the news of war, as of any commodity, is that is at one and the same time "astoundingly esoteric and absolutely eccentric to itself" (Eagleton 1981, 29). The particularities of war reportage *must* be mystified in order to achieve the invisibility that allows for war to report itself.

This autonomy allows the meanings given in news of war to seem natural, obvious, axiomatic, even as they respond to a social consensus and work in the service of hegemonic projects. But what exactly *is* this social consensus on war, and how does it win credibility in relation to the conduct of war? What are these hegemonic projects, and how does war reportage—even war reportage presumed to be critical of war—advance the interests of war-making powers? We turn now to these questions of war's meaning.

War reportage presents its names, numbers, characters, and categories in all their self-evidence. As delivered in the news, war seems spontaneous. As a commodity, however, war reportage relates to a specific field of existence, a set of conditions that determine, in advance, the possibilities for the emergence of war as news. Relations, desires, and interests already presuppose the presence of a protagonist fighting the good fight in war, or of a number that accurately attests to the atrociousness of atrocity. And these determining conditions must be effaced for the things they condition to maintain their fetishistic allure. What remains, in news of war, is the victim suffering, the battle raging, and the journalist there to tell us what it's like.

INTERLUDE

Available Stories

Ethnographer: I really miss that moment in Erbil, when everything was in full swing, and all these people—journalists, fixers, medics, mercenaries, soldiers, writers, analysts—they had some sense of something happening, something terrible maybe, but something that was momentous enough that a story was necessary to tell. Not even, like, a news story, but just, *Scorpion Checkpoint was busy today.* Or, *the Tal Afar refugee camp is really muddy.* Or even just drinking a beer and talking about something totally unrelated. Or not talking at all. But knowing where we were and what was around. Stories were available. *There sure are a lot of ways to die.* And, *I saw you on CNN—you looked terrible.*

Journalist: Yes. I guess the surety is that things always pass, and the dispersal was inevitable, but it's sad and I miss it too in many ways. That dusty neighborhood with its cracked pavement and gutters full of sewage. Its neon pickles and tea vendors and mobile phone sellers cracking pumpkin seeds. And the knowledge that Rami will be at the Teachers Club, and probably some half-cut fixers and other friends too. And some newly arrived travelers, wastrels, freelancers, with the social awkwardness that requires drink and a place as seemingly nondescript as the Teachers Club. Or a more senior correspondent, like a peacock, throwing out stories like crumbs and drinking with a sense of weary professionalism. I'd go back tomorrow.

PART II

The Meaning of War Reportage and Its Exclusions

THREE

Extermination as Protection

Depoliticizing War, Remoralizing Violence

> Your ideas are terrifying and your hearts are faint. Your acts of pity and cruelty are absurd, committed with no calm, as if they were irresistible. Finally, you fear blood more and more.
> —PAUL VALÉRY

A Map to a Meaning

"In Mosul, they want you to cover the bodies." This is what a journalist in Erbil told me when I asked about the focus of her reporting. "Journalists cover the suffering of people," a journalist in Beirut remarked, explaining, "You interview someone, and you're looking for a quote about being hurt. They give you a political screed, and that's not what I want. The strictures of the discourse demand accounts of immediate bodily suffering and not the layers of historical grievance." And here is a journalist after a long day of reporting from Mosul: "I went by the Tigris to see if there were any bodies. There were. It was bad for me personally but good professionally."

The battle for Mosul began in October 2016, quickly becoming the world's largest military operation since the 2003 US invasion of Iraq. By 2017, the battle had grown into the most destructive urban combat since the Second World War. The battle included airstrikes and ground forces, guerrilla tactics and siege warfare, more than a dozen state militaries as well as informal militias and soldiers of fortune. It included chemical munitions and suicide bombings, drone swarms and forced displacements. Operations officially ended in July 2017 with the declared defeat of the Islamic State in Mosul. Through the nine-month battle, journalists embedded with various Iraqi and Kurdish combat units or commuted to the war from flophouses and hotel rooms in nearby Erbil. The conflict was extensively covered, but this coverage, according to interviews and observations I conducted in and around Mosul throughout the battle, maintained a particular focus and intent.

In this chapter and the next, I assess the kind of meaning journalism makes for war today. Analysis of the coverage of Mosul reveals the meanings now prominent in war reportage and renders visible the contingencies of journalism's representational authority. As a case study, the battle for Mosul allows us to assess the potential of war reportage as an institution purporting to "speak truth to power" and to thereby ascertain how power is understood through journalism. For as James Carey (1997) notes, the history of journalism is not only a history of technologies, institutions, and political-economic arrangements; the history of journalism is also a history of formal shifts in social comprehension of the world. The history of journalism is a history of how the world is *thought*, and war reportage can reveal the emphases and omissions of how the world of war is *thought now*. For if "war is a force that gives us meaning," as journalist Chris Hedges (2002) asserts, then war reportage is the force behind the force—a dynamic effaced in Hedges's account of war's meaning even as he parses the meanings given by war. The reportage from Mosul crystalizes a moment in social cognition, a moment in which war is assigned meanings responsive to, and reproductive of, a dominant way of thinking.

This chapter maps this way of thinking about war and journalism's critical role therein. Here I assess the humanitarian valence of contemporary war reportage, tracking an emphasis on war's morality and the attendant erasure of war's politics. This dynamic posed a particular problem in the battle for Mosul, where journalists attempted to square the protectionary rationale for anti–Islamic State operations with the harm these operations committed. Their attempt reveals the limits of war reportage today and, thereby, of popular understandings of war in the Middle East and beyond.

Journalism's Humanitarian Desire

Throughout the battle for Mosul, the international press focused not on the strategic progress of the battle, nor on the political dynamics perpetuating war in Iraq, nor on the historical factors that underpin armed conflict in the region. The narrative focus remained on the lives saved or harmed amid the conflagration. These lives were topologized through the categorical imperatives of contemporary war reportage: Humans in Mosul were civilians or combatants, guilty or innocent, victim or perpetrator, dead or alive.[1] Violence against bodies was the abiding content of the reportage from Mosul, wherein the detonation of a vehicle-borne explosive device, the impact of an airstrike, and the suffering that resulted from these and similar acts became the primary matter of much day-to-day media coverage from the battle. Violence and the suffering it caused were emphasized as the central issue of war—its most striking, and most significant, manifestation. But this violence was particular: not the structural violence of the authoritarian or insurgent state, nor the politics of violence as resistance or imperialism or sovereign will, nor the "slow" violence (Nixon 2011) of corporate weapons sales or cultural erasure or environmental collapse. This was violence against bodies—bloody and immediate, corporeal and individuated.

A journalist, standing on Mosul wreckage, was firm: "An abandoned child in Sinjar is more important than where the frontline is." A journalist in Baghdad remarked, "I don't have the sense of a wider narrative, I'm just trying to humanize when people are being killed. Once you lose the sense of human individuals, you stop giving a shit." War is winnowed, then, from a "wider narrative"—which might entail historical trajectories, financial imperatives, political implications—to "human individuals" harmed or killed.[2] The effects of violence on singular bodies becomes the matter at hand in war reportage, while war's existence as a matter of policy and economics and law cedes narrative ground. "How civilians are affected is primary to what's important about war," a journalist in Erbil insisted. But this "how" mystifies a narrative choice between the immediate causes of civilian harm and the reasons that civilians are harmed in war. "The human angle *is* the story," a journalist in Beirut told me. "You highlight the human story. Human stories always resonate more than stories of the facts of policy and territory."

Why the journalistic focus on individuated and somatic suffering? Is this the natural purview of reportorial representations of war, or can we trace some practical-historical basis for this focus, some political economy driving its hegemony? For journalism is a power that prescribes what Didier Fassin calls "a certain form of legitimate discourse" and that authorizes certain kinds of experiences and certain ways of categorizing those experiences (2012, 203). By emphasizing particular types of violence at the exclusion of others, by employing particular criteria for justifiability and rationality in the expenditure of violence, and by essentializing subjects through the use of particular categories, war reportage reproduces a prevailing liberal worldview I will shorthand here as *militarized humanitarianism*. Journalistic representations of war follow the trends of humanitarianism whereby, according to Fassin, "domination is transformed into misfortune, injustice is articulated as suffering, violence is expressed in terms of trauma" (2012, 6). While the humanitarian impulse prompts journalistic focus on violence and suffering as the central matter of war, the meaning given to that violence and that suffering is shaped by humanitarianism's moral commitments and representational concerns. Enacting the humanitarian discourse, war reportage transforms war from the effects of policy on populations to the effects of violence on the innocent.[3]

A central claim of militarized humanitarianism is that the urgency of saving human bodies, and a violence employed to do so, is an exception to any violence premised merely upon political analysis or historical truth. Humanitarianism operates as a "culture of transcendent moral sentiment," over and above any national or international politics (Hopgood 2013, x). As Samuel Moyn argues, humanitarian justifications for violence "make a difference not through political vision but by transcending politics. Morality, global in its potential scope, could become the aspiration of humankind" (2010, 113). Humanitarian's moral claim to legitimacy in the use of violence, in supersession of the political, depends upon a series of typologies that war reportage articulates: the innocent victim, the cruel perpetrator, the virtuous protector. War reportage authorizes and disseminates the norms of humanitarianism, naturalizing those norms as the transparent reality of war. It is through war reportage that what everyone "should know" about war becomes what everyone "does know" about war—a common humanitarian sense (Slaughter 2007, 6; see also Burke 1957).

What everyone knows is that violence that causes human suffering is unjustifiable, and that such violence must be stopped, even with counterviolence. Everyone knows that this reactive violence is, because protective, justified. Everyone knows that civilian victims of war are innocent, and that the effects of violence on the innocent is the most important thing about war. This is the common sense disseminated to global news consumers, and it codifies a war understandable in particular ways through a journalism authorized to tell us what war is like. Violence and suffering are made recognizable by war reportage in a manner amenable to humanitarian's moral and discursive logic, wherein a protectionary violence is essentially just even if incidentally destructive. War reportage does not, then, merely reflect the reality of war so much as constitute and regulate it for publics removed from war, fashioning how subjects in the war zone are imagined, articulated, and—consequentially—affected.

We see this theme realized in the Pulitzer Prize finalists for 2016, 2017, and 2018—the years of the battle for Mosul and its immediate aftermath—which included quite a few nominations for Mosul coverage. Nominations were given to the Associated Press staff for stories that "vividly showed the human cost of the US-led defeat of the Islamic State in the northern Iraqi city of Mosul"; to the staff of the *New York Times* for stories that "demystified the rapid rise and enduring strength of the Islamic State"; and to an individual journalist at the *New York Times* for "dissecting the power and persistence of the ISIS terror movement." The overwhelming thrust of these stories dealt with what journalists call the "human cost of war": the impact of the war with the Islamic State on human individuals, particularly noncombatants. The focus of these Pulitzer-nominated stories—and of those stories produced by the journalists I interviewed and observed—exposed the inhumanity of conflict by attending to the individuals experiencing it, those injured, killed, or otherwise suffering the conditions of wartime violence. Attention to suffering in the news signals its importance for understanding what war *means*.[4]

It is in the post–Cold War period, argues Robert Meister, that the "iconology of human suffering has become the cultural frame through which human rights abuses everywhere are made to appear as such" (2015). Stephen Hopgood invokes the suffering individual as a totem that impels humanitarianism action, often militarized (2013). If violent conflict is now recognized primarily as the unjustified abuse of individual humans, this recognition relies upon a conception of life's goodness that is both homogeneous and universal. The "human" to which militarized humanitarianism responds requires a universal cast for the marshaling of justification for counterviolence; contextual rationales for human suffering—revolution, state building, community defense—can thereby be seen to violate an inviolable and natural human innocence irreducible to class, ethnic, religious, cultural, national, or other difference. For the humanitarian mandate, the human must exceed any political, cultural, or historical context that might limit or condition the necessity of humanity's protection. The ethics of humanitarianism, according to Meister, "is here identified as the imperative to pull recognizable forms of physical violence out of context so that politics can never again be a reason for allowing generically human bodies to be maimed and murdered" (2015).

Humanitarian's moral claim as well as its geographic mobility depends, then, on a generic victim whose suffering is irreducible to context and thus to contextual justification. Such a sufferer, writes Costas Douzinas, takes on a "universal essence" in the humanitarian imagination; it is a being "without differentiation or distinction" and "united with all others in an empty nature deprived of substantive characteristics" (2000, 187). The generically human body synchronizes, discursively, with the generically violent event: Human lives, everywhere the same because identically sacred, are either harmed or saved by a violence whose historical or political basis is trivial compared with the suffering it causes or prevents. In this manner, as Fassin and Mariella Pandolfi note, the "humanitarianization of intervention," wherein the primacy of aid to victims obscures political context and historical particularity, results in the "neutralization—or depoliticization—of war" (2010, 13).

Representations of the universality of the human, a human that deserves saving if under threat of violence, are achieved through the reduction or purification of humans to a biological essence that registers pain identically across cultural, political, and social contexts. Talal Asad (2007) explains how the biologization of the human entails an essentializing of pain as purely somatic and therefore extra-contextual. Where humans are bodies, corporeal suffering becomes what humans experience in scenes of violence, despite contextual distinctions between such scenes. Journalism's tendency to decontextualize suffering as bodily pain (rather than political persecution, or cultural oppression, or economic destitution) is a factor not only of pain's obviousness and thus its representational ease. It is not only, that is, attributable to the demands of a twenty-four-hour news cycle and a lack of resources for deeper investigative reportage. Bodily suffering is also inherently understandable within the universalizing humanitarian frame ascendant in the post–Cold War period. Journalism's decontextualization of suffering as bodily pain is also, then—and in humanitarian fashion—its depoliticization, an erasure of the particular political conditions, foundations, and aims that make suffering happen. In its journalistic rendering, the violence expended in war, as well as the subject suffering this violence, comes to transcend any particular context undermining of humanitarianism's universalist claim. The assignment of a generic victimhood allows for a straightforward moral accounting of the violence that is victimhood's cause.

This figuration of the subject of violence is instrumental to identifying individuals worthy of protection and empathy, and to advancing a specific understanding of war. As Eyal Weizman argues in his study of humanitarianism, "The globalization of compassion meant a view of humanity based on the figure of the victim" (2011, 38). Such a view operates in contemporary war reportage, where a suffering victim stands for the universal figure of humanity in the story of war, and news consumers are the empathetic witnesses to (as well as, presumably, supporters of intervention to prevent) human suffering. Thusly universalized, the victim is no longer a subject with a social class and a familial history and an ethnic or religious or gender identity, but a body with a story about violence, an allegory for an experience of conflict that journalism is authorized to tell. The imposition of victimhood as a status borne on a biologized understanding of life and the corporeal essence of suffering simplifies more complex and shifting relationships in zones of conflict, flattening political and historical distinctions into a legible narrative schema of suffering victim, extremist perpetrator, justified intervener. These figural elements are suitable to a worldview premised on moral certitude as opposed to political analysis.

Journalism authorizes and manages such a worldview, pulling a dyadic violence-suffering out of context in order to activate universalist meanings for war and the harm it does. "There are facts that need to be turned into a story, it has to sizzle," a journalist told me at a checkpoint near Mosul. "It has to be fair and true, yes, but there should be universal themes." Universality in war becomes central to a journalism that both elicits and satisfies consumer desire for what war means, and "universal themes" make violence interesting and important in the news marketplace. "Syria is not interesting from a news perspective," a journalist remarked in Beirut. "It's been going on so long. So we spotlight particular issues—human stories—and this connects with foreign audiences." The connection at issue is about meeting consumer expectations for war's reality, expectations premised on the legible victimhood that journalism provides.[5]

The result of this conception of a universal body and a homogenized suffering, realized in the representation of the individual victim, allows for a deployment of violence by the powerful on behalf of the biological life—though not, as Mahmood Mamdani argues, the political aspirations—of the powerless. These purified powerless are deserving not of the political rights of the citizen but of the biological right to survival, a right "summed up in one word, protection" (2010, 54). Justified counterviolence is premised on protection, and the language of a "responsibility to protect" (R2P, in the policy jargon) articulates a distinction between sanctioned, legitimate violence and the unjustified violence harmful to human victims. According to Anne Orford, the language of R2P has colonized the debate around the use of violence since its codification by the International Commission on Intervention and State Sovereignty in 2001. This manner of speaking about militarism shifted the discourse from one of fighting for rights or controlling populations to one of "responsibility" for human suffering (Orford 2019, 209; see also Hehir 2012). Here the suffering innocent—the "natural human," pulled from political and historical context—can be used to underwrite demand for military action (Hopgood 2013, 72).[6]

Today's militarized humanitarianism operates as a doctrine for representing the violence of the powerful as at least potentially justified because of its stated intention, premised on the responsibility of a so-called international community, to protect victims from the violence prompted by politics, history, or culture—that is, by context (Meister 2011; Shklar 1984). Humanitarian interventions, however violent, become—because "responsible"—beyond ethical repute.[7] Stripped of context, the victims intended to be saved are recognizable by news consumers as individuals like all individuals, suffering as anyone would. Difference is overcome and moral certitude achieved.

In its humanitarian mode, interventionist violence and contemporary war reportage operate on a shared discursive premise: Victims are the primary characters of war, and a violence that produces victims requires attention—whether representational or military. Both the humanitarian responsibility to protect and the journalistic responsibility to represent address a violence and a suffering stripped of context, and both grant meanings to war that are moral and universal. War reportage both responds to and reproduces humanitarian desire. And as humanitarianism came to shape understandings of war and suffering in the post-war era, war reporters assumed the mantle of humanitarian witness, transmitting suffering in ways that enact an implicit humanitarian worldview.

The humanitarian valence of war reporting, while shifting and inconsistent across modern conflicts, becomes especially salient where civilian harm is made central as a news object, as it was during the battle for Mosul. Where civilians are harmed at scale, and where journalists find this harm newsworthy (with the worn adage, "it bleeds, it leads," kicking in), a humanitarian organization of war's meaning becomes especially apparent. In such cases, journalism's narrative frame captures an immanent violence that can be judged legitimate or extreme; a suffering mostly shorn of political and historical context; a separation of innocence from guilt, victim from perpetrator. This narrative frame suits a reigning doxa on war.[8]

Checkpoint Captives

The Aqrab, or "Scorpion," checkpoint is a funnel at the cusp of Kurdish Iraq for traffic into and out of Mosul. It's July 22, 2017, and it's 115 degrees. Several journalists, their fixer, and I arrive late—well past dawn—and those manning the checkpoint seem caffeinated and supervised enough to give a shit. The checkpoint consists of a two-room bunker set between the east-bound and west-bound lanes of traffic. Inside the bunker is an overstuffed couch, a plywood desk, piles of ledgers, a struggling table fan, and young men in military uniforms. Automatic weapons lounge about. Outside the bunker is a dusty scene of pickups piled with family belongings, fuel trucks belching grit, goats on tethers. Along the eastern lane, outbound from Mosul, soldiers are checking the paperwork of all fighting-age men.

Checkpoints are a prominent feature in the lives of working war reporters.[9] As a chokepoint for the access on which stories—and, especially in the case of freelancers, livelihoods—depend, checkpoints can severely impact the ability of journalists to do their work. Checkpoints are one of the few places where wartime dynamics work against foreign journalists, who are forced to leverage whatever they can—contacts, jokes, flirtation, fame, money, perseverance, guile, comradery, cigarettes—to pass through. Checkpoints can also be a barometer for official regard for the media. As a journalist at a checkpoint near Kirkuk, Iraq, explained, "One factor that suggests the achievement of journalism is that more journalists are stopped at checkpoints before big offenses, so someone must think that journalists affect the military's reality and their ability to cover things up." At specific moments in the Mosul battle, various news organizations, including Reuters, were banned from passing through checkpoints.

Most plainly, checkpoints are a place where journalists spend a lot of time. Here is where novels get read, Arabic gets learned, emails get sent. While various strategies are employed to move swiftly through checkpoints, the whims and personalities of those manning the checkpoint are often decisive factors.

Around Mosul and the greater region, checkpoints differed markedly in sectarian orientation, in relationships to the central Iraqi state and the US military, and in general regard for international media. The ability to read checkpoint culture became an important skill for journalists and their fixers. But biding time at checkpoints was, on the whole, inevitable when reporting on Mosul, and the checkpoint game could be wearying. "I'm pretty good at checkpoints," a journalist told me while waiting to cross the Syrian border from Iraq. "I know what to laugh about, which leaders to curse, but I still don't fully get what's going on, what's dangerous and what's not."

At the Aqrab checkpoint, I watch the journalists negotiate with Iraqi soldiers as their paperwork—official permits, passport photocopies—disappears into a scrum of files. We've been here ninety minutes, and the journalists have already cycled through a checkpoint repertoire: stately professionalism, obsequious politesse, dirty humor, sly flirtation, measured anger. My observation of the negotiation grows tedious in the heat, and I wander over to the garbaged strip between the east- and west-bound traffic lanes. A goat picks listlessly in the shadow of a Humvee. From the checkpoint bunker, a soldier saunters toward me, his cap rakishly poised. "I show you something," he remarks upon earshot.

He pulls me by the hand over to the Humvee—a vintage model, probably from the immediate post-invasion years—parked in the dust near the bunker. "Look in," the soldier commands. It's difficult to see through the armored windows of the vehicle, almost mirrors in the high-sun glare; at first I see only my own face. But my eyes adjust, and there in the back seat is a man stooped, hands bound behind a contorted frame. It must be an ungodly heat inside the vehicle. The zip ties binding his arms are the only thing of brightness in the cab, their chalky sheen in stark distinction from the shadowed human wither. Almost imperceptibly, the man's head wilts in my direction; the peripheral of his left eye must be swinging me into its line of sight. He gazes up and through me. With the heavy darkness inside the truck and the bright sunshine outside, he must see me better than I see him. What I do see is a teenager, maybe fifteen years old, who'd been apprehended as an Islamic State fighter and whose execution loomed.

Is the possibility of this kid's execution a matter of war's inhumane excess or its central logic, a moral lapse or a juridical design? Is his vulnerability to state power a problem of protecting innocents or exterminating enemies? Is he not a *guilty* victim, or an *innocent* perpetrator, categories transgressive of journalistic order? Is he a human body violated amidst war's immanent violence, or is he the subject of historical grievance, a civil war lost, the sovereign decision to pardon or to kill?

The journalists are finally given permission to continue their journey to Mosul, and we pile into our dust-caked SUV. As the checkpoint recedes, I voice my displeasure about the boy in the Humvee. The journalists seem miffed that their fixer hadn't alerted them to the presence of the prisoner, a figural representative for the receding battle for Mosul. I didn't mention him first, though; our driver, friendly with the soldiers at the checkpoint, had also been invited to glimpse the boy, and he'd passed around his cellphone photos to the journalists in the car. Now a topic of discussion, I ask the journalists how the boy could be made into a news story and what must be left out. He is a victim, but of a difficult kind, the journalists agree. They consider appealing to his age and bodily harm (as I have done here) as a means to elicit empathy for an alleged Islamic State fighter.

When perpetrators are victims, when protection become punishment, when law inverts to unlaw, journalism's discursive norms are threatened. The entwinement of saving and killing marked a troubling political reality of the war in Mosul, a reality too often displaced by the moral certitude of the humanitarian frame.[10]

Protective Violence

The Mosul battle kicked off in October 2016 with the bombing of Islamic State targets by the US-led Combined Joint Task Force Operation Inherent Resolve.[11] By that time, reporting had already sedimented particular meanings for the violence associated with the broader Islamic State conflict, which had been underway for some years. During this period of initial coverage—roughly from 2013, when the Islamic State broke from the local al-Qaeda franchise and distinguished itself in brand and strategy from a former incarnation in the post-invasion insurgency—the Islamic State was made knowable to international news consumers as the purveyors of a violence lawless, unjustified, and extreme. Atrocities stacked up—the beheading of American journalist James Foley in August 2014, the burning alive of Jordanian pilot Muath al-Kasasbeh in January 2015—and journalists in the region responded with objective, fact-based accounts of the horror.[12] The *New York Times*, in an article from November 21, 2015, offered a standard appraisal: "There was no way to avoid seeing the [Islamic State] organization as the wanton killing machine it was" (Moaveni 2015). Choice of noun and adjective in this typical description entail a judgment about Islamic State violence hidden beneath the normativity of the meaning journalism makes.

In international reportage from the region, Islamic State violence thus came to symptomize inhumane harm. Such violence, expended for purposes political or theological, was from the vantage of humanitarian morality a quintessentially unjustified and unjustifiable violence, demeaning of the supreme good of bodily protection. And the violence expended against the Islamic State—or rather, against the human suffering it caused—figured journalistically as an acceptable counterviolence whose effects, *even if excessive*, were presumed justified. Another *New York Times* description, from an October 16, 2016, article, is similarly routine: "Forces will fight to enter a city where for weeks the harsh authoritarian rule of the Islamic State . . . has sought to crack down on a population eager to either escape or rebel" (Nordland 2016).

In narratively arranging the conflict around an unprovoked terroristic violence and a reactive, protective violence, US-Coalition forces can figure only as a righteous actor deploying a violence whose aims are pure, while the Islamic State can figure only as an illegitimate actor perpetrating a violence for purposes abhorrent.[13] The conflict in Mosul became calcified in its journalistic representation as a heedless insurgency violating innocent bodies and thus necessitating responsible military intervention, rather than a civil war in which the United States joined one side rather than the other. The former framing—of an unprovoked, cruel violence and a reactive, protective violence—suits a humanitarian worldview, wherein an outside intervention becomes legible as the responsibility to police certain forms of suffering, a legibility premised upon a moral distinction between preventable inhumane harm and incidental inadvertent harm. The later framing—of a civil war between the Islamic State and the Iraqi state, in which the United States backs one side—muddies this distinction, as the violence becomes predicated on political rather than moral claims. In a civil war, the notion of a responsibility to protect is displaced by a will to win, and preventing human harm is relegated below strategic aims. Either framing—civil war or humane protection—can be made "factual" or "accurate"; any number of narrative possibilities exist in the representation of a war. But only one such framing perpetuates a dominant consensus regarding the meaning of US war in the Middle East. It is this framing that has become conventional in war reportage today.

Prior to what many news organizations came to call the "mother of all battles" in Mosul,[14] journalists in the region did a commendable job indicating why the Islamic State, with a force estimated at just 800–1,500 fighters, was able to capture Mosul, Iraq's second-largest city, in which 30,000 Iraqi Army soldiers were garrisoned alongside 30,000 Iraqi federal police. As journalists explained, Mosul's majority Sunni population was long disaffected with the central Iraqi state, a circumstance that resulted in the infiltration of Islamic State sleeper cells, an absence of organized local resistance to Islamic State forces, and the defection of many Iraqi state soldiers and police. Corruption in the Iraqi state military meant an overestimation of troop strength, and many soldiers stationed in Mosul from Iraq's Shia-majority south lacked a will to fight on behalf of a Sunni-majority city and simply absconded. But this historical and political context, background for the reportage produced on the Islamic State rout of Mosul, tended to drop off the narrative radar as the international fight to retake the city came underway. In the relevant reportage, Mosul soon became a humanitarian crisis attributable to Islamic State violence and not to those problems that laid the groundwork for the success of the insurgency. The circumstances that allowed the Islamic State to capture and hold the city; Iraqi government corruption, ineptitude, and abuse; the services provided by the Islamic State, and which may have induced some to remain in the city; the longer history of destabilization, polarization, and US military domination, including in the Mosul Nineveh campaign of 2008: These factors went largely unmentioned in the daily reportage from Mosul once the battle for the city began.

As long as some forms of suffering are authorized as necessary or inevitable and others as extreme or terroristic, some forms of war "can be understood as humane" and their infliction of suffering a matter of responsibility

(Orford 2019, 210). The language of "liberation," very frequently employed by journalists during the battle, establishes the authorization of certain violences and the prohibition of others. That Mosul should be "liberated" by US-Coalition forces (rather than "taken," "occupied," or "seized") is a polemic naturalized by journalism as the true meaning of the war.[15]

Civilian Harm as Discursive Tension

In the final months of the battle for Mosul, following an intensified US-Coalition air campaign, many journalists began to question government and military claims concerning the civilian impact of anti–Islamic State targeting. Dogged reporting systematically threw into doubt Pentagon assessments of US-Coalition operations, as it was soon revealed that these operations killed many more civilians in Mosul than initially presumed—*more, even, than the Islamic State*. In attributing more and more civilian harm to US-Coalition forces, journalism assumed a critical posture toward the official humanitarian rationale framing the Mosul battle. The *Washington Post*, the *Los Angeles Times*, the *New York Times*, the Associated Press, National Public Radio, BuzzFeed News, and other news organizations brought attention to the inaccurately low death tallies offered by official US organs. Once largely supportive of anti–Islamic State operations, journalists assumed an oppositional stance to the interventionary action. But the nature and effects of this journalistic opposition require scrutiny.

On May 1, 2017, reporters for the *Los Angeles Times* published a story about civilian casualty reviews in the US military, finding that "the military failed to report 80 civilian casualties from airstrikes during the last two years" (Hennessy-Fiske and Hennigan 2017). Through investigations in Mosul and elsewhere in Iraq, and by comparing independent monitors' estimates of civilian casualties with those of the US military and Coalition partners, the reporting demonstrated officials' underestimates of the number of those killed by US-Coalition forces. On November 2, 2017, BuzzFeed News published a story detailing discrepancies in US-Coalition accounts of civilian death in Mosul: "The Coalition . . . has not kept pace with the flurry of allegations of civilian casualties that have emerged" (Giglio 2017). Through reporting in Mosul and elsewhere, BuzzFeed News was able to document civilian casualties that had not received attention from US military investigators. On December 20, 2017, an Associated Press investigation from Mosul revealed that "the number killed in the nine-month battle to liberate the city from the Islamic State group marauders has not been acknowledged by the US-led Coalition, the Iraqi government or the self-styled caliphate" (George et al. 2017). The article continues, "What is clear from the tallies is that as Coalition and Iraqi government forces increased their pace, civilians were dying in ever higher numbers at the hands of their liberators." Focusing on individuals' traumatic experiences and a body count supplied by the Mosul morgue, the Associated Press found that the US-Coalition "liberators" severely underreported the scale of death resulting from the war against Islamic State "marauders."[16]

In response to this coverage, the US military at first denied the reported scale of civilian harm from US-Coalition operations. US-Coalition spokespersons consistently defended official figures on civilian casualties in interviews and other statements. Col. Joseph Scrocca told the Associated Press that lower numbers from US military accounts indicate a more careful investigative process used to "get to the truth" of the civilian casualties (in George et al. 2017). A Coalition spokesperson told BuzzFeed News that some of the reported incidents of civilian deaths were "not credible" (in Giglio 2017). Responding to *Los Angeles Times* reporting on an airstrike in Mosul that killed civilians, Pentagon officials found "insufficient information to be able to determine if civilians were present or harmed" in the incident (in Hennessy-Fiske and Hennigan 2017). Regarding other reported civilian deaths, Scrocca told the *Los Angeles Times*, "All we have is an allegation, no proof or way to interview victims" (in Hennessy-Fiske and Hennigan 2017). In general, then, US officials flatly denied many incidents of civilian harm. US military assessments of civilian harm were themselves publicized as an indication of humanitarian concern.

As proof of civilian harm from US-Coalition attacks proliferated, and outright dismissal became harder to maintain, officials argued that such harm was either rare and inadvertent, or unavoidable and thereby necessary given Islamic State use of civilian shields and the density of urban combat. In a September 2017 column for *Foreign Policy*, Lt. Gen. Stephen Townsend, the commander of the US-Coalition war in Mosul, staked a claim: "I challenge anyone to find a more precise air campaign in the history of warfare" (Townsend 2017b). This despite the fact, Townsend notes, that "the Islamic State had nearly three years to prepare for the defense of these cities and then cowardly used civilians as human shields to protect themselves even further" (Townsend 2017b).

Because Townsend commanded the US-Coalition war in Mosul, and because his published remarks on that conflict are indicative of official framing of other recent conflicts, close attention to his argument is warranted. In the *Foreign Policy* article, Townsend offers a number of justifications for the US-Coalition campaign in order to dispute or defend the alleged scale of civilian harm it inflicted. First was the need to "protect our partner forces and Coalition service members." Civilians are relegated below US-Coalition soldiers in a hierarchy of worth, and self-defense is affirmed as justification for harm against civilians, even as the necessity of self-defense need not be proven. Townsend then insists that the Coalition "strikes only valid military targets after considering the principles of military necessity, humanity, proportionality, and distinction. . . . The Coalition's goal is always for zero human casualties."[17] This is a defense of civilian death when proportional to military goals, and which articulates the humanitarian toleration for violence when considered protective and thereby virtuous. While noting that allegations of civilian harm are "unsupported by fact," Townsend also charges that such allegations "strengthen the Islamic State's hold on civilians, placing civilians at greater risk." This, Townsend explains, because greater hesitancy to kill civilians on the part of the US-Coalition leaves civilians vulnerable to the Islamic State's own "disregard for human life." Better to be harmed accidently by virtuous violence, Townsend seems to suggest, than purposely by terroristic violence.[18]

Townsend then enumerates Islamic State cruelties, noting that if civilians "are not liberated they will also surely die, either at the hands of the Islamic State or from starvation." Townsend in this way shifts blame for civilian death (including lack of food, a result of siege conditions imposed by the US-Coalition) to the Islamic State. "The Islamic State brought misery and death to this region," Townsend argues, "and it is responsible for the plight of civilians in the areas its fighters hold." Those civilian deaths attributable to the US-Coalition are in this way blamed on the Islamic State for resisting defeat.[19] To destroy the Islamic State in Iraq and Syria, Townsend argues, would also prevent death "in our homelands across the globe," and thus future lives can be protected at the expense of Iraqi lives in Mosul.[20] Townsend concludes his article by arguing, "The only way to save the people . . . is to liberate them from the Islamic State." The *possibility*, even the *likelihood*, of killing civilians becomes, in effect, a necessary condition for their protection. Here the worldview of militarized humanitarianism—in which violence, even deadly violence, is justified by the intent to protect—is fully realized.[21]

Journalistic challenge to officials' defense of the harm committed against civilians consisted, in humanitarian fashion, of an emphasis on the suffering of innocent civilians, a suffering that legitimated the US-Coalition use of force in the first place. This challenge drew wide praise. Journalists were seen—by media critics, liberal politicians, and large segments of the news-consuming public—as occupying the role of oppositional "fourth estate," contesting official claims and thereby "speaking truth to power." Here was the foreign press corps living up to the ideals of great war reportage past, particularly from the war in Vietnam, when journalists (as popular history has it) disassembled Pentagon deception and revealed the truth of war behind the official veil. The 2018 Hillman Prize, honoring "excellence in journalism," was awarded to the "The Uncounted," a report on civilian casualties in Mosul from the *New York Times Magazine* (Hillman Foundation 2018). The award states, "These journalists stepped up to do what the governments and institutions did not," namely, account for US-caused harm.

As a result of this reportage, the exact number of civilians killed in the US-Coalition offensive in Mosul became a matter of serious contention. Yet the nature and implications of this contention are not entirely clear. Accuracy is a primary value of journalism, of course, and producing an accurate number of war dead carries professional and discursive significance for the institution of war reportage. But is meaningful contestation about civilian death primarily a matter of numerical accuracy, or is the reason that people were killed the more consequential matter? For while the reportage on civilian casualties in the US-Coalition air war in Mosul stubbornly questioned the accuracy of official assessments, it did not question the rationale on offer: that such killing is an accidental exception or a necessary excess to a humane and thus well-intentioned intervention. In focusing on the bodily effects of war—counting the casualties, describing the suffering—and in frontloading violence against victims as the central meaning of war, the rationale for war, its meaning and intent, is never called to account. Tracking the scale and horror of death, while an important journalistic practice (and especially where underestimations suit the interests of a particular party to the conflict), does not in itself challenge the premises upon which this death is dealt. The coverage of civilian harm in Mosul became a contestation around accurate tallies, but this contestation implicitly accepts the inadvertent or unavoidable nature of the harm at issue. Harming civilians remained a moral dilemma, and the violence expended by the US-Coalition was still represented in the news as protective in intent and thus morally justified.

Through difficult reporting, some journalists revealed what appeared to be US war crimes: Civilians were killed by the US-Coalition in very large numbers. Yet this reporting never amounted to a reconsideration of the humanitarian justification for war in Mosul, a justification that underpinned official defense of the harm committed. The figuration of the US-Coalition as humanitarian savior may have been dampened by the revelations of outsized civilian harm, but the structural features of the war reportage narrative—victims as innocent, violence as the central problem of war, the anti–Islamic State offensive as virtuous—held firm. Journalism from Mosul testified to the excesses of US-Coalition warfare, its mistakes and regrets, but the war remained essentially legitimate because of its intention to protect innocent bodies. Journalism's challenge to the official narrative of the battle can be seen, then, as part of the sanctioned code, what Stuart Hall and coauthors (1978) would describe as a permitted, preinscribed deviance rather than a decisive break. Journalism's disenchantment of US deception in Mosul—its piercing of the veil of official obfuscation, its disclosure of the real behind the mask—was widely regarded as a pinnacle for journalism in the War on Terror. Yet journalism's disenchantment was also a re-enchantment: War remained meaningful through a humanitarian register—it remained about the suffering of bodies—and this meaning mystified the systematic and possibly punitive logic of the violence narrated to be protective in intent. The revelation revealed another mask.

For the circumstance in which civilian death in US air war is an *excess*—an incidental necessity or unintended consequence of otherwise careful targeting protocol—rather than a *design* of war would be an historical anomaly. The history of US air war—over Dresden and Tokyo in World War II, during Operation Rolling Thunder and Speedy Express in Vietnam, against the Federal Republic of Yugoslavia in Kosovo, in the NATO intervention in Libya—is a history in which civilians were not killed unintentionally (Appy 2000; Gregory 2015; Searle 2002; Selden 2007; Turse 2013). Rather, communities under bombardment were typically understood by war planners as populations hostile to the United States and supportive of enemy forces. Civilian suffering was not an excess to war making but its architecture. Here life was not figured as sacred, but only some lives in some places; victims were not innocent but guilty by association; civilians were killed not unavoidably in the protection of bodies, but strategically, as politicized populations killed for the purposes of military victory. The killing of civilians entailed a political-strategic rationale, not a lapse in otherwise protective warfare.[22]

On the one hand, the framework of humanitarian intervention—the use of justified violence to stop an unjustified violence—admits inadvertent death. International humanitarian law allows for civilians to be killed "incidentally" as long as these casualties are not disproportionate to the military advantages gained (Crawford 2013; Fenrick 2001; Orford 2019). Civilians can be lawfully sacrificed when "military objectives" are deemed to require it.[23] On the other hand, if the number of civilian dead, whether 6 or 6,000, is thought too high by the publics on behalf of which humanitarian intervention is purportedly waged, we must ask *why*. Why did the news of outsized civilian deaths in Mosul strike news producers, and presumably news consumers, as newsworthy? Was it simply a matter of the divergence between official and journalistic tallies, and thus the exposure of Pentagon perfidy regarding the "smart" bombs and "precision" munitions advertised to more humanely wage war? If the suffering wrought by humanitarian counterviolence is thought to be disproportionate to the aim of protecting bodies, then why exactly does this disproportion disturb, given the allowance for—in fact, the likelihood of—civilian death in war, whatever its political or moral premises? If civilian death is inevitable in war, then is the scandal of such death its quantity or its systematicity? Is the hidden scale of war's violence the decisive issue, or is it the logic of a war where civilians are killed at scale?

Journalistic emphasis on the toll inflicted upon civilians by US-Coalition violence—a toll rivaling that inflicted by the violence the intervention was advertised to stop—belies meanings absent in the reportage from Mosul. For the concern of US-Coalition officials may be less about the protection of innocents from violence than about who gets to use violence in the world, and which violence is deemed justified, rational, lawful, humane. Col. Thomas Veale, a spokesman for US-Coalition forces, revealed this slippage to the Associated Press (in George et al. 2017):

> It is simply irresponsible to focus criticism on inadvertent casualties caused by the Coalition's war to defeat ISIS. Without the Coalition's air and ground campaign against ISIS, there would have inevitably been additional years, if not decades of suffering and needless death and mutilation in Syria and Iraq at the hands of terrorists who lack any ethical or moral standards.

Veale's pronouncement suggests that the operation against the Islamic State is about the claim to righteous violence against an immoral, extreme violence, irrespective of the effects of that righteous violence on those otherwise subject to the violence deemed immoral. For as Carl Schmitt ([1934] 1985) notes, the authority to administer righteousness and legitimacy, the authority to decide the rules of violence and define exceptions thereto, is the very essence of sovereignty. An act of death dealing superseding politics as such, militarized humanitarianism manifests the sovereign right to kill even as it performs a moral, protective function.

Journalism from Mosul effectively questioned the success of this performance without questioning the performance itself. Because the journalism that contested the number of deaths dealt by a humanitarian intervention never contested the sovereign power to deal death in the name of humanity. By reporting civilian harm as an inadvertent mistake or incidental necessity of war, a *moral* bug—rather than a structural property of war, a *political* feature intended to produce particular results—journalists normalized the meanings for war suitable to a ruling order. Inhumane acts such as the killing of civilians, which can be classified as a war crime, become humane—become merely proportional, merely "collateral damage," and thus legal—by virtue of assumed intent. War reportage authorizes this assumption for its publics. Here protection can serve as an alibi for destructive power, the very power that can cause the suffering to which journalism attends. The victims central to contemporary war reportage are indeed "collateral": They are the narrative deposit necessary to legitimate interventionary action and humanitarian violence.[24]

Humanitarianism, as a representational premise, does have a particular appeal for those publics on behalf of whom war is waged and much war reportage produced. The *ur*-experience of humanitarianism, its primal instantiation, is the conceptual severing of humane violence from extermination (mark of colonialism, imperialism, revolution, and other politically inflected violences). The notion that the United States or the "international community" invades a city to kill its population is, in a humanitarian era, a journalistic category error, and a notion popularly disavowed. The international news from Mosul, in its representational emphases, disowns that notion on its audience's behalf. The importance of contentions over numerical accuracy in accounting for civilian harm is premised on the idea of war as protection and thereby avoids reckoning with the idea of war as extermination. In reporting the effects of violence on the innocent rather than the effects of policy on populations—in representing the battle for Mosul as protection, even failed protection, rather than extermination—journalism saves its audience from a return of what humanitarianism represses: the strategic dimensions of civilian killing. For minus journalism's representational emphases, there is little to distinguish the killing of civilians under humane conditions from the killing of civilians, full stop. Devoid of humane justification, war remains—as Kurtz, Joseph Conrad's colonial agent, puts it—the extermination of the brutes. One role of the war reportage from Mosul was to say to its audience, *This is not mass murder.*

Disarming Critique

While focus on civilian harm from US-Coalition operations in Mosul presumes a critique of US air war, the humanitarian register of war reportage relieves the critical impulse. Emphasis on victimhood, prevalent in the reportage produced from the battle for Mosul, becomes complicit in the perpetuation of the official rationale for interventionary violence. As Evelyn Cobley points out, "Critical commentaries overlook such complicities because their thematic approach ignores ideological implications of formal strategies" (1993, 5). The formal conventions of journalism—victims separated from perpetrators, lawful and legitimate violence distinct from excessive and terroristic violence, the individuating narrative frame—articulates an ideology in its very structure. Features inherent to contemporary war reportage thus prevent a more complex treatment of civilian death and foreclose a more critical examination of official responses thereto.[25]

In interviews, I asked journalists why official accounts of US-caused civilian harm as inadvertent or unavoidable were rarely challenged. Journalists cited, most often, a professional resistance to imputations of motive. "Sticking to the facts" in Mosul meant reporting conditions on the ground and the responses of those involved. US-Coalition spokespeople attributed civilian death in anti–Islamic State operations to unintended accidents—the so-called fog of war—or to incidental necessity given the conditions of battle, and such responses were duly reported in the news. More precisely, such responses *are* the news. And this news of what US officials say about civilian casualties disabuses the journalist of having to take a position on the truth or falsity of official claims, or of having to question the policy underpinning official claims. By excluding interpretation, journalists are exercising "news judgement" in accordance with basic conventions of objectivity and accuracy (Hallin 1986, 71). The practical routines of news making (e.g., interviewing official sources) and the institutional ideals of journalism (e.g., objectivity and accuracy) convene to shape the meanings war reportage makes.

"Journalism as empirical inquiry is limited to what can be proven, and internal mind states or motivations are extremely difficult, if not impossible, to prove." This is what a journalist told me on a long drive through northern Iraq. We were headed to a village east of Mosul recently taken from the Islamic State by US-Coalition forces. "One issue is time and space," he continued. "Investigating the underlying motives of individual humans is time-consuming and difficult at the best of times. Deadlines, word limits, and the costly, constrained conditions of reporting in conflict zones means most journalists have to take people at their word." Pancaked buildings passed the car window, and I asked why the motives of US policymakers and military commanders, specifically, are underexamined, given that the expressions of Islamic State members are not accepted uncritically by the international press. He replied:

> There's a generalized acceptance, among liberals in particular, of government as essentially good. Under eight years of Obama, a generation of journalists came of age believing that the progressive American dream could work, and that if the government was still doing things that appeared to be exploitative, imperialist, arbitrary—if Guantanamo was not shut, if Yemeni weddings were still being incinerated by Hellfire missiles, and if obscure, unaccountable branches of the national security establishment and private subcontractors were still waging shadow wars in impoverished countries—this was not because the policymakers themselves held ill intentions. We implicitly trusted officials' intentions. It was because of some hangover from a more brutal time, the Bush era, which was now being washed away as the arc of the moral universe bent inevitably toward justice. Journalists are not in the habit of questioning the motives of government policymakers or wondering whether anyone could ever do something as repellent as developing an explicit policy to terrorize or collectively punish civilians. It's hard to believe that these people are lying to your face, and harder still to prove.[26]

Other journalists suggested space constraints, deadlines, and a general presumption about the humane intent of US-Coalition policy as reasons for accepting official narratives regarding civilian harm. In reporting the official line without comment, however, the news reproduces that line and thereby functions, essentially, as an instrument of state power (Barnoy and Reich 2020; Zaller and Chiu 1996). An official claim as to what war in Mosul *is*—and what the War on Terror, broadly, means—is preserved and indeed enhanced through journalism, which offers this narrative "objectively," at face value. A rational violence is used to counter an extreme violence, and civilians are protected from harm but are sometimes killed in the process. Here officials become the "primary definers" of reality, shaping how stories of war are told in the press (Bennett et al. 2007).

Journalists were also reluctant, they told me, to report that some people chose to stay in Mosul under Islamic State rule. Such a story could imply that civilians were harmed by US-Coalition forces not accidently as innocent victims, but strategically as populations supportive of an international enemy. While the choice to remain in Mosul does not necessarily entail support for the Islamic State (the alternative—losing one's home and becoming internally displaced—is not a bright one), it is the case that, for some, there were good reasons to remain under Islamic State rule. Alienation from a Shia-dominated central government in Baghdad and grievances about Iraqi state corruption were not uncommon among Mosul's Sunni majority before the Islamic State took control. The Islamic State did offer, at least initially and for specific communities, more security and better social services (trash collection, electricity, health care) than Mosul's previous government. Some Mosulawis had familial and communal ties to the Islamic State.[27]

Journalists reported these dynamics prior to the battle for Mosul, but once the battle was underway, attention to popular support for the Islamic State became journalistically impalpable. As a journalist in Erbil told me, "There is a well-intentioned, generally unconscious humanistic desire among many journalists to contradict a perceived mainstream narrative in the US and Europe that all Muslims are 'terrorist' sympathizers, which produces an implicit bias toward narratives that suggest large Muslim populations are anti–Islamic State." Of course, in avoiding the demonization of Muslims through more "humanizing" narratives, journalists are ignoring the history and politics that contextualize the choice to resist the US-Coalition intervention. They are also denying the complexity of human behavior in wartime.[28]

"In Islamic State–held Iraq," the same journalist continued,

> The journalist finds herself in an awkward position. If you write that the residents are pro–Islamic State, you risk empowering a pernicious domestic narrative among your presumed audience, fed by decades of *Homeland* and *American Sniper* and *24*. In order to relate a narrative in which Muslim subjects are *both* pro–Islamic State (or at least Islamic State tolerant) and "sympathetic" or "humanized," you must disturb many deeply rooted narratives and assumptions among your audience, who are often used to thinking of the Islamic State as a sort mythological creation on to which they can displace anxieties and fears, and who are also used to thinking of their own governments in the savior role. Upsetting these narratives by relating a long, complicated history of political and economic exploitation of which your audience is largely unaware is hard work and takes space. It's easier to accept an anti–Islamic State population narrative for Mosul.

In accepting this simplified account, however, America's strategic rationale for the killing of civilians (in Tokyo, Vietnam, Kosovo, Libya, and elsewhere, including Iraq) can never enter the narrative frame. By representing civilians in Mosul as innocent victims, the possibility of their strategic elimination by US-Coalition forces is elided. Humanitarian justification for violence obscures any political rationale.[29]

A story narrating rational, or at least willful, reasons to remain in Islamic State territory risks granting the Islamic State legitimacy as a governing body, and this opens a difficult discursive terrain for journalism and its humanitarian impulses. For such an admission can give credence to the group as an actor whose use of violence, while horrific (as all violence can be), may yet be justified in the defense of a supportive population. Islamic State violence *too* becomes protective. Such a narrative threatens the US-Coalition monopoly on justified violence. To narrate the battle in this fashion entails that legitimacy in the killing of civilians is no longer the sole possession of only one party to the conflict. This expansion of sovereign authority would necessarily call into question the right of the "international community" to intervene militarily in Mosul, a right that grounds the institution of humanitarian order. If what counts as rational, justified, lawful violence is contested, then the humanitarian consensus cannot hold. Suddenly, the United States appears to be intervening not on behalf of an international community, protecting civilians as a moral responsibility, but as the backer of one side of a civil war, protecting its own interests as geopolitical strategy. "Civil war" is a term never used in the international news to describe the battle for Mosul and the extended war against the Islamic State in Iraq. For such framing readmits the political in a way dangerous to the moral basis of humanitarianism, which professes to supersede politics. Violence, in this account, would be about something other than saving. It would be about winning.

Moreover, an account in which the Islamic State is granted legitimacy as a governing body throws into relief the violence of international humanitarian law, revealing law not as a mechanism for the protection of human individuals, but as a carapace over the exercise of violence for strategic purposes. If what counts as lawful violence is in contention, journalism is then faced with particular category errors disruptive of its humanitarian perspective. Suddenly, there are guilty victims—those who chose to stay and support, or at least tolerate, the Islamic State—whose death registers not as the incidental excess of humanitarian protection but as the strategic elimination of enemies of state. Here journalism's humanitarian edifice is threatened.

When journalists embrace a humanitarian paradigm in order to resist anti-Muslim narratives, as journalists themselves suggest, journalism is then expelling the idea that the US military is in Mosul killing Muslims, even as this is what the US military was doing. The expulsion of this idea, in the retreat to humanitarian meanings for war, displaces political context with moral intention. The work of journalism in war zones becomes the work of repression. Reporting war as the effects of violence on the innocent, rather than the effects of policy on populations, is not simply a matter of failing to tell the real story. It is the fulfillment of a desire, pervasive in the liberal democracies supporting wars in the Middle East and beyond, that people are killed as a matter of protection rather than a matter of extermination.

More recent reportage indicates that civilian harm in the US-Coalition air war against the Islamic State amounted less to incidental necessity or accidental excess than to systematic disregard for civilian lives, a disregard whose scale and consistency make it indistinguishable from a coherent policy. A series of articles appearing in the *New York Times Magazine* in December of 2021 revealed that the US military logged many more civilian casualty incidents that had been publicly acknowledged.[30] Most of these incidents were categorized by the US military as comprising civilian casualties proportional to the military objectives achieved in a given strike operation, or as based on claims of harm deemed non-credible and that could then be dismissed. This reportage, however, demonstrates that US military claims of proportionality were largely unfounded and that dismissal of casualty events often relied on faulty or superficial investigations.[31] Of 1,300 military assessments of civilian casualty incidents, not one resulted in a finding of wrongdoing. Moreover, despite the scale of civilian harm recorded by the US military, no changes were made to the pace or processes of airstrike operations. The looming question, unasked in the *Times* articles, is whether faulty proportionality assessments and investigatory flaws allow the US military to ignore accounts of civilian harm in order to maintain offensive operations while still advertising humanitarian concern.

The publication of this classified strike data undermines previous Pentagon assurances about the transparency of military operations, the precision of US weapons systems, and the accidents attendant to the "fog of war." The data shows, instead, the US military's awareness of the scale of civilian harm in anti–Islamic State operations and their failure to do anything about it. The military's collection of civilian casualty data can indeed be seen as a pretext for ignoring it. By tracking accounts of civilian death in order to affirm their proportionality or dismiss their credibility, impunity is assured in the continued execution of air war.[32] As with the attention to civilian casualties by journalists in Mosul, attention to civilian casualties by the US military can justify war on the basis of intent, transforming a siege into a liberation by virtue of an assumption of purpose that cannot be proven.

While the war reportage from Mosul granted the benefit of the doubt to Pentagon claims of necessity or accident in the killing of civilians, this more recent reportage could (but explicitly does not) grant the benefit of the doubt to Pentagon claims about proportionality or non-credibility in the killing of civilians, killing now exposed as neither accidental nor necessary. US military tracking of civilian harm can become proof of humanitarian intent, since the classification of such harm as proportional or non-credible can also justify the continuation of a war deemed humanitarian. This recent reportage, then, is yet subject to interpretations still in contention. In response to this recent reportage, a US military spokesman explained, "You have in your possession more than a thousand investigations into strikes that were alleged to have caused civilian harm, which is clear evidence that we have strove to understand and acknowledge the mistakes we have made." But the understanding of US-caused civilian harm as *mistake*, rather than *policy*, is precisely what this reportage calls into question.[33]

It should be noted, however, that this reportage on the US military's strike investigations—published years after the conclusion of the conflict in question—relied on documents released through Freedom of Information Act requests and court order; on anonymous sources in the US government; and on interviews conducted at blast sites in Iraq and Syria long after combat operations ceased. This journalism, that is, revelatory for an understanding of the Islamic State conflict, is not war reportage in the normative sense. We must ask why, then, the war reportage that was undertaken during the conflict did not produce meanings similarly skeptical of official claims to humanitarian intent and of the rationale given for civilian killing.

Why does today's war reportage reproduce one meaning for war and displace others? What are the conditions—social, political, discursive—determining the meaning war is represented to possess? How do empathy, objectivity, and presiding notions of "the human" impact the way war is journalistically rendered? The determinations of war's meaning is the next topic to assess.

FOUR

Power Speaking to Truth

Struggles with the Problem of War

> I had come to think the newspapers are right
> after all, and man was born good.
> —CHARLES BAUDELAIRE

War's Control

The meaning journalism made from Mosul—the meaning accrued through a representational focus on civilian suffering—is that violence is the central problem of war, and stopping that violence is a form of virtue. This is the prevailing sense of contemporary war reportage as it is the grounding principle of militarized humanitarianism. The presupposition of this account of war is that civilians are innocent; that the suffering of civilians manifests individually, corporeally, and in a universally recognizable manner; and that this suffering should be stopped even at the cost of violence. If war can be undertaken free of suffering, the logic goes, the central problem of war is solved. A humane war, where only combatants are killed, would seem to solve the central problem of war's inhumanity.

This chapter examines why reportage on civilian death in the US intervention in Mosul, reportage widely presumed to function as critique of that intervention, instead served to underwrite official rationale for US warfare. I aim to show how "speaking truth to power" can indeed legitimate that power, and why war reportage tends to reproduce only those meanings for war already sanctioned by a reigning order. For the displacement of one meaning for war in service of another can clarify the relationship of journalism to the violence it represents. By looking at the choices made by journalists in the representation of the battle for Mosul, I home in on the stakes of journalism's humanitarian dynamic and indicate where a moral rendering of war both mystifies and legitimates certain political actions. This chapter, then, attempts to track those discursive conditions that perpetuate both war and its reportage.

The journalism from Mosul tended to reproduce, if implicitly, the humanitarian claim that a violence employed to stop violence against civilians amounts to care for those civilians. Yet an absence of civilian killing may not be an alternative to harm so much as its other face. It was in the nineteenth century that humanism, as word and concept, found the values familiar to today's liberal consensus, "the autonomous individual, the private self, and a public world of law and political order" (Asad 2015, 396). But one aspect of humanity and humanitarianism find roots in antiquity: that of treating others humanely. The secular enlightenment ethic of identifying with the pain of others evolved from the Christianity of good works.[1] Talal Asad (2015), tracking this pedigree, shows how medieval Christian theology both adopted this idea of compassion for the Other while clarifying, particularly during the crusades, that compassion is not incompatible with punishment. This mutual embrace of kindness and violence becomes central to the concept of humanity with Augustine, who taught that punishment for sin and redemption of the sinner must be seeped in love. While Nietzsche criticized "civilization" for its sentimental concern with physical cruelty as the worst of evils (Hollingdale 1997), and while efforts to abolish physical pain dominated the agenda of nineteenth-century social reform—from carceral policy to medical care (Moyn 2021)—the mutuality of compassion and violence continued with "civilizing" colonial wars and, today, with military interventionism, where violence is expended in the name of humanity. The sentiments of an unnamed US military officer in the Vietnam War, quoted by the Associated Press, is appropriate to this imbrication: "We had to kill them in order to save them."[2] War's inhumanity may not be so easily disentangled from humanitarian compulsions, yet the narrative impulse of war reportage elides this entanglement. For journalism, war is separate from peace, victim from perpetrator, innocence from guilt, killing from saving.

Colonial relations are a crucial stage in the genealogy of humanitarianism and in the history of its militarized application, particularly over the course of the long nineteenth century. A proto-humanitarian ethic was central to the "civilizing" rationale of colonial imposition, in which imperial powers provided education, medical care, and religious services to the colonies. As Calhoun explains, these colonial missions "contributed to the development of a 'welfarist' notion of human flourishing . . . that helped underpin new doctrines of state legitimacy in which kings ruled in order to make the lives of their subjects better" (2010, 39). A critical aspect of this orientation toward the Other—one that maintains amidst the rhetorical shift from "civilizing" to "saving"—is a disregard for those contextual dynamics that might cause a society to require outside provision of things like medical care. Efforts to legitimize colonialism on the basis of the inability of colonized societies to self-govern ignored the effects of colonialism on those societies, which weakened the political and social structures that Europeans took to be uncivilized. Thus, while colonial powers ascribed social disorder "to the backwardness of local populations, in fact, such conditions were often as much the result of earlier Western 'explorations' and armed trading projects" (Calhoun 2010, 40). While many conflicts in the Middle East—from border wars to sectarian tension—result from the foreign intervention also utilized as a response to these conflicts, this recursivity is absurdly pronounced in the case of the Islamic State war. There, a conflict in Iraq prompting US intervention, and which was advertised to save Iraqis, is the direct result of American intervention in Iraq merely a few years prior, an intervention also advertised to save Iraqis. And just as colonial discourse abstracted the human in need of civilization from the political context of colonization, so do humanitarian and journalistic discourses often abstract the victim to be saved from the harm that humanitarian interventionism may entail.

The figural resonance of the victim—central to contemporary war reportage—can work in the service of military power irrespective of whether civilians are saved or harmed by that power. Because the story of civilian suffering legitimates and rationalizes intervention premised on humane protection whether or not that aim is met. I am speaking here of something more or other than the "CNN effect," a 1990s term of art for the impact of news mediation on foreign policy processes, an effect that is in any case debated (Robinson 2002). Rather, and with respect to recent war coverage, the coincidence between the meanings war reportage makes and the rhetoric of military intervention is not so much a matter of cause and effect than it is of convergence in a common sense suitable to the operations of a dominant order. And unlike classic cases of the (supposed) CNN effect, such as in Kosovo in 1999, journalistic focus on the suffering victim in Mosul was used to *indict* the intervention as well as to justify it. The issue, then, is less whether the meanings made by war reportage incite intervention than it is how these meanings support a status quo that normalizes militarism, irrespective of the support or opposition to militarism such meanings might appear to suggest in any given circumstance. To be clear, many journalists will readily criticize the way humanitarian rhetoric is applied in the War on Terror (Hammond 2004). This criticism, however, does not itself disrupt the way that contemporary war reportage makes meanings conducive to US militarism in the Middle East and beyond.

Whether subjects are protected or harmed through the intervention of a foreign military, the imposition of power over the subjects in question is confirmed rather than avoided. As the executive pardon of the death-row inmate is not a lapse in the sovereign power to execute but its very instantiation (Fiskesjö 2003), so a lack of civilian killing may not be a gentler warfare so much as war's destructive power held, for strategic reason, in abeyance. A war free of innocent death—a war that fully satisfies humanitarian desire—may not disrupt the architecture of war but rather sustain its institution. For while a humane war would seem to appease those who see war's inhumanity as its central fault, such a humane war could then continue forever (as America's anti-terror wars seem to be doing), without news-consumer opposition or public protest, in the control of populations and the institution of selective domination. Samuel Moyn argues that a "new consensus" on warfare leverages inhumane violence—including America's own "descent into lawlessness" during the US torture program—to "strengthen a selective agenda of humane war" (Moyn 2021, 254; see also Abu El-Haj 2022). Focus on the cruelty of suffering, and thus on the morality of warfare, can align with the political imperatives of "forever war."[3]

We can see the risks of a war satisfying to humanitarian desire—endless perpetuation, non-lethal dominance, an individuating and managerial gaze—in the genealogy of US weapons development. In the post-9/11 era of global conflict, as America's War on Terror expanded to include nearly every country on earth (with nearly 800 US military bases in at least 80 countries and special operators deployed in about 150 countries), the use of armed drones provided an opportune alternative to ground troops and other forms of conventional warfare. The drone combines individualized targeting, management of distant or difficult to police populations, and an avoidance of the high political stakes of overseas troop deployments. The most frequently used payload for drones is the Hellfire missile, an ordinance originally developed to pierce Soviet tank armor. When fired from drones, the Hellfire missile, as modified in 2002, became the choice weapon for targeted killing, allowing for the incineration of everything within a tight, 360-degree blast radius (Gusterson 2017).

America's leaders were quick to see the strategic value and political convenience of drone warfare, as well as its humanitarian capacity. In 2013, then-President Barack Obama gave a speech at the National Defense University at Fort McNair in Washington, DC, in which he lauded the drone's promise of more humane warring. Obama declared,

> Simply put, these strikes have saved lives. . . . Remember that the terrorists we are after target civilians, and the death toll from their acts of terrorism against Muslims dwarfs any estimate of civilian casualties from drone strikes. . . . Conventional airpower or missiles are far less precise than drones, and are likely to cause more civilian casualties and more local outrage. And invasions of these territories lead us to be viewed as occupying armies, unleash a torrent of unintended consequences, are difficult to contain, result in large numbers of civilian casualties and ultimately empower those who thrive on violent conflict.[4]

Drone warfare, a more precise and thus more humane warfare, is advertised to solve the central problem of war's inhumanity. Obama further explained that "by narrowly targeting our action against those who want to kill us and not the people they hide among, we are choosing the course of action least likely to result in the loss of innocent life." Drones are on the side of life; their deployment is a humane and justified act in the face of illegitimate, terroristic violence.

The political appeal of drone warfare—its low casualty rate (when compared with siege warfare or mass invasion); the difficulty of assessing death (journalistically and otherwise) in remote areas outside of regular military operations; a remote managerial dynamic that avoids on-the-ground troop commitments—allows war to expand. Hellfire drone strikes are used where missile strikes would pose too great a risk to civilians, and they are therefore used more often and in more places. Drone strikes are low-cost financially as well as politically. And so a more humane war, because it can be mostly ignored and thereby proliferated, may cause *more* civilian casualties than a conventional war, which is likely to stimulate public objection and is restricted by various legal and pragmatic considerations.

This impulse to a more humane, and thus more acceptable, way of war is not new. The Gatling gun, an early rapid-fire weapon and the most well-known forerunner to the modern machine gun, was created in response to proto-humanitarian concerns. Richard Gatling designed his weapon to fire continuously with very few operators in order to reduce the number of individuals needed on the American Civil War battlefields and thereby decrease the number of deaths caused by combat and associated disease (Wahl and Toppel 1971). However, the convenience and killing power of the new weapon precipitated its wide use—not only in America, but later throughout Africa and Asia in the Boshin War, the Anglo-Zulu War, and beyond. The Gatling gun's rapid-fire design allowed for more inflicted casualties from a single weapon then was previously possible. The desire to protect bodies led to an intensification of their vulnerability.

The genealogy of humane weaponry unfolds. In the aftermath of the Mosul battle, I heard rumors—during bingo night at the US consulate in Erbil, at the Classy Hotel bar—of a new weapon, identified in 2019 as the R9X. It is a further variant of the Hellfire missile but stripped of its 20-pound explosive charge. The weapon, now with warhead inert, relies on force of impact; its six 100-pound blades, fanning out as the weapon is launched, are designed to kill a single individual while reducing harm to proximate others. Nicknamed the "Flying Ginsu," this new weapon is intended to pose no danger to innocent bystanders, a welcome development for those agitating for more humane forms of warfare.[5] But like its predecessor, the weapon carries particular risks. The ability to kill a single individual surrounded by others who are not targeted frontloads the necessity of solid intelligence, intelligence that often proves unreliable. More to the point, any method of killing seen as more precise can lead to increased employment, particularly in remote areas where oversight is spotty, in spaces outside declared war zones, and in circumstances where confidence in precision lowers the threshold on execution. More humane war, in this case too, means more war.[6] The journalism from Mosul, attending to civilian suffering and the necessity of its amelioration, implicitly endorses a form of warfare able to profit from moral concern.

A Decent Story

In the spring of 2017, I accompanied a journalist to an internally displaced persons (IDP) camp on the eastern outskirts of Mosul. The battle for the city was then raging, with large numbers of Iraqis fleeing Mosul's old city for camps, nearby villages, and cities farther afield. The camp we were visiting was, as these things go, unexceptional: windblown strips of blue UNHCR tents on a hard-caked dirt expanse; chain-link fencing; a rickety guard post. And a journalist eager to investigate.

"There's a good story here," the journalist insists. Her silky black hair is gathering dust, and her dark eyes graze for a target. After completing a master's degree at an American journalism school, this journalist worked freelance through Africa and the Middle East before landing a staff position at an American news outlet. She has a wariness about her, some sense of a trust frequently tested.

"Has anyone here lost a family member?" the journalist instructs her fixer, a squat Kurdish man, to ask the women roaming among the tents. The fixer, Mazar, is incredulous. Mazar has seen a lot as a fixer; he worked in Mosul most days of the battle, doing more "frontline shit," as journalists cavalierly put it, than could be reasonably expected of the sane. He's known as a good fixer, and especially in combat situations; brave but not stupid, with an eye for the gruesome and the spectacular. Mazar had been twice shot by Islamic State snipers and is proud of the scars; he liked to show off harried cellphone video of firefights and stately photos of dead kids. He has worked with almost every freelancer around, and many of the staff people too, and his impressions of the journalists in Iraq at the time—who is intelligent, who impulsive—largely matched my own. Mazar knows which journalists are good at their job, and he has doubts about our present company.

The journalist in question trudges around the camp, poking her head through tent flaps and employing the Arabic she knew. A receptive household is soon found, and the journalist, Mazar, and I enter a ten-by-ten-foot tent crowded with two babies, three toddlers, two young women, and an elderly matriarch.

With Mazar translating, one of the young women explains that her husband was taken by the Iraqi military as a suspected Islamic State fighter. The woman herself was injured in the flight from Mosul, though it is unclear whether her bandaged leg is the result of an Islamic State sniper or a hasty scramble onto a departing truck or some other war-zone obstacle. The woman gesticulates in long arcs drawn through the dusky murk of the crowded tent. The smaller children reach for the woman's arms as she points, as if in accusation, toward her old home in Mosul. She denounces the Islamic State, the United States, the Iraqi military, the United Nations, the Kurdish Peshmerga forces, the irregular Shia militias, and the news media.

"Ask her what happened to her and her husband," the journalist interjects. Mazar translates, and he and the young woman engage in a long exchange. The woman explains how Mosul was long neglected by the government in Baghdad and mentions recent distrust between local policemen and Iraqi soldiers from the south. She speaks about the exodus of Assyrian Christians after a series of murders and the increasing shortage of doctors, electricity, and jobs. She does not mention her husband.

"Ask her about her injury though, and about the Islamic State," the journalist insists. Mazar delivers the injunction, which the young woman duly disregards. She talks about the future taken from her children, her mother's declining health, the filth and scarcity of the camp, the loss of home and possessions, and the pointlessness of talking to the press. Children scrabble about, tugging the adults' abayas.

The journalist, impatient, ducks out through the tent flaps. Mazar then interrupts the woman to thank her for her time. He shares goodbyes with all the adults and children present, and he and I leave the tent together.

"What a waste of time," the journalist remarks outside. She's smoking a cigarette and scanning her phone. "We need a better refugee," she says, and Mazar unsuccessfully hides a grimace. "We need someone who can tell a decent story about the escape from the Islamic State."

This journalist, admittedly, was among the least professional of those I observed, and exemplified to the sharpest degree a focus on individual victimhood at the expense of historical and political context. However, and as discussed in the previous chapter, the focus on individuals as a way of universalizing wartime suffering remains a basic trait of contemporary war reportage.

Here is Janine di Giovanni, a prominent war reporter, speaking about her coverage from Syria on National Public Radio in 2016:

> People are going to turn off the television set if they see too many mass graves, too many bodies, too much bombing. But a good in-depth story is going to capture the attention of people, particularly when it has a narrative. And that's what I do. Go on the ground, spend months and

months, sit on the floor with people and talk to them. For instance, one of the characters in my book is Nada, a young activist. She was detained, raped, basically her life completely shattered. So what I did is used her as a vehicle to tell the story of rape in Syria.

Di Giovanni is clear that the subject of her reportage in wartime Syria is both a person in the world—with a life and a context—and a "character" that can be "used as a vehicle" to express the meaning of war. While "too many bodies" may provoke reader fatigue (perhaps because they lack the enticement of a story—that is, they are only literal), the victimhood established for Nada through her narrative emplotment transforms her into a "victim of war," a formal element that gains meaning in relation to news-consumer expectations about war and its violence. Nada becomes "Nada": Nada the synecdoche, Nada the allegory, Nada the fulfillment of suffering as the prefigured reality of war. Di Giovanni implies that Nada's suffering as a victim of war is what gives traction to her story; it is what allows a journalist to "capture the attention" of news consumers. Innocent suffering is valuable, in today's news marketplace, as both a primary meaning and central problem of war, and it demands a frame both individualizing in its application and universalizing in its symbolism. In her narrative figuration as "the victim of war," Nada overcomes the historical and political singularity of the Syrian conflict to enact the universal and generic meaning anticipated by news-consuming societies.

As Mazar, the journalist, and I leave the refugee camp, driving eastward away from Mosul, I scan the horizon of auburn pastureland and the occasional burnt-out sedan. We pass through various checkpoints—Mazar somberly at the wheel, the journalist tweeting from the passenger seat—while I record my observations in a notebook.

The next night, back in my room in Erbil, I receive a text message from the journalist. It's a screenshot from a television program on which the journalist appeared earlier that evening. On a graphic introducing the program, the journalist's visage appears next to that of Abu Bakr al-Baghdadi, the leader of the Islamic State at the time, against a background of churning flames. Whatever story the journalist found, it was good enough for the evening news.

Producing Empathy

The production of empathy—a central goal of the journalists I interviewed and observed—suits the universalizing claims of humanitarianism, the associated evacuation of political context, and the focus on corporeal suffering as the primary problem of war. "Empathy is emotional understanding," a journalist in Erbil told me. "A huge part is portraying suffering in a way that's intelligible."

Empathy implies intelligibility insofar it presupposes an understanding of the suffering of others. Victimhood, in war reportage, requires a universalist cast such that the legibility of suffering, and thus of war as journalistically rendered, is achieved for news consumers. The question remains as to how wartime suffering is transformed through its journalistic depiction to meet the expectations of a faraway audience regarding what suffering is like. The production of empathy is itself the production of war's legibility, which entails a journalistic taxonomizing suitable to *a priori* understandings. Suffering is individual, it is corporeal, it is beneath politics and culture, it expels context: These dynamics are necessary to secure consumer understanding.[7]

Asked about reporting strategies, a journalist in Beirut told me, "I've been focusing on one family. Trying for audience empathy. Peoples' stories get more attention." Individuation is required when audience empathy is presumed to be determined by relation to a fellow human being, a person whose position as a victim a news consumer could imagine themselves in. This requires stripping from victimhood those cultural or political elements to which a faraway news consumer cannot relate. As another journalist remarked to me in Baghdad, "A story should have tension and universal themes. Joy and sorrow. Once you're a mom, you're united with all moms. I'm no different than that mom in Syria." But in avoiding interpersonal difference, motherhood must be stripped of cultural inflection—it must be purely biological and extra-contextual—in order to function as a vehicle for global empathy.[8]

The overcoming of contextual distinction is key to journalistic empathy production and necessitates the supersession of the politically and culturally particular. This is what the "humanizing" of others, a common journalistic aim, *does*. The reduction of subjects to biological bodies establishes a baseline of relation, and the reduction of suffering to somatic pain does the same. But the attempt to "humanize" Mosulawi civilians as innocent victims—as individuals a news consumer can empathize with, and in this way understand—functions as a *de*humanization insofar as it strips from Mosulawis their political agency, historical experience, and cultural identity. Such dynamics, moreover, are fundamental to the complex choices people make amidst war and violence. Whether to stay in Mosul and live under Islamic State rule, or whether to leave Mosul as an internally displaced subject, is a choice weighted with considerations about ethnic identity, economic prospects, communal networks, political ideals—considerations with which a faraway news audience may have difficulty relating. The journalistic production of empathy, by flattening subject identity, wrests control of an event from the designated victim of that event, defining their subjectivity for them and "compartmentalizing the person" into the status of victim rather that presenting them as "a mutually interacting partner" in the production of wartime news (Taussig 1992, 100).[9]

The biologization of subjects, and the thinning of social relationships inherent to the journalistic application of victimhood, entail the occlusion of other ways of narratively organizing conflict. While competing models of antagonism—revolutionary/counterrevolutionary, insurgent/state, minority/majority, believer/infidel—all carry a certain political, historical, and collectivist context, the victim/perpetrator model makes no such claim and remains free of class-based, racial, ethnic, religious, or geographic entanglements. The use of victim/perpetrator as an organizing narrative principle produces identifiable, classifiable, individuated, and everywhere polarized figures, what Kenneth Cmiel calls a "thin" culture of victimhood that floats atop historical or political context, "communicat[ing] without nuance across thicker culture divides" (1999, 1248). Victimhood can be judged "as is" by a universalizing humanitarian morality, freeing it from the political analysis necessary to assess other modes of subjecthood embedded in a particular historical conjuncture.

With respect to war reportage, we can note that the assignment of victimhood as an individual's subjectivity, and suffering as his or her condition, is applied to those who may not recognize these dynamics as their own. For instance, characterizations of victimhood and suffering may be assigned to individuals who see themselves as combatants or militants or martyrs, or who consider their condition one of political domination or territorial expropriation. Victimhood and suffering, narratively applied, can in this manner mystify particular grievances, injustices, and structures of power, while their assignation as identity and circumstance can obscure other articulations and experiences of violence. As a figure in a journalistic narrative, the victim expresses the reality of war—any war—as a condition that "supersedes cultural difference" (Fassin and Rechtman 2009, 239), and war thereby loses contextual specificity in its reduction to a generic corporeal suffering. As Nicolas Guilhot notes, "'Victim' loses any discriminatory and explanatory power it may have once possessed" once victimhood is deployed as "a universal condition that can be claimed by actors inhabiting incommensurable situations . . . and these situations lose historical intelligibility" (2012, 91). This loss of context suits a narrative framework designed to elicit empathy among global news consumers.

An early test of humanitarian morality came with the imperial adventures of European powers, whose encounters with the Other threatened the identity of the colonizer as one apart from the colonized. According to Lynn Festa (2009), one method for reasserting the identity of the European abroad was to frame relations through sympathy, the natural asymmetry of which could express a necessary imperial antithesis: The suffering, colonized subject could now be marked apart from the sympathetic, colonizer subject, where each depended on the other for solid and seemingly independent identities. This kind of sentimentality—one that continues to mark journalism, especially war reportage—becomes not simply an ideological veil for exploitation or domination, as some have argued (e.g., Bishara 2012). It forms the basis for a complex emotional relationship that shapes both domination and subjugation.[10]

The journalistic commitment to empathy production is in this way more complicated in its effects than may at first appear. For the ability to know another—to feel empathy for the psychic or material state of a fellow human—is not incompatible with the urge to dominate. As one of the major contributors to US counterinsurgency doctrine (and frequent cable news commentator), Maj. Gen. Robert Scales, writes in *Armed Forces Journal*, "Understanding and empathy will be important weapons of war" (2006). The idea that contemporary war reportage prompts empathy for suffering others and is therefore on the side of the dispossessed thus deserves scrutiny. For the ability to *feel like* and to *empathize with* another is dependent upon the vulnerability of that Other, and vulnerability is thereby necessary to elicit audience empathy. Empathy becomes a condition of control, a means of manipulating conditions (social, psychological, and otherwise) for the purpose of marking a separation between victimized Others and an empathizing audience. As war reportage may allow news consumers affective proximity to the victims of war, it also reinscribes their material distance. The journalistic focus on suffering, required for empathy production, can distract from those structures that perpetuate suffering—structures that may benefit an empathetic news audience.[11]

While knowledge of suffering Others may provoke a will to peace, the recent history of humanitarian interventions suggests it is often peace as pacification, "a form of 'necessary' violence directed at the uncontrolled violence of territorially peripheral populations" (Asad 2015, 406). That is, feelings of empathy inspired by humanistic war reportage can spark desire among news consumers for an end to Others' suffering, and this desire can be leveraged as support for military intervention. Nowhere in journalism's production of empathy is an understanding of what causes suffering, or of how interventions may stop or increase suffering, necessarily activated. And nowhere does the ability of sufferers to change their own conditions—or their own narrative figuration—necessarily appear. Where the problem of war is limited to the suffering it creates, a response to that suffering need not grapple with the histories, policies, and actions that cause this suffering, nor the non-military resources available to resist it.

Joseph Masco describes how affect "becomes a kind of infrastructure for the security state, creating the collective intensities of feeling necessary to produce individual commitments, remake ethical standards, and energize modes of personal and collective sacrifice" (2014, 202; see also Rutherford 2009; Stone 2018). Empathy can be understood as just such an affective infrastructure, wherein the relation of feeling of the news consumer to the individual victim, universalized through the humanitarian paradigm, helps to justify the use of violence and distract from its punitive effects. As the preceding chapter argues, reporting on the suffering that well-intentioned militarism may *cause*—the reportage from Mosul so widely lauded, and which also produced the empathy cited by journalists as a central aim—may not undermine militarized humanitarianism so much as reinforce its ideals, heretofore unmet. For a story indicating that powerful militaries are not perfect in their protection of human life may not function as a critique of militarism so much as emphasize militarism's power, its capacities for humane improvement, and thus its further necessity. As Jesse Hearns-Branaman quips, "Saying the emperor has no clothes acts more to assert that the emperor is an emperor than to embarrass him for his lack of clothing" (2016, 139).

As long as empathy for suffering Others can justify violence in their name, the actual effects of that violence—up to and including the killing of the Others in question—becomes a concern secondary to suffering's amelioration. The intent of militarized humanitarianism supersedes its effects, and the morality of warfare overcomes its politics. As an affective infrastructure, empathy can help to mediate the contradictions of a murderous intervention understood as humane.

The Teachers Club

"Our agenda defines what we see." This is what I'm told over drinks at the Teachers Club, a restaurant and café in Erbil. Waiters shuffle among crowded tables as Rami, a freelance journalist for Middle Eastern and British news outlets, cradles a beer. Rami has moist, unkempt hair and a week of dark stubble; he laughs easily, and his eyes squeeze to cheerful crescents when he speaks. He is one of the younger journalists around—late twenties, perhaps—but being from the region, his knowledge is granular, his language abilities robust, and his networks sturdy. Rami had spent a long day conducting interviews with people fleeing Mosul, and I was asking him about the kind of story he was looking for. "Client desire drives coverage," he says. "And frontline reporting is what people want." He fumbles for a cigarette caked with the dust of summertime Iraqi roads.

The Teachers Club is busy. Photojournalists in black t-shirts hunch over empty whiskey bottles discussing kinetic operations. Ex-Marines, now volunteer medics or soldiers of fortune, mingle with lithe Italian aid workers. Businessmen and diplomats suck down Gitanes cigarettes and debate postwar reconstruction. Journalists based in Istanbul, London, and New York nod intently as those based in Iraq offer crucial logistical tips for reporting the ongoing assault: which fixers are available tomorrow, which Iraqi divisions control which parts of the city, how different segments of the Kurdish regional government are responding to shifting political winds. Rami is speaking about an injured man with juicy quotes.

"Hopefully I'll be an editor at some point and pay less attention to victimhood. As a journalist, I know it makes for good narratives and good reading. The victimhood of marginalized people is important, but it has the capacity to shape or distort a story." Rami sips his Almaza and considers a woeful kebab. "The flipside is how Western media has distorted the value of victimhood, selectively applying it. There's not a right/wrong way to be a victim. Life is more complicated than that."

I ask Rami if he feels that all humans suffer the same way, given similar conditions of war and violence. Is suffering universal?

"No, suffering is not universal. And if you don't suffer correctly, you are seen as threatening, and this drives our fear of the Other. We see that people are willing to die for causes, or commit spectacular acts of violence, and this seems a matter that is dangerous." Rami mentions suicide bombers, who can pose a categorical challenge to journalism's conventional distinctions between life and death, victim and perpetrator, civilian and combatant.

Just then another journalist lumbers over from a more crowded table. Robert is of stocky build and brusque manner, with thick gray hair slicked back imposingly across his scalp. He got his start in the Bosnian war before turning to the Middle East as a staff journalist for a French news organization. A Teachers Club regular, Robert is generous with backslaps and journalistic lore. He lands roughly into a plastic chair with a bottle in one hand and a pack of cigarettes in the other.

"What do you do about suicide bombers?" Rami asks the recent arrival. "They kind of interrupt the value we always want to give to human life, no? As something to protect? They challenge certain narrative givens."

"There was a point in Iraq when all we wrote were car bomb stories," Robert replies, probably in reference to the bad post-invasion years of the mid-2000s. "A better job would be explaining the rifts in society and why this is problematic. But the car bombing, the suicide bombing—it's easier to just describe the harm."

Rami seems to consider the point while draining his beer but changes the subject instead. "What are you working on then, mate?" he asks his older colleague.

"Usual stuff," Robert replies. "Story on migrants. Story on the Golden Division."

The Teachers Club—more than the frontline, more than the refugee camp, more than the press conference—was a prolific space of meaning making for the war in Mosul. Here was where stories were tested, information traded, narratives compared. Here the official hermeneutics of journalism were nightly unfolded: Who to count and what to cut, which topics are important and which extraneous. This process was never specified and rarely direct, but through the interactions constellating, night after night—across the dozens of tables where journalists met to relax, argue, and debrief—the news about the battle for Mosul solidified. As a space of journalistic negotiation, the Teachers Club was at that moment only the most popular of options in Erbil; the Chaldean Club, the German Beer Garten, the bar at the Classy Hotel all fulfilled this hermeneutic function.

A holdover from the days of Baath Party workers associations, the Teachers Club quickly absorbed the sociality created with a nearby international war zone—the proliferating press, diplomatic, and NGO corps come to soak up the conflict. It had the space. In the cold Kurdistani winters, patrons gather in the Teachers Club's voluminous ballroom, which stretches under soft disco lighting from a cordoned-off kitchen, across a vast expanse of tables, to wood-grained plastic siding on the far end. In the thick Iraqi summers, patrons move outside, to a wide lawn bordered by spindly pine trees and an inflatable bouncy castle. In each space, indoor and out, some hundred tables begin the night in orderly formation, with maroon tablecloths and menus nobly perched. But soon tables are pushed together to accommodate unexpected dinner guests; tablecloths become blankets as balmy nights turn chilly; chairs are cast aside amidst dramatic hugs and spilled wine. Indoors and out, the tables recede into a shadowed periphery; the spaces are so big that it's easy to lose one's way in the table maze, stumbling into conversations that derail the search for one's intended destination. Waiters in smart, vaguely seventies-style suits—extended collars, tight vests, creased slacks—hurry among the crowds bearing whiskey and steaming meats.

The patronage at the Teachers Club can be remarkably diverse. Besides the ex-pat rabble, middle-class Kurdish couples hold hands in the dusk while their children wrestle in the grass. Old Maronites play chess and feed nicotine habits. Large and genteel Arab families—three, four generations—mingle with neighbors displaced by the Islamic State. The entire business is contained in a large compound surrounded by a high stone wall. The entrance, near a church in a tidy section of Ankawa, a majority-Christian neighborhood, is nondescript. A few sturdy Kurdish men in leather jackets lounge about the front entrance; a foyer contains the manager—a professorial man in thick glasses—and a guy with a rifle. Arab men tend to receive a pat-down for weapons and in tenser times are refused entry.

The two journalists, after some prodding, discuss the limits to their narrative endeavor and whether journalistic conventions might be challenged by a different kind of story. "It's not permissible to describe al-

Qaeda as a revolutionary movement," Rami remarks. "This is a question that should be asked: Why you can't interrogate whether a group can be both terroristic and revolutionary."

"But this is general," Robert responds,

> It's a social failure, a failure of educational institutions. A revolutionary terrorist undermines the meaning assigned to terrorism. I've been careful to explain that some people did initially support ISIS, that ISIS symbolized an escape from the Iraqi state. That may as well be revolutionary. Those people just don't support ISIS while the bombs are falling.

Robert offers cigarettes before teething one out of the pack for himself.

"Yes, okay. Journalism requires pure categories," Rami replies, declining the cigarette. Then he adds:

> People are uncomfortable with categorical fluidity and unanswered questions, which leads to simplified treatments of complex matters—9/11, beheadings, eating a soldier's heart. The important question here, I guess, is why does that happen and what does it say about the level of animosity? Can such a person be part of the future Syria or wherever? Tough questions without satisfying answers.

"Indeed," Robert mutters. He takes a long drag and nods at a hefty Kurdish fixer striding past our table. "But the media is focused on the horror, instead of what pushed this person to do this. The questions don't disappear though. And if you don't deal with them in the media, people will answer them on their own."

Rami glances downward, then at me. "The media is training audiences to look for the bang," he pronounces. "Without context, you, the consumer, put in your own context."

The Value of Casualties

Militarized humanitarianism (as outlined in Chapter 3) demands the depoliticization of its violence in order to legitimate the moral claim to the protection of innocents and delegitimate any other rationale for civilian harm. In like fashion, journalists narrated the casualties caused by US-Coalition operations in Mosul as a moral failing, and largely overlooked any possible political rationale for the harm officially described as unintentional or unfortunately necessary.

Consider, though, the "non-combatant casualty cutoff value," variously abbreviated as NCV or NCCV, a measure of military engagement designed to manage, but not prevent, civilian harm. As a US senior legal advisor explained, "The NCV represents a number of civilians that could be killed, that might be acceptable under certain rules, not international law, but under whatever restrictions the US government has put on us" (in McDonell 2018, 136). Through surveillance and other means, the US military levies predictions for the number of civilian dead within a proposed blast radius, as from a drone strike, airstrike, or other offensive deployment—what US military doctrine refers to as a "proportionality analysis" (US Department of Defense 2016)—based on "pattern of life," population density, the specific weapon being used, the kind of structure being targeted, and related factors. This predicted tally must fall below a certain threshold—the NCV—before a strike is authorized.[12] The NCV shifts over time and across zones of conflict, and while the criteria for the NCV in a particular area of military operations is classified, the specific allowance for civilian death seems to oscillate in response to political considerations. The number of civilians authorized to be "inadvertently" killed in a strike is a political calculus—premised on preventing blowback and managing optics—not a moral one.[13]

The NCV in Afghanistan, prior to the US withdrawal, was thought to be zero, and it was thought to be so because of the diplomatic friction *any* civilian deaths caused between the US and the former Afghan government. According to leaked documents, the NCV immediately following the 2003 US invasion of Iraq was thirty.[14] As Eyal Weizman interprets it, "In this system of calculation twenty-nine deaths designates a threshold. Above it, in the eyes of US military lawyers, is potentially 'unlawful killing'; below it, 'necessary sacrifice.'" Weizman argues that the NCV threshold employed in post-invasion Iraq was "likely chosen for reasons of its potential resonance in the media" (2011, 132). Media attention to human death, and the reaction of a news-consuming public, was presumably assessed by US military officials, and to the extent that twenty-nine Iraqi deaths was unlikely to dominate news coverage or public attention, it became acceptable to US war makers as an incidental necessity of war making.[15] Air war seems to adhere to a circular logic here, premised on the politics of appearing accountable rather than the moral virtue of accountability. In employing an NCV, the US military appears to be gauging how little humanitarianism can be instituted while still affirming its humanitarian concern. During the battle for Mosul, the NCV is thought to have been twenty.[16]

Was civilian death in Mosul a moral failing, then, the necessary price or inadvertent excess of humanitarian protection? Or was civilian death inherent to an intervention premised on defeating enemies, and thus a matter of political calculus and strategic enterprise? Military intervention may be narrated as a way to save bodies exposed to cruel violence—a humanitarian response to a humanitarian problem. And yet the fact that the intervention did not uniformly do so—the fact that US-Coalition operations harmed more civilians in Mosul than the Islamic State, whose harm the intervention was advertised to stop—makes sense when read through a political, rather than moral, register. Put otherwise, that the US-Coalition killed more civilians in Mosul than the Islamic State is darkly ironic only if the purpose of the operation is humanitarian and protective rather than political or punitive: to save rather than to win. For the Islamic State is not only an affront to the sacrality of human life; it is an affront to the political order instituted by US-client states in Iraq and elsewhere. An intervention, one that may cause widespread civilian death, is a response to *that* problem—a political problem—even if it is not a very good response to the problem of human suffering as such. That the US military kills rather than saves may be insensible humanistically, but it is perfectly sensible (if not actually strategic) as a way to win a war.

The war reportage from Mosul and throughout the region offered an Islamic State whose primary offense is their lack of compassion for civilians, and who place territorial expansion or theological passion above human life. They are trying to win, rather than to save, and their violence is in this manner a humanitarian offense. But for the US-Coalition who fought the Islamic State in Mosul, is the enemy's violence an offense to humanity, or is their politics an offense to national security? Journalists in Mosul tended to report the former, but US military action is historically predicated upon the latter. Why, then, are civilian deaths narrated in war reportage as an inadvertent element of a humanitarian action premised on protecting innocents, rather than a routine element of a military action premised on defeating enemies? Why is US military activity represented in journalism as operating, even if poorly, on the side of innocent life against unjustified death, rather than on one side of a conflict against another side? Attention to humanitarian responsibility, and to the unfortunate harm that can result, mystifies the national security and geopolitical bases for attacking those deemed politically—and not merely morally—threatening.

Objectivity's Interests

A war reportage able to express skepticism regarding the protective claims of militarized humanitarianism would be a war reportage that takes seriously the politics of violence. Thusly politicized, such a war reportage might appear sharply partisan, insofar as it will challenge a reigning consensus concerning war and violence. This war reportage will make meaning not in coincidence with a universalizing worldview—such as that currently built around victimhood and suffering—but rather in the situated, positioned, and partial manner expressive of a specific constituency. Such a war reportage might not produce empathy for individuated and decontextualized bodies, but rather solidarity based on class, race, religion, or other shared context.[17] It will be a war reportage in which violence becomes meaningful not as an abstract moral aberration but as a structural condition of a specific historical conjuncture. In seeking such a war reportage, it is useful to glance backward at a more politicized era of journalism in America. Though not without its problems, industrial and epistemic, America's "yellow press" period provides the basis for conceptualizing a war reportage able to overcome some of the pitfalls present today.

"There is a sentiment gaining ground to the effect that the public wants its politics 'straight.'" So an American journalist wrote in 1901, at a time when advertising had grown from just a fraction of newspaper revenue to more than two-thirds of total revenue at America's 18,000 newspapers (in Lepore 2019). With the growing dependence on advertising dollars came a shift in the political content of newspaper coverage. From a partisan press, supported by constituent subscriptions and political parties, newspapers transformed into a commodity supported by advertising. Readers, once seen as voters whose political inclinations could be courted, became consumers whose personal politics mattered less than their buying power. The new advertising-based business model that came of age in the United States with the turn of the last century flattened political acuity in order to reach the largest possible segment of the population. Absent a partisan perspective, no particular segment of the American readership was alienated by political disagreement, and the greatest number of eyeballs could be converted into the biggest advertising dollars. As Jill Lepore explains, "Newspapers stopped rousing the rabble so much because businesses wanted readers, no matter their politics. . . . Newspapers sorted themselves out not by their readers' political leanings but by their incomes" (2019). With the turn away from a partisan press, objectivity gained prominence as a journalistic ideal. This ideal, however, was elevated not in response to a need for "better," or more transparent, or more truthful representations of reality. Rather, objectivity was elevated, during a transition away from newspaper partisanship, in response to business interests (Baker 1995). Journalistic objectivity presumed depoliticization, not a generic truthfulness.

The elevation of objectivity in the post–yellow press period suited journalism's professional claim to legitimacy. As Daniel Hallin (1986) argues, the journalism environment in nineteenth-century America—small and numerous papers reflecting specific partisan concerns—could appeal to the First Amendment and free market ideology in defense of their role in American political life. With the consolidation and corporatization of newspapers, and the increasing dependence on advertising revenue and thus on big industry, this basis for legitimacy was undermined. Journalism required another source of validity for the meanings it made, and another source of credibility for responding to criticism of the power of mass media in society. Objectivity served this legitimizing function. As newspapers chose nonpartisanship as a way to attain larger circulation, objectivity itself operated as a commercial product, a way to achieve economies of scale in the production of meaningful truths (Hamilton 2006).

The turn away from explicitly partisan representation in meeting the demands of industry advertisers implied an increased autonomy of journalists from the political sphere. Journalistic representation was no longer beholden to political interests and could, presumably, produce more transparent, accurate, balanced truths. But does the absence of explicitly political meaning making simply abstract journalism from the political as such, or does this absence necessarily defer to the political perspective of the status quo, now mystified beneath the gloss of objectivity? Which meanings are occluded in the journalistic adherence to an extra-political mandate, and which political conditions fail to surface in the authorized, objective accounts of journalists? Now guarantors of objective representation, journalists are forced to defer to normative understandings of the world in order to make the meanings previously grounded in partisan perspectives and associated political analyses. In attaining legibility for an audience no longer differentiated by political position, only broadly normative understandings of the world will serve as an adequate basis for journalistic representation. The source of this narrative normativity, as theorists from Hegel to Hayden White note, is the presiding social order. "But it is the State," Hegel writes, "which first presents subject-matter that is not only adapted to the prose of History, but involves the production of such history in the very progress of its own being" (1956, 61). As the "first draft of history," journalism is implicated in Hegel's charge.

James Carey (1986) observes that the departure from an explicitly partisan journalism deprived journalists of a point of view from which to explain the world they reported, and this vacuum was filled by a status quo established by the state. In the absence of partisan perspective, centralized state power became the arbiter of what was acceptably real and conventionally meaningful in journalistic depictions of the world. Sure enough, as the era of the yellow press waned, journalists increasingly relied upon government officials for information and points of view, and the state became the central source for the reality reported as news (Bennett et al. 2007; Sigal 1973; Winston and Winston 2021). What Edmund Burke called, in the eighteenth century, the "Fourth Estate," a designation indicating journalism's independence from other governing bodies and social institutions, became, by the twentieth century, "an integral part of the governing process" (in Hallin 1986, 69). As Hallin puts it, "Journalists depended on their relationship with the state to make objectivity work as a practical form of journalism, and objectivity, in turn, was essential to the new role the press was playing as a 'fourth branch of government'" (1986, 70).

Journalists covering war are aware of objectivity's limits. "True objectivity is hard to maintain," a journalist in Erbil told me. "Objectivity is aspirational," another remarked in Beirut. "You never get to full objectivity, but you can get closer to it." A third, also in Beirut, said, "There is no objectivity in warfare. All you can do is try to portray the perspectives of all parties." Yet another journalist, in Baghdad, explained, "I believe objectivity is aspirational but not possible or achievable." Other journalists view objectivity as the ground for credibility and as a means to determine war's truth. A journalist in New York told me, "Objectivity means to me telling it as fair and accurate as you can and keeping your biases out, and I know you can because I've done it." A journalist in Beirut insisted, "There's a baseline of objectivity for credibility: the number of people killed." Another journalist explained in Erbil, "The biggest hurdle for objectivity is choosing what to write about. There is a herd mentality. But some stories are obvious, like airstrikes that killed civilians." For some, then, objectivity remains necessary for determining war's truth, the basis of which is found in unjustified death.

While journalists may be critical of objectivity as an ideal, its centrality to the profession nonetheless persists, and this leaves journalists open to manipulation by government officials (in the case of war reportage, often officials from defense departments, interior ministries, and state militaries). For even as the relationship between journalism and officialdom can be adversarial, these respective institutions, and the individuals working therein, rely on one another to achieve their distinct goals. Though a single political party can no longer command a newspaper as they could in a previous era of American journalism, it is no longer necessary for a political party to do so. The views of politicians and segments of the state—including the military—are guaranteed transmission through major media outlets as primary sources of information, and they are protected against attacks of partisan manipulation of the press by virtue of their authority as sources.[18] As state power sets the standards for acceptably truthful representations of reality, it is the position of power, rather than any particular perspective, that now allows institutions and individuals access to the communicative instrument of journalism, whose legitimacy in turn depends upon an objectivity tied to the normatively true. As Stuart Hall and coauthors argue, "The very rules which aim to preserve the impartiality of the media, and which grew out of desires for greater professional neutrality, also serve powerfully to orientate the media in the 'definitions of social reality' which their 'accredited sources'—the institutional spokesmen—provide" (1978, 58; see also Boyd-Barrett 2021). Objectivity rationalizes the connection between war reportage and the state, and it creates the dependency of war reporters on the state's truth of war.

Along with other shifts in the culture of mass mediation, early twentieth-century journalism also capitalized on the prestige of science and assumed the values of scientific distance (Pettegree 2014). Journalists "position[ed] themselves outside the system of politics . . . [and] above the fray of social life" (Carey 1997, 335). This left journalists to describe events but never to explain them, insofar as explanation requires (and perhaps especially in the case of war and conflict) a political-historical position from which to cast an analysis.[19] As Carey notes, the transition away from the yellow press "displaced not merely partisanship but an explicit ideological context in which to present, interpret, and explain the news" (1986, 163). In its objective, post-partisan mode, war reportage is limited to those meanings seen as neutral or apolitical, and a focus on civilian casualties—the suffering of individuated, decontextualized bodies, considered *already* understandable as a moral problem—accepts these constraints. An increasing attention to "human interest" stories after the late-nineteenth-century abandonment of journalistic partisanship is predicable, then, since such stories entail "material that, however charming, was inexplicable" in terms of world historical import (Carey 1986, 166). The meaning of "human interest" content—such as the experience of individual suffering in war—can be assumed at face value; insofar as such content requires no political or historical grounding, it is designed to fit established categories of understandability. And so a journalist, at a press center near Raqqa, could explain to me exactly why war reportage is easy: "You don't need to make meaning because meaning is already there." Such meaning is severed from the political as such.

Questions about why people die, the structural conditions that perpetuate their suffering, and the political content of their lives and deaths are subsumed in the humanitarian discourse, a particular mode of understanding life, death, and suffering designed to be post-partisan. As discussed, militarized humanitarianism is understood to supersede political considerations (Hopgood 2013). Civilian harm becomes self-evident: not the result of policy decisions made far from the war zone, nor the explanation for a party's triumph or loss in battle, but an exemplification of the inhumanity of war. Civilian death becomes something to be described but never necessarily explained. The meanings made by war reportage are meanings that fit already established expectations, where victims are innocent, suffering is corporeal, and violence is cruel though sometimes necessary to confront such cruelty. This is the dominant common sense of war, enshrined in the humanitarian paradigm, to which war reportage responds. The failure of war reportage to make meaning in relation to historical and political conditions serves war-making powers by disregarding those explanations that might inform skepticism about the aims and strategies of such powers. Explanations for violence that account for the politics of civilian death dealing may cause news consumers to question the justness of a war promoted as humanitarian or the deaths assumed to be accidental or unavoidably incidental.[20]

The objective, transparent, neutral gloss applied to war and violence in contemporary war reportage mystifies both the ideological position of journalism's representations as well as the economic and historical basis of objectivity and related ideals. Otherwise put, the conditions of a journalism that renounces partisanship in the objective presentation of events performs the erasure of its own ideological position. "Every authority," writes Michel de Certeau, "bases itself on the notion of the 'real,' which it is supposed to recount. It is always in the name of the 'real' that one produces and moves the faithful" (1986, 203). As an authority on war's reality, the politics bound up in journalistic meaning making must be erased; the economic and historical basis for journalistic notions of the real must be obscured. Objectivity performs this work.[21]

The meaning of war delivered by war reportage, now primarily the suffering of civilians, depends upon the legitimacy of war reportage as a reality-delivering enterprise, and this legitimacy is in turn predicated upon an objectivity arbitrated by a reigning order. No position on civilian casualties is likely to be taken other than that already normatively established. In an era of militarized humanitarianism, the established position is that civilian suffering is bad. It is a moral claim. No position, then, will be taken on the policy that results in civilian casualties—the institutional factors and objectives that might perpetuate civilian death for strategic gain—nor on the politics of intervention in which humanitarian concern might be leveraged for domination and control. Such positions would be considered partisan, and thus undermining of journalistic credibility. As a status quo orders the meaning of war—victims innocent and perpetrators guilty, suffering corporeal and individual, violence justified or extreme—an objective journalism can reproduce only those meanings thusly ordered.

"The point of journalism, the whole thing, is to hold up a mirror to what is happening for people who aren't there," a journalist told me in Erbil, adding,

> They can feel what people there are feeling. So the value of objective frontline coverage is, if you want to feel what war is like, go to the front line. Explaining the situation is important, but it's also important to tell people not in a war what war feels like, objectively. A child with his eyes burned out is more important than explanation. Why should a guy in London give a shit about the political analysis? Stories are for their own sake, that's all we can do. Beyond that, it's politicization.

Is empathy an adequate substitute for analysis? Should feeling trump explanation? Is political analysis less worthy than a story "for its own sake"? The structures of power that instigate and sustain war can remain intact if explanations of those structures remain secondary to displays of the suffering those structures cause. The yellow press suggests an imperfect model for what non-objective war reportage might achieve. While the humanitarian grounds of the journalism from Mosul indicate the persistence of an ideology in contemporary war reportage, it is an ideology concealed beneath the normativity of accurate, factual, balanced news. News consumers were left to read about the battle for Mosul, to feel bad about its violence and empathize with its victims. But news consumers could rarely understand the conflict. For real understanding entails the abandonment of conceptual consensus in favor of explanations—almost necessarily partisan—for why war happens the way it does.

Liberation or Siege

The recent wars in Syria and Iraq have been determined thus far by five sieges: in Kobani, Mosul, Raqqa, East Aleppo, and eastern Ghouta (with a sixth, ongoing, in Idlib). In Mosul, Raqqa, Aleppo, and Ghouta, hospitals and schools were destroyed alongside bunkers and weapons depots. Fighters died; civilians died. In East Aleppo and eastern Ghouta, siege was conducted by Russian and Syrian state militaries; in Mosul and Raqqa, siege was conducted by US and Iraqi state militaries. A comparison between these sets of sieges is illuminating.[22]

In the international press, civilian suffering in East Aleppo and eastern Ghouta was largely attributed to committed local resistance to Syrian state domination and illegal Russian airpower. Many news organizations designated these conflicts part of a "civil war." The *Wall Street Journal* described how Russian and Syrian forces "laid siege" to East Aleppo "to reclaim areas under the control of rebels" who were attempting to "break the regime-imposed siege" (Marson and Raydan 2016). Reporting on the battle for eastern Ghouta, the *Financial Times* described "President Bashar al-Assad's government attempts to crush one of the last rebel holdouts in Syria" (Solomon and Khattab 2018). As indicated in Chapter 1, these typical descriptions, designations, and framings did not—and could not—appear in coverage of Mosul or Raqqa, where civilian suffering was attributed to foreign jihadists or to their use of human shields amidst a US-led intervention premised on saving innocent life. Civilian harm in Mosul and Raqqa was not the unjust effect of political resistance to foreign incursion, but the sacrifice necessary for humanity's protection.

Absent the application of a humanitarian morality, the major battles in Iraq and Syria are in many ways identical: A mix of local and foreign fighters, primarily Islamist, defended territory crowded with civilians. The territory was contested by a central government of distinct sectarian persuasion, backed by a foreign, Western military. The violence expended was asymmetrical, with one side commanding airpower and advanced weaponry. Why, then, the distinct, if not converse, journalistic depictions? Why "siege" and not "liberation," "rebel" and not "jihadist," "civil war" and not "intervention"? Why an attempt "to crush rebellion" rather than an attempt to protect civilians?

One reason for this difference in international news coverage can only be political: The meaning invoked for war in Mosul and Raqqa—America's battlefields—simply could not function for Aleppo or Ghouta without appearing partisan. The meanings war reportage made for the battle for Mosul, the meanings considered objective, would appear highly subjective when applied to Aleppo and Ghouta, as such meanings would apply rationality and extremism, innocence and guilt, in a manner contentious to a prevailing status quo in the United States, Europe, and other centers of international news consumption. Applying journalism's narrative framework from Mosul or Raqqa to East Aleppo or eastern Ghouta conflicts with popular assumptions about whom to root for in foreign affairs, about who can claim humane intent in the use of military power, about whose violences are legitimate and whose lawless, about which rebellions are terrorism. As Géraldine Muhlmann argues of the US war in Vietnam, the bare facts of violence remain secondary to the logic in which they operate and the context in which the facts come to make sense. "The real problem" Muhlmann writes of violence against civilians, "was to know what had led to this event, precisely what sort of event it had been, and what had made it possible. . . . It is clear that it is the general atmosphere surrounding the event, rather than the facts, that is the crux of the problem" (2008, 323). What civilian death comes to *mean* for news consumers depends less on the material dynamics involved in death—the facts on the ground in Aleppo or Mosul or anywhere else—than the context within which these elements come to make sense in the news, their figuration in a narrative design.

The facts at play in these parallel sieges of Mosul/Raqqa and Aleppo/Ghouta are, as mentioned, largely identical: Bombs dropped, bodies rent. But they were reported differently, and here a latent politics seeps into the "crypto-normativity" (Bargu 2014) of the news narrative. Who are the good guys, who the bad; which Other is to be feared, and which populations protected; with whom does the justification for violence lie, and whose cause is righteous: These are *political* questions displaced by the moralism normative to international news.

While those in a war can only see the forces harming them as antagonistic, and their own will to live as valid, these factors are narratively manipulatable, and the order enacted in the journalistic practice of meaning making will exert its pressure. Whether war is a matter of protection or extermination, whether a conflict is about liberation or siege: These meanings are, in many cases, already determined by the social consensus that conditions journalistic representations of war.

Narrative Resistance

Journalists are aware of the contingency of meaning in wartime. Asked about the discursive constraints on reportage from Mosul, a journalist in Erbil was frank: "The Islamic State are the bad guys, Iraqi Security Services and Coalition partners are good, with excesses excusable because of the evil they are confronting. It's just easier to talk about monsters than people with mothers who made a decision from a number of options available."

I asked a journalist in Erbil whether normative meanings for war influence news content. She replied,

> One time I was forced to put ISIS in the lead even when the attack had nothing to do with the Islamic State. So the paper wants to fit the news into these narratives. What we find is important, but not in a way that people outside care. Is my job to make people care about this stuff, or only the stuff they're used to caring about? Am I beholden only to the narratives out there and tested?

Often, the journalists I interviewed and observed were adamant about their freedom to represent the world as they saw it. Most journalists told me they could pitch stories they were genuinely interested in, that they were at liberty to travel where risk and logistics allowed, and that they could report in ways that might conflict with powerful interests. And yet the stories journalists produced from the battle for Mosul are, generally, of narrow focus and similar perspective, and they tend to reproduce meanings that adhere to a reigning status quo. If journalists, or at least some journalists, are aware of the ideology operating in their stories of war, why do journalists continue to hew to a narrative suitable to a ruling order? Or, as Hall asks, "Precisely how is it that such large numbers of journalists . . . do tend to reproduce, quite spontaneously, without compulsion, again and again, accounts of the world constructed within fundamentally the same ideological categories?" (1985, 100–101).

"The temptation of narrative fulfilment is hard to resist," a journalist told me in Baghdad. "The seductions of narrative are so strong. Maybe because I've been trained like that, I don't know. But it's almost existential, given that my ability to be employed—and thus to feed myself—more or less depends on reproducing the accepted narrative." For this journalist, material realities and discursive pressures were tightly entangled. The perception of an ideology bearing down is no guarantee of the ability to resist it.

Hall describes journalists as "inscribed" by an ideology to which they do not consciously or explicitly commit themselves. Ideology, he insists, "writes them" (1985, 101). While war reporters can identify the ways in which normative concerns and narrative conventions produce narrow meanings for war and violence, the humanitarian grounds of war reportage—central to the profession as it operates today—nevertheless circumscribe the endeavor. The subjective identification of the journalist to a particular ideological formation is thus inconsequential to the expression of that ideology though journalism.

Hall's assessment of how journalism "writes" the journalist echoes Ivan Illich's understanding of professionalism, in which the profession has "power over the work its member do" (1978, 25). For Illich, the profession, and not the individual professional, is the source of authority. Journalism does its ideological work even *despite* the journalist. The power of this professional authority is established "by concession," writes Illich, "from an elite whose interests it props up. As a clergy provides external salvation, so a profession claims legitimacy as the interpreter, protector and supplier of a special 'this worldly' interest of the public at large" (1978, 25). The profession of war reportage assumes the authority to narrate war by virtue of a ruling order, and war is narrated in the manner this order demands.[23] Even as an individual journalist may disagree with the prevailing meaning of a war or an event therein, journalism as a profession already predetermines the kind of meaning that can be produced. Its authority depends on it.

"People want their image of what a war *is* to be confirmed," a journalist remarked in Baghdad.

You are defined by what your readers expect. It's based on a dominant narrative. We end up having to structure reality in a way that's understandable to readers. The Islamic State comes to take precedence not, or not only, because it's an existential threat, but because it's easy to cover—it fits into a model that's by this point well-established.

Consumer expectations about war are met by journalists, whose authority is entwined with the order that establishes those very expectations.

"It doesn't matter what I actually find," a journalist told me on the road to Mosul. "The meaning is there waiting for me."

Desiring Order

In an analysis of historical narrative, Hayden White (1987, 14) considers a dynamic evident too in the reportage from Mosul:

> If every fully realized story, however we define that familiar but conceptually elusive entity, is a kind of allegory, points to a moral, or endows events, whether real or imaginary, with a significance they do not possess as a mere sequence, then it seems possible to conclude that every historical narrative has as its latent or manifest purpose the desire to moralize the events of which it treats.

In telling the story of the battle—even in an objective, factual, truthful way—war reportage endows war with a meaning it does not of itself possess. We might, then, understand the purpose of war reportage, latent or manifest, as the desire to moralize the war it narrates—to grant war significance—and to do so in alignment with a hegemonic consensus.

Where there is ambiguity or ambivalence in war—where war can be a liberation or a siege, protection or extermination—the closure provided by storytelling is troubled. Applying meanings satisfying to news consumers, war reportage asserts narrative control, moralizing war in coincidence with "the social system that is the source of any morality we can imagine" (White 1987, 14). In determining war's meaning through a humanitarian register, war comes to cohere with the expectations of a social system, expectation undermined by meanings that remain open, incomplete, and thereby contestable. War—and the subjects, plots, and figures of war—achieves, thereby, the narrative fullness demanded by a popular consensus and by the news marketplace it underwrites. The meaning of war made by war reportage, and which displays a significance that can *only be made*, confirms the morality of the authority already arbitrating what war is commonly thought to be.

For discourse analysts like Tuen Van Dijk, news is produced to be "consonant with socially-shared norms, values, and attitudes." He writes: "It is easier to understand and certainly easier to accept and, hence, to integrate news that is consonant with . . . the ideological consensus in a given society or culture" (1988, 121–22). The ideological consensus on matters of war is that violence that harms human bodies is wrong, and that violence used to stop such violence can be justified. The ideological consensus is that the problem of war is the suffering it creates, and that suffering can be healed without addressing what caused it. These things constitute what Hall and coauthors call the "knowledge stock" to which the news responds (1978, 64). Telling stories of harm committed by the US-Coalition in Mosul—and in this way "speaking truth to power"—is not, then, as subversive as it might appear. Broadcasting civilian death to an international public, even civilian death caused by the violence of the "international community," can be the speaking of truth to power only insofar as it remains a truth that power recognizes, enables, legitimates, and even demands. The truth of the innocent victim who suffers corporeally and individually; the truth of the essential goodness, if unfortunate excesses, of militarized humanitarianism; the truth of a distinction between protection and extermination, victim and perpetrator, liberation and siege. Such is the truth hegemonic in the societies for which much war reportage is produced. Such is the truth that confirms the morality established by a presiding order. To report on wartime suffering in the manner normative to contemporary war reportage is only to affirm that suffering happens the way it is expected to. Such representations affirm the already assumed meaning of war rather than resituating or challenging orthodox understandings. The basic "knowledge stock" about war is maintained for a news-consuming public rather than called into question or to account.

In transforming war from the effects of policy on populations to the effects of violence on the innocent—in representing the battle for Mosul as protection rather than extermination, as liberation rather than siege—war reportage may be repressing one desire for the satisfaction of another. By narrating civilian death in Mosul as an accidental exception or a necessary excess to justified violence, war reportage chooses *not* to fulfil a societal desire for the extermination of those presumed to threaten that society. But the US military, by its own admission, was in Mosul to do whatever was necessary to protect American interests; it went to destroy in Iraq what could otherwise, it was asserted, harm "us" "here." War reportage, in its narrative insistence, allows news consumers absolution from the guilt of the extermination that *did* ensue in Mosul through focus on the righteousness—even if unfulfilled—of responsibility and rescue.[24]

Journalism, in this manner, represents its audience to itself as compassionate witnesses to incidental suffering rather than indifferent bystanders to strategic killing. And in disavowing the desire to exterminate others through a narrative of humanitarian protection (again, even unfulfilled protection), war reportage justifies military intervention on the grounds of presumed intent. If war reportage can make meaning for the battle for Mosul as mismanaged protection rather than effective extermination, as excessively violent liberation rather than predictably violent siege, then war reportage can justify the killing of civilians under the pretense of a possibility that cannot be proven. The reportage that revealed US-Coalition manipulation of civilian casualty counts, assessed in the previous chapter, may function as a sharp criticism of a liberation, but it functions as an implicit endorsement of a siege. The meaning for war offered by war reportage is, then, of utmost consequence. In a liberation, murder is a bug; in a siege, it is a feature.

But what happens when journalists' experiences of war clash with the meanings that their journalism demands? What are the effects of a conflict between journalists' understandings of war and the reality their journalism must deliver? The next chapters turn to the practice of war reportage to examine the consequential tension between experience and expression in wartime journalism. It bears emphasizing, however, that competing meanings for the battle for Mosul are not distinct economies of representation: one treating the humanitarian intent of war and its incidental excesses, another treating the political design of war and its strategic consequences. Rather, these different narratives are interchangeable insofar as they describe the same deception, a deception in which every variety of narrative lives. The meaning of war can be made radically contrary to accepted norms (and norms, of course, do change), but this meaning would still be an effect of narrative. Regardless of the meanings made, the news will deliver a reality seductive to its consumers. Narrative "makes the real desirable," says White (1987, 21), and it does this by imposing upon events the formal coherence of a story. The reality of warfare, as given in the news, appears to "speak for itself" by displaying a coherence that is already desired by news consumers, a coherence that "summons us from afar" in its articulation of a reality we are already primed to demand (White 1987, 21). This desire will be explored in the chapters to come.

The task at hand is not, then, to see the truth of extermination over the falsity of protection, but rather to ascertain how all meanings moralize war in relation to a dominant order. The task is to disassemble the coherence of war that war reportage attempts to make total. The task is to challenge conventional meanings for war by understanding how particular they can be and how authority is constituted through the displacement of this particularity.

INTERLUDE

What to Make of It

Ethnographer: How have you been? We haven't talked since Iraq. You said something happened?

Journalist: I had a weird thing in London the other week when there was a loud thunderclap, and I was convinced it was an explosion for a few seconds. And everything sort of slowed down. And I looked at the people around me, and some men grinning, and it looked macabre and like a horror shop hall of mirrors for a moment. I remember thinking it was so fucked up that these men were smiling when a bomb went off. It occurred after a night of drinking and not much sleep, almost none, and I think my nerves were frayed or I was more sensitive to these things and already feeling a doubling of time and an otherworldliness. To me it didn't sound like a thunderclap, it was sharper and louder and more sudden and jarring, like a rift through space on a rainy North London street. Life became fragile and precious. Memories collide and time zones merge. Suppose it also occurred in a longer period of sleep deprivation, not eating much and multiple time zones and travel to Iraq-Ukraine-Iraq-Palestine. Only in Ukraine was I under fire, but in the other places the threat of escalation surrounded in its perfected use of power. It was certainly a surreal moment of placelessness or dispossession. A general sensitivity to the world seen and the world unseen, to quote the Sufis. It also occurred on All Saints Day, first November in the Christian calendar, the day before the celebration of the departed in All Souls Day or the Day of the Dead. What to make of it all?

PART III

The Practice of War Reportage and Its Contradictions

FIVE

Writing Conflicts

The Tension Between Experience and Expression

> Dreams have started wars, and wars, from the very earliest times, have determined the propriety and impropriety—indeed, the range—of dreams.
> —WALTER BENJAMIN

The Dream Life of Journalism

Diane was covering her first major war for the international press. A freelance journalist for British and American news outlets, she is austere in dress and manner, with pensive brown eyes and the reticent wisdom of a failed soldier.

While reporting on the Islamic State's enslavement of Yazidi women, Diane experienced a recurring dream. We spoke at her home in Erbil, in northern Iraq, where many journalists covering war with the Islamic State then lived. Sitting in plastic chairs on a withered lawn, we shared the heady exhaustion of a place where war is the ligature of all work, all social relations, all conversation. I'd been interviewing and observing Diane for months—at nervous checkpoints, amidst urban ruin—but the conveyance of dreams was her initiative. The dreams mattered to her.

Diane dreamed about being raped by masked men. Wearing black and with faces obscured, the men barged in and pounced. The scene of ferocity and panic mirrored those described to Diane by her Yazidi subjects. The dream content syncopated with the reportage then filling Diane's spiral-bound notebooks. But this latent connection was not apparent in the news Diane produced. For the professional imperatives of war reportage necessitate a fissure between the object of news and the experience of its representation.

Diane's dream reflects the twinned burdens of war reportage: the violence that saturates journalistic life and the demands of an authoritative narrative genre. The confusions, ambiguities, and distress of both war and its narration comprise the foundations of journalism in wartime, yet the effects of this disturbance are obscured by the forms and ideals of the profession. "Those who could not flee were killed and buried in mass graves," Diane's published story explains, before elaborating on the massacre of Yazidi men and the enslavement of Yazidi women. But the effect on the reporter of what is reported is not elaborated, as the accuracy, impartiality, and facticity of Diane's journalism conceals this connection. An intimacy between Diane and the object of her journalism, evident in her dream life, is concealed by third-person prose, a distanced and definitive account, the ideals of objectivity and neutrality—in short, by journalism.

Can war reportage be understood without assessing this hidden intimacy? Stuart Hall, in an analysis of mass media, insists, "What is shown or seen, in representation, can only be understood in relation to what cannot be seen, what cannot be shown" (1997, 266). The experience of reporting war is mystified within the news commodity but never quite erased, and an assessment of the stories delivered by war reportage requires examination of what is hidden therein. While the reifications and refusals of news narrative signal a tension between the practice of journalism and its product, this tension is not merely conflictual. For the production of war news is precipitated precisely by what is excised from that news. This chapter and the next track the tension between journalist and journalism as the pressures of war and its narrative commodification bear down. Experience and expression, however divergent, form a relationship essential to war reportage.

By observing the practice of war reportage across Iraq, Lebanon, and Syria, as well as in Afghanistan and Ukraine, and by interviewing journalists about their professional routines, a certain excess to the news is exposed, something latent but displaced in the texts journalists produce. A focus on the activities of news making amidst war and violence reveals another side to the products of journalism, an "unmarked space" of everything unaccounted for by journalistic meaning and the narratives carrying that meaning (Luhmann 2000, 37). This chapter identifies this journalistic remainder in order to assess both its danger to journalism and its generativity. In examining the practice of war reportage, my aim is to position the news as the satisfaction of desire for a legible, knowable war, and the practice of journalism as that which both propels and threatens that satisfaction. In this chapter and the next, we find journalists navigating the contradictions between experience and expression amidst a life of deadlines and destruction. In what journalists do and make is glimpsed both a desire for a war that can be journalistically ordered and a struggle to ever fully erase the disorders of war.

To focus on the practice of journalism in wartime, then, is to focus not only on how the news is produced—the interviewing of victims, the encountering of suffering, the meeting of deadlines, the narrating of events. Such focus also demonstrates how journalists' experiences of war are managed by the discursive constraints of war reportage and the generic conventions though which news of war is communicated. My focus on practice is intended to show the inherent misalignments of the life of war reportage and to question, with Michael Taussig, "whether the story the storyteller of war might want to tell us is freely available, anyway" (1992, 65). War as experienced by journalists may be outside or beyond journalistic communication, even as the experience of war is foundational to the professional activity of war reportage.

In considering this circumstance—in which an excess to journalism is also fundamental to journalism—the psychoanalytic register is strategic. For in tracking the tension between practice and discourse, between journalist and journalism, I am tracking what could be called *journalism's unconscious*: the site of connections, experiences, and anxieties withdrawn from the conscious operations of journalism—what could be called *the news*—and yet impacting these operations as a hidden impulse, a latent spirit. In this site we find Walt Whitman's "real war" that "will never get in the books" ([1855] 1995, 80). We find journalist Michael Herr's "dripping, laughing death-face," hidden "in the back of every column of print . . . an after-image that simply wanted to tell you at last what somehow had not been told" (1977, 218). What has not been told as news still affects news production, exerting its influence on the techniques, conventions, and ideals of journalistic professionalism. As with the Freudian unconscious, this journalistic unconscious does not become available to examination until it "admits of communication or observation" (Freud 1950, 402): the nagging dream, the sick joke, the bewildering gaze, the person or place whose significance can be neither ignored nor fully explained. These matters, common among journalists reporting from war, are occluded by journalism but available to ethnographic interpretation and psychoanalytic diagnosis. What can be recognized as the repressed of war reportage surfaces outside the constraints of the genre, and this return is revealing. Interviews and observation reveal both the fantasy that the news *is* as well as the latent processes percolating beneath the news-making endeavor.

Dreams are one site among others for the reemergence of what is innate to war reportage yet displaced from the news commodity. Gananath Obeyesekere approaches dreams as "one conduit between . . . fantasy and culture" (1990, xix) and as a primary link between ethnography and psychoanalysis (what Obeyesekere calls "psychoethnography"). Anthropologists have long considered dreams as "communicative processes in culture," wherein the information presented by dreams becomes an interpretive key for the investigation of cultural forms (Mageo 2003, 7; see also Eggan 1952; Mittermaier 2015; Tedlock 1992). Particularly relevant for war reportage is Wojciech Owczarski's (2020) understanding of dreams as the communication of what is otherwise "unspeakable" of an experience of violence. For the communicative potential of journalists' dreams is precisely the disclosure of an "unspeakability" in journalistic representations of war. The culture of war reportage is communicated through what is unexpressed in the professional language and sanctioned meaning of war reportage.[1]

Initially, journalists volunteered their dreams to me after meeting an early morning deadline or after a long day on Mosul's frontline. Tired of discussing editorial negotiations or the politics of access, many journalists wanted to tell me something they would not tell a colleague. The space of ethnography became a space for what exceeds journalism, and I became a vessel (though not an impartial one) for what journalism keeps hidden. Of course, ethnographers similarly struggle with the tensions of translating those people and events they encounter. My relationship to the ethnographic material I record here is troubled—by uneven access, emotional attachments, incomplete understanding—just as the relationship of this material to my theoretical concerns is troubled by mediation and its borders. But as Donna Haraway (2016) reminds us, trouble provides a basis for thinking alongside those with whom we share danger.[2]

Journalists helped me to observe the latent processes percolating beneath the news-making endeavor, and to identify the return of this journalistically repressed. The self-evidence of news narratives can here be resituated as a claim to order and control. For a surplus to journalism, surfacing in the practice of journalism, reveals the fantasy that the news *is*: its satisfaction of consumer desire for a particular reality of war, a reality shaped by societal norms, market incentives, and institutional expectations. This fantasy of war, delivered by war reportage, is propelled by what the fantasy elides; an excess shapes war reportage from its outside, throwing its particularity into relief. A bond between the latent and the manifest is thereby inherent to war reportage, driving the enterprise onward.

The subject of this chapter, then, is not an individual journalist's unconscious (the concern of psychoanalysis proper) but rather journal*ism*'s unconscious, the storehouse for what does not surface in journalism. I use the term "journalistic unconscious" heuristically, and in order to illuminate a process unfolding in the Middle East and other war zones today.[3] While anthropological engagements with media and with psychoanalysis do not often converge, the process of abjection (literally, "casting off") suggests a link. What disturbs reason—and, thereby, the consensus that underpins a social order—must be expelled; abjection is in this way "coextensive with social and symbolic order" (Kristeva 1982, 68). This process pertains to both psychoanalytic and media anthropology. Experiences inherent to but displaced by journalism can be understood to threaten, in psychoanalytic fashion, the control over meaning that journalists enact. The abjected and the normative thus retain an essential relationship in journalism, a relationship whose structure can be elaborated. Ethnography registers what is implicit to journalism as a cultural practice, while psychoanalysis registers the repressed and its return.

This chapter's focus on journalistic practice is intended to tease out the conflict between the meanings and texts of war reportage and the activities and routines of war reporting. The journalists I engage are employed to encounter conflict and to transmit the reality of this conflict through narrative. Firsthand experience of war is a professional requirement for these war reporters. Yet the effects of this encounter with war—the effects of the experience of war's devastation, war's absurdity, war's confusion, war's beauty—must be excised from the news these journalists produce, which presupposes a war factual, certain, and knowable.

Transforming the disorder of war to meet the standards of war reportage thereby entails contradictory pressures. For even as the authority and authenticity of war reportage depends upon journalists' intimate encounters with violence, the conventional truth of reportage—the sense it makes of war—entails the narrative suppression of just these encounters, which can challenge journalism's discursive demands. The practice of witnessing is central to a genre premised upon proximity to war (Palmer 2018a; Zelizer 2007), yet what is witnessed by journalists can conflict with their generic mandate: to order war in alignment with consumer expectations for coherence.[4] Firm borders—between war and peace, guilt and innocence, rational and irrational, lawful and extreme, us and them—must be maintained in journalism even as they are known, through the practice of journalism, to blur. Journalists' encounters with violence in Raqqa, Mosul, and other conflicts disturb news-consumer assumptions, generated and reproduced through journalism, about what war *is*. And in this manner, something is repressed in the news, something that both conditions and threatens the production of news. War reportage denies its unconscious even as this unconscious permeates the practice of war reportage.

The war experienced by journalists and the war expressed as journalism are mutually implicated in the process of news production even as they conflict. These elements can be considered dialectical in that their tension, internal to war reportage, can never be resolved. The language of repression becomes useful in suggesting the persistence *in* the news of what is mystified *by* the news. While many have noted the fissure between experience and output in discourse production, we should interrogate the finality of this apparent break. The "constitutive outside" (Laclau 1990, 9) of war reportage is always lurking at journalism's discursive border, and this surplus cannot be finally banished. Journalism is incapable of truly expelling what it cannot admit, while journalists are unable to fully suture the cut between experience of war and news of war. This tension—and its productivity—provide an opportunity for considering war reportage anew.

Karl Marx's writing on the mystifications of labor power is compelling here, as it indicated a productive capacity hidden away in the objective presence of the commodity produced. This capacity animates or spiritualizes that commodity, Marx argues, as for a fetish. When wood becomes table, he fabulously notes, it does more than simply stand with its feet on the ground; the table "stands on its head, and evolves out of its wooden brain grotesque ideas, far more wonderful than if it were to begin dancing of its own free will" (1976, 163–164). Can we seek the grotesque ideas about war evolving from the inky brain of the news? Can we seek the complexities, ambiguities, and intimacies innate to the making of the news commodity—innate to the practice of news production—that are hidden away in the objective presence of the news? Is it possible to excavate from war reportage the contradictory pressures of war and its production, pressures that authorize journalism even as they are repressed in journalism?[5]

Recent scholarship in media anthropology (e.g., Bishara 2012; Boyer 2013; Peterson 2001) usefully clarifies the fissures inherent to journalistic production—the fissures between the practice of news making and the news product—by exposing the contingencies of objectivity, facticity, sourcing, and related ideals and techniques. Yet more attention must be paid to the generative power of this fissure and to the structure it exhibits. Tracking the ideological complicities and rhetorical performances of journalism is not enough to discern how war reportage is shaped by war, and through both war's encounter and war's erasure. For the self-fashioning of war reporters, and the fashioning of the meanings war reportage makes, takes place amidst the expulsions innate to war reportage—a matter recognized in anthropology's so-called reflexive turn. As this "turn" clarified, anthropological professionalism is not merely a matter of producing proper ethnography, but of properly managing those things that both exceed the ethnographic text and yet beset its production. The basis for this "turn" in the theorization of ethnographic fieldwork persists in journalism too, where professionals are likewise sent to a faraway field to produce texts that select, shape, and otherwise delimit what that field is recognized to be. The displaced "outside" constitutes the sanctioned "inside," and when the fieldworkers are journalists, and the field is war, particular dynamics will ensue. This chapter places war reportage within the "writing culture" frame (Clifford and Marcus 1986), drawing out journalism's displacements as the basis for what war reportage now *is*. In its topic and in its tension, call it *writing conflicts*.

Journalistic Distortion

Max hurried into a mosque where locals were keeping the bodies after a massacre. His job was to count them—a basic routine of war reporting. Some bodies were badly burned, placed on slabs of ice to fight the rot. One body was so thoroughly charred that only a chunk of torso remained. An elderly woman squatted over it, howling. "My son!" she cried. "My son!" The body—if it could be called a body—lacked identifying features;

it was more blackened mush than deceased child. Max speculated that the woman knew her son was dead but couldn't find his remains and had settled on the most unidentifiable body—the one that couldn't be known—as a proxy to mourn.

Max is a bookish Midwesterner, swift and lanky and quick to a pun, with deep-set blue eyes and a Leninist goatee. He worked for a British wire service before freelancing around the Middle East for American newspapers and magazines. Max's published report on the massacre conveyed certainty and assurance, and it frontloaded the number of dead as the critical matter. "A reporter saw [number] of bodies in [name] mosque."[6] As the conventions of his news organization dictate, Max staged his own disappearance as a subjective experiencer of violence, replaced by "a reporter" whose account is both authoritative and removed. Deflected by this rhetorical position is any sense that "a reporter's" encounter with violence may impact the news produced, and any sense that the news produced might displace an important dimension of the violence encountered by "a reporter."

Here is what Mark Pedelty calls "objectivity as absence": The journalist's "primary duty as that of *not* becoming located" (1995, 172). War reportage demands Max's exclusion as both author of a narrative and experiencer of an event. This exclusion is reflected in journalism's language—the use of third-person prose, the avoidance of explicit opinion, the staged simultaneity of an event's occurrence and its narration. And it is reflected in the objective, impartial frame that is both the narrative standard and institutional ideology of war reportage. Max's self-effacement in this way responds to the demands of the profession and thus fails, as Pedelty argues, to engender a sense of the "interconnectedness linking individuals to the larger world in which they live" (1995, 25). Yet the interconnection endures. Max is discursively absent from the text he produced and the meaning it made. But the practice of encountering war's events, of counting war's bodies, links Max ineluctably to the violence he reports. Max is very much located in war—the practice of war reportage demands it—even as this presence is mystified by the generic demands of the news.

"But there was no 'son' there," Max murmurs into a beer in Baghdad some months after the encounter. Max did his job as a practicing war reporter—he'd encountered the casualties and counted them for the news. But Max hasn't moved on; an unknowable body still lurks behind the death he enumerated. Max is troubled not, or not only, by the extremity of the violence he witnessed, but by the professional necessity to make that extremity legible. While the conflict between experience and expression in the context of violence is treated in recent scholarship (e.g., Butler 2009; Jameson 2013), the relationship between the practice and product of war reportage—between the routines of news making in wartime and the meanings of news texts—is particular. For both the experience of extremity and the application of legibility are inherent to the profession of war reportage, and these things can clash. Both elements—the devastation that challenges narration and the narration that displaces devastation—are innate to the job, and their discordance weighs upon journalists like Max even as it remains structural to journalism. Seeing uncountable bodies can be necessary to seeing the bodies that are counted; what is not tellable persists within the news told. As a journalist in Erbil remarked, "There's a disconnect between the dynamics of what you can understand in terms of the facts and what it actually feels like to experience violence. There is a visceral brutality, an aggression, that feels different than the explaining." This difference is not a matter of representation's limits, but of the inherent conflict between journalists' practices of encountering war and the narrative modalities available to journalists.

Though only in mid-career, Max has covered several conflicts in the Middle East, and he knows well the symbolic power of a death toll. "We fetishize numbers at the expense of context," he tells me in a voice rasped and hollow. Casualty counts enact a claim to verifiable truth and thereby reify the reality articulated as news. As a discursive element, casualty counts manifest the legibility pivotal to the news product. However, presumptions about a number's relationship to reality neglect what cannot be counted, and what cannot be counted bothers Max still. Max is normally self-assured, a professional at ease in his work. Now the pen habitually spinning between Max's fingers sits deserted on the bar of a fortified hotel.

The fantasy that casualty counts are the complete reality of an event in war covers a hole in the ability of the news to contain what war *is*, even as journalists confront this hole in their daily labors. The woman clutching a torso, howling for her son, can thus be seen as a *distortion* in the doubled sense noted by Freud: that which "change[s] the appearance" of something, and that which "wrench[es] apart" its reality (1939, 70). To change the appearance of the violence reported and to wrench apart the reality produced as news: Charred flesh, clutched by a woman in agony, distorts journalistic truth. It is a distortion attendant to the practice of war reportage, effaced by the news product but burdening the news producer.

We can add a third, medial sense: distortion as an alteration to a sound wave during its processing, where news is the purified signal, and the twinned pressures of war and its narration the distorting noise. War as narrated in the news may seem seamless—a reality that can be classified, defined, counted—but the lives of narrators in war rarely are. Freud writes, "In many textual distortions we may count on finding suppressed and abnegated material hidden away somewhere, though in an altered shape and torn out of its original connection" (1939, 52). Torn from the news narrative, altered as dream or humor or foul mood, the distortions to journalism live on with journalists. Freud concludes that this abnegated remainder is difficult to recognize but never disappeared. The relationship between news practice and news product is not only a matter of disjuncture, then, but of connection, and of what this connection provokes. As both practice and product, war reportage is driven by its internal tension; a remainder is abnegated but never disappeared, and this process propels war reportage.

The distortions of war and its laborious representation travel beneath the signal that is news, and attention to the practice of war reportage presents the effects of this antithetical foundation. For the experiences of journalists, observable in the spaces of journalistic life, can trouble the narratives of war even as such experiences underwrite the authority to narrate. This relationship between experience, meaning, and text can be observed and assessed; ethnography recognizes an abnegated remainder to war reportage, and psychoanalysis diagnoses its repression. We must then ask: What are the professional narratives of war, and how do they meet news-consumer expectations? What is the consumer desire for an *un*distorted reality—a reality as pure signal—and how does journalism both enable and satisfy this desire? In addressing these questions, the generativity of journalism's internal tension is clarified. This tension is generative insofar as the expulsion of the journalistically illegible allows the news to become itself: a seamless representation of a knowable world. This is the fantasy that the news elaborates, a dominant fantasy of a purified war.

The fantasy expressed as journalism instantiates social desire for a particular wartime reality. Narrative categories, standardized tropes, stock characters, and other generic conventions create legibility in accordance with societal expectation for what war *is*. War is thereby, as Hall and coauthors explain, "brought within the horizon of the 'meaningful'" (1978, 57). This desired reality is one where violence can be typologized through its means and ends; where the guilty and innocent can be parsed, with the former punished and the latter saved; where war is an unfortunate interruption to global peace rather than an extension of that peace. It is a desired reality where violence is immanent rather than structural, corporeal rather than political, spectacular rather than bureaucratic. Operating as what Allen Feldman terms a "regime of facticity," war reportage essentializes its object, applying a typology in which any exclusions are effaced by the structure of typification itself (2015, 6). But this fantasy is one journalists experience, in their practice as journalists, as permeable. By assessing this discrepancy—by locating what the news is *not*—we see how the production of a fantasy of war both requires and expels what exceeds that fantasy.[7] Lurking at the frontier of established binaries and conventional categories is a war that, as for Fredric Jameson, "ceaselessly tempts and exasperates narrative ambitions" (2013, 257). This temptation to narrate, and the exasperation that results, is evident in the spaces where journalists live and work.

"In coverage of war, what *is* is chaos." This is what a journalist told me in a newsroom in Beirut. "I've felt pressure to add meaning when there hasn't been meaning."[8] Journalism transmits the intelligibility of a newsworthy event, and it must thereby omit those aspects of war that challenge journalistic sense making as such. For even as journalism can index the expected means and ends of war, its plot and its characters, journalists yet attest to what their texts are designed to elide: a violence that is other than the categories applied and the purposes reported. This "a-significance" of violence (Bousquet 2011) is a dynamic archived by journalists—in dreams, in humor, in little orange bottles behind the bathroom mirror—even as it is displaced by journalism in the reproduction of conventional meanings within standardized news texts. And in this manner, journalists come to inhabit what Kathleen Stewart describes as "a haunting double epistemology of being in the midst of things and impacted by them and yet making something of things" (1996, 4).

For the ability to make something of war—to make it intelligible, to make it news—is not accomplished through an autonomous gaze that assumes a mastering of the ruin at hand. Rather, the news commodity made from war is contiguous with the pressures of its production. For Diane and for Max, an intimacy between the journalist and the object of journalism endures even as it must be concealed. Untallied flesh, as from a body that doesn't count as a body; the resonance of assault, as from a rape that is other than the rape reported. What is repressed in journalism still affects journalists and thus journalism. This tension is unresolved even as it remains inherent.

"Death is unfathomable," a journalist told me outside a press conference in Erbil. "It doesn't make sense. Death and violence disrupt all norms, and understanding that we can't understand it is an important part of the job." Journalists must understand that which is not understandable *as* news, and this "important part of the job" indicates how a hidden tension remains productive. Knowing what to omit from war reportage hinges on an encounter with the journalistically inadmissible.[9]

The uncanny, then, retains in journalism its Freudian description as the "secretly familiar" (1919, 245). The uncanny of war is the secretly familiar of the news, percolating just below the accurate, objective, factual surface. The uncanny challenges journalistic meaning making even as it remains a feature of the practice of wartime journalism. For the border between real and surreal, sense and nonsense—held in place by the meanings war reportage is tasked to make—becomes, in the practice of war reportage, a borderland through which the journalist must travel. "The more securing the regime of facticity in war becomes," Feldman writes, "the more it is permeated by the disturbing specter of an invasive otherness" (2015, 5). Facticity and otherness are kindred in war reportage even as they contradict, and this conflict frames journalistic life.

What, then, do journalism's formal commitments to a seamless reality—to an objective, accurate delivery of war—*do?* A war narratively organized in a particular fashion, and the displacement of what does not meet this standard, allows for control over war's meaning. Here the social role of journalism becomes apparent. Yet this control is nevertheless permeated by the uncontrollable.

Fear on the Road

Emily is quick to laugh but can be deadly serious on assignment. One of the better Arabic speakers of the regional foreign press corps, she is committed to her stories and despondent over minor mistakes. She moves in long, eager strides and speaks with a directness at turns authoritative and childlike. The daughter of Latin American–based journalists, she worked for a wire service before securing a staff job at a British newspaper.

Emily was chasing an interview through northeast Syria when fear overtook us. The interview, with a local community leader, had been arranged well in advance, in a town recently taken from the Islamic State. We arrive in late morning to a concrete office building. Inside, men in beige kaftans study old ledgers in dimly lit rooms with ashtrays overflowing. Emily offers greetings and is soon instructed to drive to the leader's village, where we will be welcomed for the interview at his home. Emily is wary; any change of plans entails risk. But the interview is important to her story of the ongoing battle in Raqqa. So we get back into the car—Emily and I and Emily's driver, Mustafa—and we head out.

The town recedes. We pass through a checkpoint controlled by friendly Kurdish forces, and then another a few miles on, before coasting into the empty umber spaces of Syria's hinterland. Scrub ebbs toward every horizon; the wide highway ribbons into blurred heat. Emily reviews notes in the passenger seat, Mustafa cranks up a pop-radio hit, and my mind begins to drift. Time and desert wander by. At some point, two men on motorcycles approach our car and speed away. More time passes; a brutalist granary shimmers in the distance. And abruptly the highway asphalt cleaves apart before us, like a wave upturned in turbulent seas: A recent US airstrike has blasted into the roadway, and we careen to a halt before our rent passage. Shifting the vehicle into the scrubland, we continue off-road beside the highway until the asphalt is again intact. We ride along in silence then, happy for a smooth road and functioning air conditioning, but still with no village in sight. Where are we? When was the last checkpoint? Emily consults her map as another man on motorcycle bolts by. And Emily looks up with a start; she and Mustafa lock eyes in recognition. We've driven into contested territory.

A drastic U-turn crumples me across the back seat as panic permeates the car. Emily is frantic, shouting at Mustafa, who curses above the engine roar. After the deaths of James Foley and Marie Colvin, the vulnerability of foreign journalists in Syria is well known and acutely felt. As we hurtle back toward town, fear seems to hold us in abeyance; I remember little of those moments except the clammy relief of recognized safety.

Fear is the patron saint of war reportage, invisibly guiding its progress, respected but ethereal. And in this way fear is congenital to wartime journalism, a dynamic integral to, if abstracted from, the news produced in war. Fear is everywhere and nowhere in war reporting, determining which stories get told, in what manner and at what cost, but fear is rarely acknowledged in narrative. For while chaos, uncertainty, and distress constitute war reportage as practice, their admission in the war report constitutes a generic breach. Fear cannot make the meaning institutional to journalism; what is unexpressed propels but never appears in the expression produced.[10]

I'd seen and felt fear while observing journalists before—there was a dodged sniper round in Tripoli, an errant mortar in Kabul—but the fear on the road with Emily was more sustained, a thick and sweaty thing whose source was both sharp and obscure. Emily eventually landed her interview, and the story she published was informative and measured (by the standards normatively applied), erasing the fear on the road. For the news must conform to a logic of disavowal as it concentrates its narrative power. Emily's story prioritized the news object—an interview, and what it explained—at the expense of how this interview came to be, and what was leveraged or lost, encountered or endured, in the process.

From Emily's story, the news consumer received the "anomalies of Syria's six-year civil war," the "reality on the ground," the "charred buildings lying in ruins." The story provided crucial insight into regional political transformations and added important details to the record of the war in Syria. But the difficulties of producing the story are repressed. In Emily's case, such difficulties also included the possibility of Syrian state reprisal, prompting her story's anonymous publication in the newspaper where Emily has worked for many years. The byline of the story, where Emily's name would usually appear, was replaced with "a reporter." The repressed, then, leaves its textual trace; an undesignated byline gestures to the fear that is structural to the story but never explicit. Reading for absences—here, the absence of a name—allows for a glimpse of what both exceeds and precipitates war reportage.

From Hell to Trauma

Certain narrative dynamics can cover the breach between insensible experience and sensible meaning while also suggesting the prominence of this breach in the lives of war's representors. *Trauma* presents a particular cogency in this regard. For trauma is both a discursive convention of contemporary war reportage and a sign for what exceeds the limits of war reportage.

I heard a story once, about a bomber who self-detonated in a public square during the battle for Mosul. A group of journalists were lounging outside a party at an NGO compound in Erbil, sucking French cigarettes and passing a bottle of whiskey. The moon dodged thin clouds, and two helicopters sliced across the warm-breeze night. "Her body vaporized," one of the journalists remarked between drags. "But her head, with long, flowing hair, remained intact. She looked serene almost, at ease without the rest of her." The journalist described how the bomber's head was placed gingerly in the square and how, before long, a comb was retrieved. Iraqi soldiers, teenagers, and stooped, angular women brushed the beautiful hair on this disembodied head while their neighbors took cellphone snapshots. "And it *was* beautiful hair," the journalist mused for effect. "Flowing down like that. It was beautiful hair . . ." The bottle continued its passage. Through the darkness I saw another journalist shake her head and smile.[11]

I relayed the story some months later, at a dinner party in California with a group of artists and tenure-track academics. It was a chilly spring evening, outside on the deck after a vegetarian meal, and my audience responded with sharp disgust. I'm not sure why I told the story, or why I didn't anticipate this reaction; someone surely asked about my research, or about Iraq, which was then front-page news. War does horrible things to people, the group agreed after their shock was duly registered. The trauma of war does horrible things. It makes sense, then—the story makes sense—with the trauma and the war.

Had I told the story wrong? Maybe it wasn't clear, or maybe I didn't get the details right. Because the story of the head with beautiful, flowing hair is not about the repulsive depravities of war. The story is not about war's trauma, or about what trauma is expected to do. The story is not sensible in a way the news demands, but rather expresses, as stories swapped around parties in Erbil tended to do, what is journalistically inexpressible. The story is about the absurd humor of life amidst death—the life of Iraqis, and the life of foreign journalists too. It is about an abnegated remainder surfacing, for a moment, at the margins of a dark but ordered world. It is not a horror story at all, but a story intended to thwart such restrictive classification. It's a story told, amidst horror, to make you shake your head and smile.

What does this story do for journalists in Iraq that it does not do for intellectuals in California? For the former, the story releases a latency to the reality produced as news, an excess that cannot be properly commodified. For the latter, the story delivers the reality expected of war today, a reality reproduced in and as news. While the content of this reality shifts through the history of war reportage, from the Somme to Khe Sanh to Kandahar to Kyiv, the structures of reality-delivery persist. Journalistic emphasis on traumatic victimhood in today's ongoing anti-terror wars shares a logic with an emphasis on the glories of combat in the Crimean War, considered the first modernly reported conflict.[12] Both emphases make war real in relation to reigning social expectation.

Paul Fussell's (1975) analysis of a transition in imaginings of war is instructive. For Fussell, the First World War precipitated a decisive break in the meaning war popularly made. The so-called Great War—its massive scale, its organizational disregard for human life—disenchanted particular notions, then persistently axiomatic, regarding the meaning and reality of conflict. While the old verities of honor and glory retained their explanatory power in the England of 1914, the young men who went off to fight the new war saw these values die in no-man's-land. In its nineteenth-century narrative portrayal, war made a kind of sense that corresponded with established notions of heroism and history, and the First World War disrupted this way of thinking. After the industrial-scaled horrors of the Western Front, and as a result of the narrative labor of First World War writers, the hellishness of combat began to supplant its glory as the defining reality of war.

This transformation demonstrates how the necessity of sense making in wartime adjusts through the history of conflict while maintaining its integrity. From the First World War, Fussell argues, social cognition had been altered and a dominant form of understanding challenged and replaced. The "maps of meaning," in Hall and coauthors' locution (1978, 57), which form "the basis of our cultural knowledge," had shifted, and wartime representation responded to and reproduced newly acceptable ideas of war's reality. What was latent, surfaced: The insensibility of war—its hellishness—became newly sensible. A discursive structure, which makes knowable the reality of war, endures even as the contents of that structure modify to suit evolving expectations for war's reality.

Fussell's analysis can be extended. For today the trauma of war is the reality coincident with widespread social expectation. Trauma makes war real the way it is now supposed to be. By Vietnam, American society was familiar with the figure of the traumatized veteran, popularly held in fear and reverence. The reality of war as traumatic has since intensified—from "post-Vietnam syndrome" to PTSD—as a principal organizing topos. The authority of wartime experience, and of that experience as traumatic, now underwrites social truth about war. Roy Scranton suggests how the story of war's trauma "frames and filters our perceptions of reality through a set of recognizable and comforting conventions. It works to convince us that war is a special kind of experience that offers a special kind of truth, a truth that gives those who have been there a special kind of authority" (2015). Didier Fassin calls trauma "the new vocabulary of war" (2012, 202).

Since the 1990s, write Fassin and Richard Rechtman, "the human being suffering from trauma ... became the very embodiment of our common humanity" (2009, 23). Over the last few decades, then, "trauma had become an essential human value, a mark of the humanity of those who suffered it and of those who cared for them" (Fassin and Rechtman 2009, 23). It is the very commonness of trauma, its presumed universality as what all humans experience in scenes of violence, which has made it so prominent a lens through which to view the world. Trauma can be applied to victims, witnesses, and perpetrators alike, regardless of cultural, historical, social, political, temporal, or geographic difference. As understood after the Holocaust—the quintessential, if only retroactively denoted, traumatic event (Felman 2002)—and with the recognition of post-traumatic stress disorder in the third edition of the *Diagnostic and Statistical Manual of Mental Disorders* (or *DSM-III*) of 1980, trauma became the way many societies see, understand, and respond to war today, as "a suffering without borders, a suffering that knows no cultural barriers" (Fassin and Rechtman 2009, 239). Trauma became what violence like war does to people—any war, any people.[13]

The *DSM-III* defines the criteria for PTSD as the experience of "an event that is outside the range of usual human experience and that would be markedly distressing to almost anyone." Current popular understanding is that any person anywhere can be *expected* to suffer trauma of essentially the same kind in the face of something as abnormal as the violence of war. And because of this universal quality of trauma, media consumers of violence become secure in their abilities to know trauma when they see it and to feel empathy for those who suffer it. This is what Fassin and Rechtman describe as "communion in trauma" (2009, 18). Trauma informs the way many of us see, understand, and respond to violence today.

"Trauma" makes sense of violence, but it displaces an insensibility in this very act of discursive containment. As trauma became a primary meaning of the encounter with violence—a "special kind of truth" about war—the authority of journalism fused with consumer expectation for traumatized journalists. War reporters, covering chemical attacks in

Douma or airstrikes in Raqqa, are presumed traumatized. Yet the confusions and irrealities associated with trauma—the nightmares, gallows humor, impulsive behaviors, self-destructive tendencies, the fear—are repressed by the conventions and ideals of journalistic professionalism. "Trauma" makes war intelligible to news consumers, delivering the reality expected, but this traumatic reality must expel its excess, which includes the traumas experienced by journalists in the course of their labors. As a journalistic gloss, "trauma" displaces but never disappears the insensibility it claims to capture. Here again, the irreconcilable persists; an excess to journalistic expression both challenges and underpins the journalistic pursuit. The contradiction of "trauma" is such that a prominent journalistic signifier hides the reality it purportedly signifies, and this tension is evident in the spaces of journalistic life.[14]

In Beirut I stayed with Daniel, a confident journalist—brash, even—quick to declare solutions to the region's problems. Daniel has a long face, stubbled and crowned with thin brown hair, and a notepad perpetually peeks from his breast pocket. As a student journalist for his university newspaper, Daniel arrived in New York City the day after the 9/11 attacks. Since then, he's worked freelance and staff jobs for British, Middle Eastern, and American news outlets. Daniel angers easily, and his sleep is erratic. I'd often find him fixing things—window frames, a bathroom faucet—never broken to begin with. While covering the war in Syria, Daniel was abducted, held in a dark room, and forced to undergo mock executions. "You're congratulated when you survive," Daniel told me. "Many journalists want to skirt death, and the closer they come to the edge the more pats on the back they get." Death-skirting is professionally encouraged while its effects are secreted away.

Tasked to write about his abduction, and thereby certify his professional threshold for risk, Daniel produced a story that was informative and dramatic. His published narrative explained how kidnapping had become the price of reporting from the war in Syria, and it gave meaning to his ordeal through an account of regional events. "I was recently abducted," Daniel's story begins, employing a rare first-person frame. The story describes being strip-searched, handcuffed, and blindfolded. It then enumerates, in a spare and straightforward manner, the organizational history of his abductors. As the strictures of war reportage dictate, Daniel preserved a certain professional remove, narrating even his own kidnapping with objective distance and clean factuality. Daniel the reporter and Daniel the abductee are dissociated.

The events Daniel reported are clearly traumatic, but the trauma of the event Daniel experienced is nowhere in evidence. If Daniel's anger, or his preoccupation to fix, are effects of the trauma of war reporting, this was not a trauma that ever appeared in his reportage. His trauma exceeds, as trauma always does, the trauma conventional to news of war. Daniel remains tethered to his experience in Syria in a way that both perpetuates and disrupts the news he makes. A disorderly reality is suppressed, but cannot be disappeared, by the frictionless reality suitable to an enduring fantasy of war.

So what does "trauma"—like "soldier's heart" in the Civil War, "shell shock" in the First World War, "battle fatigue" in the Second—actually signify other than that remainder to the experience of violence that cannot be journalistically articulated? Trauma is an attempt to answer an unanswerable question, to explicate the inexplicability of war. For what is traumatic about war is precisely the otherwise unnameable. The "thousand-yard stare," a gloss emerging from Second World War reportage (and further discussed in Chapter 6), captured the psychic distress of combat precisely because the object of the soldier's stare is obscure. As a language frequent to war reportage, "trauma" allows the otherwise unassimilable to be pulled into socially acceptable significance; opacity is pierced and war's reality recognized. But what is really traumatic about war lurks *un*signified. The unnameable can be named as symbols are found and deployed, but the potency of unnameability bears down.

Trauma usefully particularizes the internal tension of war reportage, for here the journalistic effort to name, typologize, and certify both mystifies and relies upon that which escapes such efforts. The omission in Fassin and Rechtman's account of trauma-as-discourse is some reckoning with a traumatic reality that exceeds discursive constraint. Journalism controls the insensibility of violence through generic ascriptions like "trauma," yet something insensible nevertheless affects journalists (as well as those they write about) as sensible meaning is crafted amidst war. Trauma is an expression for what threatens expression, and yet the inexpressible still makes its presence felt. The irreconcilability between journalism's narrative of war and journalists' experience of war—between a consciously named and an unconsciousness unnamed—remains formative in the lives of journalists, and this fissure retains a generative power in the production of the news.

I lived in Diane's home in Erbil while she covered war with the Islamic State. One afternoon, CNN contacted Diane to request a live interview. It was to be a short segment—just a few basic questions about the ongoing battle in Mosul. Before she went on air, we cooked dinner and joked about recent military ineptitudes. Diane seemed in good spirits: quick to laugh, glad her work was being recognized, and happy to appear on TV.

In the interview, Diane looked pale and gaunt in a black turtleneck, her dark hair pulled tightly back. She sat at a wooden desk and stared intently into the computer camera. Behind her was the bedroom-office wall, once whitewashed, bare but for the cracks wandering through peeling plaster. Diane's lamp threw a hard bleached light across the scene. The CNN anchor, important and refined, asked about death, and then about loss, and then about hope. Diane answered with stony articulation, producing population figures and revealing character sketches. The content she delivered was certain and deliberate. She also seemed wrung out, a brave expert exhausted by the weight of her professional duty. Diane's gaze met the viewer, unblinking.

Diane performed a role as a traumatized journalist, authenticating her status as war reporter and authorizing her knowledge of violence. Diane was aware of the superficiality of this performance, and of the ideological character of the conventions at play. However, war did affect Diane. It was not performed on CNN but expressed in conversation and in habit; her nightmares, rather than her pallid television complexion, testify to war's impact. What can be named, performed, and professionalized does not exhaust the potency of war's impact, even as this impact seems to determine the performance given. And thus a crucial element of journalistic labor power is concealed as it assumes the form of the news commodity. The news orders war to suit consumer desire for the classifiable and understandable, the defined and enumerated, while the disorder of war is submerged. Trauma can be journalistically institutionalized even though, and contrary to the claims of the genre, trauma cannot be contained by journalism. Ethnographic interpretation and psychoanalytic diagnosis here converge: Trauma is implicit to journalism as a cultural practice, and it is repressed in journalism as an abject disturbance.[15]

Fantasy as Form

Amy was covering the battle for Mosul, though she'd recently returned from the war in Syria. She has a freckled complexion, with a thin, stubborn smile and eyebrows often arched in disbelief. Amy grew up in South America and has freelanced for several years for American newspapers. At the time of our meeting in Erbil, Amy was having a recurring dream of some torment. In the dream, Amy was running down a dusty alleyway while something frightening—an armed drone, an impending airstrike—stalked her from above. The dream was a torment not because Amy knew so well from Syria the death that the sky can bring. Rather, Amy was tormented by an awareness that she was not in Syria at all, but in Iraq. The alleyway was the same, the fear was the same, but the delivery of death wasn't authoritarian and Syrian. It was humanitarian and American.

Amy's dream expresses a political illegibility. As discussed in Chapter 4, the major battles of the recent wars in Iraq and Syria were in many ways identical: a mix of local and foreign fighters defended territory crowded with civilians. The territory was contested by a central government of distinct sectarian persuasion, backed by a foreign, Western military commanding advanced weaponry. The international press, however, reported the battles differently. Conflict in East Aleppo and eastern Ghouta was largely reported as committed local resistance to the domination of the Syrian state and its Russian proxy. Conflict in Mosul and Raqqa was largely reported as the tenacity of foreign jihadists and the suffering of their captive civilians amidst a US-led intervention premised on saving lives.

Applying the narrative framework normative to international news coverage of Mosul or Raqqa (US-Coalition air wars) to East Aleppo or eastern Ghouta (Russian-Syrian air wars) disrupts the meaning of war currently prevalent in those societies consuming much of the reportage from these war zones. Such a reapplication conflicts with reigning assumptions about whose violences are lawful and whose extreme, about which rebellions are terrorism. Amy's dream indicates that what war *is* depends less on the dynamics experienced by journalists than on the representations through which these dynamics come to make sense. Whether war is a matter of protection or extermination, whether it is a liberation or a siege, is determined by the social order within which journalism becomes intelligible. The anxiety of Amy's dream marks this slippage, demonstrating—quite literally— John Pauly's contention that "we dream the forms of social order as we enact them in the practice of communication" (in Carey 1997, 314). The torment of Amy's dream—the anxiety of a self-evidence undermined—marks the return of journalism's repressed. It marks the effects of the established meaning of war on those tasked to reproduce that meaning in discord with their experience of war. It is the torment of an illegibility displaced: the effect of the practice of war reportage on the practitioner.[16]

Amy's published journalism identifies conflict in Aleppo as a "regime-imposed siege" and in Mosul as "the liberation of an Iraqi city" even as she experienced—in her labor and in her dreams—the fragility of these designations. A professional war reporter, Amy produced an impartial account of war that concealed the order underwriting impartiality and journalistic claims thereto. But by examining what is repressed in journalism, the news can be understood not as the representation of a naturally given reality, nor even as the representation of a partial, manufactured reality. Rather, war reportage can be understood as the representation of a reality that satisfies consumer desire, desire shaped by a prevailing order, and that must then excise any disruption thereto. Amy's dream indicates just this.

How does the hidden tension of journalistic labor disguise itself in the seamless transmission of war's narrated reality? What is guiding the expressive power of journalism such that it can always meet consumer expectations for the legible truth of war despite war's experienced illegibility? How does journalism maintain a border between practice and meaning, experience and expression, journalistic unconscious and objective commodity? And does the maintenance of this border serve a social role?

Examining a divergence between journalists' experiences of war and the reality of war they report is not enough for understanding the work journalism does. Or, as Allen Feldman asserts, "To propose the disjuncture between factuality and actuality is not to arrive at a determining, uncontested ground beyond masking ideologies, but rather to explore the fissure itself as a generative power" (2015, 5). For if journalism fails to faithfully reflect reality, as many have argued (most prominently, perhaps, Chomsky and Edward 1988), the question remains as to *how* journalism sustains the perception of reality-reflection through the activation of particular expectations and the manipulation of particular desires.[17] The fissure in war reportage—between journalist and journalism, between the insensibility encountered in war and the sense made thereof—is generative indeed, because this fissure generates a social fantasy of war.

Rather than revealing the secret buried within the news—rather than explicating the ideology lurking beneath objectivity, or the rhetorical performance upon which facticity is predicated—we might instead attend to the form that the news takes. Rather than scrutinizing journalism's content—exposing the unreliability of official sources, or the partiality of an event's description—we might instead consider the ways such content organizes the world. We are looking, in this case, at why the reality delivered by journalism assumes the form of the news commodity, and at how this commodity satisfies consumer desire, whether editorially provoked or societally structured.[18] For the turn to consumer desire and its satisfaction gets us beyond a reckoning with war reportage as simply "constructed" to an understanding of the productive capacity of journalism's internal tension. By looking at what is inherent to news making yet repressed in the news text, the form and power of a social fantasy can be gleaned. My approach to "writing conflicts"—as displacement that yet generates the enterprise—demonstrates how the reality represented in war reportage may be less that of Iraq or Syria than it is the background for journalism's own social reality, a reality whose particularity is exposed through journalistic practice. A fantasy of war, formally constituted as the news commodity, does not illuminate faraway conflict so much as it does the producers and consumers of that fantasy.

That this fantasy may be "constructed" is only part of the point. For what Yael Navaro-Yashin calls the "force of fantasy" (2002, 16) indicates how war exists as a desired object, and how journalism delivers that object through a process laden with contradiction. While war reportage can be critiqued on the basis of its ideological complicities or its discursive particularities, the turn to fantasy shows how war reportage endures despite these deconstructivist critiques. Fantasy does "everyday maintenance work" for war reportage (Navaro-Yashin 2002, 4), allowing it to thrive amidst its inherent tensions. Constructivist analyses of mass media entail an exterior position from which to judge the authenticity, legitimacy, or truth of the object of media narrative. By shifting emphasis from what war reportage *means* to how it *happens*, and to the tension between them, we can begin to see how journalism's contradictions effectuate a persistent fantasy.

Hayden White asks the pertinent question: "What desire is gratified ... by the fantasy that real events are properly represented when they can be shown to display the formal coherency of a story?" (1990, 4). In the case of war reportage today, the fantasy that reality displays the coherence of a story gratifies consumer desire for the finality of a death toll, the trauma of combat, the rationality of humanitarian violence in the face of irrational terroristic violence. And the fantasy that reality displays the coherence of a story allows these things to be offered without much complexity, hesitancy, ambiguity, or context. What is too ambiguous, too strange, too uncertain for this fantasy may be omitted, but this abnegated remainder powers fantasy production still.

For Hegel, a historical account must not only narrativize the past but must do so in alignment with a social order. Much war reportage reflects a political-social order in its account of insurgency, militarism, and suffering. And thus, even as it may abjure explicit partisan messaging in the post–yellow press era, war reportage adheres a political position in the very normativity of its narrative, which adjudicates the accurate and the real. Representing the essential legitimacy of state violence and the extremity of any other; representing an immanent violence, rather than the structures that drive it, as what is unjust about warfare; representing individual victims desiring our empathy, and individual perpetrators deserving our wrath, rather than collectivities exercising political will: Here a social order operates in and as narrative.[19]

Journalism, following White, "achieves narrative fullness by explicitly invoking the idea of a social system to serve as a fixed reference point by which the flow of ephemeral events can be endowed with specifically moral meaning" (1990, 22). It is, then, the social context of the news commodity that provides the parameters of intelligibility within which the news comes to make sense. That which journalism excludes—that of war and violence which fails to gain sanctified journalistic meaning—does so in relation to a social context of production. "You need to create a narrative, one that people can understand," a journalist told me in Duhok, Iraq. "War is a difficult case. You have to make clear something that often provides no clarity at all. If it's not easy enough to explain we'll drop the story." What has no clarity—often, the experience of war and violence—is the grounds for the production of clarity, and narrative covers this gap. But clarity becomes so only in relation to an imposed order. Ease of explanation is dictated by societal expectation.

Of course, neither the experience of war nor its news narration should be accepted as "the real" itself. Rather, examining the news as fantasy allows us to glimpse what is otherwise obfuscated by expectations for war's reality, and thus by the economy of desire that accompanies journalism. For this economy manifests the fears, hopes, and vulnerabilities expressed as war reportage. An Islamic State threatening liberal freedoms; civilian death in US-Coalition airstrikes as necessary or inadvertent rather than punitive or strategic; violence that can be categorized, counted, and thereby known: Here the fantasy, as news, does its work. The news, in this case, is not some "fake" or constructed reality, which would entail a kind of false consciousness. The news is a social truth, the effectiveness of which depends upon consumer investment. The elements of journalistic reality—ruthless insurgents and innocent civilians, quotable experts and broken soldiers, a journalist bearing witness to ruin—particularize the fantasy structure of war reportage and articulate a reigning understanding of war.

Instead of simply interpreting the fantasy that guides journalists' productions, then—instead of deciphering the ideology of the reality that the news produces, of war's reality as glory or hell or trauma, as siege or liberation, as civil war or counterinsurgency—we can recognize what Mladen Dolar calls the "profound consistency" and "total contingency" of fantasy as a structure attempting to cover a void (1998, xii).[20] Journalists living and working in war confront a void in journalism that war never ceases to open up. The fantasy that *is* news covers this void, suturing the absences rent by ambiguity, intimacy, incompletion, classificatory transgression. Consistent and contingent both, the news does its work. Ethnography allows us to follow journalists as they encounter a void and attempt to fill it, marshaling their semiotic and institutional resources as the pressures of representational authority weigh down. Glory, hell, trauma; "Iraq at a crossroads" and "Syria on the edge": There is a void in what can be known of war, and the fetish, as object of belief, fills this void.

The news is that fetish. The news satisfies a desire for the coherence of war even as what counts as coherence shifts, and even as the incoherence of war may be inherent to the practice of news production. The news performs expected closure even as indeterminacy directs the performance. The fantasy structure can thereby persist irrespective of the precise content of the fantasy, and regardless of the fragility of that content for those producing the fantasy. And so the phantasmic quality of journalism as commodity disguises its irreparable lack, and the producers of the commodity live within that lack while they live within war. Journalism is laid bare as a practice primed to fulfill a social role, while the repressions attendant to that practice return in journalists' dreams, in their anxieties, in stories told at the bar.[21] A fantasy of war, premised on consumer belief in a presupposed knowledge, is thereby maintained. And as particular beliefs are reproduced, a status quo retains its power.[22]

We might, in this case, follow Paul Rabinow's (1996) injunction to exoticize our conceptions of reality, enabling journalism's self-evidence to reveal its contrived and contingent nature. The defamiliarization of fantasy—what Lacan would call an "estrangement effect" (Dolar 1998, xii)—allows us to see the news as a stable form with fragile contents responding to and reproducing social desire. Such an estrangement is provided by what journalism represses. What could be called journalism's *marginalia*—dreams, fears, confusions—permit us to see the news enacting a "foreign correspondence" between war and expectations of war, between an ambiguous experience and a yearning for fixed and reliable meaning. Journalism lets one become the other, even as journalists struggle with what this process disavows. An emphasis on casualty counts and professional distance, on definitive classifications and bearing witness to suffering: These narrative mechanisms do the fantastic work while journalists live the limits of these mechanisms. By estranging fantasy through an examination of what it hides, we spy a social order exerting itself. Ethnographic interpretation of journalists' experiences of war, and psychoanalytic diagnosis of the repressions that result, allow fantasy *as* fantasy to be grasped.

But fantasy does not simply procure a phantasmic object to satisfy desire, as where the traumatized victim or the Islamic extremist is procured by journalism to satisfy news-consumer desire. Rather, the fantasy of war enables news consumers to assume *any desire at all*. There is, then, a circulatory form to the fantasy that journalism is. War as glory or war as trauma, war as liberation or war as extermination: Journalism attempts to fill the void that *it itself* evinces; it phantasmatically satisfies a desire for war's reality that *it itself* perpetuates. And for journalists, who experience the journalistically insensible and must apply the discipline of sense, the abjections of war agitate at the margins of what news consumers expect.

Dreamwork

Some weeks after his encounter at the mosque, Max had a dream. He is standing backstage at a theater, set to perform for a large crowd. It is late, and the audience is waiting. Max desperately situates his jacket and tie, attempting to cover for his exhaustion and lack of preparation for the event ahead. Hastily combing his hair, Max realizes the audience won't be convinced of his performance. Now Max is meeting with his editor, who explains that Max's recent story on the battle for Mosul is incoherent and not befitting a journalist. Now Max is trying to move his possessions into a room too small to fit them. There are strangers in the room, reading his reportage.

News consumers await the reality of war, but will they be satisfied with the war that journalism delivers? Are journalists prepared to perform the fantasy expected? For the excess of war, as lived by journalists in war zones, clashes with the coherence demanded by the societies within which much war reportage circulates. As I have argued here, the professional negotiation of this tension remains fraught. The possessions of journalists—the nightmares recurrent, the experiences uncategorized, the encounters called traumatic—cannot quite fit into the space of the news, even as such possessions constitute news making in wartime. But if the news is a room too small, the foundations of this room are expansive indeed, buttressed on official—though unseen—ground. Repressed impurity and proffered fantasy: These elements, in their tension, structure the practice of war reportage.

Considering the news as fantasy provides clues to the strange efficacy of journalism as a truth-providing, reality-delivering enterprise. For here, in fantasy, is a key to understanding the status of journalists as subjects beholden to practices shaped by desire, where journalistic practice and desired text form a relationship whose structure can be elaborated. In fantasy we encounter the secrets of those narratives shaping knowledge of war—the secrets of disavowal and control—and which are revealed through what fantasy expels. For behind today's journalistic truth is a phantasmic seed that effectuates it, and which discloses an economy of desire that makes it function. Behind every news commodity is a journalist's labor, redolent of the journalistically insensible, yet displaced by the objective presence of the reality delivered. The next chapter seeks to recover the insensibility hidden within the practices of wartime journalism—in the notes scribbled, the tropes deployed, the ideals enacted.

A journalist at a dusty checkpoint near Raqqa explained, "My experience is that war is strange. Reality doesn't make sense anymore. It's nonsensical." Then she went back to work.

SIX

Agitation at the Margins

Return of the Journalistically Repressed

So there's a fog of war, Brian, and also the fog in covering war.
—TOM BROKAW, ON BRIAN WILLIAMS'S DISPROVEN
STORY OF AN ATTACK IN IRAQ

Repression and Representation

"There's a structural desire on the part of journalists to find explanations when things don't make sense. Journalism must create sense for the insensible." This is what a journalist explained to me on the road to Damascus.

Journalism's formal commitment is to a sensible reality for war. Yet an insensibility ever lurks for war reporters, reappearing (as the previous chapter showed) in dreams, in humor, in impulsive behavior. This insensibility can emerge in substance abuse, in anger, in addiction to the frontline. And it can surface in the practice of war reportage itself, amidst the processes of selecting a story, interviewing sources, writing up the facts. This chapter tracks these returns of the journalistically insensible in order to demonstrate both the alienations of journalistic labor and the lurking presence of what challenges journalistic convention. Here I read against the grain of the news for that which news of war denies. I am reading, that is, for the residue of those ambiguities, uncertainties, and absurdities of war saturating the practice of news production yet normatively excised from the news text. In glimpsing this excess, we glimpse the fragility of an attempt—central to war reportage—to control what war *is*. In journalists' interviews, in their efforts to bear witness, in their attempt to describe what may challenge representation itself, the manifest content of the news reveals what so often remains latent. These practices of news making thereby disclose both the distance and the intimacy between the experience of war and the expressions produced therefrom. The practice of war reportage may demand the repression of certain dynamics of war, but the repressed can yet return in wartime news.

"If the world is not a jumble of random and chaotic events," insist Stuart Hall and coauthors (1978, 54),

> then they must be identified (i.e. named, defined, related to other events known to the audience), and assigned a social context (i.e. placed within a frame of meanings familiar to the audience). . . . This process—identification and contextualization—is one of the most important through which events are "made to mean" by the media.

But what happens when journalists must identify—name, define, and relate—what destabilizes journalistic identification, what outstrips journalism's expected categories and familiar contexts? What can journalists produce when the world indeed becomes "a jumble of random and chaotic events," events to which the journalist applies professionally mandated meanings ultimately unsuited to the world journalists experience? Where does an excess to war reportage bleed into the commodity of war news?

Sourcing the Insensible

One emergence of the journalistically insensible can be glimpsed amid a primary practice of war reportage, a practice designed to create legibility and sense. Interviewing is a central means by which journalists gather information about war, and talking with politicians, aid workers, combatants, diplomats, and average people exposed to conditions of conflict is a near-daily routine of wartime journalism. Interviews are sometimes conducted by phone (particularly when an in-person meeting is prevented for reasons of safety, politics, or logistics), but most of the interviewing I observed took place in offices, homes, cafés, or on the street. Sometimes interviews were arranged in advance, often in the case of a specific individual or category of professional (a doctor, a human rights lawyer) whose perspective on an event is key to a given story. But I also observed interviews conducted spontaneously in refugee camps or near sites of combat that aimed to personalize the events being covered (displacement, injury, combat). Often, journalists would speak among themselves about "good characters" in the war—morticians and barbers and soldiers who were especially evocative in their description of events or poignant in their answers to journalists' questions. Such "characters" were prized for the "color" they could add to a story.

While the subject and circumstances of an interview were specific in each instance, interviewing itself, in the case of the journalism I observed, entailed a set of procedures and experiences that varied little. In the case of politicians or other powerful individuals in Lebanon, Iraq, and Syria, journalists underwent various security screenings upon arrival at the interview; they offered copious greetings to the assembled assistants and hangers-on; they received tiny bottles of water or tiny cans of Pepsi. Amongst shimmering, over-stuffed furniture and expansive desks, the questions and answers commenced. In more modest abodes, from family living rooms to UNCHR tents, journalists distributed greetings just as generously; the hosts might retrieve thin mats for assembly on the floor; available refreshments were offered insistently; neighbors and neighbors' kids would arrive to observe the proceedings. In interviews conducted on the street or near scenes of conflict, a safer and quieter corner would be found for a quicker exchange. In each instance, journalists placed their hand-held recorders on a table or a knee, notebooks were opened, and pens were poised. Often these interviews relied on a translator traveling with the journalist, adding another layer to the dance of interlocution.

Charles Briggs (2002; 2007a) demonstrates how interviewing is informed by regulated processes of discourse production, and journalists' question-and-answer format, as I observed it, does tend to reproduce those meanings already normative to news of the events addressed in the interview. An opposition politician provides an oppositional political perspective; a refugee provides the despondency of displacement. Interviews in this way furnish the intelligibility for war already demanded by the discourse of war reportage. By offering articulate subjects, experiential knowledge, and professional expertise, interviews make news texts seem "like direct embodiments of the encounter between interview and interviewee" while hiding the power and the politics that always undergird and propel the interview process (Briggs 2007a, 554). Interviews shape the events of a war in ways acceptable to the discourse of war reportage.

Yet here too is a practice of war reportage that registers an outside to the borders it attempts to police. Here too we find that which both exceeds and precipitates discursive capture. In producing only meanings suitable to the news discourse, the practice of interviewing allows us to discern what is elided in this process of production. An insensible remainder—attendant to the practice of interviewing but mystified by the sense that interviewing is designed to make—is yet available for observation and analysis. While the text produced through interviewing is imbricated in a dominant consensus about war's reality—a consensus underpinning war reportage broadly—the practice of interviewing results in effects that challenge journalism's discursive norms.

In the process of journalistic interviewing, note-taking is standard. In addition to the answers given to questions asked, journalists might record the age or profession of the subject interviewed, and they might jot down some details about the scene or context of the interview. Journalists sometimes allowed me to peruse their old notepads, and I was struck by the errant inscriptions many journalists left behind. Aside duly transcribed interview answers, free-form reactions often percolated across the notepad page. In clumsy sketches and scribbled addendums, the notepads revealed anguished faces, dark quips, unspoken accusations. "How could he do this?" a notepad in Kobani contained, beside a crude face wearing a merciless frown. "Survive" was written, sidelong, in a notepad I inspected in Beirut. More than once, I spotted a dark knot of scribbles in the center of an otherwise blank page. A journalist at a checkpoint outside Mosul, after hearing about my interest in notepads, offered me hers. I saw this scrawl: "I'm scared."

Notepads also contain the jarring juxtaposition of the momentous and the mundane. Beside interviews and notes on the wartime suffering that is the primary focus of contemporary war reportage, notepads carry shopping lists, expense tallies, to-do reminders. At the American University of Beirut, I was invited to view the papers of the journalist Anthony Shadid, who covered conflict in the Middle East for several US news organizations, and who died on assignment in Syria in 2012. The archive contained a few old notepads. Beside an interview containing weighty ruminations on sacrifice and justice, there is a grocery list: "eggs, rice." One page contained something illegible on yogurt; the next, "Left hand two fingers blown off."

The professional routine of interviewing exposes an excess to journalism. The notepads reveal both the banality and the insensibility inherent to the life of war reporting but erased from the commodity of war reportage. Journalists' notepads contain—in the most literal way—the margins of journalism: those reactions and emotions and meanings marginalized by the practice of producing proper news. Here we find a surplus stewing at the edges of what journalism formally speaks and sanctions. It is the practice of interviewing itself—a practice foundational to the coverage of conflict—that expresses this excess. On the notepad page can be glimpsed the residue of journalism's unconscious, the displaced that is never quite disappeared. The notepad, in psychoanalytic fashion, displays the structure of displacement and condensation: that which is repressed in journalism, and where, precisely, the repressed returns.

In tarrying with what may trouble journalism's discursive mandate, the interview can also provide journalists a particular resource. For interviews allow journalists an opportunity to signal what normatively exceeds the meanings journalism makes. The voices of those experiencing violence can express that which the news must otherwise dismiss, and this expression thereby gestures beyond journalism's generic limit.

A *New York Times* story about the war in Syria includes a question asked by the disembodied, objective journalist and answered by a source on the ground: "Was there a military purpose? 'Absolutely not,' he said. 'The war has no meaning anymore'" (Barnard 2016).

Meaninglessness, generically speaking, is anathema to journalism, which insists on making meaning in accordance with societal expectations for war's reality. While a lack of acceptable meaning may be frequently experienced by journalists and others in the war zone, the disavowal of this lack is necessary for the professional claim to representational authority.[1] But by appearing to simply reproduce voices experiencing violence—rather than selecting, curating, and staging those voices—journalists can smuggle into their journalism that which exceeds journalism, even as they retain the distanced professionalism of an objective, rational reporter. Journalists can thereby suggest war's discursive challenge to journalism while relegating this challenge to the experiences of the nonprofessional, the traumatized, the victim. Authority over violence is narratively maintained even as violence can be shown to trouble narrative authority.

Another story on the war in Syria appearing in the *New York Times* includes a similar discursive transgression (Barnard and Saad 2016):

Malek, an activist who said he hoped to join his pregnant wife in northern Aleppo Province, and who asked to be identified only by his first name for fear of being killed, said that "the scenes are unbearable." He added: "I would say that life is becoming harder than death. People are dying for nothing, without any justification. Humans are no longer human."

Can the journalistic narrative deliver humans who are no longer human? Otherwise put, is the "nonhuman-human" an acceptable figure within a discourse premised upon categorical purity? Journalism typically denies such typological perversion in the pursuit of definitional certainty; victims are other than perpetrators, death is everywhere distinct from life. Yet such perversion is common to conditions of violence and familiar to many war reporters. By presenting the categorical impurities of war through the expressions of sources on the ground—characteristically *not* journalists—the transgressive dimensions of war become admissible even as the professionalism of journalists, and the narrative realism of journalism, are sustained. Interview quotes both domesticate the insensible of war and preserve some suggestion of its otherness.

Interviewing, Briggs argues, deploys discourse "highly adapted to producing the precise types of information that will be recontextualized in the books, articles, reports, media productions, and the like that are envisioned as the final product." Interviews "provide the nation-state and its institutions with representations . . . that confirms the hegemonic status quo" (2002, 911). Interviews very often reproduce the status quo demanded by a prevailing consensus regarding the meaning of faraway war. In the practice of interviewing, the information received is circumscribed by the questions asked, the power relations attendant, and the meanings expected.[2] Yet maintenance of journalistic authority—and of the authority of the meanings for war that journalism makes—entails strategies for coping with discursive challenge. Quoting from interviews is one such strategy.

A very common discursive challenge, in the context of conflict in the Middle East, concerns the category transgression presented by martyrdom. Martyrdom troubles the boundary between victim and perpetrator, insofar as the suicide bomber (the prototypical martyr in the context of Middle East war reportage) becomes a victim of their own perpetration. Martyrs propel themselves into lives beyond deaths, transgressing a boundary basic to journalism, while calling into question both the supreme value of biological survival and the supreme negativity of biological death—dynamics foundational to the humanitarian culture of war reportage (addressed in Chapter 4). Suicide bombers are both human bodies and offensive weapons—they are what Banu Bargu (2014) calls "human weapons"—and in this manner too they scramble the categories essential to both war reportage and humanitarianism. Martyrdom thus marks a discursive frontier for journalism, and it demands a sense other than that conventional to the news. By exposing the limits of journalistic typologies, martyrdom suggests how war and violence can escape such typological capture. But because of its commonness as figure, idea, and event, war reportage in the Middle East is forced to reckon with martyrdom even as it finds ways to avoid engaging with the discursive danger martyrdom can pose.

A search for the word "martyr" in the *New York Times*, the *Washington Post*, and the *Wall Street Journal* between 2014 and 2018 offers some revealing trends. Martyrdom appears almost as frequently in reportage on domestic US events as it does in reportage on war in the Middle East.[3] In US domestic reportage, "martyr" assumes the meaning of a sacrificial hero (former Senator Al Franken is a "martyr" for the #metoo movement, for example). This sacrifice is never absolute; no death is associated with martyrdom in this common journalistic deployment, and thus the life/death category error presented by martyrdom is abstracted.

When martyrdom does appear in the context of war, it appears most often through the expressions of interviewed sources.

> "I'm not afraid, because this is jihad," he explained. "When I die, I will be a martyr." (Morris 2014)

> "Now it is a matter of faith," said Abu Noor Al Jaberi, a commander with Kattaeb Sayed Al Shuhada, a large militia involved in Tikrit's liberation. "Do your job to the best of your ability and if you die you are a martyr. You go to paradise." (El-Ghobashy and Abi-Habib 2015)

> "Our youth was a special martyr," the chanter said of Mr. Moshajjari, whose portrait on a stage showed him in a forest wearing a pair of shooting glasses and a jungle vest. (Erdbrink 2014)

Quotations from interviewed sources allow martyrdom to appear in news text without disrupting the meanings, categories, and definitions normative to news of war.[4] As an idea, experience, or event that exceeds journalistic discourse—as something disruptive to the very basis of that discourse—martyrdom can surface in quotation while the potency of its transgressions are hidden away. In these instances of its textual appearance, martyrdom becomes either a general gloss for sacrifice or an exotic cultural expression, while its meaning for those expressing or experiencing martyrdom is obscured. Martyrdom is suggested but never quite grappled with, and thus its disruptive characteristics are left to fester at the edges of journalistic representation.[5]

When encountering the journalistically insensible, the journalist confronts a narrative problem: whether to domesticate this insensibility—transforming it to suit discursive norms—or whether to simply present what cannot assume a normative journalistic sense. In a comparative history of journalism, Géraldine Muhlmann puts the problem this way: "Should [journalists] try to show a radical otherness, at the risk that it will no longer have any meaning for their readers, and that readers will, ultimately, be little affected . . . ? Or should they, on the contrary, resign themselves to taming the otherness so as to make it have an effect?" (2008, 31). The activity of interviewing, and the routines of its narrative deployment, allows journalism to have it both ways. Those dynamics of war that threaten journalistic discourse can be suitably narrated through the quotations of others, while the potency of the discursive threat is erased. The practice of interviewing provides one strategy for coping with the excesses of war experienced by war reporters but denied by war reportage.

The Practice of Proximity

A half dozen journalists are gathered around a plastic table in a tiled kitchen in Erbil, in a cinderblock house a short walk from the Classy Hotel. The residents in the house tend to rotate—a newspaper photographer leaves for Raqqa; a wire reporter moves in—but a staff photographer and two freelance journalists are steady tenants. The photographer keeps close attention to a small lawn; it remains lush in defiance of Iraqi summer.

The journalists are discussing the logistics of access to the frontline, a steady and critical topic of conversation. Some are planning a trip to west Mosul in the morning, a week before the military offensive there will officially end. That day a Kurdish fixer was killed in Mosul's old city, and two French journalists injured, when they set off an IED while dodging Islamic State sniper fire. The French journalists will later die from their wounds. The journalists around the table reason these casualties a mistake: a scramble down an alleyway that hadn't been properly checked for explosives. One of the journalists insists that it is not frontline proximity that is to blame here, but inattention to surroundings amidst the confusions of combat. The other journalists nod without commitment. A pause descends, and the conversation has nowhere to go; it seems crass to press the issue, or just bad luck. A freelancer breaks the silence. "So should we rent a car or get a ride with an Iraqi division?"

One of the journalists in the room will not join the trip. Later, the kitchen empty, she explains her decision. "Most of the work that's produced from the frontline—mine too—is the same. It's exciting but rarely thoughtful, mostly just fast and disposable news. Proximity is not what's needed. The literal approach of 'being there and seeing it' can be an ideological folly." Through the kitchen window I see a flak jacket slumped in the grass. She continues:

> What you get, when you go on reporting trips to Mosul, is confusion. Where is this convoy going? Where is the frontline? Can we trust these guys we're talking to or traveling with? What was that *bang*? What we don't know is everywhere, and getting a story out of *that* is a miracle every time.

Proximity to war is perhaps the essential practice of war reportage, a practice institutionally glossed as "access." Access can refer to the direct encounter with any journalistically important object: governmental and corporate personnel, courtrooms and crime scenes, transcripts and documents. For war reportage, however, war is the fundamental object of access. War is a location from which to observe, an event to encounter, and a source for information. And more: Proximity to war functions for war reporters as proof of authenticity, as a symbolics of truth. In a primer on war reportage, journalist James Rodgers writes, "Access is the starting point of all coverage of conflict. It enables the journalist to watch, to listen, to ask the questions that yield the information needed to tell a story" (2012, 28). Yet the relationship between access and information is not as straightforward as this description suggests.

I leave aside here the politics of access in wartime, most pronounced in the practice of embedding, wherein journalists report from within a military unit. This issue—and the self-censorship, military control, psychological dependencies, and critical myopia that can result—has been given much scholarly attention (e.g., Carruthers 2011; Robinson et al. 2010; Schechter 2003; Tumber and Palmer 2004; Tumber and Webster 2006), and its dynamics need not be rehashed here. I am interested, rather, in how proximity to war registers a confrontation between experience and text, and how that confrontation is both represented and displaced. In "accessing" war, journalists are encountering what may trouble their realist narrative enterprise, and there the boundaries of journalistic representation come into view. Journalists must find ways of reckoning with this limit.

As the preceding chapter showed, those aspects of war disruptive to normative news narratives are often effaced, reappearing in dreams, for example, or in stories told at the bar. But journalists can also attend to the tension between the experience of war and its expression through a language suitable to journalism's generic conventions that yet suggests what exceeds journalism's discursive constraints. The use of particular tropes is one way that journalists mark war's journalistic illegibility from within the eminently legible news text. Here the ambiguities, confusions, and irrealities confronted in the practice of war reportage can be translated into the certainties, facts, and truths of journalism. The "blank stare" is one such trope.

> I walked across the fields Saturday morning, climbing through barbed wire and passing over a steep embankment, to find myself face to face with a German cavalryman who had been shot through the head, his eyes fixed in a blank stare. (*New York Times*, dateline: Carentan, France [Gorrell 1944])

> A bone-thin infant lay next to the body of her mother, her eyes frozen in the blank stare of death. (*Washington Post*, dateline: Congo Town, Liberia [James 1990])

> These acts of destruction had taken place long before I had arrived—some minor form of cleansing, perhaps, that had occurred at the beginning of the war. What I was seeing was a kind of uniform joylessness. The blank stare. (*Ottawa Citizen*, dateline: Zagreb, Croatia [Itani 1994])

> There was just one rusted window, with two wires protruding through it. Hamed held them to his neck and shuddered. They were used to electrocute prisoners, he said. His eyes showed no anger, just a sad, blank stare. (*Independent*, dateline: Basra, Iraq [Edwards 2003])

> Most of the time, though, Haitians I meet have been stone-faced as they recount their harrowing stories, displaying the same blank stare I have witnessed on faces in other parts of the world where struggling never stops. (*New York Times*, dateline: Port-au-Prince, Haiti [Lacey 2010])

> With a blank stare, he replied coldly, "Regarding your soldiers' death toll, when they travel that far to fight a war they are definitely not going to be presented with flowers and there will be deaths for sure." (*Mirror*, dateline: Peshawar, Afghanistan [Hughes 2013])

> For the men at the front, the strain is visible: in the dead-tired eyes of a police chief after another day leading his men in a bombarded city; in the blank stare of a commander who had just lost one of his best soldiers. (*New York Times,* dateline: Dnipro, Ukraine [Gall 2022])

These are selected appearances of a language that functions as an opening to what exceeds journalistic capture. That the journalistic deployment of the "blank stare" is so often coincident with violence suggests the limits of certainty, facticity, realism, and related conventions and ideals in the context of war's narration, specifically. The "blank stare"—a trope habitually used in the published news of the journalists I interviewed and observed—is an example of a language engaged at the frontier of journalistic representation.[6]

In its image of absence, of a negative space, the blank stare indicates a lack of what can be realistically or factually reported. The blank stare marks, narratively, the horizon of meaning under conditions of violence. To search for the meaning of the blank stare would be to attempt a symbolic interpretation that presupposes a truth to be excavated beneath the surface; journalism could then discover and dispel a symbolism clouding the truth and narrate that truth directly. But the blank stare is *all* surface, its "blankness" an evacuation that denies this hermeneutic conversion. If there is symbolism to the blank stare, it is in some way undispellable: There is nothing to verify behind the sign, no underlying truth to report. Tropes like the blank stare articulate a breach in the interpretive authority of journalism and the failure of its promise to archive an intrinsically intelligible event. Such tropes provide an opening to the indeterminacy often experienced by journalists in war, an opening to that nonmeaningful remainder—attendant to the practice of proximity—that cannot be properly defined or categorized within journalism's realist narrative frame. The blank stare suggests the persistence of what journalists encounter but which journalism must disavow.[7]

Eric Santner points to this potentiality when he notes how "the tropological resources of language" can be used to "heal wounds that language never ceases to open up." He continues: "Poetics . . . is presented as a concern with language to the extent that it is radically, even violently, cut off from its semantic rootedness" (1990, 14). The rootedness of journalistic language in its denotational and hermeneutic functions, and the loss of a stable referent that is the severing of these roots—a loss common to encounters with violence—impels the turn to poetic language as a means to evoke what is otherwise journalistically unaccountable.

The loss of a stable referent, and the poetic resources available under such conditions, is assessed too in Paul de Man's reading of Rilke, wherein the "absence of a reliable referent . . . designates the impossibility for the language of poetry to appropriate anything, be it as consciousness, as object, or as a synthesis of both" (1979, 47). The loss of a reliable referent is a circumstance that realist representation cannot endure, and here war reportage, bounded by realist intent, meets its limit. For war can disrupt the referential reliability upon which journalism, as realist narrative, depends: a death, as for the martyr, that does not end life; a guilty victim or an innocent perpetrator; a body that is not a body. As J. L. Austin asserts, "Reference is necessary for either truth or falsehood" (1962, 50), and journalism's production of truth thereby depends upon a reckoning with the referential instability of war. Here a poetic language becomes strategic. The violence encountered in the practice of war reportage can disrupt narrative stability even as the war reporter must narrate violence's truth, and the blank stare—a poetic language—expresses this irreconcilability. The trope manages a tension between wartime experience and news text, revealing a discursive threat often hidden beneath journalism's realist control.

The very image of an absent referent, the blank stare suggests the failures of journalistic narrative to cope with the discursive depletions of war and the journalistically ineffable dimensions of violence encountered. Such failure, for Santner, is why "the speaking subject is perpetually in mourning: for the referent . . . for meaning . . . for stable terms of orientation, because these losses are always already there as soon as one uses language" (1990, 15). A loss of stable orientation may well be inevitable to language, but the inability of journalism to discursively control violence—to produce its final meaning, to explain its certain truth—is particularly disorienting for journalists who live with war while attempting narrative mastery. Journalism appropriates, designates, classifies; it makes meaning while disguising its function as meaning maker. These journalistic operations, however, presume a stability undermined by journalists' wartime experience. The turn to poetic language, as Santner and de Man show, indicates a sloughing off of appropriation and an acceptance of the unknowable and nonmeaningful, of that which realism cannot represent nor language fully discipline. As trope, the blank stare is a narrative resource for gesturing to what the practice of war reportage confronts: the exhaustion of events to be categorized, Others to be defined, referents to be ascertained, truths to be known.[8]

In a newsroom in Beirut, I met with a journalist who'd recently returned from the war in Syria. A mentor to many regional journalists after a forty-year career for an American newspaper, she possesses deep institutional knowledge and dark, languid eyes. She seemed exhausted by the trip to Syria but also satisfied with the journalism she'd been able to produce. I asked her about violence and the challenges of its representation.

"What's more violent," she replied,

> an explosion or its aftermath? We were in Homs after the government airstrikes, and it was terrible—worse, perhaps, than during them. What's more scary, more impacting, is not the explosion but the aftermath, the blank stare of those who've just lost their entire family. The trauma that you have to absorb in order to represent it. That's how I work. It makes my work good, but it takes a heavy toll.

The practice of war reportage, this journalist explains, necessitates the "absorption of trauma" in order to represent what may otherwise challenge representation. This challenge—the "impact" of war—is glossed by the journalist as the "blank stares" of those who've experienced tremendous loss in wartime. The blank stare is used to suggest the trauma whose experience by the journalist allows for "good" journalism; it suggests the journalistically unrepresentable hidden within—and yet precipitating—the news text. The blank stare seems to cover a gap between the journalistically representable and that which threatens this narrative enterprise.

Julia Kristeva, in her analysis of abjection, addresses such a circumstance: "The writer, fascinated by the abject, imagines its logic, projects himself into it, introjects it, and as a consequence perverts language. . . . With such literature there takes place a crossing over of the dichotomous categories of Pure and Impure, Prohibition and Sin, Morality and Immorality." Kristeva shows how a writing "implicated in the interspace that characterizes perversion . . . implies an ability to imagine the abject, that is, to see oneself in its place and to thrust it aside only by means of the displacements of verbal play" (1982, 16). The explosion can be written up as an event in the news, but the absoluteness of its violence—the full impact experienced—can distress journalistic representation. What is needed, amid this confrontation with violence, is a narrative resource able to transgress conventional narrative bounds, a writing able to "displace" and "pervert" a more normative language.

Mass graves, interrogation centers, ammunition, policy papers, chemical agents, discarded belongings, targeted assassinations, smuggled oil, price-gouged bread, bloodstains, weapons manuals, unpotable water, the ruin of a family home: All the categorizable material of war, subject to definition and explanation, and thus to the facticity and accuracy of the journalistic account, is unable to add up to violence itself. What is required, then, for the journalist who "absorbs trauma in order to represent it," is indeed a perversion of that language that attempts to cover the hole in knowability. The journalist, fascinated by the abjection confronted while reporting war, can deploy a poetic language transgressive of conventional generic dynamics, and in this way signal the collapse of meaning otherwise displaced in the news. The blank stare indicates what of war can be "accessed" by journalists but never discursively controlled.[9]

Even Barack Obama, addressing insurgent violence in his memoir, employs this tropological strategy: "It's impossible to penetrate the blank stares of those who would murder innocents with abstract, serene satisfaction" (2004, x). The penetration—of human necks by Islamic State knives, of insurgent bunkers by American missiles—is the bloody lead for the journalist, the content of the news they produce. But the blank stare, an unreadable sign, cannot be so penetrated. The blank stare thwarts this kind of appropriation, becoming "the point of departure of scription as the laying bare of meaning" (Kristeva 1982, 154). The limits of meaning making—a central concern of journalism as discourse, as "scription"—are revealed and indeed overcome by the blankness of the wartime stare. The nonmeaningful excess of war, experienced by journalists as practice yet repressed in journalism as text, returns tropologically with the blank stare, expressing both the tension inherent to war reportage and that tension's generativity.

The Voices Given

What of the trauma that the journalist above attempts to "absorb in order to represent" war? As discussed in the preceding chapter, trauma is widely understood as inherent to the experiences routine in war reporting— "trauma is inevitable in war," a journalist in Erbil told me—even as trauma can thwart journalism's discursive command. The acceptance of trauma as a dynamic of war reportage is clear from the attention recently given in the news industry. Illustrative of the "culture of trauma" tracked by Didier Fassin and Richard Rechtman (2009), a profusion of workshops and retreats are now available to journalists experiencing trauma, and numerous centers and institutes (such as the Dart Center for Journalism and Trauma at Columbia University's Graduate School of Journalism) are devoted to the matter. Scholarship on journalistic trauma has grown apace (e.g., Buchanan and Keats 2011; Dwoeznik 2007; Rentschler 2009). "There's a pathologization of trauma," a journalist in Beirut explained, "where war correspondence is seen as qualitatively different from other reporting." A journalist in Erbil told me, of Mosul, "It's hard to imagine a society that's so traumatized. It's hard to convey that. So I just tell stories." The acknowledgment of trauma as a clinical condition and a professional identity suggests that the culture of war reportage embraces trauma even as its appearance in the news text can pose discursive difficulties.

In the relevant theoretical scholarship, trauma troubles narration; it conflicts with the ability to properly document, and thus come to terms with, the event that caused subject trauma. Mimetic reflection becomes impossible as realist representation falters against the traumatic break (Rothberg 2000). In the culture of trauma now prevalent, however, narration is also a therapy for trauma (Das 2006; Das and Kleinman 2001; Hacking 1995; Herman 1992; Kafer 2016). Epigenetics—the cutting edge of trauma studies—asserts the right of self-narration as central to self-healing, wherein "narrating a traumatic memory can help to defuse it" (Brison 2002, 71). Trauma may disable narration, then, but a cure for trauma is found in having one's story told, and in becoming capable of telling it. "Giving voice to the voiceless"—a well-worn journalistic ideal in coverage of war and other hardships—can be understood in this therapeutic register, as a journalistic practice primed to evoke, and thereby begin to heal, the trauma that cannot be otherwise expressed. "Voicelessness" becomes "voice" through the care of journalists and the attention of journalism to the extremity of the experience of violence. A journalist in Baghdad suggested as much: "Giving voice to war actors is what we should all be doing, of course."

"I often feel bad about asking for stories," a journalist remarked in Erbil, adding:

Some people are happy to talk, though. It's catharsis. But particularly the pieces with lots of journalists there, like vultures, and people will ask, "What am I going to get out of this?" I can give you a voice. If there are no journalists there, the Iraqi Army would flatten Mosul. The mere presence of journalists changes things. I'm not sure about the relationship between stories and humanitarian assistance, but if journalists didn't make a fuss, would people be so likely to attend to it?

Telling one's story to a journalist, then, is either a form of emotional catharsis or a strategy for material assistance, and in either case, "giving voice" to those experiencing war becomes an exercise of care. A journalist in Beirut explained, "You can humanize, give people a voice, in order to understand them. This is journalists' work: Give them a voice in order to understand what the danger is and maybe confront it." Giving voice operates under the sign of humane concern.

The ability to give voice presupposes the power of war reportage to grant voice as it sees fit and to translate that voice through the narrative idioms and designs of the news. The dialogic dynamic of "voice giving" in war reportage—in which subjects in war are encountered by journalists, with their stories then negotiated among parties—is erased in the apparently transparent delivery of the Other's expression. Any misunderstandings, mistranslations, and mystifications embedded in this transaction disappear. A more expansive issue concerns the way that giving voice symptomizes certain emphases in war reportage at the expense of others. If the ability to tell a story of violence amounts to concern for traumatic experience, a notion also prevalent in humanitarian discourse (Dawes 2007), we must consider how proximity to war and the narration of war's experience invites catharsis at the expense of analysis. The truth at stake in capturing subject trauma in war—realized practically through proximity and narratively though giving voice—is the truth of emotional experience rather than critical inquiry. In the "combat trauma imaginary" (Abu El-Haj 2022, 2), pathologizing the experience of war can amount to a depoliticization of war as the language of care replaces the language of politics. Journalism's representational focus demonstrates a certain moral sentiment, wherein war reportage becomes a practice and form concerned with war's emotional toll rather than its political conditions.

"The Israel-Palestine conflict, it's an important problem to solve," a journalist in New York, who was formerly based in the Middle East, explained to me. "No matter the level of suffering, it won't end softly. And I'm not sure what the coverage will do to help. But it can give voice." "Scenes of suffering can be exploited by journalism for sensationalism," a journalist in Baghdad remarked. "But there are areas where we're allowed a little leeway for advocacy. We can't advocate for a side [in a conflict], but refugees get a little space. Voice for the voiceless—this slogan produces some of the best journalism." Journalistic attention to war's suffering, then, realized through the practice of giving voice, may say less about the events encountered and their specific dynamics than it does about the cultural currency of war reportage and the imposition of this culture in war zones. That is, giving voice in war reportage, as a practical instantiation of journalism's concern for war's effects, both exposes and conceals. The traumatized Other, silenced by war, may be encountered by a journalist accessing scenes of conflict; her voice may be "given" through journalism as the trauma of war is narrated. But the rhetorical *topoi* managing this presentation are hidden away, as are the cultural concerns they institute.

I want to suggest, in this case, that the *practice* of giving voice exposes that which journalism attempts to elide: the cultural particularity of journalism. The effort to "give voice to the voiceless" undermines the self-evidence of journalistic representation and the accuracy, transparency, and factuality it claims. While trauma may challenge narration, the *intention* to represent trauma already positions journalism as a discourse for documenting war's subjectivation rather than war's political, historical, or economic dynamics. Journalistic emphasis on war's morality over and above its political context was discussed in Chapter 3. Here, I mean to specify the practice of war reportage as the collection of war's traumatic stories and, thereby, as the display of care for war's trauma, rather than as the transmission of what these stories may contain. For while the stories told to journalists in war zones may transgress journalistic conventions in their nonlinearity, their insensibility, their strangeness (dynamics prevalent in traumatic testimony, as discussed below), and while the stories' message may convey the complexity of war's historical and political dynamics, such content may be less important for war reportage than the activity of story-collection itself. Because the practice of giving voice reflects journalism's concern for war's emotional toll, a concern that supersedes interest in war's political substance. It is the formal commitment to voice-giving, and not the content expressed by the voice, that matters.

Even as journalism can indicate, as through the blank stare, those things that trouble war's journalistic representation, the practice of war reportage—the practice of collecting blank stares—indicates something else. Such a practice indicates the ambiguity of war reportage as a transparent delivery of reality that yet selects what that reality is supposed to be. The indeterminacy between positivism and relativism—constitutive of the war reporting enterprise—is revealed by practices like giving voice, which attempt to transmit the real experience of war while at the same time emphasizing only certain elements of war's experience. The practice of collecting testimony to war's trauma—testimony invoked to be transparent, mimetic, accurate—itself testifies to the culture of war reportage today, a culture invested in the traumatic reality of war. The ambiguity of journalism as a truth-delivering/truth-selecting endeavor saturates war reportage even as it is denied by war reportage, and the practice of voice-giving in this way reveals what journalism attempts to hide.[10]

Of course, many journalists are skeptical of voice-giving as a practice or ideal. "Journalists can trick themselves into believing their own assumptions," a journalist in Beirut told me. "I try to avoid the orientalism of, say, capturing 'the voice of Middle East women.' The danger of implementing your own schemas." Another journalist in Beirut explained,

> Journalism can take agency from the people whose stories we're trying to tell. Whose voices are heard? "Voice for the voiceless"—what's that? It's a problem; the orientation of the power dynamic there. That's what my brown ears hear. It's not meant with malice, but it's invisible.

For these journalists, the discursive impositions of war reportage reflect relations of power.

"When you cover violence, there's a sense of impotence," a journalist in Los Angeles, previously based in the Middle East, remarked. She continued,

> Now a culture of safety is emerging. There's lot of ego and adventurism. Jim Foley wanted to save these people, but he was there for the wrong reason. "Giving voice to the voiceless"—I'm suspicious of this. I don't seek war; I did it because I spoke the language and was in the country. Marie Colvin in Homs gave voice to the voiceless, then she goes back to stand with the people of Homs, and the editors said don't. It's not her job to stand with the people as they fall. She should not have been allowed to cover conflict because of her motivations. She was on a mission, like Foley.

The skepticism of this journalist, and others, registers a discomfort with what giving voice reveals about the selectivity and culture of war reportage. But if giving voice is too imposing a practice of journalistic selection, or too reflective of journalism's cultural particularity, there is another practice better inclined toward the neutrality and objectivity journalists so often want to claim. Here the emphasis shifts from the testimony of the Other (however ventriloquized) to the journalist's own.

Configuring the Witness

Perhaps the most prominent gloss for what journalists *do* in war zones today is witnessing or "bearing witness." Many of the journalists I interviewed spoke of bearing witness to war and violence as a primary goal and professional ideal. A reporter in Beirut put it succinctly: "Witnessing is paramount." A journalist in Baghdad expanded on the sentiment: "There have been instances of journalists holding governments accountable, of articles being cited to enforce sanctions and intervention. Bearing witness is instrumental in this regard." For this journalist, witnessing allows access to the otherwise unknown or unnoticed, a truth that, when witnessed and reported, can spur juridical, political, and even military action. A journalist in Erbil told me, "A lot of what we do is bear witness, and the suffering and inhumanity must be reflected in the reporting." A report from Columbia University's Graduate School of Journalism begins, "Throughout the twentieth century the core proposition of foreign correspondence was to bear witness."[11]

The unreliability of witness testimony is well-attested in psychological, sociological, and criminological scholarship. The capriciousness of memory, the inconsistency of subjective accounts, the influence of confirmation bias, the context of testimony: These and other factors limit the usefulness of bearing witness for a mimetic presentation of past events. In the context of war reportage, bearing witness is of course imbricated in the larger problem of what counts as truth. For Stuart Allan and Barbie Zelizer, "Truth-telling . . . is necessarily embedded in a cultural politics of legitimacy; its authority resting on presence, on the moral duty to bear witness by being there" (2004, 5). Allan and Zelizer emphasize the institutional dynamics of journalistic presence, and the way truth's dependence on "being there" and "witnessing" can be distorted by military, economic, and technological factors. "A journalist's capacity to be present"—and thus to deliver the truth granted by witnessing—"was limited, undermined, or even denied when the battleground was placed off limits, the military barricade went up, the cameras broke down, or sources refused to talk" (Allan and Zelizer 2004, 5). Rather than focus on these institutional constraints to witness-bearing (also discussed in Inglis 2002; Katovsky and Carlson 2003; Seib 2004), I am interested in what bearing witness reveals about the relationship between the practice and text of war reportage. How might the ideal of bearing witness mediate the contradiction between the insensibility of journalists' experiences of war and the necessity of producing journalistic sense?

The gap between historical truth and witness testimony, assessed most extensively in Holocaust historiography, is in many ways analogous to the gap between the journalistic practice of proximity and the meanings rendered in journalistic texts. Martin Jay understands witness testimony as an insufficient guide to the events of the Holocaust since the basis of such testimony remains incongruous with a fact-based historicity of the event as such. This incongruence between factuality and narrativity marks, for Jay, "the opposing temptations of thinking history is mimetic reproduction and thinking it is subjective imposition" (1992, 107). For Christopher Browning (1992), the difficulty of witness testimony with respect to Holocaust historiography is the risk of aestheticization inherent to any and all narrative production. But according to Hayden White, this difficulty is not methodological but representational; it is the "problem" of the story form as such (1999, 81). Whether witness testimony can count as a truthful rendering of a violent reality, or whether the very narrativity of testimony—its particular dynamics of storytelling—forces a reconsideration of what counts as truth: This is the matter at hand for witness-based accounts of the Holocaust as it is for journalism in war zones.

I want to consider witness-bearing not as the transmission of truth—however partial or aestheticizing or "constructed"—but as a figural element of war reportage and thereby see the practice of bearing witness as itself a fulfilment of the promise of journalism to deliver war's truth. Witness-bearing is a legitimation of journalistic truth, in this case, *not* due to the practice of providing facts (facts that are thought to constitute the content of journalistic truth) but due to the *practice* of being a war reporter who bears witness. That is, in being proximate to war, and thereby bearing witness to war, the war reporter enacts—figurally—the authority to tell the truth of war. This authority is unmoored from any specific experiences of war, including those insensible to or transgressive of a fact-based account of war. It is the *form* of witness-bearing that matters, not its content, a content that may be disruptive to the meanings for war that journalism normatively provides. Witnessing allegorizes, rather than contains, truth.[12]

Journalistic witnessing is not, then, a matter of a journalist's experience of war subsequently expressed in war reportage. Rather, this experience, when authorized as witnessing, "is already a figure and, insofar as it will serve as a content or referent of a further representation, it is a prefiguration that is fulfilled only" in the news text (White 1999, 93). Journalism, in this sense, is not the container for the content that is the facts of war witnessed by a journalist. This would necessitate the practice of proximity for the purposes of information, and journalism would be harmed when that practice resulted in information unsuitable—due to the extremity, or ambiguity, or complexity of war—to journalism's factual, distanced, objective narration. Rather, journalism from war zones is the fulfillment of the figure of the journalist as witness-bearer, and thus the insensibility of war as witnessed has little bearing on journalism's ability to provide a suitably sensible account of war. The journalist's experience of war—the bearing witness to violence, suffering, ruin—is allegorized as the truth of war irrespective of whether that experience accords with journalistic standards for truthfulness.

Focusing on the factual instability of witness testimony thus obscures the purpose of bearing witness for war reportage, which is not to deliver the facts of wartime events but to authorize the facts narrated as news. Witness-bearing is the figural element that closes the gap between war as experienced, however insensibly, and the factual, legible realism of war as reported. While journalists may understand witness-bearing as the practice of gathering information, its function as a journalistic ideal is to indicate something beyond itself. More than information gathering, bearing witness is a legitimation of the representational authority of war reportage as such.

It is the figuration of witness-bearing, and not the factuality of what is witnessed, that authorizes the news commodity as a truthful transmission of reality. Here the practice of war reportage becomes less a matter of observing and understanding the events of war than of being amidst violence for its own sake—that is, for the sake of legitimizing journalism's truthfulness regardless of the content (or displacement) of that truth. Whether what is seen or experienced by a journalist is journalistically legible is inconsequential to journalism's formal commitment to seeing and experiencing. Considering the practice of bearing witness as figural allows us, then, to understand how the meanings delivered in news texts can be read as truthful despite the obviousness of journalistic mimesis as a generic conceit and despite the obviousness of facts as selected and fashioned rather than found and given. Bearing witness is the embodiment of a rhetoric of truthfulness, a rhetoric that supersedes the truth or falsity of the correspondence claimed between facts reported and events "on the ground." The fulfillment of consumer expectations for truthfulness—the satisfaction of audience desire for what war is like—is the salient element of journalistic commodification of war, an element realized in bearing witness, regardless of the contradictions that the experience of witness-bearing presents for news making.[13]

With respect to consumer expectation, the figural dynamic of journalistic witnessing exhibits another function. If the focus of contemporary war reportage is the suffering war inflicts, as argued in Chapters 3 and 4, then the witness testimony to that suffering, delivered to news consumers, affords those consumers *too* the position of the witness. In relation to the humanitarian valence ascendant in news of war today, journalists become surrogate witnesses for their audiences, testifying to the suffering those audiences would have witnessed had they been there at the scene of the crime. Because, through the news, they *are* there—figuratively speaking—witnessing war's suffering through their journalist proxy. If witnessing in war reportage is about establishing presence—a presence that also authorizes the facts of war witnessed, primarily facts about suffering—then that presence is marked by the traumatic shock of the encounter with violence. Journalists today are *traumatized* witnesses, insofar as trauma, as discussed in the previous chapter, is the expected response to the experience of war (Fassin and Rechtman 2009). And as news consumers become witnesses to war through journalistic consumption, journalists themselves become victims of the violence they encounter, experiencing trauma on their audiences' behalf. In this figural schema, news audiences are transformed from indifferent bystanders of war's violence to compassionate witnesses to that violence, and journalists become the traumatized victims sacrificed to make war's atrocities known.[14]

These formal dynamics of witnessing abstract the political and historical context in which the witnessing of war takes place. Where social struggles become a matter of individual psychology, where violence is transformed into psychosomatic trauma, there, according to Nicolas Guilhot, "a political understanding of social situations is displaced by an emotional response directed at depoliticized victims" (2012, 84). The implications of this approach to war are treated in previous chapters; here I mean only to emphasize the affordance of journalistic witnessing for underwriting this moral economy. For the witness testimony provided by war reportage is not the testimony of a court of law, used to indict or exonerate an alleged perpetrator. Such testimony would emphasize content over form—the truth witnessed rather than the truth of witnessing. While war reportage can and has been used in this capacity (for example, after the 2005 Haditha massacre in Iraq), this does not appear to be a primary function of news of war. In the case of much contemporary war reportage, where witnessing's figural capacity is its primary modality, journalists' testimony becomes a form of therapy, allowing news consumers to become the compassionate witnesses that absolves them of the guilt of indifference to human suffering—a cardinal humanitarian sin. Journalistic testimony figures as the indirect first-person account of what it would be like for consumers of news to be in the journalist's place. As witnesses to war, journalists can represent its audience to itself as those who would, like the journalist, be concerned with war's suffering and traumatized by war's violence. It is the figural dynamic of witnessing—the *role* journalists assume—that allows this transference to take place.[15]

And yet, if bearing witness is figural, then why does the journalist feel a need to undertake anything but the most superficial encounter with war? If the practice of bearing witness is not a matter of information gathering but simply of being there for its own sake, then why do journalists continue to expose themselves to danger, to emotional distress, and to the dynamics of war that can challenge the meanings their texts are designed to make?

On a sweltering night in Erbil, I met Peter at a café to discuss the practice of reporting from the battle for Mosul. Peter has the sturdy brow and earnest jawline of a war-movie hero, with a resigned gait and firm handshake. He is in his early thirties and has been freelancing in the region for several years. Peter had been spending a lot of time in a frontline medical clinic, witnessing the wounds of warfare inflicted on children, the elderly, and others fleeing combat. The clinic was run by a group of US Marine veterans who, I was told, came to Iraq to fight the Islamic State. They found as much action, and less compromised glory, using their emergency medical training to run a much-needed clinic near Mosul's frontline. The situation was a boon for freelancers like Peter, who could catch a ride to the front with the medics and station themselves at the clinic. They got good stories of violence and suffering without the expense of a fixer or driver.[16] The clinic boasted some of the goriest, saddest stuff that war can offer, and Peter had seen much of it.

"I was out near the clinic when a suicide car exploded," Peter told me of a recent trip to the front. "I wanted to see it. I wanted to see the brains leaked on the road. I didn't have to go, it wasn't relevant to the story I was working on. But I needed to see it in order to write authoritatively about the conflict."

Here Peter articulates the ideal of bearing witness, where the practice of proximity to war legitimates the authority of the journalist and of the journalism they produce. In conversation at the café, it was clear that Peter understood the contradiction at issue, wherein the practice of exposing oneself to war may entail experiences unfitted—threatening, even—to the narratives of war that must be produced. But Peter continued: "Then I thought about it, and that wasn't true," he said. "I wanted to see the brains for no other reason than that. There was no utility."

Peter's first comments suggest the figural importance of witness-bearing to war reportage, wherein the practice of encountering war authorizes the news reported, even if the encounter signals what exceeds the news. Peter's latter comments indicate that while witness-bearing may be figural, something else remains to the practice of proximity. The narrative utility of what is witnessed by a journalist may be extraneous, and the professional utility of the activity of witnessing may also be incidental. Because sometimes a journalist just wants to see it. Even if the authority of experience is more important than any information that experience provides—even if bearing witness is figural—the practice of war reportage still conflicts with purely professional concerns. A journalist, in her office in Baghdad, gestured to this remainder: "Journalism is good cover for getting close to the mystery that is death," she told me. And here journalism becomes the institutional carapace under which a journalist's own desire for reality—a reality unbounded by journalism—stirs.

This is the journalist "fascinated by the abject" (Kristeva 1982, 16). The production of war reportage may displace what is journalistically insensible, and it may gesture to that insensibility through poetic language or interview quotes. But the practice of war reportage confronts the insensible, and here the lived reality of journalism cannot be contained by journalism.

The Uncovered

If journalists are fascinated by the abject, this fascination is yet selective. For there are stories of war, important to global understandings of war, that are simply not encountered by working war reporters and that do not then appear in their published reportage. And if what is unreported of the experience of war produces one kind of displacement in the production of war reportage, what is unexperienced of war produces another.

Journalists must choose what to cover, of course, and cannot be expected to produce, like Borges's famous mapmaker, a representation that covers the exact dimensions of that which it represents. Yet, insofar as unreported stories cast in relief those stories that do appear in the news, the unreported can be understood to percolate at the margins of published journalism. The unreported of war particularizes what journalists *do* choose to report; this hidden remainder to the news betrays war reportage as a practice of selection and regulation.

In March of 2019, in the wake of territorial loss, the Islamic State retreated to the small town of Baghuz in eastern Syria, on a Euphrates riverbend just across the border from Iraq. While the potency of the Islamic State as an insurgent force had not altogether dissipated, the loss of major urban centers in Mosul and Raqqa significantly reduced their military and governance capacities. Some journalists left Iraq and Syria after the major battles with the Islamic State had concluded, while those who remained continued to focus on the defeat of the group, the grinding Syrian civil war, and related matters of conflict and its effects across Syria, Iraq, Lebanon, and the wider region. A few journalists managed to reach eastern Syria to cover the last major military confrontation with the Islamic State; others, in Baghdad and Erbil, reported on Islamic State–related events in Iraq; still others covered the wars in Syria and Iraq from Beirut or cities further afield—Istanbul or Abu Dhabi, Paris or New York.

By March, US-Coalition forces had encircled the bulk of remaining Islamic State forces, along with a significant civilian population, in and around Baghuz. Some ten thousand fighters and civilians were crammed into a square-mile area and surrounded, for weeks, by the US-Coalition. US airstrikes and Coalition-partner ground units (mostly Kurdish and Iraqi troops, along with US Special Forces) attacked Islamic State positions around Baghuz until their last strip of territory was in Coalition possession. Victory against the Islamic State was declared on March 23, 2019.

Prior to the victory that quickly dominated coverage of the Middle East, stories of the battle for Baghuz were not as prominent as one might, in hindsight, assume, given its narrative importance as the "last stand" of the Islamic State. According to journalists interviewed, the difficulty of accessing the battlefield in Syria, an inability to time reporting trips to the final defeat of the Islamic State and, after the months-long conflagrations in Mosul and Raqqa, lack of audience and editorial interest in yet another battle, prompted journalistic attention to other stories. Some journalists did report from Baghuz; the *Wall Street Journal*, the Associated Press, CNN, and a few other organizations published stories on the "last holdout" of the Islamic State, focusing on the plight of civilians and the tenacity of US-Coalition forces. But many journalists reporting from the region during the days before the declared victory produced stories unrelated to this battle.

Between March 17 and March 23, 2019, the day Baghuz fell, *New York Times* journalists in the region published a story about Islamic State fighters targeting Iraqi mushroom foragers and another story about the arrest of alleged organizers of a bombing that killed four Americans in Syria the previous January. *Wall Street Journal* journalists in the region also covered this arrest, along with the reopening of an Iraq–Syria border crossing, and the Islamic State's calls for revenge after a mass shooting at a mosque in Christchurch, New Zealand. *Washington Post* journalists in the region published a story about the drowning of Iraqi "revelers" after the capsizing of their holiday boat. The international news narrative that emerged from Iraq and Syria during the final week of the Baghuz battle was of a terrorist enemy on the verge of territorial defeat yet still able to inflict violence against civilians in an unstable and war-torn region.

But something else occurred during the final days of the battle for Baghuz, something not reported in the international press until years later. On March 18, 2019, five days before victory was declared against the Islamic State, an American F-15 dropped a 500-pound bomb on a crowd of women, children, and wounded men huddled in a depression by the Euphrates riverbank on the outskirts of Baghuz. They were wrapped in blankets, laying in rows, and according to accounts, fifty to seventy individuals were killed. Soon thereafter, another American F-15 dropped two 2,000-pound bombs on the same group, now consisting mostly of wounded stragglers from the first bombing. This was one of the largest civilian casualty incidents of the years-long war with the Islamic State. The strike was not publicly acknowledged by the US military, nor identified in military records, nor was it reported in the international news at the time. It was not until a *New York Times* investigation of the bombing was published on November 15, 2021, that the public was informed of this event.

From the *Times* story on the Baghuz airstrike, we learn that US military lawyers, who witnessed the bombing and its effects remotely from a US base in Qatar, considered the strike a possible war crime, but that no investigation of the strike was conducted by the internal watchdog agency tasked to assess strike procedures. We learn that the strike, conducted by a Special Operations Force called Talon Anvil, which operates outside the regular US military chain of command, was justified on the premise of defense against imminent danger to US-Coalition ground forces, a danger that was neither apparent at the time nor verified subsequently.[17] We learn that the US military quickly ordered the blast site bulldozed and that the relevant strike logs were falsified or incorrectly registered the requisite casualty information.[18]

We can consider the airstrike in Baghuz, unreported at the time of its occurrence, as something hidden beneath the stories that do appear in the news. Journalists spend their time pitching ideas, conducting interviews, gathering facts, cultivating sources, reporting from the scene, writing up their findings, and waiting for their coverage to be edited, fact-checked, headlined, formatted, and otherwise processed for publication. Yet there remain other stories not covered, and the occurrence of this excess suggests the contingency of the reality represented in news of war, a reality dispensed as illustrative if not complete. The existence of stories not covered disrupts the pretension of journalistic omniscience in wartime, and it indicates a war where the selection of which reality to report amounts to circumstantiality if not capriciousness. Stories not covered suggest that reportage on war is illustrative not of war itself but of the interests and capacities structuring the production of war reportage. Stories not covered shadow those that are. As a journalist in Iraq explained, "Journalists have a choice of whether they're there or not. That choice is a steel door." Journalists make practical and representational choices in wartime, choices that shape news-consumer knowledge of war.

The circumstance in which stories from war remain uncovered in the news may seem both obvious and unavoidable, a consequence of finite journalistic resources and the literal endlessness of news stories that could be made from any given reality. But the use of limited resources—the specific attention of journalists in the field, and the specific attention of news institutions to which fields their journalists cover—is not, of course, value neutral. The use of journalistic resources is contingent upon perceived consumer interest, cost and logistics, the editorial prerogatives of a given news organization, and the management of media by more powerful institutions. And the endlessness of news stories available to a journalist indicates how narrative is always a choice, one informed by the precise position—cultural and political, geographic and professional—of the journalist-author. "Choices are constrained by the context of production," a journalist said to me in Beirut. Another journalist in Beirut explained, "I'm typical in my choice of topics—mostly migration, suffering. Part conscience, part stories I come across."

Setting aside the political-economic content of international news coverage (where resources are spent, and why), we might understand the occurrence of stories not covered as another form of displacement. The stories that might have been—stories like the Baghuz airstrike—are often stories that *would* have been reported had journalists known then what they know now. A problem, however, when it comes to US war crimes, is that journalists very rarely know then what they know now. As events from the My Lai massacre to the abuse at Abu Ghraib suggest, US misconduct in war is rarely covered by journalists at the time of its occurrence. Military management of the foreign press, the exigencies of timing, the difficulties of access, editorial and consumer demand: These and other factors combine to limit the stories journalists tell—or *can* tell—from the scenes of warfare. In assessing published news alongside what is not published, war reportage comes to seem less a natural or self-evident purview of war's reality than the arbitrary or prescribed deployment of finite narrative resources. The stories not covered form a domain effaced from the content of the news yet innate to the practice of its production, which is always a matter of selection and capacity.

"You have to make choices," a journalist told me in Erbil. "But truth is larger, always, even with a thousand pages. We don't have the tools, the ambitions, to consider this. I don't grapple with this." The reality reported of war is discriminating, and the practice of this discrimination amounts to sanctioning one reality for war over others. Yet the unselected reality is still present outside the news. "Journalism promises to give you a reality," a journalist in Erbil remarked. "But it's ironic to say that, because you can't tell the whole story. Yes, you spend a couple of hours with someone, but what happens after you leave? There's a human process that continues." And so the manifest content of journalism obscures a hidden remainder. For what fails to surface in published news does not, of course, fail to exist, and this existence can trouble the news published. Where resources are applied, where access is granted, where audience interest is thought to lie: These factors determine the news that is reported, even as something unreported may make trivial—if only in hindsight—the determinations made.

The unreported airstrike in Baghuz is a matter more important, in many ways, than arrested bomb plotters in Syria or targeted mushroom foragers in Iraq (as interesting or newsworthy as these latter stories may be). The Baghuz airstrike is more important in illustrating how the recent wars in the Middle East work. The event shows that US-caused harm to civilians can be hidden from the US military's own disclosure and investigatory processes, processes advertised to work as safeguards for the rule of law. It shows that chain-of-command protocols in place to ensure against civilian harm can be bypassed by special operators justifying violence on the premise of an imminent danger that need not exist. It shows that US military targeting may be less precise, and US assessment of civilian harm less transparent, then regularly promised. And it shows that the use of violence by US and US-allied forces may be less about protecting civilians from terrorists than about defeating perceived enemies, regardless of the cost to those populations that the US military publicly claims to protect. Such matters, revealed by the Baghuz airstrike, illustrate what American war *is* today—a newsworthy matter for a global (and especially American) news audience. By focusing on a capsized party boat or on the harm done to civilians by the Islamic State, the international press sublimated one reality of warfare in the selection of another. But the sublimated reality, reflected in stories not told, does not disappear.

In the case of the Baghuz airstrike, the event was reported, if only eventually. A consequential reality, disappeared behind the news reported at the time, resurfaced years later. The reportage revealing the airstrike and its effects is certainly commendable. It is important to note, however, that this resurfacing was not due to the efforts of war reporters. The reporting on the Baghuz airstrike was based on anonymous sources inside the US military, who sought accountability for the strike first from their chain of command, then from the Air Force Office of Special Investigations, then from the Department of Defense Inspector General, before going to the press. The story was then reported by US-based journalists operating out of US news bureaus. Other recent revelations about the conduct of US-Coalition forces in Iraq and Syria, reported in 2021 and 2022 and discussed in Chapter 4, relied on court-ordered and Freedom of Information Act–released documents.

A question then presents itself: If some of the most critical matters of war are reported through anonymous sources in Washington, DC, or from documents obtained through court order, rather than encountered by journalists in Syria and Iraq, to what extent does war reportage conducted in areas of conflict inform its audience about what war *is*? Even as war, of course, may contain multitudes—of realities, of stories, of meanings—we must ask whether accessing a zone of conflict, listening to those suffering war, and bearing witnessing to war's ruin are enough to give news consumers an understanding of war's reality, or of those aspects of war's reality we might deem most important. Are the critical aspects of war ascertainable by way of the primary practices of war reporters?

War reportage, as a practice, remains subject to its unavoidable selectivity, and to the outside produced thereby. The stories not told become yet another dimension of the displacements inherent to the practice of war reportage, yet another register in which to track what the news is *not*. The stories not told cast in relief the particularity of what the news of war now *is*. With the later coverage of the Baghuz airstrike emerges the power of the previous reportage for regulating the reality of war, and the function of journalistic practices—interviewing, accessing, witnessing—for certifying that reality. Terrorist targeting of mushroom foragers, Islamic State calls for revenge: Practices of news production illuminated a particular war while eclipsing another. Coverage of the Baghuz airstrike then returned the journalistically repressed: a war in the Middle East other than the one reported at the time.

Yet the war reporter remains *there*, in the space and time of war. Unlike other representations of conflict—the realist war movie, for example—the production of war reportage entails the encounter with what threatens discursive control. Journalists must face, rather than merely render, a war that exceeds commodification. While the autonomy of the news elides the social basis of its production, while names and numbers manage what war is understood to be, another reality yet waits for journalists in the war zone, a ruined reality resistant to the narrative tools at hand. The fissure between war and its representation may be concealed by the commodity form of the news, yet this fissure continues to be lived by war reporters, who know how fragile their representations can be. Here possibilities emerge for representing war otherwise and, thereby, for knowing war anew. It is to these possibilities that the conclusive chapter turns.

I once saw a journalist near Mosul, pale with shock. "I'd forgotten," she said, "that legs have bones in them." Then she averted her gaze. A war unexpected still makes its presence felt.

INTERLUDE

Leaving Mosul

Journalist: So that's the ending of Mosul, and it's not a happy thing. We all miss the purpose of Mosul, to be perfectly honest. "I'm here to do Mosul. I'm here to cover this offensive." "What are you doing today? I'm going to Mosul." So it's an exhalation now, but it's not a joyful, relaxed exhalation. It's like, "Oh shit, where do I get my purpose now?" And Mosul was such a long campaign. For all of us, it was really significant for our careers.

Ethnographer: There seems to be a general pause around town, a moment of reflection that is, in my estimation, much needed. And asking, "What am I going to do now?" is a reflexive instinct.

Journalist: Yes, and we've all been having these conversations about how we covered it. How we all got caught up with the CTS [the Iraqi Counterterrorism Services] or ISOF, how we weren't critical enough, all that shit. Collectively, we were reflecting. And yeah, there was a pause, there was a break. At the time I was happy it was finished. Now it feels weird. Going back there to Mosul feels really nice, such a fucking great city, gorgeous. We sat by the Tigris. They have this little arcade there, all the families are there eating dolma and kids playing in the water. But it feels weird because the city's moved on now. My memories of it are history. It doesn't reflect how the place is now. Kind of bittersweet to go back.

Ethnographer: It's left you behind. Is there anything you'll miss about covering Mosul?

Journalist: It was emotionally engaging. We were living and breathing it. When we are going to the frontline clinics and seeing wounded and dead children, that was the emotional tenor of it, and it sounds wrong to say that was engaging, but we were all feeling the same things at the same time. So we were buoyed by the emotional currents of that conflict that we were engaged in. We felt a part of something. So we had this collective emotional response of each element as it went through, each part of it, and you have to put your own emotions into it. I think that's why I'm exhausted now. You wouldn't take this home to your family. But being here, it comes with this cost, which I'm going through now, which is this wrench. . . . Sorry, my mom is texting. She sent me a picture of a kale pie. See? Incongruous.

Ethnographer: Incongruous, definitely. What can a kale pie mean to you here?

Journalist: It's not a life that I lead. I spend a couple weeks there every year. It's not my life. What I'm trying to do now is to make a life that's not this, but not that either. Something geographically in the middle and emotionally in the middle. Not soul-destroyingly boring and not waking up in a conflict. It is like a breakup, leaving this place.

Ethnographer: It makes sense. Breaking up means leaving some of your personal history with another, a shared history, and you can't take it with you.

Journalist: Grief. That's what I have now. But I can't really live here anymore, and I can't really explain why. It's just the day-to-day stuff. It almost feels like an extended student lifestyle, with the smoking and drinking, all the same people in one neighborhood. We used to have more parties. When [redacted] was here during Mosul, it was more social. Well, you remember those times.

Ethnographer: There are less people here now. Or rather, less journalists. Teachers Club is just as crowded, but I don't recognize as many people. I'm still struck when I see journalists run into each other after time apart, though. I was with [redacted] in Ain Issa when he ran into a photographer he hadn't seen since Libya. I don't think he really likes her, actually, but they have a connection. I came across Jim Muir's reflections on Marie Colvin recently. These two people have seen each other in a lot of—

Journalist: Stressful situations. Yeah, that's it. And that's why we have that bond. When I go home, my family and my friends there, I'll fall back on clichés. "It was grim." There's a fascination with what is laid bare: what it's like to see a bombing, what it's "*really* like." And journalists say, "It's not interesting for me to explain what it's like, because you don't know, so let's just talk about what you've been up to." People don't know how to pose the question.

CONCLUSION

War's Exit

Entangled Possibility in the Age of Endless Conflict

Surety, then ruin.
—INSCRIPTION ON THE GATE AT THE ORACLE OF DELPHI

Border Wars

Why is war reportage the way it is? This book aimed to show how war reportage works by examining its language, meaning, and practice, and in this way assess what journalism says about war and what it allows us, thereby, to think. By attending to the lived experience of war and its representation, I hoped to scrutinize journalism's commitment to the delivery of war's reality and discern what is displaced in the process of reality-delivery.

This project necessitated critique. Investigating how war reportage works required interrogation of the interests served by war reportage, the ideology flowing through the discourse, and the meanings journalists do not make. In this concluding chapter, I turn from critique to possibility, seeking capacities embedded in war reportage for representing and understanding war *otherwise*. I want to consider "another way of telling" war (Berger 1982), but one endemic to the rules and limits of contemporary war reportage. For in addition to critique, this ethnography offered glimpses of the representational opportunity hidden in the generic conventions, enduring meanings, and normative practices of war reportage. I do not mean to suggest that the limits of war reportage, as currently constituted, can simply be overcome. Rather, these limits themselves present the potential for generative transgression. By looking sidelong at the activities and narratives of journalists, certain possibilities already entangled in war reportage can be ascertained. These entangled possibilities become available both *through* and *despite* the discursive constraints and social forces regulating news production in wartime.[1]

The preceding chapters demonstrated how the univocity achieved in war reportage necessitates the exclusion of what the discourse cannot accommodate and how the excluded yet lurks. This operation of "order by exclusion" is embedded in relations of power, wherein closures of meaning are accomplished in the interests of particular hegemonic projects (Chouliaraki 2002, 91; see also Laclau and Mouffe 1985; Torfing 1998). But in tracking the way meaning is fixed in war reportage, I have also attempted to indicate where this fixity is threatened—where, that is, a surplus stalks the borders of the sense war reportage makes. This approach to discursive vulnerability denaturalizes the war delivered in war reportage—the war organized as death tallies, suffering victims, the inhumanity of violence— and suggests a war open to classificatory struggle and contested meaning, a war of ambiguity and absurdity and contradiction confronted by journalists amid their labors. While attempts to fix the meaning of war can be seen as a strategy of closure in the service of a dominant order, this discursive regulation always yields that which cannot be suitably controlled. The "constitutive outside" (Laclau 1990, 9) of war reportage is always waiting at journalism's discursive border, and this surplus is frequently encountered by journalists in wartime. Journalism's incapacity to finally banish what it cannot report, its inability to finally suture the fissure between war and news of war, provides an opportunity for considering war reportage anew.

For Ernesto Laclau and Chantal Mouffe, the possibility of a truly democratic politics lies precisely in the "continual tendency towards the affirmation of the 'constitutive other'" (in Coombe 1998, 291). As every effort at closure is subject to inevitable failure, as every will to hegemony is unable to finally totalize the field of signification, a challenge to any control of war's meaning is already inherent to what is expelled. The conditions of possibility for thinking war in relation to interests other than those currently dominant, and for remaking the social order to which war reportage responds, is evoked by journalism's constitutive contingency, this "other" that war reporters—though rarely war reportage—continually affirm. It is with the realization of an outside to the meanings fixed in news of war, an outside lived by journalists, that a resistance to normative assertions about war can be grasped.

In contemporary war reportage, war becomes self-evident, a thing-in-itself, whose meaning is sought in bodily suffering and whose reality is ordered by the conventions generically applied. But by narrowing war to meanings authoritatively journalistic, and reproductive of a reigning common sense, war reportage already initiates an opening though which to glimpse war in other ways. In traversing the border between the totalizing conceptions of war organized by war reportage and the surplus this hegemony emits, the fragility of journalistic order can be realized and a knowing *otherwise* activated. Tracking this border, and the possibilities it both accommodates and conceals, *itself* becomes a means to question the authority constituted representationally and to engage the contestations that result.

Grimness and Estrangement

Research presented in this book indicates that the meaning recent wars in the Middle East made for journalists—that war, in general, makes—can exceed or differ from that made by journalists in the news they produce. This gap may be expected of storytellers who invariably experience the world in ways other than the stories they produce can oblige. Yet war and war reportage present unique circumstances. Violence, suffering, death: These are slippery things, notoriously elusive of discursive capture. Meanwhile, and as I have tried to show, the persistence of a gap between war and news of war undermines what is essential to the value of war reportage as a commodity on a market: the direct and transparent delivery of war's reality.

To be sure, many news consumers must suspect that the reality presented as war reportage is not the only reality journalists encounter in the course of their work. As discussed in this book's introduction, speculation concerning journalism's "constructedness" is now rife. Journalists often mentioned to me a circumstance in which this suspicion is actively confronted. Upon returning to hometowns—in Manchester or Christchurch or São Paolo—some cousin or childhood friend of the journalist expresses their curiosity about the reality behind the war articulated as news. "What is it *really* like over there?" they ask the journalist, after catching up over drinks at the neighborhood bar, or smoking cigarettes on the front stoop outside the family home. "What is war really *like*?"

The question implies some intuition that the journalist—with whom the questioner shares a childhood, or a college romance, or inside jokes, and for whom the journalist is not *only* a journalist—isn't telling the whole truth in the news they produce. Among news consumers encountering a journalist who is more than a journalist, who is more than a figure of authorized reality-delivery—but a buddy, or an in-law, or an ex-lover—some breach is revealed. The person they know is not the same as the byline in the news, and this distinction prompts a desire to close the divide between war's mediated reality and some experienced reality, a divide that war reportage is designed to conceal. If the journalist they know is more than a journalist, than the war that journalist experiences must be more than the war commodified as news.

The journalists I spoke to, however, had very little interest in confirming this suspicion for their friends and family back home. Rather, journalists seemed to resent the suggestion outright. "There's a social border between my journalist and non-journalist friends," a journalist explained in Tripoli, Lebanon. "I don't want to talk to the latter about war. We don't have that shared experience. What a body is like—journalists can joke about it. We know what it smells like." A journalist in Erbil told me, "I'm not interested in explaining how war really is to those who haven't experienced war. So I just say, 'it was grim,' and leave it at that."

"It was grim" is a deflection I heard often among those avoiding disclosure of their experiences in Mosul or Raqqa, Aleppo or Homs. "When you go back home, it becomes hard to engage with friends and others," explained a journalist in Baghdad. "And it's hard to be conscious that you're in a bubble here, where violence is normal, but it's not really normal." The relativity of normalcy can cause feelings of disconnection after leaving sites of war. "I have that feeling, coming home from the frontline, with friends and family, you feel alien." This is what a journalist said to me in Erbil toward the end of the battle for Mosul, as he prepared to leave for home. "There's a collision of cultures, and you realize you are the contact between the local and the foreign, where the foreign is this danger, the violence, war." As a contact or connection between here and there, "peace" and "war," the journalist is caught between worlds, and "grimness" covers for the despondency of this position. For these professional storytellers of war, the ability to produce a story *not* dictated by the exigencies of war reportage can feel strange. "What is war *really* like?" a journalist in Baghdad mused. "Where do I start?" Without the rules preconditional to journalism's representations, without the professional ideals that structure the meaning war can make, without a shared education in a body's fetid rot, journalists are left without a net in expressing war's reality. The armature of journalistic storytelling fallen away, the story of war becomes difficult for journalists to tell. And so, "it was grim."

Grimness marks this essential estrangement, not only of the war reporter in peacetime, but of the producer of a commodity that elides the processes of its production. Grimness expresses both the isolation felt by war reporters displaced from the violent conditions of their reportage, as well as the alienation of journalists from a commodity that denies its own sociality. On the one hand, war reporters returning to places considered peaceful feel a sense of separation between themselves and their home communities, a sense resulting from their encounters with war as quintessence of the foreign and as basis for the strange life they choose. The journalist, *as* a journalist, is alone, cut off from those who understand war as they do—those who can recognize, and joke about, what human death is like—and who understand the life war reporters lead. They are disconnected from a place where war is atmospheric, the basis of all social relations, and they are left instead where war is abnormal, aberrant, and strange. The expression of war's grimness—a deflection of eager inquiry—marks this gulf.

On the other hand, the commodity that war reporters produce always hides the intimacies, emotions, and dependencies essential to the work of war reportage, and here the journalist is estranged from journalism. As long as war remains self-evident in the news and to news consumers, all the connections a journalist might have to war are abstracted. The journalist quoted above, who acknowledged telling curious friends back home that war is simply grim, is also the journalist who stood on a table in Erbil to recite a Wilfred Owen poem for an Iraqi soldier killed by the Islamic State. The soldier was well-liked in the journalist community in Iraq; he was a character in the news, but he was also a friend to news producers. This friendship, and the emotion of the recitation given in its honor, is excised from the news even as it remains fundamental to the production of the news. Something essential to the life of the war reporter is unmoored from war reportage, and its absence can be especially difficult for journalists removed from war. Grimness marks this passage too.

The figure of the Iraqi soldier in a news story—a hero, perhaps, or a source, or an integer in a death toll—is no longer the guy who helped you out, or made you laugh, or saved your ass. He is a figure only: a synecdoche, an allegory, a symbolic truth, and commodifiable as such. This figure offers itself as compensation for the trials of journalistic labor—for the work of interviewing and reporting, of sharing danger with others and sometimes loving them too—of which this figure is also the product. Cut loose from the spaces of their labor and confronted with the echo of what their commodity denies, journalists may even miss war. They may miss what their journalism displaces: the fullness of a life lived but rarely reported.

Knowing War Otherwise

In delivering war the way it does, war reportage can be seen as doing the work of closure. Its figural design, its categories and emplotments, its certainty, its moralism: These elements meet a demand for resolution in representations of war and they satisfy consumer desire for what war *is*. Here again is the theodicean dimension of war reportage, its delivery of reliable meaning for otherwise insensible suffering. Here again is the order that war reportage substantiates, narrating and thereby controlling the terror, the trauma, the extremity threatening to news-consuming societies.

Yet closure is something rarely attained by war reporters themselves. Many journalists are aware of their ability to bestow meaning upon events; they understand the craft of narrative, and they understand the fragility of the stories they "get." And in understanding their own constructivist power, journalists cannot but remain outside its influence. The "systems of equivalence" that Stuart Hall calls "closures," and in which "what could be assumed about the world" becomes, in journalism, identical with "what could be said to be true" (1982, 71), breaks down amidst the lived experience of war. Journalists live outside the paradigms they apply, they live outside the systems of closure they institute, because they encounter a war distinct from war's representation. While they look for a good story, while they seek characters and color and plot in war, journalists recognize themselves apart from these dynamics and thus removed from the closure their commodities maintain. "Grimness" marks a recognition of this conclusive failure of closure, but as gesture to journalism's constitutive outside, grimness marks an opening too, a potential for other ways of knowing.

"To articulate the past historically does not mean to recognize it 'the way it really was,'" Walter Benjamin writes. "It means to seize hold of a memory as it flashes up at a moment of danger" (2006, 391). This is, precisely, how journalists can articulate war. In conversation, in notepads, in dreams, war reporters do not recognize wartime "the way it really was" in any normative journalistic sense. While war reportage attempts this mimetic performance, it is the ambiguity of war, its humor and abjection and eccentricity, its irony and its pathos, that flash up for journalists. This flashing up is dangerous—for journalists, and for journalism too. As war proliferates and transforms—from counterinsurgency to "great power competition" to the "hyperwar" of algorithmic control—knowing what war *can* be, as opposed to what it is expected to be, is a dangerous prospect for those charged with representational closure. In providing categories and enumerations, in provisioning legibility, in reproducing a commanding common sense, war reportage delivers war the way it really was, and as it is expected to really be. But as it flashes up amidst danger, the seizing hold of wartime experience is something else. It is such moments of danger—discursive and professional and existential danger—that allow for and indeed create what Michael Taussig (1993) calls "mimetic slippage," wherein reproduction explodes into metamorphosis, and the representational force of journalism becomes the transformative force of thinking anew. Reality may always be "discursively mobilized," as Judith Butler and Joan Scott note—war reportage, after all, must fashion war's reality in discourse—yet different "reality effects" are nevertheless available depending on the mode of this mobilization (1992, xvii). Possibility exists even where discourse maintains its control.

What is required, then, in establishing new ways of knowing war, is not only a deconstruction of the discourse through which war is constituted. We must, too, consider war in terms of the social order that constitutes war reportage as a discourse, and thereby enable the rearticulations of war that can arise in contest with that order. By scrutinizing practices such as witness-bearing as a figural instantiation of consumer fantasy, by denaturalizing the meaning given to war in its convergence with a militarized humanitarianism, by inspecting generic conventions as a set of rules ordering what war can be: Here the self-evidence of war is particularized, and the interests buried within this self-evidence can surface. Taking stock of the "contingency of universality" (Hoy and McCarthy 1995, 172) allows us to identify where the totality of war reportage might be punctured and what new ideas about war might flow forth. The commonness of the sense underpinning journalistic representation is in this way disputed and the parameters of war's intelligibility redrawn. The experience of war's representors affirms this potential.

The lived experience of war, and of war's representation, indicates that more than journalism's definitive account of war is warranted, more than an account conducive to a reigning common sense. For Hayden White, the aim of interpretation is complexity not simplicity; its point is to "create perplexity in the face of the real" (2009, 74). War reportage, of course, elides interpretation in its transmission of the self-evident. Journalists thus find themselves in the very unique position of representing something as personally perplexing as war and violence and death, but with so simple a set of discursive tools. "On good days, journalists are engaged in meaning making. On bad days, we prop up the edifice of war in such a way that readers can think they understand war and thus have an informed view." I was speaking with a journalist in the lobby of the Classy Hotel in Erbil. Armed with a prestigious British education, this journalist had freelanced around the Middle East before joining the staff of an American news outlet. Her dark curls bobbed as she glanced furtively around the room. It was peak wartime at the Classy, with aid workers spending "danger pay" at the bar, television crews disassembling dusty gear on large dining tables, journalists in the lounge swapping jokes.

"But that's an illusion," the journalist continued,

> Readers don't get war. It can't be fully explained, and thus we are not engaged in meaningful exposition but in duplicitous excuses. It's not that journalists are creating fiction. The problem is the estrangement between the reader not in a war and the journalist's perception and description of war. Readers assume they understand more than they do of war.

Journalists are tasked to explain what "can't be fully explained" while denying that journalistic explanation can ever fall short. Consumer desire for a meaningful account of war becomes a desire for a limited economy of truth. War reporters may advance this wartime economy, but they know it for what it is because they live its limits.

How to reckon with this estrangement, then, this gap between war and representation, expectation and experience? How to occasion that "rigorous sense of partiality" that James Clifford sees as a source of representational tact, a way to present "an inherently imperfect mode of knowledge, which produces gaps as it fills them" (1986, 7)? It is, to be sure, a dangerous suggestion when it comes to war and violence, where the stakes of comprehension and reaction could not be much higher. What would it be, then, to embrace a journalism that retains its mimetic function—that delivers war's reality in a realistic fashion—but which yet sloughs off narrative closure for the rifts that narrative realism represses? Here would be the representation sought by Theodor Adorno, which "consists of giving form to the crucial contradictions of real existence" and thereby "give[s] voice to what ideology hides" (1991, 39). Here would be a realism in which, as Michael Rothberg insists, "the scars that mark the relationship of a discourse to the real are not fetishistically denied, but exposed" (2000, 106). Here would be a journalism that reveals its limits. For challenge to normative news of war need not amount to dismissal of a need for knowledge of war. Nor does the insistence on the political implications of representation need amount to a retreat into the epistemological weeds while violence strikes all around. Rather, understandings of war and analyses of representation depend on each other insofar as the experience of war continues to challenge both understanding and representation.

This is, perhaps, the crux of the dilemma that declining trust in mass media presents to war reportage specifically. As the taboo fortifies the ritual, so does the journalistic taboo on fiction—intensified amidst the proliferation of "fake news" accusations and broad suspicion of mass media—fortify the rituals of objectivity, factuality, accuracy, certainty. The most prominent institutional response to the crisis in media trust is the doubling down on truth as normatively understood. Fact-checking articles abound; transparency in news production ascends.[2] Such a rearguard positivism is unlikely to close the media trust deficit or convince a newspaper's detractors of its honesty. In the case of war specifically, the intensified insistence on facticity and truthfulness serve to further obscure the ambiguities inherent to war and inherent to what war's belligerents often prefer disguised. Industry insistence on the performance of definitive truth amounts, in war reportage, to a smoothing over of those contradictions that the operations of war making *also* attempt to hide. Torture, suicide attacks, automated assassination, staged executions, weapons supply chains, nuclear stockpiling, classified strikes, artisanal mining, psychological operations, sexual enslavement, private military contracting, black sites, empire, money: These elements of war can defy the representational mastery of war reportage as currently constituted. These things outstrip, in their categorical transgressions and definitional inversions and calculated insensibility, the kind of stories war reportage is designed to deliver. An inability to document the heterodox and irreconcilable, the conflicted and contradictory, amounts to a failure to represent war.

The peace characterized as the absence of war, the humanitarianism always other than counterinsurgency, the perpetrators who cannot be victims, the dead who cannot be living, the liberation distinct from a siege, the "there" that is never also "here": The disavowal of such wartime anomalies allows the omissions, aversions, and white noise of war making to perpetuate. Allen Feldman describes writing about violence as "shooting blanks": a writing that "center[s] on the empty spaces around the manifest scripts and graphemes of war machines." The task of the writer of violence, Feldman argues, is "to rewrite that labyrinth of violence, to remap it in-situ in order to think it otherwise" (2017). The embrace of ambiguity is essential to the enterprise of representing war as it now *is*, even though the way war *is* may challenge what normatively counts as realistic representation, and even though uncertainty will be the representational result of this embrace.

In examining war reportage on the levels of language, meaning, and practice, it is possible to discern a displacement of ambiguity in each instance. The ambiguities of war's reality are displaced by the discipline of journalistic language. The ambiguities of war's interpretation are displaced by the normativity of journalistic meaning. And the ambiguities of journalists' experiences of war are displaced amidst the protocols of journalistic practice. In considering war reportage as a series of displacements, we might account for war as something that agitates at the margins of what war reportage delivers, and for war reporters as those traversing an interstitial space between war and its representation. To return something of this interstitiality to journalism—some of what Roger Caillois (2003, 322) calls the "fruitful ambiguity" of the poetic arts—would be to attend to insight rather than truth, and to take seriously the fantasies that condition popular conceptions of war. Here would be a style of war reportage for which knowledge is something we *do* rather than something we possess, a knowledge embedded in how news producers live and how news consumers imagine rather than a knowledge exchanged unaltered from owner to owner. Instead of more certainty—moral or political—consumers would grapple with a process of journalistic interpretation always open and ever shifting. Instead of war as an object to perceive, it would become a relation to engage, an intersubjective arena that allows for—demands, even—an encounter with alterity and with what we may *not* be able to definitively understand.

Uncommon Sense

Throughout the preceding chapters, I have pointed, if obliquely, to places in which to seek an outside to journalism's economy of truth. The knowledge of fixers—a "situated knowledge" (Haraway 1988) of war, discussed in Chapter 2—accommodates a war reportage more open to contestation and more accountable to the context of its emergence. The journalism of Ali Arkady, discussed in Chapter 1, and which revealed the violence of purported protagonists in the recent war in Iraq, muddied narrative distinctions between good and bad, ally and enemy, justified and extreme. Arkady was able to challenge realist presumptions of war's categorical fixity and thereby question the customary sense that war makes. If the names journalistically applied in war are subject to preconditions and thus open to contestation, as I argued in Chapter 1, this circumstance suggests that other names are indeed possible. The potential of journalism to name the things of war *otherwise* is the potential to push against predetermined norms and reconceive how war is made knowable.

The yellow press period, discussed in Chapter 4, suggests that war reportage can make meaning not only in alignment with the power underpinning a social consensus, but in convergence with the worldviews of specific constituencies and with the struggles of particular groups. Such a war reportage would abandon objective distance and the manufacture of universality for articulations embedded in political and social conditions. Empathy, which reinscribes the distance between the consumer of news and the object of news, would cede discursive ground to a solidarity based on shared wartime context.

In Chapters 5 and 6, journalists' dreams, notepad scribblings, casual conversations, and emotional attachments indicate further resources for embracing the illegibilities of war. Journalists' use of particular tropes (like the blank stare) and of quotations from sources on the ground become ways to smuggle into war reportage that which threatens its generic closures.[3] Such narrative practices can account for experiences otherwise expunged from war reportage. These sites and strategies throw into relief the boundaries that war reportage enacts and the surplus generated thereby.

In interviews conducted on the language, meaning, and practice of journalism, several journalists seemed intimately aware of the politics of the knowledge they produced, the tensions inherent to its production, and the limits imposed on its public presentation. As quotes offered in the preceding chapters demonstrate, these journalists have already internalized many of the critiques deployed in this book. Some journalists are skeptical of how certain designations, such as "terrorist," are applied in news from the Middle East. Some discern how trauma frames, and thereby limits, popular understandings of both war and the practice of journalism. A few journalists grasp the danger of taking the humanitarian intentions of military and state officials at face value. The internalization of critique does not in itself amount to changes in the operations of war reportage. It does, however, indicate the subversive capacity of journalistic self-awareness—and the possibility for pushing back against a dominant order of knowledge.

There remains a gasping need for stories of war that run counter to prevailing narratives. Such reportage will require a suspicion of the frictionless pronouncements of official sources, of leading geopolitical imaginaries and militarized moral projects, and of the force of empire in the Middle East and beyond. It will entail skepticism of humanitarian claims and an overarching distrust of power. It will necessitate a rebalance between the focus on individual suffering and investigation of the systems that perpetuate suffering. And such reportage, because it defamiliarizes war, will generate conflict with audiences, editors, officials, and with other journalists, who prefer a war directly apparent and imminently knowable.

In abandoning a war without complexity, a war of self-evident facts and moral truisms, we face instead the insistent perplexities of contemporary warfare and the consistent contingencies of its representation. In the years to come, war reporters can expect an increase in remote, cyber, and proxy warring in the Middle East, with more limited and more difficult access to the events of conflict. As US "force postures" realign toward "near-peer" conflict with China, as NATO's cusp becomes the site for "great power" proxy conflict and military profiteering, as powerful militaries resurrect the embedding system and target unwanted journalists, journalism's investigative role may become more prominent than its witness-bearing one.[4] Analyses of the political and economic systems perpetuating violence may be necessary to deepen consumer knowledge while relieving journalists of the pressure for exposure to the worst of wartime violence. Amidst financial pressures and waning consumer interest, local journalists may well assume a larger role in international news production; their "situatedness" can impact the way reportage is practiced, the meanings it makes, and the language used to order those meanings. As cyberweapons undermine conventional military strength, as drone technology democratizes, as surveillance capacities expand, journalists may find increasing need to make meaning not in coincidence with a reigning status quo but in affiliation with positions of opposition. Solidarity could become more necessary than empathy, strategic insight more valuable than universal truth. As war becomes yet more spectral, yet more technologized, yet more intertwined with a peaceful global order, so journalism may need to be less certain, less organized, less accountable to normative affirmations of sense. Rather than the fulfilment of a prefigured notion of war, war reportage may need to index what doesn't seem to count as *war* at all.

Such a refusal of fulfillment points to a final matter here at the closure of this book. War is represented in war reportage to correspond with war as it is expected to be. This correspondence remains consequential regardless of the representational possibilities journalists engage—regardless of the contextual richness or nuanced ambiguity that might be journalistically applied to war. If war reporters remain committed to reporting what they encounter *as war*, then the limit at issue for war reportage is not only the suppression of representational possibility, not only the generic boundaries maintained, but the very notion of war itself as popularly imagined. For as long as war is the common denominator to which all armed conflict can be reduced, and through which all such events can be represented and thereby known, then war remains a product of war reportage as a paradigm for what journalism is supposed to be: the satisfaction of consumer desire for reality. War fulfills this desire, but it does so with the loss of what war is not yet imagined to be. Energy extraction, migration controls, military-industrial influence, population transfers, sanctions regimes and asset freezes, trade and monetary policy, ecological decline, poverty, debt: Do these matters fall within the scope of war reportage? Should they?

Only when peace is understood as conterminous with war—only when those things *not* considered the purview of war reportage are accepted as essential to what war is now—can war reportage truly reckon with its object. For when the intimacy between war and those things excepted from war is realized, war becomes meaningful in a way that can account for present global conditions. But if this were the case—if war reportage could accomplish the representation of everything war is, including those things not imagined as war—the very existence of war reportage would be threatened. In reporting war as it now is, war reportage might become something else entirely.

EPILOGUE

From Mosul to Mariupol

So have I heard and do in part believe it.
—HORATIO, *HAMLET*

"I've never felt more censored." So said a journalist from one of the world's leading news organizations. We were in a hotel bomb shelter in Ukraine a few months after the Russian invasion, as American and European military aid escalated and narratives of the conflict ossified. Air-raid sirens had wailed since lunchtime, though many chose to ignore the warnings until the workday was done. In the shelter, aid workers and hotel employees chatted amicably, stared into mobile phone screens, or lounged about on bedding retrieved from more vulnerable spaces above. The bomb shelter was a new site for me, ethnographically; as the sirens announced an unseen danger, I considered war from a distinct angle. James Clifford's description of field research as "deep hanging out" (1997) became miserably literal.

But what did the journalist mean? "Censorship" is not a word used in the preceding chapters, and even as I have traced the constraints of war reportage as a representational form, the term seems reductive of the ambiguities, contingencies, and struggles of conflict journalism. And yet, as this journalist explained, the foreign press corps was indeed subject to considerable restrictions in Ukraine. Whose victimhood matters, whose violence is justified, whose territory is sacrosanct—such questions, displaced in coverage of the Islamic State wars, were becoming further obscured. For this journalist, who'd reported from Syria, Iraq, and Lebanon, the conflict in Ukraine presented renewed challenges.

By the spring of 2022, many journalists I knew from the Middle East were based in Lviv and Kyiv, or were reporting from sites of Ukrainian displacement, such as Poland, or from areas of combat to the east. A sizable majority of the journalists I interviewed and observed for this book were in Ukraine at that time, or had recently been there, or would soon arrive. Ukraine was then the biggest story in the world, receiving more minutes of American television coverage, for example, than any international conflict since the 1991 Gulf War.[1] Resources, journalistic and military, were streaming into the country, though to what effect was not yet clear.

If the conflict in Ukraine presents a challenge for war reporters, is this challenge unique? Do the journalistic mechanisms I tracked through conflict in Iraq, Syria, and the greater Middle East apply to this new war in Europe? How are the language, meaning, and practice of war reportage transformed in the transition from one international war zone to another?

On the level of journalistic language, technical terms like "genocide" and "war crime" were being applied to Russian violence in Ukraine with such indiscrimination as to render these terms principally symbolic—less a technical description of violence than a moral denunciation. This choice of language in the news from Ukraine mirrors that deployed by the US government, which had recently transitioned from sanctioning International Criminal Court judges (and their families) over claims of US war crimes in Afghanistan, to promoting the court's jurisdiction over Ukraine.[2] The linguistic accord between war reportage and Western officials concerning the war crimes of Vladimir Putin in Ukraine follows their past convergence regarding the war crimes of Manuel Noriega in Panama, Slobodan Milošević in Yugoslavia, Saddam Hussein in Iraq, and Muammar Qaddafi in Libya. In each case, journalists reported on the prevalence of war crimes to societies whose governments were waging war against the accused. The symbolic charge of this rhetoric carries consequences: The violence of the war criminal, as for that of the terrorist, makes retributive counterviolence not only permissible but morally obligatory, foreclosing inclinations toward a negotiated peace. The strategic interests embedded in the language of a "war on terror" are realized, too, in a war against a war criminal.

Such selectivity in journalistic language is broadly apparent in Ukraine. A journalist for a French news organization, speaking live on television, was direct: "Imagine, we're in the twenty-first century in a European city, and there are cruise missiles as if it was Iraq or Afghanistan." Where violence should be expected and where, in contrast, its infliction most shocks are distinctions linguistically encoded—as we saw in the case of southern Beirut. Whose resistance is heroic, and whose violence is noble? Whose sovereignty is inviolable, and whose territory subject to invasion? Who is deemed worthy of support, and who can be dismissed, denied, deported? Such choices are naturalized, through language, as common sense.[3]

The language used by journalists in Ukraine reflects the contingency of the meanings journalists make. In Ukraine, as in the Middle East, reportorial focus remains on individual victims of war, on their bodily suffering, and on that suffering as the central problem of war. Harm to innocent civilians continues to justify, implicitly and sometimes explicitly, a violent response to violence. Suffering in Ukraine, as in other recent conflicts, is framed as a rationale for an intensification of war, even as that intensification will lead to further suffering. "Resilience" has become a central trope in Ukraine-based reportage, and Ukrainians are the fulfillment of a prefigured reality of resistance to foreign incursion.

This figuration marks a certain inversion from the narrative design of recent war coverage. Rather than passive victims of terroristic violence, journalists often frame Ukrainians as resilient heroes to despotic aggression. Rescue through direct US-European intervention in Ukraine (thus far unlikely) is less prominent as a journalistically elicited desire than is support—moral and material—for those fighting to save themselves. Journalists, then, are no longer addressing an omnipotent audience, an audience who empathizes with innocents and is poised to support a militarized rescue. Journalists are instead addressing an impotent audience, an audience deterred by the threat of nuclear confrontation and relegated to zealously hanging their newly recognizable Ukrainian flags. As the US military seizes the opportunity to launder its image as a defender of state sovereignty and international law, as the shift to proxy war provides unique rhetorical subversions, so journalists are adjusting to a conflict in which the focus on civilian suffering does not directly implicate their readership, whether through the guilt of association or the "responsibility to protect."

And yet some meanings persist. In much of the news coverage produced from Ukraine, "our" violence is made distinct from "their" violence, and who "we" are now extends to the Russian border. As a journalist for Al Jazeera put it, "What's compelling is just looking at them, the way they're dressed. These are prosperous middle-class people. These are not obviously refugees trying to get away from areas in the Middle East [or] North Africa. They look like any European family you would live next door to." Ukrainians are narratively positioned as people distinct from others experiencing similar conditions, people more like "us" than like "them." Yet the meanings made for war—its justifications, its cruelties—maintain. As a moral claim to military action once again obscures its political content, the differences between saving victims of war and defeating a wartime enemy once again collapse. The prospects of negotiated settlement as a way to end a war rarely register in the reportage from Ukraine; rather, and as representations of suffering proliferate, a humanitarian rationale for warfare—and the necessity of outright victory in the face of irrational cruelty—comes, expectedly, to dominate. The protection of civilian life must be achieved, the reportage from Ukraine suggests, through increased military engagement—an engagement that comes at the expense of civilian life. In this, the city of Mosul prefigures the cities of Mariupol, Kharkiv, Bakhmut.

Even more than recent conflicts elsewhere, the invocation of militarized humanitarianism is widespread in Ukraine. In the runup to the invasion in February 2022, Russian officials continually cited the protection of innocent civilians as a central rationale for militarism. A new Russian foreign policy doctrine, approved in September 2022, justifies intervention as a "humanitarian policy" to "protect, safeguard, and advance" Russian values and peoples (Reuters 2022). The US-Coalition's preferred narrative about the wars against the Islamic State—and the West's preferred justification for interventionary violence broadly—is universalized in the war in Ukraine, a war in which all sides claim a humanitarian mandate. Journalists rarely acknowledge this irony, even as their journalism is forced to reckon with its contradictions.

The practice of war reportage, conversely, became formally easier as war reached Europe. In Ukraine, the wireless internet is steady and the mobile phone networks reliable. A freelance journalist can travel toward the front by punctual train and cheap taxi instead of requiring expensive fixers and drivers. Europeans and Americans—the bulk, it seems, of the foreign journalists based in Ukraine—are widely welcomed, supported, encouraged in their journalistic labors. But the narrow pool of sources quoted to explain the conflict, the deepening currents of Ukrainian nationalism, and the restrictions placed on reporting frontline conditions, military casualties, and other central matters of war leaves much of the coverage myopic and its production deceptively straightforward. "It's easy to get stories here," a freelance journalist told me in Kyiv on his way east. The easy stories, however, obscure difficulties of access and limitations on content with which journalists are daily forced to contend.

According to several journalists I interviewed, access to the frontline is tightly regulated, often consisting of two-hour visits to a trench chaperoned by a government minder. Many stories about the frontline are secondhand accounts from military leadership or generated from visits to areas where active combat has ceased. Ukrainian officials consistently threaten to revoke the press credentials of foreign and local journalists in response to undesirable coverage or behavior. At least two major foreign news organizations almost lost their press credentials after visiting the frontline without a government minder; another had a prearranged interview with Ukrainian President Volodymyr Zelensky canceled after officials deemed their coverage too critical; a third stopped producing news from Ukraine in protest of overbearing restrictions.[4] A *New York Times* journalist, who reported on the Ukrainian military's use of internationally banned cluster munitions, had his press credentials revoked and his renewal denied in separate incidents, according to a *Times* spokesperson.[5]

Journalists expressed frustration with the refusals of Ukrainian officials to provide casualty estimates or detailed progress reports, while the constraints on frontline coverage make it hard for journalists to confirm the optimistic combat assessments of their sources. While much Ukraine-based journalism offers definitive accounts of Russian military weakness and Ukrainian military capability, journalists in Ukraine were less certain about the trajectory of the war. Many news organizations seem to be prioritizing fragile access at the expense of forthright coverage.

I found journalists in Ukraine grappling with these matters of language and meaning and production, matters we'd discussed in the Middle East. The problem, some journalists agreed, is not that Ukrainians don't deserve supportive coverage; the problem is that such coverage is not granted widely enough. The problem is not that war crimes are being so frequently reported; the problem is that they are being reported impulsively and selectively. Individual journalists can bear witness to suffering, they can give voice to the voiceless, but journalism, as a signifying system, continues to control the representation of war and to hide the impacts of this imposition. Once again, journalists reporting from conflict find themselves in conflict with journalism.

"Even as much of my audience will be sympathetic to Ukrainian suffering and supportive of Ukrainian resistance, there seem to be particular pressures." This is what a journalist told me at a café in Kyiv before a nightly curfew ended our interview. "We report that Russia makes 'false claims' about the war. Why *false*? Why not just *claims*? This kind of insistence is . . ." The journalist searched for a word in the empty city. "It's consequential," he said. "It is consequential, and it is selective."

So was the journalist in the hotel bomb shelter being *censored*? On May 19, 2022, the *New York Times* published a column from their editorial board asking for clarification on US policy in Ukraine. "Is the United States," asked the board, "trying to help bring an end to this conflict through a settlement that would allow for a sovereign Ukraine and some kind of relationship between the United States and Russia? Or is the United States now trying to weaken Russia permanently?" (Editorial Board 2022). The column was published during my time in Ukraine, and it asked many of the questions I'd been considering with journalists on the ground. Such questions, however, remained journalistically off-limits to many of those with whom I spoke. Good coverage, for these journalists, meant applying once again a clean separation of resistance from perpetration, saving from killing.

According to a *Times* journalist in the region, the editor in charge of coverage from Ukraine resented the editorial board column, which risked undermining the reportage he oversaw. For this reportage was indeed in conflict with the issues raised by the editorial. The *Times* coverage, like much of the reportage from Ukraine, granted benefit of the doubt to military and political officials—Ukrainian, European, and American—concerning the purpose and execution of the war, concerning what victory might look like, concerning why civilians were dying and what could be done about it. This benefit was given without any transparency about the gift.[6] But even as human suffering and the necessity of its cessation became the focus of the reportage and, thereby, of the meaning granted to the war, US Secretary of Defense Lloyd Austin announced a contrary US aim: "to see Russia weakened." Joe Biden asserted that Vladimir Putin "cannot remain in power."

What *is* the war in Ukraine, then? Is it a war of democracy against autocracy, as US and NATO officials claim, a war of good versus evil once again? Is it a civil conflict, in which powerful outsiders back opposing sides? Is it a war of imperial conquest, in which Russia plays the role of the United States in Iraq, and the United States plays Iran, supporting the native resistance? Is it a war to preserve the "rules-based international order" or over the right to arbitrate and institute that order? As in news coverage of the War on Terror, only some narratives win credibility in convergence with a dominant consensus.

As the prominence of Ukraine in the news begins to ebb, as the war grinds on, journalists are once again struggling in the wake. After covering war in Iraq, in Syria, in Afghanistan—and, for some, in Libya and Chechnya and the Balkans—war reporters in Ukraine confront familiar challenges in new contexts. The sanctioned language that mystifies the conditions of its appearance in the news. The authorized meanings that occlude the transgressive ones. The professional practices that erase what war is experienced to be. The medieval "censor" was the official judge of cultural production, empowered to assess books and plays for the immoral, the subversive, and the heretical. What is censorship, then, but the displacement of a simmering narrative threat?

In the hotel bomb shelter, the journalist excused herself to struggle with a story on Ukrainian language schools—increasingly obligatory for Ukrainian Russian speakers displaced to western Ukraine. In her story, the journalist hoped to suggest the risks of cultural erasure. But she had to incorporate quotes that uniformly praised Ukrainian repudiation of anything Russian.

I too tried to work, shuffling through a new course syllabus and proofs for a forthcoming article. My mind wandered, and I found myself staring up at the ceiling of the shelter. I gazed toward my field site from the safety of a bunker deep below. There was war's soft underbelly, its amorphous sheen, a story ready to be told this way or that. As war shifts around the globe, as it is experienced and represented, practiced and performed, inflicted, leveraged, and suffered, war remains there, waiting. Soon the air-raid sirens ceased. There was nowhere to go but up.

ACKNOWLEDGMENTS

This text, like those it examines, is embedded in social relations stretching through decades and across continents. While its faults are my own, its existence results from efforts collective.

The History of Consciousness Department, where this book began, casts its peculiar shadow. There, Robert Meister pointed the way through long years and myriad drafts, providing vital insight, administrative wit, and a sensitivity to the project and its struggles. James Clifford gave wisdom and reassurance at every step, cutting through entanglements and grasping the matter's heart. Banu Bargu lent shrewdness to this work, care to its progress, and discernment to its production. Don Brenneis offered recognition amidst uncertainty and vision through the haze.

Two guides did not live to see this book completed. Hayden White and Helene Moglen mark the work from start to finish, as they mark my formation as a thinker and writer. Hayden's encouragement and acuity still resound. Helene gave illumination and spirit to my research and to much more. Their broad erudition and easy grace are a rare combination in the academy today, and my gratitude for their counsel is unbounded. John Perry Barlow, who too left along the way, gave something essential to this work and to the work of living.

Teachers of all kinds furnished the conversation, critique, and care without which a long-term project cannot sustain. Nathaniel Deutsch offered reflection and advice at critical junctures; his composure left a trace.

Daniel Hallin and William T. Vollmann provided intuition and good judgment. Support came from Dorian Bell, Margaret Brose, Nancy Chen, Michael Davidson, Muriam Davis, Allen Feldman, Carla Freccero, Matt Lasar, David Marriott, Morten Pedersen, Eric Porter, Thomas Serres, Max Tomba, and Rob Wilson. Nelson Foster, and everyone at the Ring of Bone, gave guidance on roads winding. Thanks to Ryo Imamura, Carl Bielefeldt, and Curandero Miguel for pushing me along. Thanks to Ken Rodgers at *Kyoto Journal* for the chance in Afghanistan that led to this book.

Colleagues offered perspective, consultation, and courage. Matthew O'Malley and Ryan Lee were steady comrades. Jack Davies, Dylan Fagan, Jane Komori, and Gabriela Salvidea intervened in moments of struggle. Robert Cavooris, Asad Haider, and Delio Vasquez cleared a path through the thicket. For their encouragement, I thank Lana and Ken Andre, Ozan Asik, Jessica Calvanico, Adrian Drummond-Cole, Stephen Engel, Jared Gampel, Patrick King, Natalia Koulinka, Janina Laurenas, James Longley, Michael McCarrin, and Miriam Stone. Rocky and Marco were faithful companions. Chris Chitty's influence abides. Other friends gave heart: Ariel Blake and Caroline McCarthy, Raphael Blake and Kory Trinks, Anne-Lauren Graham, Stephanie d'Arc Taylor, everyone in the Apes Collective. Thank you.

In Beirut and Iraq, hospitality came from Jackson Allers, Giacomo Galeno, Fabiola Hanna and Toni Rouhana, Nisreen Kaj, Lina Khoury and Szymon Urbanczyk, Charbel Maskineh, and Laure de Selys. Their warmth sustained my research.

At the American University of Beirut, my gratitude goes to May Farah, Waleed Hazbun, and Rami Khouri for their accommodation. At the AUB archives, Kaoukab Chebaro and Nada Jahshan gave time and consideration. At the University of Southern California, I am indebted to Tom Hollihan and Jenny Chio, whose support was unwavering. Ajay Batra and Ella Klik were keen interlocutors and savvy coconspirators. Further succor came from Hector Amaya, Mike Ananny, Daniela Bleichmar, Nick Cull, Jennifer Petersen, and Cristina Visperas.

Generous funding from the Wenner-Gren Foundation was essential for this administratively and existentially difficult ethnography. I am grateful to Mary Beth Moss and Danilyn Rutherford for believing in the project at the outset. Further support came from The Humanities Institute at UC Santa Cruz, which continues to nourish strange projects in times of austerity. Thanks especially to Irena Polic for her commitment. The Hoover

Library and Archives at Stanford University, the Society of Fellows in the Humanities at USC, and the Center on Communication Leadership and Policy at USC buoyed this work tremendously.

At Stanford University Press, Dylan Kyung-lim White grasped the project and guided its completion. His care, humor, and discernment made the difference. Austin Araujo, Melissa Chavez, Cindy Lim, Chris Peterson, and David Zielonka shepherded the book through production, while Jennifer Gordon and Fred Kameny granted expertise and ingenuity. I thank the anonymous reviewers of the manuscript for their prudence and insight. Thanks, as well, to the editors of *HAU: Journal of Ethnographic Theory*, *Journal of Applied Journalism & Media Studies*, and *Media, War & Conflict*, where materials from this book first appeared.

My family furnished the necessities. Fox and Adam, Zoe and Hannah, Eileen and Irwin, Miriam and Jack, Amy and Perry and Beth—no thanks are enough. Jack in particular, whose stories of war were as playful as they were bewildering, leaves a deep impression on this work.

Those who gave the most to this research cannot, strangely, be thanked by name. The journalists and fixers whose words and deeds proliferate across these pages are those without whom this book would not exist. Some participated repeatedly and over many years, others more briefly but to incisive effect. These journalists took me through checkpoints, told me their stories, invited me inside—all for a project whose conclusions they may ardently contest. This circumstance is illustrative of a group of journalists working with selflessness and without judgment. They know who they are. I thank them, most deeply, for their generosity and for their trust.

My eternal gratitude to the ten thousand things of Mystery Canyon, Branciforte watershed, on the unceded territory of the Awaswas Nation, where I wrote this work. Gassho.

Finally, to Katherine Andre, who teaches me the most important thing. Without her, little of this project would have worked and little would be worth it. My admiration for her intellect, compassion, and spirit grows unceasingly.

NOTES

Preface

1. I have struggled with what to call the conflicts subsumed under this official designation, which presumes no limits to war's location, duration, or scope. The use of the "so-called" qualifier, as well as scare quotes, are often employed in critical scholarship to draw attention to the ideological saturation of the name, its dubious political and strategic premises, and its moralistic overdetermination. Hereafter, and for ease of reading, I use War on Terror without such modifications (further discussed in Chapter 1). The convenience of the name should not indicate acceptance of what it sanctions, distorts, and obscures.

2. As of writing, the tenor of the Islamic State conflict in Iraq and Syria is much reduced yet still ongoing. The United Nations estimates that over 10,000 Islamic State fighters remain in that region, with cash reserves between $25 million and $50 million. Some 50,000 US troops are stationed in the Middle East, about as many as during the Obama administration, with 2,500 in Iraq and 900 in Syria (not including special operators, contractors, and other irregular forces). In March 2023, the US Department of Defense requested nearly $400 million to help combat the Islamic State, and US military raids against the group's alleged leaders in Syria remain consistent. Islamic State franchise groups continue to grow across Asia and Africa, yet news-consumer interest in the group, and foreign journalistic presence in Iraq and Syria, have declined precipitously.

3. This is not to say that those justifications for civilian death central to the US War on Terror were not being emphasized in the news on Gaza. On October 25, 2023, after thousands of civilians killed in Gaza, and as Israeli airstrikes averaged ten fatalities per casualty-causing strike (Action on Armed

Violence 2023), the *New York Times* reported on the claims of Israeli officials: "To Israelis, there is a necessity and a method to their strikes, which they say are not about retaliation but defense. . . . They argue that strikes that ease an Israeli ground advance will help reduce the loss of life for Palestinian civilians and Israeli soldiers alike, once the invasion begins" (Kingsley 2023). Disseminated here is an official defense of mass killing common to the conflicts treated in this book, wherein civilians are killed for the purposes of their protection. This claim is examined in Chapters 3 and 4.

4. The politics of war's journalistic representation is quickly becoming a mass politics. As Israel began its ground invasion of Gaza, a protest was staged at the headquarters of the *New York Times*. As the Israeli military killed dozens of Gazan journalists while embedding foreign journalists, some journalists in America resigned in opposition to their networks' coverage. News of war is a terrain of popular struggle. In the wake of the deadliest conflict for journalists on record, with media consumers politicized and modes of consumption proliferating, the stakes of war reportage have never seemed higher.

Introduction

1. Names of journalists and fixers have been changed to protect subject anonymity.

2. Just as war reportage employs its own chronotopes (Bakhtin 1982), its own time-space configurations for making meaning in narrative—the frontline, the battlefield, the refugee camp, the morgue, the *war zone* itself—so does the Classy Hotel function in this introduction as a time-space interface indicating the image of the journalist in ethnographic inquiry. As the time frame of the war with the Islamic State thickens into history, as the war takes on the flesh of description, so the war-zone hotel—among other spaces discussed in this book—becomes charged with the movement of scholarly plot. Such spaces organize my story of war because they indicate where war reportage becomes itself.

3. In this manner, ethnography readmits the experiences of war ignored by Baudrillard's account of news and postmodernity. Baudrillard incisively captures the hyperreality of media consumption in a simulacral society. However, and as Robert Stam (1992) observes, Baudrillard fails to indicate the differences between those captivated by mass-mediated warfare and those subject to the violence so mediated.

4. Ethnography too engages in such impositions, as where an individual journalist, situated by the generic conventions of this book, fulfills the role prefigured by the arguments developed in these pages. Self-awareness concerning these discursive dynamics is one means by which to distinguish this text from those under study. Another is the distinct conceptions of truth exercised in different genres of representation. Yet another is the difference in the relations of power inherent to the transformation of particular subjects into discursive objects. An ethnographic account of war's journalists is different, in this sense, from a journalistic account of war's victims.

5. While I do not mean to overstate the influence of journalism, its entanglements with ascertainable sources of power—including governmental and military institutions—is apparent. That war reportage both enhances and reproduces prevailing understandings of war in the Middle East is no inert fact but a circumstance upon which power depends, to at least some degree, for its operation. On this point, I wager a distinction between the so-called CNN effect, wherein reporting on human suffering can push government and military leaders to action, and something more subtle and more diffuse: the ability of media to fix the meaning of war in relation to a "structure of dominance" (Althusser 1971). In a CNN article on Syrian war reportage, journalist Arwa Damon writes, "There were moments when I wished I could transport the decision-makers to Syria so they could bear witness to the extreme suffering and injustice. We tried to depict it, report it as best we could, as raw as we could, but it seemed not to phase [sic] them." Here the possibilities of the "CNN effect" are confused with how dominant interests become dominant and journalism's relation thereto. I return to this matter in Chapter 4.

6. While a number of Middle East–based journalists who participated in this study traveled to Ukraine for brief reporting trips in 2014–2018, the considerable broadening of war in Ukraine in 2022 drew a tremendous influx of journalistic resources. Many of those I interviewed and observed in Iraq, Syria, and Lebanon relocated to Ukraine for extended periods after the Russian invasion in February of 2022, and my fieldwork in Ukraine that spring was intended to survey how war reportage was adjusting to a conflict with distinct political, cultural, and historical conditions. While my findings from Ukraine are suggested in the chapters that follow, and while that war is treated specifically in an epilogue to this book, my research from the Middle East forms the basis for the arguments ahead.

7. I also researched in the personal papers of prominent journalists who covered conflict during World War II, the American War in Vietnam, and the US occupation of Iraq. This archival research was conducted at the Hoover Library and Archives at Stanford University and at the American University of Beirut.

8. As Lindsay Palmer (2018a) notes, it is rare to encounter war reporters who do not work, at least to some degree, across multiple forms of media. The boundary between print and digital is also increasingly porous. Newspaper reporters used to file once daily, their story appearing in the following day's paper. Today, newspaper reporters may file multiple times per day in order to update stories appearing on their newspaper's website (and which might also include photographs and video). This reporting priority was once called "digital first," though the declining use of the term indicates the collapsed distinction, from the perspective of news producers, between digital and print formats.

9. My focus on English-language war reportage, and to a lesser extent French and Arabic war reportage, is intended to support analyses of a single body of journalism in its internal consistency rather than divergence within

this body, for example, between liberal and conservative news organizations, or between public-funded and corporate-funded news. (Much of the war reportage from major French, German, and Arabic news organizations is also published in English; some English-language coverage of the Middle East is also published in Arabic.) This approach to a discourse produced in a certain place, at a certain time, and on a certain topic enables me to reckon with what war reportage, *in general*, is and does, a matter I believe to be both vital and understudied. What war reportage is and does—how human suffering is accounted for, what witness-bearing entails, which words are used and to what effect—must be understood in general before an examination of what war reportage is and does at any specific news organization becomes tenable. Moreover, it is the case that war reportage functions, empirically, as a single body. As will be shown, journalists in war zones often write the same stories, in the same way, as their colleagues from competing news organizations. "Editors will ask me to report what the *New York Times* reports," a journalist in Kobani told me. "There's a herd mentality," a journalist in Beirut insisted. "If the [*Washington*] *Post* covered it and I didn't, I freak out."

10. Oliver Boyd-Barrett (2019) observes that news organizations based in the West are overrepresented in international news reportage, an imbalance reflected in war reportage from the Middle East. The colonial history of war reportage (Hamilton 2009; Spurr 1993) is one source of this disparity; the considerable political and economic capacity required for war coverage is another. Perhaps the most significant institutional absence in this ethnography is Chinese journalism, a growing presence in war zones, though still minor compared with American and European coverage. Shixin Ivy Zhang argues that while Chinese journalists have covered foreign wars since the 1990s, it was only with the 2011 conflict in Libya that Chinese-language media made a "collective debut on the world's battlefield" (2016, 3). Chinese journalists covered the wars treated in this book, but their reportage is outside its scope.

11. For many of the foreign journalists in this study, Iraq, Syria, and Lebanon functioned as a contiguous beat. Many Beirut-based journalists also covered Syria, either through short reporting trips or entirely remotely after that country become less hospitable to consistent journalistic presence. A few Beirut-based journalists also made regular reporting trips to Iraq. Many journalists in Iraq occasionally reported on Syria, traveling over the border from regular posts in Baghdad or Erbil (the latter city becoming more central during the battle for Mosul, and logistically easier with visa-free entry for many foreigners). Journalists who primarily covered Syria tended to base themselves in Istanbul or Beirut, and less often in Erbil, after the risks of long-term reporting from the country increased.

12. The conflict in Syria may be the most documented war in history. Even the recent absence of foreign journalists in much of the country has not lessened the endless stream of cellphone footage, satellite imagery, and local Syrian journalism representing the now teenaged war. However, the ability of this alternative documentation to gain widespread attention in the media

marketplace—and its capacity to expand or otherwise alter perceptions of the war—remain limited. It should be noted, too, that many mainstream news organizations deploy citizen journalism on their own platforms (and for their own purposes) without offering compensation to its producers (Palmer 2012). A study by Colleen Murrell (2018) indicates that Reuters, the Associated Press, and Agence France-Presse were sourcing Syrian citizen videos from YouTube and passing them to news clients. On the biases inherent to remote reporting on Syria, see Oliver Boyd-Barrett (2021) and Richard Pendry (2015).

13. The potential audience for the kind of war reportage engaged in this book is probably a few hundred thousand print subscribers and a few hundred thousand online pageviews, though proprietary data and social media circulation make consumption rates difficult to track. This estimated rate of daily consumption is sizable, though it remains relative; a *Washington Post* blog post on the war in Syria, titled "9 Questions on Syria for People Who Are Underinformed," received 9 million pageviews, much more than a news story in the same paper reported from Syria (Kaphle 2015). We can assume that consumption rates for war reportage are subject to wide swings, given the alternating importance and banality of faraway war for most news consumers.

14. The ever-declining number of newspapers able to support foreign coverage often do so through a broad-church approach, subsidizing such reportage through cooking recipes, puzzles, live events, merchandizing, and other income-generating enterprises.

15. Historical examples can be found for most of the major problems often treated as novel in the news industry today. "The Problem of False News," a 1932 address to the League of Nations on behalf of the International Association of Journalists Accredited, diagnoses misinformation and its social impact in a manner strikingly contemporary: "the delicate problem of the dissemination of false news liable to trouble the maintenance of the peace and understanding of the peoples" (Streit 1937, 67). This address inveighs, in familiar terms, against the intensity of the news cycle ("we have against us too the speed with which the news must be gathered, written, transmitted, edited, put in type, printed, and distributed" [65]) and the dire economic conditions of journalism ("the news, although it is an extremely costly thing to gather and distribute—and the more accurate, the more costly—is the one necessity for which no one anywhere is willing to pay anywhere near what it costs to produce" [66]). The solutions offered in the address to the problems of misinformation and financial distress are also identical to those being proposed today: state subsidies for news production, independent fact-checking institutions, better press access to government bodies, "freedom of the press" broadly.

16. At a campus talk with a journalist who covered the US war in Iraq, a theorist of some renown was heard to ask, during the Q&A, "How could you be so brave?" The question asked (if one can call it a question) suggests the way that war reportage is often exempted from critical inquiry into its obvious— perhaps *too* obvious—discursivity.

17. The most influential intervention in reception studies of journalism is

probably Nick Couldry's (2014). On the "audience turn" in journalism research, see Irena Costera-Meijer (2016). For a study of audience responses to war reportage in the early War on Terror era, see Jean Seaton (2003).

18. Such spaces become, as chronotopes, both a cognitive concept (a means to understanding the practice and discourse of war reportage) and a narrative feature (a way to express what war reportage is like). They are, for this text, both fact and figure.

Chapter 1

1. Here, and throughout this book, I consider war reportage as a narrative form originating in the West but today thoroughly globalized. My research indicates that journalists working for international news outlets based in Doha and Abu Dhabi engage in similar work routines, employ similar narrative tropes, and make similar meanings for war as those working for organizations based in New York and Paris. War's reality, as rendered in war reportage, is not the domain of any specific nation or culture but the reflection of a dominant knowledge functioning across cultures, a hegemonic worldview operating over and above other ideas (some locally produced) also always in operation. While meanings for war particular to a Paris or a Doha certainly exist, and distinctions among consumers' reception of war reportage are no doubt myriad, the "common sense" reproduced in war reportage is not geographically bounded thereby. The advertising prerogative to reach the broadest possible news audience; the digital dispersion of news de-coupled from any national economy; the topical character of war and its presumed global importance; and a reigning neoliberal context within which information circulates all serve to abstract war's meaning, as delivered through war reportage, from the particulars of any located consumer base (Appadurai 1996; Hepp and Couldry 2009; Mattelart 2009). To assert war reportage as globalized is not to deny the distinct "house styles" and editorial lines of any individual news organization, nor to overlook the varied reciprocal influences between media and local institutions. I do not mean to suggest that national media systems, nor news organizations based within a single nation, cannot be compared. My position, rather, is that war reportage—a subgenre of journalism operating under specific conditions—is engaged with practical and discursive conventions now globally pervasive.

2. The primary purpose of news organizations' style manuals is to standardize use of language. It is through regularity in spelling, grammar, and other linguistic elements that the presence of language itself, as a signifying technology, can more easily escape notice. The mimetic performance of the news is thereby preserved. Differences in narrative style among a news organization's articles, or inconsistencies in the use of a particular phrase across the body of a newspaper's coverage, can suggest the contingency and craft of language, revealing a gap between reality and its representation that journalism attempts to obscure.

3. To examine war reportage as a narrative production does not entail a

rejection of journalistic truth claims as illusory, fictive, "fake." Rather, such an examination indicates how war reportage elaborates war through a system of organization and control, a system that shapes what war *is* for news consumers. The news is no more fake than any discursive production, even as it must still be affirmed that some truths remain better than others. I return to this matter in the book's conclusion.

4. For this work, Arkady won the prestigious Bayeux Prize (Bayeux Calvados-Normandy Award) for war correspondents in 2017 and the Free Press Unlimited's Most Resilient Journalist Award in 2019. His work was exhibited as part of the 2017 Venice Biennale.

5. In a study of crime reporting in Venezuela, Charles Briggs notes that "communicable maps and the people interpellated by them are generally projected in moral and ethical terms—as being heroic, rational, and agentive by virtue of their placement in desirable subject positions or malevolent, irrational, ignorant, or passive because of their insertion in villainous slots" (2007b, 344). Briggs argues that this narrative placement can help us understand the way moral positions on a given event are created and naturalized. Chapters 3 and 4 address the moral valence ascribed to war in war reportage; here we can note how the narrative positions granted to subjects in war cohere with a dominant moral order.

6. Two other factors relating to Arkady's reportage should be noted. The first is his medium. As a photographer, his evidence of "protagonist" violence landed differently than a written account would have, and it confronted the distinct dynamics of visual epistemology in realism. (On visual realism, see Millar 2011; on realism in photography see Ray 2020.) The second factor is that Arkady is Iraqi. His localness may have been decisive in the access he was granted to the ERD and the trust he evidently earned. The stakes of Arkady's decision to publish his images were also higher than they would have been for a foreigner. Arkady risked much for this reportage, and he continues to inspire Iraqi journalists especially. I address the matter of localness in the following chapter; see also Blacksin 2022 and Blacksin and Mitra 2023.

7. In 2022, I spoke with Ali Arkady in Paris, where he remained in exile five years after the publication of his footage of the ERD. Arkady's reputation in Iraq has recently improved, however, after one of the soldiers featured in that footage was implicated in the shooting of Iraqi citizens during mass protests in 2020. (The soldier was sentenced to life in prison in 2023.) In Paris, Ali is completing a degree in fine arts, producing mixed-media works that combine photography, lithography, and sculpture, and he recently undertook a journalistic project in Ukraine. I asked Arkady if there was anything he might have done differently during the publication process that led to his exile. "I wouldn't change a thing," he told me.

8. The politics of definition has been recently addressed in studies of anti-Black racism, Islamophobia, and antisemitism, wherein viewpoints and experiences in conflict with a reigning political and legal order are shown to be obscured by the implementation of monolithic, censorious, ethnocentric, and

historically contingent definitions. Rebecca Ruth Gould, for example, argues that a "definitional turn" in public engagement with racism and antisemitism in the UK, and which lends the appearance of government action, should be replaced by a Geertzian "thick description" that can account for contradictory experiences of racism in order to achieve a dialogic, "non-definitional approach to racism outside of legal contexts" and liberal governmentality (2023, 10). The "thin" definitions yielded by ethnographic description, asserts Gould, can allow for structural changes more plausible than when "the state adopts an overreaching definition to appease specific political agendas" (2023, 12).

9. The 1999 NATO intervention of Kosovo is illustrative. The rationale for that intervention—a pattern of Serbian abuse against an ethnic Albanian minority, amounting to ethnic cleansing—could as easily be read as a low-grade civil war with casualties on both sides. To build the case for intervention, a retrospective investigation cited a process in which "ethnic-Albanian militants, humanitarian organizations, NATO and the news media fed off each other to give genocide rumors credibility" (Pearl and Block 2001). Rather than the 500,000 deaths from Yugoslavia's preintervention ethnic conflict, reported by major news organizations, it is likely that in the three years preceding the NATO intervention, some 2,000 to 3,000 people died. This number is lower per capita than the murder rates of New York, Oakland, Houston, Las Vegas, and other American cities during the same period. Yet violence in American cities is understood in ways distinct from the violence of sectarian conflict. Robberies, child custody disputes, domestic violence, and other circumstances leading to homicide—circumstances often tied to structural features of modern life in the United States and occurring within centers of global power—do not prompt calls for outside military intervention. Such violence reflects different interests, elicits different responses, and is classified differently.

10. "Officer-involved shooting," journalism's conventional designation when reporting on incidents of police violence in the United States, controls the reality of that violence by obscuring the agency of the police officer therein. Headlines such as "Rocket Kills Teenager in Iran" (*Financial Times,* April 9, 2003) and "Famine Stalks Yemen, as War Drags on and Foreign Aid Wanes" (*New York Times,* March 31, 2021) express a similar resistance to naming the agent of controversial acts of violence. (Compare the latter headline with "How Russia Is Using Ukrainians' Hunger as a Weapon of War," from the *New York Times,* March 29, 2022.) These choices reify particular power dynamics concerning the use of force and its public appraisal.

11. As with style guides, editorial influence can drive the choice of designation. "Words like 'fanaticism' creep into newspapers," a journalist explained to me in Beirut. "The deputy editor of my newspaper put 'fanatical' into my story. We argued about it." Names, especially when appearing in news headlines, can also be essential to search engine optimization (SEO) and must then correspond with the terminology an internet-searching public *already* employs. That is, SEO considerations motivate news producers to match the names

given in war news with audience expectations for how war is named, thereby reaffirming such names' self-evidence.

12. Along with "so-called Islamic State," many news organization style guides stipulate use of "self-proclaimed Islamic State" to much the same effect. The Associated Press style guide mandates "Islamic State group," a more subtle undermining of Islamic State claims to statehood.

13. There is no entry for "terrorism" in the *New York Times* style manual, the AP style manual, or many other such guides, leaving the use or avoidance of the term to the discretion of journalists and editors. The journalists I interviewed often attested to using "terrorism" adjectivally while avoided the term as a noun (e.g., a "terroristic" attack, conducted by a "gunman" rather than a "terrorist"). Philip B. Corbett (2007), a deputy editor in charge of language use at the *New York Times*, including updates to the style manual, explained: "We editors rely on the judgment, experience and accuracy of our correspondents and trust them to report events fairly and completely. It would be absurd for me, sitting here in Manhattan, to try to explain . . . what constitutes terrorism or how best to describe events in . . . troubled places. [*Times* journalists] see it, they understand it, and their only goal is to help us know what's happening."

14. Iraqis use various names for the 2003–2011 US war in Iraq, which the US military officially designates as Operation Iraqi Freedom until 2010 and Operation New Dawn until 2011, and which is subsumed under the Global War on Terror moniker. For Iraqis, it is "Bush's War" (perhaps to distinguish it from the conflicts directed against Iraq by US presidents Clinton and Bush Sr.) or "The Fall" (which carries reference to the social collapse of the post-Ottoman period). The year 2003 is known as "The Year of Change." It is vital to note, too, that many Iraqis consider the US war in Iraq to have begun with the financial and trade sanctions imposed in 1990—a timeline that defies the standards normative to international journalism concerning what can be named as "war."

15. A critical matter is whether "war" can function as an allegory for a situation that might exceed or even threaten a consensual definition of war, or whether the application of the name necessarily constrains understandings of that situation. While war reportage "entextualizes" conflict conditions in ways that are internally self-referential (Silverstein and Urban 1996), war reportage also indexes something of those conditions. The extent to which war functions differently outside journalism as it does inside—the extent to which war is reducible to the tropes that represent it—remains, I think, an open question. I return to this question in the book's conclusion.

16. This expectation coheres with a long history of Beirut as a site of foreign intervention. Along with the rest of Lebanon, Beirut was placed under French rule after the collapse of the Ottoman empire and the Franco-British colonial partition of the Middle East. During the long Lebanese civil war (1975–1990), Beirut became an arena for international conflict as Syria, the United States, Iran, Israel, France, Saudi Arabia, and other European and Middle Eastern states attempted to advance their interests directly and indirectly in the city.

Syrian military presence in Beirut until 2005, Israeli bombing of the city in 2006, and continued foreign pressures amidst Lebanon's recent economic meltdown all precondition the kind of place Beirut is thought to be. The matter at hand is how language naturalizes, and thereby legitimates, military intervention in Beirut. The history of the city as a proxy battleground for outside power does not, of itself, establish the self-evidence of interventionary possibility in Beirut; rather, the designations applied help to determine what is deemed possible. On the modern history of Beirut, see Fawwaz Traboulsi 2012.

Chapter 2

1. One of Johannes Gutenberg's earliest publications, a six-leaf pamphlet of 1454 titled *A Warning to Christendom Against the Turks*, similarly concerns the threat of violence from a distant Other.

2. As territorial gains diminish in importance both militarily (in an age of counterinsurgency and asymmetrical warfare) and journalistically (with the focus on civilian casualties and the influence of the humanitarian paradigm, discussed in the following chapter), death tallies have become a primary measure of war's progress. This circumstance has led to official manipulation of body counts, mostly famously during the American war in Vietnam. There, the "body count incentive" prompted US commanders to pad their tallies of enemy dead with civilian deaths, or to exaggerate body counts altogether (Appy 2000; Bellamy 2017). When the publication of death tallies risks unwanted anti-war sentiment, official withholding of such numbers increases. "I don't do body counts," Defense Secretary Donald Rumsfeld told CBS News in March 2002, during the early days of the US war in Afghanistan. "This country tried that in Vietnam, and it didn't work."

3. Geographic relativity folds in others: perceived social importance (where a few of "us" killed trumps journalistic attention to many of "them" killed), novelty (where a few killed in an area considered peaceful trumps journalistic attention to many killed in an area considered violent), and exoticism (where a few killed by bombing trumps journalistic attention to many killed by car crash). These kinds of distinctions are, of course, not natural but social, political, discursive—factors hidden behind the self-evidence of a casualty count.

4. According to Shannon Pufahl (2020), efforts to count the dead during the US Civil War assumed, for the first time in modern warfare, a significance beyond mere accuracy. For the families of those killed in battle, enumeration of the dead allowed for solace and closure; for the general public, it allowed for engagement with the devastation of that war. Death became manageable as death was quantified, Pufahl argues, "making [death] specific and contained, rather than abstract" (2020). The legibility of statistical enumeration became the legibility of death itself.

5. Perhaps the most well-known number of dead is the 6 million Jews killed in the Holocaust, a number that functions as something more or other than a statistical estimation: It functions as an expression of mass murder beyond the pale of reason. The symbolic power of this number, as a moral truth of the Ho-

locaust, is difficult to overestimate; were a numerical rendering of the Holocaust unavailable, one would have to be invented. But when considering the work, social and discursive, that numbers like "6 million" do, the line between availability and invention can seem to blur. The meaning of a number of dead need not correspond to its accuracy even as accuracy underwrites the meaning made.

6. According to Jay Aronson (2013), higher estimates for war casualties are often challenged—in the media and elsewhere—on technical grounds, while lower estimates, subject to the same criticisms, are rarely scrutinized.

7. For many years, journalists reported that 200,000 to 300,000 Bosniaks were killed in the Bosnian War between 1992 and 1995. The source of this number, according to Lara Nettelfield (2010) and others, was a 1992 meeting between Bosnian president Alija Izetbegivic, his foreign minister Haris Silajdzic, and his army commander Sefer Halilovic, in which the three men discussed how many deaths to attribute to Serbian military and militia aggression. Izetbegivic reportedly suggested 150,000 as a number adequate to stir international hearts and justify a foreign military intervention. During a press conference after the meeting, however, Silajdzic cited 250,000 as the number of Bosniaks killed. By the summer of 1993, it became conventional for international media to report that Serbian forces had killed 250,000 Bosniaks, and though the conflict continued until December 1995, that number was never widely adjusted. In 2003, the International Criminal Tribunal for Yugoslavia, using demographic techniques, estimated the number of Bosniaks killed as 102,622, of whom 55,261 were civilians (Tabeau and Bijak 2005). Journalists, academics, and diplomats (including Richard Holbrooke, who brokered the Dayton Peace Accords to end that war) continued to state that 250,000 Bosniaks died in the conflict. Of course, the higher estimation suited the interests of both Bosnian and US political leaders, who justified a military invasion on the premise of saving Bosniak lives.

8. By 2016, many journalists had only intermittent access to conditions on the ground in Syria. As a popular uprising descended into asymmetrical warfare, and territory friendly to international and local press shrunk, many foreign journalists began to cover much of Syria from Lebanon, Turkey, and other locations farther afield. Though reporting trips to areas controlled by the Syrian state—often tightly monitored—still occurred, and areas of northeast Syria under the control of Kurdish groups were more open to foreign media presence, large swaths of Syria remained effectively closed to the international press. The killing of journalist Marie Colvin and the disappearance of journalist Austin Tice dissuaded many news organizations from risking the safety of their reporters, and an industrywide moratorium on freelancer-produced stories from Syria (albeit porous) left coverage in the hands of local Syrian journalists and activists, on the one hand, and reporting conducted through WhatsApp, Telegram, and other remote means on the other. "In Beirut we're doing 99 percent Syria content," a journalist for a British news organization explained in Beirut. "If there was no WhatsApp, there might be no Syria coverage." The journalist showed me her phone, where WhatsApp contacts were

grouped by region in Syria, political persuasion (pro-regime, anti-regime secular, anti-regime Islamist), and role (state military soldier, anti-regime activist, etc.). She continued, "I don't see this kind of reporting as reliable or responsible. The tone used in the news is way more definitive than the reality is." On the ethical implications of remote reporting on Syria, see Richard Pendry (2015) and Oliver Boyd-Barrett (2021).

9. The estimations of these latter organizations include only those casualties that can be verified by name and often lack data for areas controlled by the Syrian state. These organizations are clear that unverified deaths are not included in their estimations, nor are war-related deaths from exposure or lack of medical care, resulting in almost certain undercounts.

10. Not all news organizations are drawn to higher casualty rates in a given instance. A journalist in Erbil insisted that the policy of his news organization was to choose the lowest estimate, so as "not to bring people back from the dead." As noted of the death tallies produced after the US invasion of Iraq, sometimes lower tallies are more likely to find resonance in the news media. Whether higher or lower numbers of dead gain journalistic prominence depends, again, on the social and political conditions undergirding a particular number's appearance in the news.

11. More recent updates to both SOHR and UN death tolls for the war in Syria indicate less an increasingly exacting process of casualty estimation than an ongoing management of the contingencies inherent to counting casualties. In citing these numbers, journalism remains downstream from this process.

12. This customary deemphasis has its exceptions. An increasing number of news organizations feature "behind the scenes" columns (such as the *New York Times*'s "Times Insider" column) wherein a journalist explains, using first-person pronouns, how they reported a given story. Such efforts may be an attempt to counter perceived distrust of the news media through the transparency and proof of presence that first-person pronouns rhetorically provide. In the age of podcasts, social media, and online influencers, such columns may also signal a trend toward personality and celebrity in news production. Where the company brand was once prioritized over any individual journalist, particularly for print publications, the shift to individuality follows the fashion of podcasting and cable news. Consider the *New York Times*, once considered an "editor's paper," where uniformity of writing—and resistance to even bylines—suited the "Gray Lady" moniker (Ritchie 2006, 12; Tifft and Jones 2000, 67). Today, a standard *Times* article includes a profile photo of the journalist and a brief bio. This shift toward authorial presence can make journalists uncomfortable. As a journalist in Erbil explained, "There's investment in reporters on the ground, and the shift to first-person is meant to show [my news organization] has people on the ground. But first-person narrative puts the focus on the journalist rather than what's actually going on."

13. Most news stories published by the wire services (Reuters, Agence France-Presse, and the Associated Press) run without a byline. Here the mystification of authorial imposition is even more comprehensive.

14. Description similarly offers proof of journalistic presence, and thus of the authority of "being there," without the complications of subjectivity. Description manifests factuality and hides the retrospective, referential, and semiotic basis of its occurrence in the news text. As noted in Chapter 6, the proliferation of description is one way to assert a text's mimetic status. This is the "reality effect" of description (Barthes 1968), wherein the inclusion of details unrelated to the newsworthiness of a given event indicates to the news consumer that reality is speaking for itself. However, the inclusion of seemingly random detail—an inclusion provided in this text too—confirms the constructedness of description, insofar as any number of details can evoke this mimetic authenticity. Description simultaneously disavows and draws attention to itself as a formal strategy of reality production (Cobley 1993), and thereby reveals the contingency it attempts to master. A journalist in Beirut told me, "My organization dissuades us from adjectival promiscuity. Hezbollah's is not a 'vibrant' flag. It terrorizes people. That language is biased. We have to strike balance in language. The language itself does work." A journalist in Baghdad remarked, "It's amazing what a little color can do to change a story."

15. The necessity of presence to the authority of news of violence is not new. Andrew Pettegree notes the considerable competition, among news producers in seventeenth-century Paris, "for windows that overlooked the prisoner's route [to their execution] or, still better, the actual place of suffering" (2014, 323).

16. In war reportage, the value of the dateline is its proof of journalistic presence in the war zone and in other sites of violence, specifically. However, in constricting the importance of presence to such spaces, war reportage downgrades the relevance of any other geographic locale. Sites of weapons manufacture, policymaking, and colonial history are sidelined. On the flattening of politics inherent to the geographic configuration of the "war zone," see Lindsay Palmer (2018a).

17. According to Shayna Plaut and Peter Klein, most news fixers have other professions and earn only a moderate income from fixing (2019, 1705). This may be true in some circumstances, but war (as for many industries) drives prices up. Fixers assisting with frontline newspaper coverage in Mosul could earn $400 per day—and much more for television production—in a country with a per capita income of about $10,000.

18. Knowledge, of course, is embodied, and here the racial, ethnic, and especially gendered dynamics of war reportage come to the fore. Particular identities can delimit the kinds of news that fixers are tasked to produce (Blacksin and Mitra 2023) as well as the access upon which journalism depends (Palmer and Melki 2018). While the hybrid racial and ethnic identities of many foreign journalists muddy some of the divides between local and foreigner, journalists and fixers—both men and women—frequently asserted the privilege of female news makers in the Middle East to access spaces gendered female under dominant regional norms. Fixers are sometimes chosen to overcome such access

limitations, as when a male journalist uses a female fixer to gain entry to women's homes, or a Sunni or Shia fixer is chosen to reach these respective communities. It is worth noting, moreover, that fixers' attunement to local gender norms can also free journalists from the same constraints. "Being a foreign correspondent as a woman actually is an opportunity to live outside the gendered rubric," a journalist explained in Beirut. "You're not treated wholly in terms of the gendered binary of the society you're in, and you're outside of your own society's gendered strictures, to an extent. Living as a kind of traveler nomad allows for a kind of androgyny that I think the early female colonial explorers enjoyed as well. But there's a discomfort there too because your 'gender freedom' is happening in the same space and time as other women are experiencing their own gendered lock-in." Gender identity, as a factor in the profession and production of news, can be experienced very differently across local-foreign divides. It is also the case, of course, that identity categories inform the structural precarities that place some individuals and populations at greater risk in war. On gender dynamics in war reportage, see Berit Von der Lippe and Rune Ottosen (2016).

19. The expectations of a global news audience can also be managed on the editorial level. A wire service editor in New York explained, "The foreign correspondent knows what's going on there, but editors know what the audience wants. That's a danger of foreign correspondence, knowing what's important in the region but not shaping stories for what's important at home." A journalist in Beirut made the same point: "The editor is closer to the home audience and acts as the representative of that audience."

20. This is not to say that local news-producers in the Middle East are always unfamiliar with the consumer worldview to which international reportage responds. Nor do I mean to deny the cosmopolitanism of fixers and other local news workers. Rather, fixers' ability to act as linguistic, professional, and cultural mediators—an ability that cuts across assumed divisions between foreign and local, professional and amateur—can be understood as a "cosmopolitan capital" necessary for fixers to "accumulate, cultivate, and leverage" in their pursuit of agency and success in journalism (Blacksin and Mitra 2023, 10).

21. The policy of rotating foreign journalists through international bureaus every few years, common to many media organizations, attests to an industry preference for a "foreign perspective" and the assumed danger of becoming "lost in the weeds" of a given beat. Localness is here assumed to disrupt the perspective essential to international news. As a newspaper editor in New York told me, "If you are living in the country, you can't help but have some stake in the conflict. We teach people to be objective, which counters this attachment. Our editors are more remote and can balance the emotional tug." On the presumed threat of affective attachment to conflict journalism, see Kotišová 2023.

22. Byline bestowal can be a matter of institutional policy or an individual journalist's discretion. "If they bring me an idea, they'll share a byline," a journalist told me in Beirut. Yet according to a recent study, out of 450 journalists

surveyed, 60 percent stated that fixers "never" or "rarely" get published credit for their work (Plaut and Klein 2019, 1705). Fixers are getting more bylines than in the past, though this trend, along with "contributor" credit at the end of a news story, seems active only at a few media organizations. It should be noted, too, that many fixers do not want bylines. Whether because of the risks of association with the international press, or lack of interest in the professional prestige afforded by the byline, some fixers reject authorial credit. "If ISIS comes to Erbil, fixers are the first people to be beheaded," a fixer told me, laughing.

23. This is not to suggest that the knowledge produced and authorized by global news organizations is any less "situated" than the knowledge of local fixers. Rather, the respective positionality of these knowledges is judged, valued, and understood differently within the culture of foreign news professionalism. The presumed universalism of war reportage distinguishes itself from the presumed provincialism of local concerns, and here the cosmopolitanism of fixers—who regularly traverse cultural, linguistic, geographic, and professional borders—is displaced by the professed totality of international news.

24. Robert Stam, in his examination of Gulf War reportage, identifies a journalistic capacity to promote "the regime of the 'fictive We'" (1992, 124). This symbolic regime, Stam argues, creates a narcissistic relationship between news producers and news consumers, in which this "fictive We" can "speak warmly about 'our side' and 'our troops' and project hostility toward whoever happens to be posited as 'them,' a 'misrecognition' with profound political consequences" (1992, 124). The journalist–audience relationship is posited to be free of any fissures, and thus, like the "Support Our Troops" slogan, disregards any divisions in a society that may be engaged in war and consuming news thereon.

25. Of course, journalism might take on a different form in a differently fetishizing society. A surrealist or fantastical account of war—commodity forms of wartime reality that may hold market value as novels, for example—can be imagined for journalism. But in many contemporary news-consuming societies, which fetishize war as they do, the prominent form for the commodity of war's representation is the realist journalistic narrative, with its particular tropes and categories, descriptions and definitions, numbers and authors. These elements are widely recognized—in America, in Europe, in the Middle East—as the way war realistically is, even as that recognition is actively cultivated rather than naturally occurring.

Chapter 3

1. The headline of a prominent 2017 feature article on Mosul from the *New York Times Magazine* establishes the relevant taxonomy: "The Living and the Dead" (Verini 2017).

2. As Leila Fadel, who covered the Middle East for National Public Radio, told *Vogue* magazine, "I don't think of myself as a war reporter. I just cover people" (in Ruiz 2022). This focus is also editorially enforced. "The stories

editors will want," a journalist in Erbil explained, "are stories told through people. Human-centered. Characters are a constant." Such narrative emphasis adheres to what Zsuzsa Ferge (1997) calls the "individualization of the social" under neoliberalism, in which broader structural forces are eclipsed.

3. Here I am tracking the humanitarian logic undergirding the meaning that contemporary war reportage makes. This task is distinct from an account of the kind of explicit journalistic advocacy for humanitarian intervention popular in the post–Cold War period (Ignatieff 1998; Rotberg and Weiss 1996; Shaw 1996) and in which mass media was tasked to depict suffering and thereby enhance consumer eagerness for "saving strangers" (Wheeler 2000; see also Boltanski 1993). My argument is that the meanings for war made in contemporary war reportage are more than procedural—more than a matter of explicit advocacy for or critique of an intervention—but arise through journalism's formal commitments. An analysis of war's meaning requires an account of how war reportage both normalizes and obscures a dominant order in its emphases, omissions, and ideals. Revealed, in this case, is how the internal logic of war reportage works in convergence with powerful interests, not as some functionalist mode of representation in service of power, but rather, and as Melani McAlister argues of cultural practices broadly, as a process in which events and interests reach a "productive, if historically contingent, accord" (2005, 8).

4. Here, for instance, is a lead excerpted from one of the stories nominated by the Pulitzer committee, "Liberation from Militants Leaves Devastation in Mosul," from the Associated Press (July 14, 2017): " 'All that's left is rubble and the bodies of families trapped underneath,' the 23-year-old said. He flipped through photos on his phone, showing picture after picture of wreckage. His own house was 'cut in half,' he said. He had to cover his nose with his tee-shirt because of the smell of buried, rotting bodies" (George 2017). Another Pulitzer Prize–nominated article, "Smothered by the Islamic State, an Iraqi Teen Dares to Dream," also from the Associated Press (December 14, 2017), showcased both individuated suffering and perpetrator extremity: "Ferah felt the gunmen looming outside her window—frightening, huge and muscular, with beards down to their chests. Her mother went pale. A simple drive to a friend's house was spiraling into disaster" (Janssen and Keath 2017). And here is an excerpt from another nominated article, "ISIS Enshrines a Theology of Rape," from the *New York Times* (August 13, 2015): "In the moments before he raped the 12-year-old girl, the Islamic State fighter took the time to explain that what he was about to do was not a sin. Because the preteen girl practiced a religion other than Islam, the Quran not only gave him the right to rape her—it condoned and encouraged it, he insisted. He bound her hands and gagged her" (Callimachi 2015). For the nominations, see https://www.pulitzer.org/prize-winners-by-category/210.

5. Mike Ananny (2020) argues that an "anticipatory news infrastructure" predisposes the press to anticipate and circulate particular kinds of news. Richard Grusin's theory of "premeditation," in which mass media focuses on

the "desire to make sure that the future has already been pre-mediated before it turns into the present" (2010, 4), further indicates how the media elicits and responds to consumer expectation. My point is more general. In an era when humanitarianism informs dominant understandings of war in particular societies (Bradley 2016; Douzinas and Gearty 2014; Iriye et al. 2012), journalists reporting to those societies will create meanings that cohere with this established consensus.

6. While military interventions were, historically, sometimes justified by the necessary defense of weak states or the imperative to support liberation movements, the protection of populations and the saving of individual lives is a justification for militarism of very recent vintage (see Fassin and Pandolfi 2010).

7. What Joseph Masco (2014) calls the "logic of preemption," in which present violence is sold as preventative of greater future violence, allows for a moral justification for humanitarian violence even *without* an ongoing violence it purports to stop. Historical and political context is replaced with a moralizing and speculative frame. On this logic, see also Lisa Hajjar (2012) and Kali Rubaii (2020).

8. Relevant here is Maxwell McComb's well-known theory of agenda setting, wherein "the enormous social influence of mass communication" works to focus societal attention on some key issues (such as victimhood in war) at the expense of others (2004, ix). John B. Thompson's related notion of "discursive elaboration" (1995), which refers to how media messages are generalized through processes of telling and retelling, is also useful for considering how a particular event of war is decontextualized through the humanitarian paradigm. Such theories tend to overlook the power and agency of journalists, however, and a more "cultural" approach (Van Hout and Jacobs 2008), sensitive to the role of journalists in news representation, seems better equipped to gauge the productive relationship between war reportage and humanitarianism. The nature of this relationship is best captured, I think, through what Max Weber ([1930] 2013), following Goethe, calls "elective affinity" (*Wahlverwandtschaft*), whereby two historically independent cultural formations join to create a bond both generative and powerful. The kinship between war reportage and humanitarianism is one of reciprocal attraction, mutual reinforcement, and active convergence. While not a substitute for other accounts of how humanitarianism and war reportage come to share reference points and explanatory paradigms, the notion of elective affinity expresses the resonance between systems of belief operating in different, if overlapping, spheres of cultural life.

9. Checkpoints, of course, are something else entirely for local people. Checkpoints restrict movement and thus operate as a mechanism of control. They demand identification and thereby work to surveille. They disrupt commerce and in this way impact livelihoods. They expand state and militia power, transform public space, instill fear as well as relief. On these and related dynamics of checkpoints in Iraq, see Omar Sirri (2021).

10. The story of Islamic State prisoners and their mistreatment by Iraqi security forces did gain traction in the weeks that followed this occurrence at the Aqrab gate, with prominent articles published on the summary executions of suspected Islamic State fighters. However, the heroism of Iraqi security forces—a crucial party to the international Coalition fighting the Islamic State—was a narrative difficult for journalists to relinquish, as discussed in Chapter 1.

11. Operation Inherent Resolve is the Pentagon's designation for the broader campaign against the Islamic State in Iraq and Syria (as well as a related campaign in Libya). That the choice to fight the Islamic State is no choice at all but rather *inherent*—a self-evident matter, not open to deliberation—suggests the broader foreclosure of questions regarding the intent of the intervention. The moralistic flavor of this designation also rhymes with other recent US operation names, such as Operation Just Cause (for the 1989 invasion of Panama), Operation Restore Hope (in Somalia in 1992), and Operation Uphold Democracy (in Haiti in 1994), as well as Enduring Freedom in Afghanistan (2001) and Iraqi Freedom in Iraq (2003). These kinds of designations mark a departure from the more whimsical operation names of the Cold War period—Operation Mongoose in Cuba (1961), for example, or Operation Menu in Cambodia (1969), or Project Wizard in Congo (1962)—when the morality of military intervention was not yet the dominant rhetorical register.

12. While much criticism, scholarly and journalistic, has been given to the Islamic State's own media apparatus, and particularly to the spectacle of violence it delivers, the charges implicit in such critique are also applicable to international media. Here is Anne Barnard, then Beirut bureau chief for the *New York Times* (February 20, 2015): "Broadcast specifically to frighten and manipulate . . . the [Islamic State's] bloody imagery, flooding social media already widely used to chronicle conflict, makes violence seem ubiquitous, even mesmerizing, and spurs a sensory overload that can both provoke feelings and numb them. . . . But while some groups want to publicize suffering in order to stop it, analysts said perpetrators like the Islamic State seek to magnify the suffering by inflicting it twice—first on the victim and then on the viewer." As will be discussed, the imputation of motive is normally anathema to journalistic objectivity. But here, the motive for Islamic State representations of violence is assumed to be the further infliction of suffering rather than the condemnation of such infliction assumed of very similar representations, including journalism's. Absent this imputation, however, Bernard's description of Islamic State media is perfectly applicable to her own news organization's reportage from the Middle East. Moreover, it bears mentioning that many Islamic State execution videos, including the killing of James Foley, are not as gruesome as they could have been (and as many previous al-Qaeda videos were). That particular video cuts away at the moment of Foley's murder. Perhaps the video was edited in a manner known to be acceptable for circulation in international news media. The Islamic State's representation of violence in this way responds to, rather than violates, the strictures of contemporary war reportage. Barbie

Zelizer (2018, 18) notes the broader structural similarities between Islamic State and US media: "[A]n orientation toward binary separations of us versus them, an emphasis on winning versus losing, an absence of structural explanation, a focus on exaggerated black-and-white descriptions of enemy character, an underlying judgment call of right versus wrong, an elision of war's signification and a dependence on the media to set things in motion."

13. My critique is not meant to suggest that Islamic State violence is not atrocious. But their executions, for example, can appear shocking in a way that state-sanctioned executions do not. Capital punishment kills more people in a given time period than the Islamic State executions did, and is sometimes carried out in similar fashion, by public beheading. In 2014, the year of Foley's execution by the Islamic State, Saudi Arabia beheaded 88 prisoners and the United States executed 35 prisoners. According to Amnesty International, more than 600 executions were carried out globally in 2014, rising to at least 1,634 in 2015 (statistics that do not include executions in China, considered a state secret). Because it is a law-preserving violence, a violence of governance replete with meaning about the nation-state and its legitimacy—and wherein the presumption of guilt on the part of those executed is inherent—less horror is instinctively registered by global news consumers and less attention given by international media.

14. The *Telegraph* (October 17, 2016): "Iraqi forces advanced Monday after launching 'the mother of all battles' aimed at retaking Mosul" (Ensor 2017). The *Mirror* (October 17, 2016): "ISIS came under devastating attack from Coalition forces as the 'mother of all battles' to liberate Mosul City got underway" (Hughes 2016). CNN (August 25, 2016): "Now Iraq's military and the US-led Coalition is preparing for what's expected to be the 'mother of all battles' in the war against ISIS in Iraq: The liberation of Mosul" (Wedeman, 2016). The spectacle, scale, and import of the conflict were emphasized through this designation, which framed the reporting that followed.

15. A typical description, from Reuters (October 24, 2016): "The battle against radical Islamists in the region will not end with the liberation of Mosul" (Nakhoul et al. 2016). Here is the Associated Press (December 20, 2017): "[T]he nine-month battle to liberate the city from the Islamic State group marauders . . ." (George et al. 2017). Some journalists and news organizations were more careful, employing the language of "liberation" only through quoted sources, as in the *New York Times* (February 14, 2017): "Iraq declared 'total liberation' in eastern Mosul" (Zucchino 2017). A journalist in Erbil remained critical: "How often do you hear about 'the liberation of Mosul'? We shouldn't be using that language. It adopts the parlance of the victor, which adopts a point of view. We're not a party to the conflict."

16. As of February 2022, the US Department of Defense reports that 1,417 civilians were killed in 342 separate incidents in the fight against the Islamic State in Iraq and Syria from August 2014 to April 2019. Airwars, a conflict monitoring group, estimates the number of civilians killed to be between 8,168 and 13,222 in 1,509 separate incidents. Other estimates of US-Coalition–

caused civilian death, less methodologically conservative, range into the tens of thousands. The symbolic value of casualty counts is treated in Chapter 2.

17. The claim to American military humanity occurs consistently across the history of US warfare. "The American army is the most humane that ever waged war," declared General S. B. M. Young in 1902, after commanding a war in the Philippines that killed perhaps a seventh of that country's population ("Kill and Burn" 1902, 499).

18. US National Security Advisor Jake Sullivan made the same argument when defending the Biden administration's decision to provide Ukraine with internationally banned cluster munitions, which are likely to harm Ukrainian civilians.

19. American officials have long placed blame for the results of US violence on those subject to that violence. Andrew Jackson, for example, deflected the genocide of Indigenous populations thusly: "I feel conscious of having done my duty to my red children and if any failure of my good intention arises, it will be attributable to their want of duty to themselves, not to me. . . . I have exonerated the national character from all imputation, and now leave the poor deluded Creeks and Cherokees to their fate, and their annihilation, which their wicked advisers has [sic] induced" (in Rogin 1987, 165). Donald Rumsfeld, at a press conference soon after the US invasion of Afghanistan, insisted, "Responsibility for every single casualty in this war, be they innocent Afghans or innocent Americans, rests at the feet of the Taliban and al-Qaeda. . . . When the Taliban issue accusations of civilian casualties, they indict themselves."

20. This was a line of argument employed in defense of area bombing and nuclear deployments at the end of the Second World War. Immediately after the atomic bombing of Hiroshima, Harry Truman proclaimed, "The world will note that the first atomic bomb was dropped on Hiroshima, a military base. That was because we wished in this first attack to avoid, insofar as possible, the killing of civilians." The necessity of preemptive violence in protecting civilians allowed Truman a rhetorical justification for the instant killing of 70,000–80,000 civilians (in Tanaka 2009, 5).

21. Townsend presents many of these same points in a press conference held in 2017 (see Townsend 2017a), though here, the moral distinction drawn between the US and Islamic State militaries is even more striking:

> I believe we should . . . inject a little moral clarity in what we're talking about here, about this issue. ISIS, their crimes against humanity must not be forgotten. . . . If ISIS really wants to prevent human suffering, they can easily do so. They are in complete control of the areas they hold in Mosul. They can leave at any time. The Coalition respects human life. . . . Although our partners in the Coalition have made mistakes that have harmed civilians, we have never targeted them, not once. On the other hand, the savages that are ISIS deliberately target, terrorize and kill innocent civilians every day. The best and fastest way to end this human suffering is to quickly liberate these cities and Iraq and Syria from ISIS.

22. While the strategic dimensions of US air war during World War II and the war in Vietnam are perhaps better known, this element is prominent even after the rise of humanitarianism as a guiding rationale for military intervention. In Kosovo, NATO spokespersons insisted that avoiding civilian harm during the air campaign was a primary concern. Yet civilians—some five hundred in total—were nonetheless killed in attacks with no discernible military target, included civilian neighborhoods (in Vranje on April 5, 1999, in Aleksinac on April 5–6, 1999); passenger trains and buses (in Grdelica on April 12, 1999, in Luzane on May 1, 1999, near Pec on May 4, 1999); refugee camps (in Gjakova on April 21, 1999); a television station (in Belgrade on April 23, 1999); as well as residential buildings, embassies, and hospitals. NATO's stated rationale for intervention—a pattern of Serbian abuse against an ethnic Albanian minority—could just as well be read as a low-grade civil war between the brutal Kosovo Liberation Army (previously denounced as a terrorist organization by the US State Department) and the brutal military forces of Slobodan Milošević, with the intervention as premised on political rather than moral concerns (Knightly 2013). The NATO intervention in Libya, led by Britain and France, was again justified by the protection of innocent civilians, yet evidence suggests that this moral rationale obscured a political strategy of regime change. The NATO alliance claimed to implement measures to avoid civilian casualties; the secretary general of NATO at the time, in a press briefing on November 3, 2011, claimed "no confirmed civilian casualties caused by NATO." However, in a report from Airwars, the conflict monitoring group, NATO strikes are estimated to have killed between 223 and 403 civilians during the war (https://airwars.org/conflict/all-belligerents-in-libya-2011/). Given the early and frequent strikes against Qaddafi's personal compounds, and NATO's decision not to intervene in arms transfers to Libyan rebel forces (in violation of UN Security Council resolutions), it is probable that a strategy of regime change, and not the protection of civilians, drove targeting decisions and military policy. In these and other post–Cold War interventions, news reportage focused on the innocence and corporeal suffering of victims, the cruelty and inhumanity of forces targeted by the intervention, and the protection of civilians as justification for interventionary violence.

23. As Francisco de Vitoria, an early thinker of just war theory, argued, "It is never lawful to kill innocent people, even accidentally and unintentionally, except when it advances a just war which cannot be won in any other way" (1991, 316). For Vitoria and other proponents of just war theory, killing civilians can be licit when accidental or when no alternative is available in the course of warfare. Today, civilian killing is considered illegal under international law if disproportional to military aims. The US military has not publicly detailed its measure of proportionality in armed operations.

24. The term "collateral damage" was first used in a military context in 1961 by economist Thomas Schelling to describe the unintended harm to civilians in the event of US–Soviet nuclear war. US military documents define "collateral damage" as "unintentional or incidental injury or damage to persons or

objects that would not be lawful military targets in the circumstances ruling at the time. Such damage is not unlawful so long as it is not excessive in light of the overall military advantage anticipated from the attack" (US Air Force 2006, 113). As Neta Crawford (2013) notes, the very law protecting civilians from intentional killing itself sanctions unintentional killing.

25. Journalistic attention to the impact of war on civilian populations, which has increased in recent decades, is no bad thing. It is important to note, too, that this journalistic focus is traceable to factors other than ideological convergence. The globalization of war reportage has forced competing news organizations to attend to matters that the priorities of governmental access and corporate sponsorship might lead some to avoid. For example, in particular instances, the popularity of Al Jazeera has moved US news organizations toward increased scrutiny of US military action in order to remain competitive (Lynch 2005). The democratization of news making has also driven journalistic coverage of civilian suffering, insofar as civilians themselves are producing evidence of suffering in war, evidence then investigated by the mainstream press (Bowman and Willis 2003). At a time of eroding public trust in mass media, the presence of journalists in war zones is critical. What they do while they're there—what meanings they make—is just as critical. While journalistic focus on civilian harm is important, we must ask what this focus emphasizes, normalizes, and occludes.

26. That officials' motives remain outside journalistic inquiry poses a significant problem for assessing the legality and responsibility of wartime killing, which often rests on the question of intentionality. As Talal Asad (2015) points out, the ethics of military killing is not concerned with effect (which can be judged necessary, whatever the scale of death inflicted) but with intention, which is measured after the fact as vicious or virtuous. On the matter of civilian death in Mosul, then, journalistic ethics and military ethics seem to align. However, questions remain regarding journalistic representation of official intention in lieu of factual discovery. Giving the benefit of the doubt to US officials may be less the problem than obscuring the fact that such benefit has been given.

27. Through a survey of 1,400 residents of Mosul, Mara Revkin (2020) found that many civilians decided to stay in Islamic State–controlled territory due to the perceived "quality of governance" as compared with that of the Iraqi state. Metrics of comparison included crime rates, electricity and drinking water availability, and the cleanliness of city streets.

28. As Evelyn Alsultany (2012) argues, positive representation of those on the receiving end of US domination can also work in the service of that domination. In Alsultany's reading of popular films and television programs in the post–9/11 era, it is no longer necessary to demonize the Other in order to justify war against the Other. Rather, sympathetic depictions of the Other allow US military action to be framed as enlightened and progressive in the act of saving suffering innocents. Positive representations of the Other in this way cohere with the logic of domination central to the War on Terror. Today, the US military often promotes its multicultural and multiracial *bona fides* (with

criticism from the American right) despite the disproportionate effects of US military violence on foreign cultures and communities of color. It is worth noting that the USA PATRIOT Act, passed after 9/11 with the stated goal of strengthened US national security, includes a section rebuking discrimination against Arabs and Muslims.

29. Civilians in Iraq may have been perceived by the US military not as individuals, to be judged on their personal innocence or guilt, but as a collective enemy population. This perception is implicit in a Department of Defense policy brief regarding payments made to those accidently harmed in US military operations: "Payments may not be offered to residents of a foreign locality or country where the population of the area *as a whole* is in a state of armed conflict or war against the United States." See https://media.defense.gov/2020/Jun/23/2002320314/-1/-1/1/interim-regulations-for-condolence-or-sympathy-payments-to-friendly-civilians-for-injury-or-loss-that-is-incident-to-military-operations.pdf; emphasis added.

30. See https://www.nytimes.com/spotlight/the-civilian-casualty-files-pentagon-reports?name=styln-civilian-casualties&region=TOP_BANNER&block=storyline_menu_recirc&action=click&pgtype=Article&variant=0_Control.

31. These problems were already made public in a 2019 report from Columbia University Law School and the Center for Civilians in Conflict on US military investigations of civilian harm. See https://civiliansinconflict.org/publications/research/in-search-of-answers. Note too that many of the internal investigations into civilian casualties from US airstrikes were conducted by the same command that approved the strikes in question.

32. A similar exculpatory dynamic occurs in other sites of military self-investigation. For example, rising numbers of reported assaults in the US armed services are advertised by military leaders as proof of attention to the problem and confidence among soldiers in the reporting process. This despite a significant lack of consequence for sexual assault in the US military, as well as a wealth of evidence suggesting that reliance on military's self-investigation creates a permissive environment for sexual assault. The US Air Force's chief sexual assault prevention officer was himself arrested for sexual assault in 2013.

33. See https://www.nytimes.com/interactive/2021/us/military-responses.html. When Azmat Khan and other *New York Times* journalists received the Pulitzer Prize for this coverage in May 2022, another Pentagon spokesman, John Kirby, used the same term, and repeatedly: "I also would be remiss if I didn't also congratulate the staff of *The New York Times* for the Pulitzer that they won in their coverage of civilian casualties caused by the United States military and military operations. . . . We knew that we had made mistakes, we're trying to learn from those mistakes. And we knew that we weren't always as transparent about those mistakes as we should be" (Richman 2022). The Pentagon's apparent praise of journalistic scrutiny in fact undermines that scrutiny; by categorizing the harm at issue as a "mistake," a *policy* of harm is mystified.

Chapter 4

1. In an examination of the relationship between charity and empire, Craig Calhoun (2010) observes that the value and activity of providing care is distinct from an effort to address the causes of the circumstances for which care is needed. This distinction is apparent in both humanitarian discourse and in the representational emphasis of war reportage.

2. This sentiment is also an adequate summation of Lt. Gen. Stephen Townsend's defense of US-Coalition killings in Mosul, outlined in the preceding chapter.

3. In this manner, humanitarianism is not so much the veil for military violence but is itself constitutive of that violence. On this collaborate dynamic, see Jennifer Greenburg (2023). On the "cultural turn" in US warfare, see Derek Gregory (2008).

4. For Obama's speech, see https://obamawhitehouse.archives.gov/the-press-office/2013/05/23/remarks-president-national-defense-university. Recent studies suggest that drones are less precise than Obama and other government officials have implied. According to a report by the International Human Rights and Conflict Resolution Clinic and the Global Justice Clinic, "Concerns have been raised about the technical accuracy of [drone] strikes. More significant, however, is the fact that the accuracy of a drone strike fundamentally hinges on the accuracy of the intelligence on which the targeting is premised. That intelligence has often been questioned" (Cavallaro et al. 2012, 126). Precision and its humanity have been advertised since the early days of air war. Army Capt. William Crozier, at The Hague in 1899, spoke of dirigible balloons that would allow for "localized at important points the destruction of life and property and sparing the sufferings of all those who are not at the precise spot" (in Scott 1920, 354). But claims of precision have a way of degrading over time. According to a congressional report conducted during the 1990–1991 Gulf War, Patriot missiles destroyed 100 percent of targeted Iraqi Scuds. In testimony to Congress after the war, that rate decreased to 96 percent. A later review by the US Army downgraded that rate to 25 percent, and a later independent review asserted a 9 percent success rate (Der Derian 2001, 283).

5. As of writing, confirmed uses of the R9X are few (some half dozen in recent years), and none were reported from the Mosul battlefields. In Mosul, efforts at "precision" strikes relied mostly on the GBU-39, a small-diameter 250-pound bomb, and the AGR-20A Advanced Precision Kill Weapon System, which fits 2.75-inch Hydra 70 unguided rockets with a laser guidance kit. These precision-guided munitions are often referred to as smart bombs and are, like drones, designed to more precisely target and thereby minimize collateral damage. We should ask, though, for whom their intelligence is advertised. William Merrin notes how smart bombs are essentially a dual-purpose weapon: Their localized destructive effect also carries a rhetorical message about the rationality—and, implicitly, the humanity—of US warring. The smart bomb is "good, intelligent, a moral force" (Merrin 2018, 10) and thus

does the discursive work that journalism also endeavors to do: of distinguishing humane violence from extreme violence.

6. Even nuclear weapons are not immune from this trend. The new W76-2, a "low-yield" nuclear warhead, is designed to be more usable because less destructive, a fact that risks lowering the threshold between conventional and nuclear war. On these weapons and their risk, see Kaplan 2020. Concern about these so-called tactical nukes has risen with the war in Ukraine, wherein a confrontation between nuclear-armed powers is once again thinkable. As the bar for use of nuclear weaponry is lowered with reduced-capacity warheads, the balance of nuclear power is upended, and the taboo on nuclear conflict weakened. No arms control treaties currently regulate these weapons.

7. In her review of conflict journalism in Africa, Susan Carruthers notes that journalists "are often wont to attribute their eagerness to establish clear-cut points of identification for sympathy and targets for blame to a deficiency in viewers' ability to grasp complexity, or a deficit in public patience to fathom it." Carruthers argues, however, that it is journalists' "embeddedness within particular cultural, political, and economic matrices which endlessly replenish the reservoir from which easy . . . explanations are retrieved" (2004, 166). Simplification is innate to the discourse. But journalistic discomfort with complexity seems widespread. A *New York Times* "Morning Briefing" newsletter (May 3, 2020), estimated to reach some 5 million people, began with this disclosure from head writer David Leonhardt: "I particularly appreciate any story that cuts through the jargon and complexity to help me really understand something" (Leonhardt 2020). Here is the *New York Times* addressing complexity as an obstacle to understanding. On the politics of complexity in public discourse, see Warner 2002.

8. As Wendy Kozol argues of the 1999 NATO intervention in Kosovo, in which photographs of mothers figured widely, "The visual trope of transnational motherhood universalizes suffering and deflects attention from the historical causes of this war" (2014, 21). The universalism of motherhood is also, of course, a gendered norm, and its journalistic deployment reflects the supposed intuitiveness of female journalists. "Men know more about rebel groups," a female journalist in Erbil explained, "and women know more about moral and emotional implications." Oliver Boyd-Barrett argues that "the humanitarian stance [of journalists] was not inherently gendered . . . but gender expectations contributed to a public perception of female war correspondents having a special moral weight in their witness of human suffering" (2021, 182). This gendered dynamic rhymes with what Jennifer Greenburg calls the logic of "military femininity" in which "the military came to explicitly value women's labor through gender essentialisms, such as claims that female soldiers were 'naturally' more emotionally equipped to 'soothe and calm' war's victims" (2023, 2).

9. This narrow approach to victimhood also maintains a gendered logic. There is, of course, a long history of leveraging women's suffering in the Middle East as justification for colonial domination and military control, and wherein

constraints on the personal freedoms of women (and, more recently, of LGBTQ+ individuals) garner more public support for intervention than do economic and political inequities (Alsultany 2012; McAlister 2005). Women in this way become props for interventionary policy, as empathy—elicited by media representation—generates a "will to intervene" on their behalf (Briggs et al. 2017). Empathy for Muslim women, as Wendy Kozol notes, "can become co-opted into emotions that reinforce rather than reject the pervasiveness and seeming inevitability of war" (2014, 7). For critiques of what Jennifer Greenburg (2023) calls "imperial feminism," see also Charles Hirschkind and Saba Mahmood (2002), Deepa Kumar (2012), and Jasbir Puar (2017).

10. Sympathy may be more inclined toward a relational asymmetry than empathy, though the capacity to recognize the feelings or experiences of another is inherent to both. And indeed, the kind of sympathy that Adam Smith placed at the center of his moral philosophy, and the kind of sympathy that George Eliot urged as the central aim of art—two influential thinkers of sympathy in the colonial period—does seem more akin to the modern concept of empathy.

11. The empathy that journalists seek to produce seems more emotional than conceptual—trying to feel "as" someone else rather than trying to understand what is happening in another's mind or body. This kind of empathy functionally asserts an identity of the empathizer apart from the emphasized without risking the inclination to act on the other's behalf. In distinguishing "emotional" from "conceptual" empathy, Paul Bloom employs a thought experiment cribbed from Mencius. Passing a lake where a child is drowning, the impetus to feel the child's suffocations is distinct from the impetus to understand the child's condition and attempt rescue (2016, 22). Yet rescue—perhaps militarized rescue—may nevertheless be justified by audience empathy of *whatever* kind, and regardless of an audience's motivation to do anything *more* than empathize.

12. A predicted level of civilian casualties exceeding an NCV threshold may not prevent the strike under consideration, which would then require special permission up the chain of command. Moreover, recent reports suggest that this chain-of-command authorization can be bypassed altogether. It now seems that many recent airstrikes in Iraq and Syria, even those predicted to result in high numbers of civilian casualties, were justified and executed without higher-level sanction on the basis of presumed threat to Coalition troops—threat that did not itself require proof (see Philipps and Schmitt 2021).

13. Reporting indicates that a similar casualty-prediction process, augmented by artificial intelligence, was operating in Israel's 2023 assault on Gaza. This suggests that civilian deaths in that conflict were neither inadvertent nor unpreventable. See Abraham 2023.

14. The document in question notes that "high collateral damage targets" include "those targets that, if struck, have a ten percent probability of causing collateral damage through blast debris and fragmentation and are estimated to result in significant collateral effects on noncombatant persons and structures,

including: (A) Non-combatant casualties estimated at 30 or greater." See wikileaks.org/wiki/US_Rules_of_Engagement_for_Iraq.

15. In an email shared with the Senate Armed Services Committee, an Air Force major explains to an Air Force lawyer that the Office of Special Investigations, tasked with assessing civilian casualty incidents, only investigates when there is "potential for high media attention, concern with outcry from local community/government, concern sensitive images may get out" (Airwars et al. 2021).

16. According to the US Department of Defense (https://dod.defense.gov/OIR/), the US-Coalition conducted 13,331 airstrikes against the Islamic State in Iraq (and an additional 11,235 strikes in Syria) as of August 9, 2017. (These are the most recent DOD figures available; Airwars, the conflict monitoring organization, estimates 14,886 strikes in Iraq and 19,904 in Syria as of February 2022. See https://airwars.org/conflict/coalition-in-iraq-and-syria/.) Allowing for up to 20 civilian deaths in each strike would amount to a total of 266,620 *acceptable* civilian deaths in the defeat of the Islamic State in Iraq, per the Department of Defense figures. The total fighting force of the Islamic State, according to Department of Defense estimates from 2016, was around 30,000.

17. A study of journalist representations of homeless populations suggests a similar distinction. "Humanizing techniques," the study argues, "tend to either evoke empathy at an individual level or enact solidarity at a community level. While both empathy and solidarity encourage concern for marginalized communities, the logic of empathy constrains this concern to worthy or exceptional individuals, whereas solidarity techniques expand the scope of concern to the entire affected community" (Varma 2020, 1–2).

18. Studies have shown that the single most important factor for journalists in determining a source's credibility is that source's "officialness," rather than the relevancy of what they know. The most reliable way to become a trusted source for journalists is to have an official role (Barnoy and Reich 2020). "Officialness" is thus determinative of accuracy or truthfulness. And since officialness is underwritten, in many cases, by a ruling order, the state can become the ultimate arbiter of the truth brokered through source quoting. As Charles Briggs argues of source quoting, "The shift from lay to [expert] voices parallels a transition to the dominance of the narrative by state voices" (2007b, 329).

19. Max Weber's critique of scientific objectivity is apropos: "The fate of an epoch which has eaten of the tree of knowledge is that it must know that we cannot learn the *meaning* of the world from the results of its analysis, be it so perfect; it must rather be in a position to create this meaning" (1949, 10).

20. Note too how the proliferation of information produced in the web 2.0 era—videos, posts, comments, memes, photographs, and data of all kinds pouring out from the battlefield—would seem to confirm assumptions about the dissipation of the fog of war and an increased understanding of conflict through more open, accessible, and transparent media. Yet, and as William Merrin (2018) notes, the opposite seems to be happening as we face the fractal disintegration of our knowledge. More information does not create more un-

derstanding when the politics of conflict are repressed in the proliferation of objective depictions of human suffering.

21. At a few larger media organizations, a recent downturn in advertising has driven a turn to subscription models of funding. Increased reliance on a core readership willing to pay for media content could presumably free newsrooms, to some degree, from a fear of advertiser estrangement and lead to journalism less constrained by the strategic mollifications of objectivity.

22. The siege of Kobani, which pitted local Kurdish forces, eventually backed by US airpower, against a largely foreign Islamic State, is the exception to this comparison and will not be taken up.

23. A recent study suggests that while journalists at state-funded news organizations (e.g., Al Jazeera, Xinhua, the BBC) emphasize their autonomy from the state in their ability to select and frame stories, these journalists very rarely use that autonomy to resist or contest their government's framing of world events (Wright et al. 2020). See also Bennett et al. 2007; Zaller and Chiu 1996.

24. A 2021 US drone strike in Kabul targeting an Islamic State member was called a "righteous strike" by Gen. Mark Milley, then chairman of the Joint Chiefs of Staff. This language confirmed the morality of US military action. However, it was soon revealed that the strike killed only civilians—ten in total, seven of them children. Though the US government pledged condolence payments to victims of the strike, as of June 2023, no such compensation had been offered.

Chapter 5

1. That the dreams presented here are not dreams as dreamt but dreams as narrated in interviews (and thus already scripted) is of minor consequence. In connecting the psychic with the cultural, the latent or manifest content of dreams is less important than the "dreamwork": the transformation of journalists' thoughts and experiences into a dream, which can then be read for what the news expels. On dreamwork, see Freud 1950.

2. My own position in the field was contested and sometimes contentious. To some journalists I was a colleague, providing a critical language for their professional, ethical, and political concerns; to others I was an interloper, a risk to journalists' bodies and careers. I was called (with some flippancy) a journalist-therapist and a journalist-whisperer; I was called (behind my back) an intruder and a cynic. While similarities between journalism and ethnography exist (Zelizer 2004), a journalist I am not, and this distinction motivated some journalists to use me as a repository for what journalism denies. However, those experiences expelled by the news, when communicated ethnographically, remain influenced by ethnography's own codes, norms, and constraints. Where anthropology addresses this issue in the so-called reflexive turn (e.g., Clifford and Marcus 1986), psychoanalysis might regard it as one of countertransference. On countertransference in ethnography, see Robben 1996.

3. Though the ahistoric universalism of Freudian psychoanalysis is debated (el Shakry 2017), here I wager on what Stefania Pandolfo calls "the transmuta-

tions of psychoanalytic knowledge" in applying this heuristic to a seemingly alien realm (2018, 136).

4. What is incoherent to journalists (and thus to journalism) may be readily intelligible to others experiencing the same events. Of course, a divergence of stakes, resources, and mobility will result in distinct experiences of war. Journalistic coherence can also be a matter of editorial negotiation. "I went to a mass grave," a journalist told me in Kobani, "and it was a grim experience. But there was also a barbecue and shisha. I wanted to put this in [the story], because it's a relief for people to find the people they've given up on finding. It's a good thing to find your relative's lost body. But my editors found this nonsensical and bizarre and cut it." Local fixers who assist foreign journalists are also of interest here, insofar as they act as translators between distinct discursive worlds. As Amahl Bishara (2012) suggests, fixers may be most familiar with the production, fragility, and market value of journalistic intelligibility.

5. For Marx, all commodities will alienate the labor of their production. In the case of the news commodity, this alienation is intensified—overdetermined even—by the idealized erasure of subjective presence. Third-person prose is one manifestation of this idealized erasure, examined in Chapter 2.

6. Searchable specifics are redacted to protect subject anonymity.

7. The content of war's fantasy may shift among news-consuming societies, but the form of this fantasy, as elaborated by war reportage, appears largely consistent. The roles of victim and preparator are prominent across the global scope of war reportage, though which individuals occupy those roles may change. Violence is frequently categorized as justified or extreme regardless of a news organization's geographic base, though the application of these categories to any particular event of violence can differ. Journalistic claims to certainty, factuality, and authority in the depiction of war are made irrespective of the society to which a given journalist reports. What war is represented to be in the news—and what is expelled therefrom—thus maintains a formal regularity among the news organizations whose journalists I interviewed and observed, whether American or Arab or French. However, only certain news organizations gain access to Middle East war zones, and my research reflects this selective dynamic. On the operation of epistemic hegemony across geographic locations, see Vázquez 2011; on the dynamics of non-Western journalism, see, for example, Mabweazara 2018 and Nyiri 2017.

8. This pressure can be explicitly editorial, even as it remains implicitly discursive. A journalist in Erbil explained, "Editors always want to know, What does this mean? Sometimes I say, I don't know."

9. In his seminal "Critique of Violence," Walter Benjamin helpfully locates the constraints of an approach to violence normative to political philosophical systems. Benjamin writes, "For what such a system . . . would contain is not a criterion for violence itself as a principal, but, rather, the criterion for cases of its use" (1996, 236). We might think of war reportage—a discourse concerned with *events* of violence—as beholden to just such a system, whereby the use of violence, and the criteria associated with this use, foreclose assessment of "violence

itself." The journalistic impulse to present causes and effects, to measure and to define, transmutes violence into a phenomenon contingent to criteria of use. In considering violence in excess of means/end calculation, Benjamin's essay indicates where journalistic discourse is constrained by its classificatory premise and limited by its fidelity to facts. Benjamin's "critique" elucidates what may be lost in the delimitation of violence to a phenomenon containable within journalistic discourse, and it allows for a consideration of violence as thought and experienced beyond the strictures of rationality, the horizon of death, the teleology of means and ends, the certainty of facts, and the judgment of legitimacy. In turning to what he calls the "principle" of violence, Benjamin recovers what may exceed the facts, explanations, and classifications that journalism inscribes—something like power or justice, which are not bound by utility.

10. It is important to emphasize here the uneven distribution of fear in areas of conflict. In Syria at the time, fear was a steady presence among those without the resources, mobility, or protection of foreign journalists. The fear experienced by foreigners in war zones can be allayed, in many instances, by the ability to leave.

11. This description coheres with many Western representations of female suicide bombers, which, according to V. G. Julie Rajan (2012), tend to focus on their physical attributes along with their sexuality and their victimization.

12. A bit of Crimean War news coverage—from William Howard Russell, the most famous of the prototypical war reporters—graces the cover of this book.

13. The history of the *DSM-III* reveals how wartime trauma achieved diagnostic credibility and thereby became, according to Wilbur Scott, "an accurate description of the objective reality of war" (1990, 295). The official codification of PTSD after the Vietnam War—the result of broad coalitional activism among Vietnam War veterans, chaplains, doctors, and others—allowed the trauma of war a self-evidence previously unavailable. Prior to the *DSM-III*, diagnostic nomenclature lacked a language for war-related trauma, and the stress of war was attributed to neurosis or psychosis unrelated to combat (such as depression, schizophrenia, and alcoholism). With the inclusion of PTSD as a diagnosable ailment, "What psychiatrists once regarded as abnormal behavior is now thought by many to represent a 'normal' response to situation of combat. With the PTSD diagnosis, psychiatrists now say it is 'normal' to be traumatized by the horrors of war" (1990, 295). As in journalism, objective knowledge produced an objective reality of war, and a "natural" experience of violence is ordered by accounts of that very naturalness. On the struggle for a PTSD diagnosis, Scott writes, "At no time was the dispute over the question of whether or not diseases and disorders exist. Instead, it turned on whether in fact there was one, PTSD, that had yet to be discovered" (1990, 308).

14. Focus on the trauma of war also displaces political complexity, since concern for physiological and psychological distress is understood to be ideologically neutral and thus post-political. As Nadia Abu El-Haj asserts of the "combat trauma imaginary" (2022, 2), moral obligation to those suffering

war-related trauma serves to sideline possibilities for debating the politics of war and its effects. I return to this matter in the following chapter.

15. Samuel Hynes stages a similar argument to that of Fussell, asserting that narrative production in the post-World War II period shifted the emphasis of war's meaning from battlefield progress to suffering and victimhood. Stories written by those who suffered in war—and the popularity of Holocaust testimonials, in particular—"radically altered the geometry of the modern soldier's tale," writes Hynes, "adding to the usual story of army against army a different war story—of armies against humanity" (1997, 223). Here the ascendence of trauma as the essential characteristic of war's experience meets the humanitarian inflection of contemporary war reportage, examined in the previous chapters. If trauma now defines war as experience, this experience can be leveraged by a humanitarian discourse claiming a moral imperative for military intervention. On the use of Holocaust trauma for military interventions, see, for example, Evans 2008.

16. One might wonder, then, how journalists can sustain in their practice of news making despite the erasure of their experiences. Journalists' motivations for reporting war (like my motivations to "ethnographize" war reporters) are myriad: Intellectual interests, political commitments, professional ambitions, and desires for adventure may all play some role. Motivations, of course, are often opaque even to oneself. On the coincidence of enabling and limiting conditions in writing practice, see Samuli Schielke and Mukhtar Shehata (2021).

17. The well-known formula of fetishistic disavowal, famously phrased by Octave Mannoni (1969), pertains: "I know very well" that war is ambiguous, excessive, and representationally contingent, "but nevertheless I believe" that war is certain, legible, and transparently delivered. Journalism instantiates this disavowal through its representational commitments. Psychoanalysis can in this way complicate an assessment of war news as "merely" constructed.

18. Alex Fattal's ethnography of warfare and marketing in Colombia is instructive on this point. Fattal shows how military branding attempts to "reconcile the irreconcilable, such as the idea of a humanitarian counterinsurgency" (2018, ix), and assesses war's commodification as it stimulates (and in some ways gratifies) consumer desire. In journalism as in the marketing campaigns Fattal examines, the commodification of war expels an excess as it maintains a social order.

19. This is not to suggest that war reportage cannot contend with powerful interests. Vietnam War reportage is perhaps the exemplar here, when the efforts of the Saigon-based press corps, though varied, produced a challenge to official narratives regarding that war's progress. However, the ability to "speak truth to power" still depends upon a language that power recognizes, authorizes, affirms. The form of war reportage—its insistence on particular categories and frameworks—imposes consequential constraints. On the limits of journalistic opposition in the Vietnam period, see Daniel Hallin (1986).

20. Otherwise put—and as argued by Hans Magnus Enzensberger (1974), Richard Dyer (1979), and Robert Stam (1992), among others—to ascertain a

media's appeal to a public requires not only an analysis of the ideology that steers people into collaboration with existing social relations. It requires, as well, attention to that kernel of fantasy exceeding those relations, and through which a media constitutes itself as the projected fulfilment of a social desire. For Fredric Jameson, the works of mass culture "deflect," in the service of an existing order, "the deepest and most fundamental hopes and fantasies of the collectivity" (1979, 144). War reportage activates the hopes of global news consumers to save the innocent and pure and to punish the cruel and violent. War reportage activates consumer fantasies of an "international community" executing humane war on premises morally virtuous. And these hopes and fantasies, deflected in the service of an existing order, are activated in such a way as to obfuscate the violence of that order, and to obscure those rationales for war that are strategically advantageous to that order.

21. There are symptoms of journalistic repression that are not addressed here, such as the high rates of substance abuse in the profession. As well, there exist other spaces where what is displaced from journalism reappears, such as the war memoir (Anthony Loyd's *My War Gone By, I Miss It So* presents one fine example of the pathos of news production). Relevant too is the site of social negotiation between journalists and sources that Mark Allen Peterson calls the "unwriteable discourse" of journalism. Peterson avoids labeling this site "unspeakable" (2001, 203) because it can be expressed outside the news commodity, as this chapter also indicates.

22. Malek Alloula's study of French postcards from colonized Algeria stages a similar argument. The colonial postcard, Alloula explains, purports to represent Algerian women while it actually reflects French desires for what an Algerian woman should be. In this manner, the colonial postcard "rests, and operates, upon a false equivalency—namely, that illusion equals reality. It literally takes its desires for realities." (1986, 4). This resonance suggests a link between war reportage and orientalism on the level of fantasy and desire.

Chapter 6

1. Meaninglessness may itself function as a meaning for war, of course, but this domestication is less suitable to a discourse premised on certitude, accuracy, and realism.

2. Gender and racial identity can also play a significant role in interviews, determining both who gets interviewed and who gets to interview. A journalist in Erbil assailed "the sexism of not being listened to, being cut off, and 'not knowing'" during interviews with military and government officials. A journalist in Beirut, who grew up in the region, lamented being "treated as a fixer" while conducting interviews. My own practice of interviewing is not exempt from this dynamic.

3. The *Washington Post* used the word "martyr" 543 times in news stories from January 1, 2014, to December 31, 2017, 134 times in the context of US reportage; the *Wall Street Journal* used "martyr" 508 times in news reportage from the same period, 122 times in the context of US news.

4. Less frequently, "martyr" appears in the context of Middle East reportage as a figure related to violence, but in a manner that never specifies the meaning of the term. The *Washington Post* (July 6, 2014): "'There is nothing between us and them,' said Suha Abu Khieder, who was still reckoning Saturday with the idea that her son, Mohammad, has become the Israeli-Palestinian conflict's latest martyr" (Eglash et al. 2014). The *Wall Street Journal* (March 10, 2016): "An important piece of government evidence was a letter saved on Mr. Pugh's laptop, which was addressed to his wife and explained his desire to become a martyr for [the] Islamic State" (Hong 2016). The *New York Times* (January 4, 2016): "Some analysts say that the arrest and trial of Sheikh Nimr—and the intense coverage by news media sympathetic to Iran—propelled his rise from a local figure into an international icon, a process completed with his execution, which made him a martyr to his supporters" (Hubbard 2016). In such instances, martyrdom suggests sacrifice amidst violence, but the implications of martyrdom as something transgressive of journalistic convention is never apparent.

5. Scare quotes are another strategy for dealing with troublesome concepts. The *Wall Street Journal*, in particular, tends to place the word *martyr* in scare quotes: "portraits of their own 'martyrs'" (Coles and Nabhan 2017), "pictures of 'martyrs' who have died fighting" (Parkinson 2014). Other news organizations also employ this tactic on occasion. As discussed in Chapter 1, the use of scare quotes and other hedges (such as "the so-called Islamic State") can be read as a hesitation regarding those topics disruptive to journalistic norms. Martyrdom causes trouble; scare quotes allow it to be expressed while its reality is nevertheless doubted.

6. A Google Ngram search for "blank stare" indicates that its use in published texts (including journalism, as well as novels and other media) increased around 1980 and continues on an upward trajectory from the year 2000. While the cause of this trend is impossible to verify, I suggest considering this increased frequency together with the prevalence of trauma as a way to make sense of violence, which intensifies along a similar timescale. The "blank stare" can be thought as an attempt to descriptively capture the experience of trauma that may otherwise evade representation. The connection between trauma and the "blank stare" is evident, for example, in the use of "the thousand-yard stare" as a gloss for what would today be considered the traumatic experience of warfare. The phrase was popularized in World War II, when illustrator and war reporter Thomas Lea's painting, *The Two Thousand Yard Stare*, appeared on the cover of *Life* magazine in 1945. The painting depicts a soldier staring vacantly out toward the painting's viewer. We might then read journalism's deployment of the "blank stare" as a narrative strategy coincident with others, such as use of the terminology of trauma, to manage what otherwise exceeds the journalistic account.

7. Is the blank stare necessarily tropological? The blankness of a stare is of course descriptive, but what exactly does it describe other than the very absence of the describable? We might posit the blank stare as figural, insofar as

the stare appears as the fulfillment of an idea of the violent encounter. But again, this metonymic dimension seems to signify only the unknowable itself. In considering the blank stare a trope, we can understand it as admissible in journalism's realist narrative while at the same time gesturing toward the limits of that very narrative. Perhaps the blank stare is a cliché, one of the most trivial clichés in all of war reportage? This may be so. But to read the blank stare as cliché does not undermine its potential to reveal the boundaries of journalism or to perform the poetic function of language. Its overuse, rather, suggests its reliability (if no longer its impact) in signaling war's ineffability.

8. Journalists cannot be poets, of course, but they can utilize the resources of poetic language to bridge the gap between professional practice and textual communication. However, as Evelyn Cobley (1993) argues, description (such as the blankness of a stare) also creates the reassurance that sense-defying events like war can be mastered through discursive control. For Roland Barthes (1968, 1986), description is designed to perform a text's mimetic status, where the most basic index of a narrative's claim to reality is the use of description through which a text appears to speak for itself. Yet the blank stare, to me, seems something more than descriptive detail. In its suggestion of what cannot be rationally understood, the blank stare indicates the limits of journalistic representation itself. In rhetorical theory, this poetic function would be called *eloquence*.

9. The power of poetic language is not, of course, only a matter of its tropological or semantic function. The form of presentation—the poetic *style*—carries an affective dimension that can overcome the limitations of realism. Style itself, it could be said, marks an unraveling of the discursive boundaries that violence also threatens. On the poetic style in journalism, see *Rebel Reporting* (2016) by poet and journalist John Ross.

10. Bernd Hüppauf observes a similar process in the history of war photography, wherein efforts to deliver a mimetic reproduction of war actually reveal the manipulations of a representational process and a worldview embedded therein. Of war photographer Frank Hurley, Hüppauf (1993, 53) writes: "While it was Hurley's aim to hide from the viewer his technical manipulations of the negative, the technique . . . exposed its artificial process in a provocative manner. The camera's inability to capture reality was not seen as merely accidental, but as a result of the nature of modern reality which was disjointed, abstract, complex, and the product of technical, including photographic, constructions."

11. This periodization is questionable. Winston Churchill's journalism from the Second Boer War (to cite a famous example from the turn of the twentieth century) was hardly a matter of bearing witness. Rather, Churchill's journalistic focus, characteristic of the time, was the honor of warfare, British victories and defeats, and the valor of the Royal Army. While attention to battlefield glory waned through the early twentieth century, focus on the progress of military battles remained, until recent decades, more of a journalistic concern than bearing witness to human suffering. A Google Ngram search indicates

that after sustained use in the mid-nineteenth century, "bearing witness" was not a popularly printed phrase until the 1990s, when its use in journalism, novels, and other print media began to spike.

12. Journalistic witnessing is in this way the successor to an early Christian progenitor, wherein the act of witnessing is itself the expression of faith. The Greek word for witness, *martis* or "martyr," was adapted by Church Fathers to suggest the persecution of Christians who bore witness to their faith, much as journalists' trauma (actual or rhetorical) becomes proof of their sacrifice for the ideals of war reportage. This Christian pedigree also links war reportage to colonial-era representation, wherein the will to save the benighted Other, activated through depictions of the Other, was understood as an expression of God's love and the work of Christian charity. In this colonial dynamic too, it is the *figure* of the charitable agent that counts, over and above the content or effectiveness of the charitable act. On Christian witnessing, see Giorgio Agamben (1999); on colonial charity, see Craig Calhoun (2010).

13. My reading of journalistic witnessing as figural also affords political possibility. Allissa Richardson's (2020) analysis of "Black witnessing" indicates how practices of witnessing, such as those that animate the Black Lives Matter movement, can enact racial justice in their evocation of a Black radical tradition. As Richardson demonstrates, the formal engagement of Black witnessing, while producing crucial evidence of anti-Black police violence, is also an activity of oppositional politics and liberatory potentiality; through the symbolics of seeing and recording, Black witnesses activate a living history of counter-public media practice and Black sociality. Even as what is witnessed can mobilize public action and lend legal weight to court challenges, the act of witnessing is *itself* a realization of the legacy of Black resistance, "an unbroken chain of brave seers" that continues to evolve (2020, 4). Contrary to Richardson's emphasis, I believe it is the *figure* of the Black witness-bearer, rather than the content of what is witnessed, that remains the most politically salient element of Black witnessing in general.

14. News consumption in this way expresses what Annette Wieviorka calls the "the era of the witness," in which the witness has become, in popular culture, "an apostle and a prophet" whose prophesy is inseparable from their trauma (2006, 127). On the moral value of witnessing in wartime see also Anne Cubilié (2005), and for a literary critique see James Campbell (1999). However, and as feminist and postcolonial scholars have long argued, such forms of witnessing can adhere to the "benevolent paternalism" that often informs Western observance of non-Western suffering. On this critique, see Inderpal Grewal (2005) and Jasbir Puar (2017).

15. Note once again that witnessing, in its early Christian adoption, is connected to both testimony and martyrdom. The witness is that person willing to suffer while attesting to a truth of which they are not the author. This valence persists in the contemporary journalistic ideal.

16. Fixers assisting with frontline coverage in Mosul earned $400 per day and more, a rate often higher than that earned by a freelance journalist for a

frontline story. While some freelancers received regular discounts from fixers who had become friends, the demand for fixers from those able to pay the established rate was often high. Freelancers sometimes pooled resources and traveled together in order to share reporting costs, but many freelance journalists in Iraq were forced to live on the prestige of war coverage alone.

17. Recently released documents indicate that, by late 2018, up to 80 percent of US airstrikes called by one Special Operations unit in the war against the Islamic State were justified by the claim of imminent danger from "hostile intent."

18. According to the "Annual Report on Civilian Casualties in Connection with United States Military Operations in 2019," from the US Department of Defense, 4,729 bombs and missiles were deployed against the Islamic State in Iraq and Syria in 2019, yet the official tally of civilian dead for that year is only 22. The strikes from March 18 in Baghuz are not included in the tally. See https://media.defense.gov/2020/May/06/2002295555/-1/-1/1sec-1057-civilian-casualties-may-1-2020.PDF.

Conclusion

1. In turning to possibilities entangled *within* contemporary war reportage, I leave aside those representational options generically adjacent to war reportage, such as memoir (as from journalist Michael Herr [1977]), oral history (as from journalist Svetlana Alexievich [1992]), and conceptual art (as from journalist Laura Poitras [2016]), as well as war fiction (see Fussell 1975). These generic alternatives and their affordances are too expansive to adequately address here.

2. Transparency is a journalistic ideal long valued in the news industry, but it has received recent institutional endorsement as a way to overcome consumer distrust (Chadha and Koliska 2014). However, and as Gabriela Perdomo and Philippe Rodrigues-Rouleau (2021) argue, "self-celebratory transparency," in which the work of contacting sources or reviewing documents is highlighted, can performatively reassert journalistic truth claims while further concealing those factors that may complicate or undermine claims to truth.

3. The journalism of Anthony Shadid exemplified this resistance to closure. Shadid once told a protégé that good journalism "doesn't claim to know too much," and his particular style of "kicker" consistently embraced ambiguity. One example, from an article in the *Washington Post* (December 24, 2009): "Only three broken bricks scarred white by bird droppings mark the grave, a rough pile of riverine gravel, mud and straw. Scrub brush, bearing thorns, grows nearby. 'We still haven't put the tombstone,' Salah said softly. 'We haven't had time.' He stood with his hands clasped tightly behind his back, one balled in a fist." In Shadid's stylist turn on this generic convention, uncertainty is emphasized rather than hidden; categories are troubled rather than secured; legibility cedes priority to a more ambivalent kind of knowing.

4. As noted in the preface to this book, waning public attention to the War on Terror does not indicate an end to the global combat operations codified

under this moniker or to the policies it initiated. For example, the 2023 US National Defense Authorization Act empowers Special Operations Forces to "mentor" foreign troops, paramilitary organizations, and mercenary groups, which can be dispatched under US direction to target US enemies. This authorization extends to new conflict contexts what was known as Section 127e (or "One Twenty-Seven Echo"), a legislative sanction for anti-terror proxy conflict and commando operations in the Middle East, Africa, and the Asia-Pacific region. While this program was set to expire in 2025, it has instead been codified beyond its original War on Terror remit. Meanwhile, foreign combat operations in Iraq and Syria continue. On May 3, 2023, the US military conducted a drone strike targeting what it called "a senior al-Qaeda leader" in Syria's Idlib province. Others claimed that the strike killed a local shepherd, whose family publicly denied involvement with al-Qaeda. US Central Command then issued this statement: "We are aware of the allegations of a civilian casualty and the outcome of the confirmation process will inform if further investigation is necessary and how it should proceed." In many ways, the War on Terror—and its obfuscations—remains active in the Middle East.

Epilogue

1. During the first month after the Russian invasion of Ukraine, the major US television news networks devoted over a third of their news coverage to the conflict—562 minutes of airtime. This can be compared to 306 minutes for the first month of the US war in Afghanistan, 414 minutes for the US invasion of Iraq, and 345 minutes for the US withdrawal from Afghanistan in 2021. See Jim Lobe (2022).

2. This transition is especially stark when considering the US Department of Defense's National Defense Strategy of 2005: "Our strength as a nation-state will continue to be challenged by those who employ a strategy of the weak using international fora, judicial processes and terrorism" (2005, 5). The indistinction, rhetorically established, between the threat from terrorism and the threat from international law suggests US government selectivity, not only concerning the writ of the ICC, but of *any* international norms that pose a challenge to American hegemony. And while the US government has agreed to assist in ICC investigations of Russian crimes in Ukraine, still on the legislative books is the American Servicemembers Protection Act—known colloquially as the "Hague Invasion Act"—signed into law in 2002 and authorizing the US president "to use all means necessary and appropriate to bring about the release of any person . . . who is being detained or imprisoned by, on behalf of, or at the request of the International Criminal Court." Relevant too are nearly a hundred "Article 98" agreements, in which signatory nations across Asia, Africa, and the Middle East agree not to surrender Americans within their borders to ICC jurisdiction. These legislative measures insulate US warfare from international legal censure, but they are largely unmentioned in the reportage on war crimes in Ukraine and US government denunciations thereof.

3. On a more granular level, the appearance of proper names in interna-

tional journalism on Ukraine reflects political positions regarding Ukrainian state sovereignty, history, and culture. The almost-universal change in journalistic usage from the Russian-derived "Kiev," once commonly employed in American and European news, to the Ukrainian-derived "Kyiv"—and many similar adjustments for places, persons, and things in Ukraine—suggests how particular understandings of a war are instantiated, though often naturalized, in the language of war reportage. (The Ukrainian government lobbied global news organizations to make such linguistic adjustments, though correlation does not prove causation in this instance.) My own use of Ukrainian designations in this epilogue marks an inability to escape from the choices, necessarily political, embedded in the use of language on war.

4. Press restrictions are in many ways worse for local Ukrainian journalists, who remain less important to the global distribution of official narratives of the war, and who are operating under new government information policies decreed under martial law. Since the Russian invasion and as of this writing, I do not believe Zelensky has granted an interview to a local news outlet.

5. An incident that occurred after my visit to Ukraine, related to me by two journalists, illustrates this tension. In September 2022, the Russian military bombed a passenger train in Ukraine, claiming the train carried arms and combatants. Ukrainian officials denied the claim, asserting that only civilians were aboard. Journalists attempting to reach the site of the bombing were denied access. Later, journalists contacted survivors of the bombed train, who confirmed that Ukrainian soldiers were indeed present. Asked by journalists for comment, Ukrainian officials accused the bombing survivors of inebriation and threatened to revoke the press credentials of inquiring journalists. One of the journalists who relayed these details to me tried to convince her editors to publish a story on the incident but was rebuffed.

6. The 2023 Pulitzer Prize in international reporting was awarded to the *New York Times* for its coverage of the war in Ukraine.

BIBLIOGRAPHY

Abraham, Yuval. 2023, November 30. "'A Mass Assassination Factory': Inside Israel's Calculated Bombing of Gaza." +972 *Magazine*. https://www.972mag.com/mass-assassination-factory-israel-calculated-bombing-gaza/

Abu El-Haj, Nadia. 2022. *Combat Trauma: Imaginaries of War and Citizenship in Post–9/11 America*. New York: Verso.

Action on Armed Violence. 2023, November 7. "Numbers of Civilian Deaths per Airstrike in 2023 Gaza at Least Four Times Higher Than Previous Israeli Bombings, AOAV Finds." *Action on Armed Violence*. https://aoav.org.uk/2023/numbers-of-civilian-deaths-per-airstrike-in-gaza-today-far-higher-than-previous-israeli-bombings-but-half-that-of-russian-syrian-attacks-in-mosul-and-aleppo-under-reporting-of-the-dead-or-less-letha/

Adorno, Theodor W. 1991. *Notes to Literature. Volume 1*. New York: Columbia University Press.

Agamben, Giorgio. 1999. *Remnants of Auschwitz: The Witness and the Archive*. New York: Zone Books.

Airwars et al., "NGO Letter to US Defense Secretary Regarding Accountability for Civilian Harm." 2021, December 2. *Human Rights Watch*. https://www.hrw.org/news/2021/12/02/ngo-letter-us-defense-secretary-regarding-accountability-civilian-harm

Alexievich, Svetlana. 1992. *Zinky Boys: Soviet Voices from Afghanistan*. W.W. Norton.

Allan, Stuart, and Barbie Zelizer. 2004. "Rules of Engagement: Journalism and War." In *Reporting War: Journalism in Wartime*, edited by Stuart Allan and Barbie Zelizer, 3–22. London: Routledge.

Alloula, Malek. 1986. *The Colonial Harem*. Minneapolis: University of Minnesota Press.

Alsultany, Evelyn. 2012. *Arabs and Muslims in the Media: Race and Representation After 9/11*. New York: New York University Press.
Althusser, Louis. 1969. *For Marx*. London: Penguin.
———. 1971. *Lenin and Philosophy and Other Essays*. London: New Left.
Ananny, Mike. 2020. "Anticipatory News Infrastructures: Seeing Journalism's Expectations of Future Publics in its Sociotechnical Systems." *New Media & Society* 22 (9): 1600–1618.
Appadurai, Arjun. 1996. *Modernity at Large: Cultural Dimensions of Globalization*. Minneapolis: University of Minnesota Press.
Appy, Christian G. 2000. *Working-Class War: American Combat Soldiers and Vietnam*. Chapel Hill: University of North Carolina Press.
Aronson, Jay. 2013. "The Politics of Civilian Casualty Counts." In *Counting Civilian Casualties: An Introduction to Recording and Estimating Nonmilitary Deaths in Conflict*, edited by Taylor B. Seybolt, Jay D. Aronson, and Baruch Fischhoff, 29–52. Oxford: Oxford University Press.
Asad, Talal. 2007. *On Suicide Bombing*. New York: Columbia University Press.
———. 2015. "Reflections on Violence, Law, and Humanitarianism." *Critical Inquiry* 41 (2): 390–427.
Auerbach, Erich. [1946] 2013. *Mimesis: The Representation of Reality in Western Literature*. Princeton: Princeton University Press.
Austin, J. L. 1962. *How to Do Things with Words*. Oxford: Oxford University Press.
Baker, Edwin C. 1995. *Advertising and a Democratic Press*. Princeton: Princeton University Press.
Bakhtin, M. M. 1982. *The Dialogic Imagination: Four Essays*. Austin: University of Texas Press.
Bargu, Banu. 2014. *Starve and Immolate: The Politics of Human Weapons*. New York: Columbia University Press.
Barnard, Anne. 2015, February 20. "Children, Caged for Effect, to Mimic Imagery of ISIS." *New York Times*. https://www.nytimes.com/2015/02/21/world/middleeast/activists-trying-to-draw-attention-to-killings-in-syria-turn-to-isis-tactic-shock-value.html
———. 2016, February 4. "As Syria Talks Fizzle, 'War Has No Meaning Anymore.'" *New York Times*. https://www.nytimes.com/2016/02/05/world/middleeast/syria-peace-talks-geneva.html
Barnard, Anne, and Hwaida Saad. 2016, December 14. "Amid Rain of Shells, Aleppo's Civilians Offer 'Final Scream.'" *New York Times*. Available at https://www.expressnews.com/news/local/article/Amid-rain-of-shells-Aleppo-s-civilians-offer-10796952.php
Barnoy, Aviv, and Zvi Reich. 2020. "Trusting Others: A Pareto Distribution of Source and Message Credibility Among News Reporters." *Communications Research* 49 (2): 196–220.
Barthes, Roland. 1968. "L'Effet de Réel." *Communications* 11: 84–98.
———. 1986. *The Rustle of Language*. New York: Farrar, Straus and Giroux.

Baudrillard, Jean. 1995. *The Gulf War Did Not Take Place*. Bloomington: University of Indiana Press.
Bauman, Zygmunt. 1993. *Modernity and Ambivalence*. Cambridge, UK: Polity Press.
Bellamy, Alex J. 2017. *East Asia's Other Miracle: Explaining the Decline of Mass Atrocities*. Oxford: Oxford University Press.
Benjamin, Walter. 1968. *Illuminations: Essays and Reflections*. New York: Harcourt Brace Jovanovich.
———. 1978. *Reflections: Essays, Aphorism, Autobiographical Writings*. New York: Harcourt Brace Jovanovich.
———. 1996. *Selected Writings: Volume 1, 1913–1926*. Cambridge, MA: Harvard University Press.
———. 2006. *Selected Writings: Volume 4, 1938–1940*. Cambridge, MA: Harvard University Press.
Bennett, Lance, Regina Lawrence, and Steven Livingston. 2007. *When the Press Fails: Political Power and the News Media from Iraq to Katrina*. Chicago: University of Chicago Press.
Benveniste, Émile. 1966. *Problems in General Linguistics*. Coral Gables: University of Miami Press.
Berger, John. 1982. *Another Way of Telling: A Possible Theory of Photography*. New York: Bloomsbury.
Bersani, Leo. 1984. *A Future for Astyanax: Character and Desire in Literature*. New York: Columbia University Press.
Bishara, Amahl. 2012. *Back Stories: News Production and Palestinian Politics*. Stanford: Stanford University Press.
Blacksin, Isaac. 2022. "Situated and Subjugated: Fixer Knowledge in the Global Newsroom." *Journal of Applied Journalism & Media Studies* 11 (3): 333–354.
Blacksin, Isaac, and Saumava Mitra. 2023. "Straddlers not Spiralists: Critical Questions for Research on Fixers, Local-Foreign News Work, and Cross-Border Journalism." *Journalism*. https://doi.org/10.1177/14648849231183838
Bloom, Paul. 2016. *Against Empathy: The Case for Rational Compassion*. New York: HarperCollins.
Bohannon, John. 2008. "Calculating Iraq's Death Toll: WHO Study Backs Lower Estimate." *Science* 319 (5861): 273.
Boltanski, Luc. 1993. *Distant Suffering*. Cambridge, UK: Cambridge University Press.
Bousquet, Antoine. 2011, September 7. "The Obscure Object That Is Violence." *The Disorder of Things*. https://thedisorderofthings.com/2011/09/07/the-obscure-object-that-is-violence/#more-4133
Bowman, Shayne, and Chris Willis. 2003. "We Media: How Audiences Are Shaping the Future of News and Information." *The Media Center at the American Press Institute*. https://ict4peace.org/wp-content/uploads/2007/05/we_media.pdf
Boyd-Barrett, Oliver. 2019. *Media Imperialism*. London: SAGE.

———. 2021. *Conflict Propaganda in Syria: Narrative Battles.* London: Routledge.

Boyer, Dominic. 2013. *The Life Informatic: Newsmaking in the Digital Era.* Ithaca: Cornell University Press.

Bradley, Mark Philip. 2016. *The World Reimagined: Americans and Human Rights in the Twentieth Century.* Cambridge, UK: Cambridge University Press.

Briggs, Charles. 2002. "Interviewing, Power/Knowledge, and Social Inequality. In *Handbook of Interview Research*, edited by James F. Gubrium and James A. Holstein, 911–922. London: SAGE.

———. 2007a. "Anthropology, Interviewing, and Communicability in Contemporary Society." *Current Anthropology* 48 (4): 551–580.

———. 2007b. "Mediating Infanticide: Theorizing Relations Between Narrative and Violence." *Cultural Anthropology* 22 (3): 315–356.

Briggs, Donald E., Walter C. Soderlund, and Tom Pierre Najem. 2017. *Syria, Press Framing, and the Responsibility to Protect.* Waterloo: Wilfred Laurier University Press.

Brison, Susan J. 2002. *Aftermath: Violence and the Remaking of a Self.* Princeton: Princeton University Press.

Browning, Christopher. 1992. "German Memory, Judicial Interrogation, and Historical Reconstruction: Writing Perpetrator History from Postwar Testimony." In *Probing the Limits of Representation*, edited by Saul Friedlander, 22–36. Cambridge, MA: Harvard University Press.

Buchanan, Marla, and Patrice Keats. 2011. "Coping with Traumatic Stress in Journalism: A Critical Ethnographic Study." *International Journal of Psychology* 46 (2): 127–135.

Burke, Kenneth. 1957. *The Philosophy of Literary Form.* Berkeley: University of California Press.

Burnham, Gilbert, Riyadh Lafta, Shannon Doocy, and Les Roberts. 2006. "Mortality After the 2003 Invasion of Iraq: A Cross-Sectional Cluster Sample Survey." *Lancet* 368 (95450): 1421–1428.

Butler, Judith. 2009. *Frames of War: When Is Life Grievable?* New York: Verso.

Butler, Judith, and Joan Scott. "Introduction." In *Feminists Theorize the Political*, edited by Judith Butler and Joan Scott, xiii–xvii. London: Routledge.

Caillois, Roger. 2003. *The Edge of Surrealism: A Roger Caillois Reader.* Durham: Duke University Press.

Calhoun, Craig. 2010. "The Idea of Emergency: Humanitarian Action and Global (Dis)Order." In *Contemporary States of Emergency: The Politics of Military and Humanitarian Interventions*, edited by Didier Fassin and Mariella Pandolfi, 29–58. New York: Zone Books.

Callimachi, Rukmini. 2015, August 13. "ISIS Enshrines a Theology of Rape." *New York Times.* https://www.nytimes.com/2015/08/14/world/middleeast/isis-enshrines-a-theology-of-rape.html

Campbell, James. 1999. "Combat Gnosticism: The Ideology of First World War Poetry Criticism." *New Literary History* 30 (1): 203–215.

Carey, James. 1986. "The Dark Continent of American Journalism." In *Read-

ing the News: A Pantheon Guide to Popular Culture, edited by Robert Karl Manoff and Michael Schudson, 146–196. New York: Pantheon.

———. 1997. *James Carey: A Critical Reader*. Minneapolis: University of Minnesota Press.

Carruthers, Susan L. 2004. "Tribalism and Tribulation: Media Construction of 'African Savagery' and 'Western Humanitarianism' in the 1990s." In *Reporting War: Journalism in Wartime*, edited by Stuart Allan and Barbie Zelizer, 155–173. New York: Routledge.

———. 2011. *The Media at War: Communication and Conflict in the Twentieth Century*. London: Palgrave Macmillan.

Cavallaro, James, Stephan Sonnenberg, and Sarah Knuckey. 2012. *Living Under Drones: Death, Injury and Trauma to Civilians from US Drone Practices in Pakistan*. Stanford and New York: International Human Rights and Conflict Resolution Clinic, Stanford Law School, and Global Justice Clinic, NYU School of Law.

Chadha, Kalyani, and Michael Koliska. 2014. "Newsrooms and Transparency in the Digital Age." *Journalism Practice* 9 (2): 215–229.

Chakrabarty, Dipesh. 2000. *Provincializing Europe: Postcolonial Thought and Historical Difference*. Princeton: Princeton University Press.

Chomsky, Noam, and Herman Edward. 1988. *Manufacturing Consent: The Political Economy of Mass Media*. New York: Random House.

Chouliaraki, Lillie. 2002. " 'The Contingency of Universality': Some Thoughts on Discourse and Realism." *Social Semiotics* 12 (1): 83–114.

Clark, Wesley K. 2001. *Waging Modern War: Bosnia, Kosovo, and the Future of Combat*. New York: PublicAffairs.

Clifford, James. 1986. "Introduction: Partial Truths." In *Writing Culture: The Poetics and Politics of Ethnography*, edited by James Clifford and George E. Marcus, 1–26. Berkeley and Los Angeles: University of California Press.

———. 1997. *Routes: Travel and Translation in the Late Twentieth Century*. Cambridge, MA: Harvard University Press.

Clifford, James, and George E. Marcus, eds. 1986. *Writing Culture: The Poetics and Politics of Ethnography*. Berkeley and Los Angeles: University of California Press.

Cmiel, Kenneth 1999. "The Emergence of Human Rights Politics in the United States." *Journal of American History* 86 (3): 1231–1250.

Cobley, Evelyn. 1993. *Representing War: Form and Ideology in First World War Narratives*. Toronto: University of Toronto Press.

Cohn, Carol. 1987. "Sex and Death in the Rational World of Defense Intellectuals." *Signs* 12 (4): 687–718.

Coles, Isabel, and Ali Nabhan. 2017, November 12. "Changing of the Guard Resets Cycle of Retribution in Iraq." *Wall Street Journal*. https://www.wsj.com/articles/changing-of-the-guard-resets-cycle-of-retribution-in-iraq-1510488002?mod=Searchresults_pos2&page=1

Coombe, Rosemary. 1998. *The Cultural Life of Intellectual Properties: Authorship, Appropriation, and the Law*. Durham: Duke University Press.

Corbett, Philip B. 2007, October 29. "Talk to the Newsroom: Deputy News Editor Philip B. Corbett." *New York Times.* https://www.nytimes.com/2007/10/29/business/media/29asktheeditors.html

Costera-Meijer, Irena. 2016. "Practicing Audience-Centered Journalism Research." In *The SAGE Handbook of Digital Journalism,* edited by Tamara Witschge, C. W. Anderson, David Domingo, and Alfred Hermida, 546–561. London: SAGE.

Couldry, Nick. 2014. "Life Within the Media Manifold: Between Freedom and Subjugation." In *Politics, Civil Society and Participation: Media and Communications in a Transforming Environment,* edited by Leif Kramp, Nico Carpentier, Andreas Hepp, Richard Kilborn, Risto Kunelius, Hannu Neiminen, Tobias Olsson, Simone Tosoni, Illija Tomanic Trivundza, and Pille Pruulmann-Vengerfeldt, 25–39. Bremen: Edition Lumiere.

Crawford, Neta. 2013. *Accountability for Killing: Moral Responsibility for Collateral Damage in America's Post-9/11 Wars.* Oxford: Oxford University Press.

Cubilié, Anne. 2005. *Women Witnessing Terror: Testimony and the Cultural Politics of Human Rights.* New York: Fordham University Press.

Damon, Arwa. 2021, March 15. "We Tell Syria's Human Stories So That the Victors Don't Write Its History." *CNN.* https://www.cnn.com/2021/03/15/middleeast/syria-anniversary-damon-analysis-intl/index.html

Das, Veena. 2006. *Life and Words: Violence and the Descent into the Ordinary.* Berkeley and Los Angeles: University of California Press.

Das, Veena, and Arthur Kleinman. 2001. "Introduction." In *Remaking a World: Violence, Social Suffering, and Recovery,* edited by Veena Das, Arthur Kleinman, Margaret M. Lock, Mamphela Ramphele, and Pamela Reynolds, 1–30. Berkeley and Los Angeles: University of California Press.

Dawes, James. 2007. *That the World May Know: Bearing Witness to Atrocity.* Cambridge, MA: Harvard University Press.

De Certeau, Michel. 1986. *Heterologies: Discourse on the Other.* Minneapolis: University of Minnesota Press.

De Man, Paul. 1979. *Allegories of Reading: Figural Language in Rousseau, Nietzsche, Rilke, and Proust.* New Haven: Yale University Press.

Der Derian, James. 2001. *Virtuous War: Mapping the Military-Industrial-Media-Entertainment-Network.* London: Routledge.

Desroisieres, Alain. 1998. *The Politics of Large Numbers: A History of Statistical Reasoning.* Cambridge, UK: Cambridge University Press.

Dolar, Mladen. 1998. "Introduction: The Subject Supposed to Enjoy." In *The Sultan's Court: European Fantasies of the East,* by Alain Grosrichard, ix–xxvii. New York and London: Verso.

Douglas, Mary. 1966. *Purity and Danger: An Analysis of Concepts of Pollution and Taboo.* London: Routledge.

Douzinas, Costas. 2000. *The End of Human Rights: Critical Thought at the Turn of the Century.* London: Hart.

Douzinas, Costas, and Conor Gearty. 2014. *The Meaning of Rights: The Phi-*

losophy and Social Theory of Human Rights. Cambridge, UK: Cambridge University Press.

Downie Jr., Leonard, and Michael Schudson. 2009, November/December. "The Reconstruction of American Journalism." *Columbia Journalism Review*. https://archives.cjr.org/reconstruction/the_reconstruction_of_american.php

Dwoeznik, Gretchen. 2007. "Journalism and Trauma: How Reporters and Photographers Make Sense of What They See." *Journalism Studies* 7 (4): 534–553.

Dyer, Richard. 1979. *Stars*. London: British Film Institute.

Eagleton, Terry. 1981. *Walter Benjamin: Or, Towards a Revolutionary Criticism*. New York: Verso.

Editorial Board. 2022, May 19. "The War in Ukraine Is Getting Complicated, and America Isn't Ready." *New York Times*. https://www.nytimes.com/2022/05/19/opinion/america-ukraine-war-support.html

Edwards, Richard. 2003, April 9. "Iraqis Gather at Smoking Ruins of Torture Centre." *Independent*. https://www.independent.co.uk/news/world/middle-east/iraqis-gather-at-smoking-ruins-of-torture-centre-5352893.html

Eggan, Dorothy. 1952. "The Manifest Content of Dreams: A Challenge to Social Science." *American Anthropologist* 54 (4): 469–485.

Eglash, Ruth, Sufian Taha, and Griff Witte. 2014, July 5. "In Jerusalem Neighborhood, an Unlikely Center of Palestinian Grievance." *Washington Post*. https://www.washingtonpost.com/world/protests-over-killing-of-arab-teen-spread-as-reports-emerge-he-was-burned-alive/2014/07/05/e1e165db-121a-4b99-bca6-01eeb8c97fb8_story.html

El-Ghobashy, Tamer, and Maria Abi-Habib. 2015, March 12. "Shiite 'Soldiers of God' Color Tikrit Battle." *Wall Street Journal*. https://www.wsj.com/articles/shiite-soldiers-of-god-color-tikrit-battle-1426204654?mod=Search results_pos2&page=1

El Shakry, Omnia. 2017. *The Arabic Freud: Psychoanalysis and Islam in Modern Egypt*. Princeton: Princeton University Press.

Enda, Jodi. 2011, December/January. "Retreating from the World." *American Journalism Review*. https://ajrarchive.org/article.asp?id=4985

Ensor, Josie. 2016, October 17. "'Isil 'Launches Suicide Attacks' on Kurdish Forces in Mosul as Bloody Battle to Retake Terror Group's Iraq Stronghold Begins." *Telegraph*. https://www.telegraph.co.uk/news/2016/10/17/bloody-battle-to-retake-mosul-begins-as-iraqi-forces-move-to-wip2/

Enzensberger, Hans Magnus. 1974. *The Consciousness Industry: On Literature, Politics and the Media*. New York: Seabury Press.

Erdbrink, Thomas. 2014, June 17. "With War at Doorstep, Iran Sees Its Revolutionary Guards in a Kinder Light." *New York Times*. https://www.nytimes.com/2014/06/18/world/middleeast/with-war-at-doorstep-iran-sees-its-revolutionary-guards-in-a-kinder-light.html

Evans, Gareth. 2008. *The Responsibility to Protect: Ending Mass Atrocity Crimes Once and For All*. Washington, DC: Brookings Institution Press.

Farsetta, Diane. 2008, February 26. "Jousting with the *Lancet*: More Data, More Debate over Iraqi Deaths." *PR Watch*. https://www.prwatch.org/node/7034

Fassin, Didier. 2012. *Humanitarian Reason: A Moral History of the Present.* Berkeley and Los Angeles: University of California Press.

Fassin, Didier, and Mariella Pandolfi. 2010. "Introduction: Military and Humanitarian Government in the Age of Intervention." In *Contemporary States of Emergency: The Politics of Military and Humanitarian Interventions,* edited by Didier Fassin and Mariella Pandolfi, 9–25. New York: Zone Books.

Fassin, Didier, and Richard Rechtman. 2009. *The Empire of Trauma: An Inquiry into the Condition of Victimhood.* Princeton: Princeton University Press.

Fattal, Alexander. 2018. *Guerrilla Marketing: Counterinsurgency and Capitalism in Colombia.* Chicago: University of Chicago Press.

Feldman, Allen. 2015. *Archives of the Insensible: Of War, Photopolitics, and Dead Memory.* Chicago: University of Chicago Press.

———. 2017, October 15. "On War, Photopolitics, White Public-Space and the Body: A Conversation with Allen Feldman." *Naked Punch.* https://www.academia.edu/35537386/On_War_Photopolitics_White_Public_Space_and_the_Body_A_Conversation_with_Allen_Feldman.

Felman, Shoshana. 2002. *The Judicial Unconscious: Trials and Traumas in the Twentieth Century.* Cambridge, MA: Harvard University Press.

Fenrick, W. J. 2001. "Targeting and Proportionality During the NATO Bombing Campaign Against Yugoslavia." *European Journal of International Law* 12 (3): 489–502.

Ferge, Zsuzsa. 1997. "The Changed Welfare Paradigm: The Individualization of the Social." *Social Policy and Administration* 31 (1): 20–44.

Festa, Lynn. 2009. "Sentimental Visions of Empire in Eighteenth-Century Studies." *Literary Compass* 6 (1): 23–55.

Filkins, Dexter. 2008. *The Forever War.* New York: Vintage.

Fiskesjö, Magnus. 2003. *The Thanksgiving Turkey Pardon, the Death of Teddy's Bear, and the Sovereign Exception of Guantanamo.* Chicago: University of Chicago Press.

Foucault, Michel. 1977. *Language, Counter-Memory, Practice: Selected Essays and Interviews.* Ithaca: Cornell University Press.

———. 1982. *The Archeology of Knowledge & The Discourse on Language.* New York: Vintage.

Freud, Sigmund. 1919. *The Complete Works.* London: Hogarth Press.

———. 1939. *Moses and Monotheism.* London: Hogarth Press.

———. 1950. *The Interpretation of Dreams.* New York: Random House.

Fussell, Paul. 1975. *The Great War and Modern Memory.* Oxford: Oxford University Press.

Gall, Carlotta. 2022, June 8. "From the Graveside to the Front, Ukrainians Tell of Grim Endurance." *New York Times.* https://www.nytimes.com/2022/06/08/world/europe/ukraine-war-front-line-trenches.html

Giglio, Mike. 2017, November 2. "BuzzFeed News Investigation Leads to US Admission It Caused Civilian Deaths in Mosul." *BuzzFeed News.* https://www.buzzfeednews.com/article/mikegiglio/the-us-isnt-paying-for-civilian-deaths-in-iraq-even-when-it

Giles, Jim. 2007. "Death Toll in Iraq: Survey Team Takes on Its Critics." *Nature* 446 (7131): 6–7.
George, Susannah. 2017, July 14. "Liberation from Militants Leaves Devastation in Mosul." *Associated Press*. https://apnews.com/article/collapse-of-the-caliphate-islamic-state-group-ap-top-news-middle-east-international-news-727cab6a7e8748dba03dee331c179543
George, Susannah, Qassim Abdul-Zahra, Maggie Michael, and Lori Hinnant. 2017, December 20. "Mosul Is a Graveyard: Final IS Battle Kills 9,000 Civilians." *Associated Press*. https://apnews.com/article/middle-east-only-on-ap-islamic-state-group-bbea7094fb954838a2fdc11278d65460
Gitlin, Todd. 2017, April 10. "As Bombs Rain in Syria, TV Journalists Fall Prey to Shock and Awe." *Columbia Journalism Review*. https://www.cjr.org/politics/syria-bombs-tv-news.php
Gorrell, Henry T. 1944, June 12. "Nazis in Carentan Defy Ultimatum; Americans in Hand-to-Hand Fighting with Germans in Outskirts of French Town." *New York Times*. https://www.nytimes.com/1944/06/12/archives/nazis-in-carentan-defy-ultimatum-americans-in-handtohand-fighting.html?searchResultPosition=1
Gould, Rebecca Ruth. 2023. "Does Defining Racism Help Overcome It?" In *Antisemitism, Islamophobia and the Politics of Definition*, edited by David Feldman and Marc Volovici, 259–280. London: Palgrave Macmillan.
Gramsci, Antonio. 1971. *Selections from the Prison Notebooks*. New York: International Publishers.
Greenburg, Jennifer. 2023. *At War with Women: Military Humanitarianism and Imperial Feminism in an Era of Permanent War*. Ithaca: Cornell University Press.
Gregory, Derek. 2008. "'The Rush to the Intimate': Counterinsurgency and the Cultural Turn." *Radical Philosophy* 150 (July/August): 8–23.
Gregory, Robert H. 2015. *Clean Bombs and Dirty Wars: Air Power in Kosovo and Libya*. Lincoln: Potomac Books.
Grewal, Inderpal. 2005. *Transnational America: Feminisms, Diasporas, Neoliberalisms*. Durham: Duke University Press.
Grusin, Richard. 2010. *Premediation: Affect and Mediality After 9/11*. New York: Palgrave Macmillan.
Guilhot, Nicolas. 2012. "The Anthropologist as Witness: Humanitarianism Between Ethnography and Critique." *Humanity* 3 (1): 81–101.
Gusterson, Hugh. 2017. *Drone: Remote Control Warfare*. Boston: MIT Press.
Hacking, Ian. 1995. *Rewriting the Soul: Multiple Personality and the Sciences of Memory*. Princeton: Princeton University Press.
Hajjar, Lisa. 2012. *Torture: A Sociology of Violence and Human Rights*. London: Routledge.
Hall, Stuart. 1982. "The Rediscovery of 'Ideology': Return of the Repressed in Media Studies." In *Culture, Society and the Media*, edited by Michael Gurevitch, Tony Bennett, James Curran, and Janet Woollacott, 52–86. London: Methuen.

———. 1985. "Signification, Representation, and Ideology: Althusser and the Post-Structuralist Debates." *Critical Studies in Media Communication* 2 (2): 91–114.

———. 1997. "The Spectacle of the 'Other.'" In *Representation: Cultural Representations and Signifying Practices*, edited by Stuart Hall, 223–290. London: Open University Press.

Hall, Stuart, Chas Critcher, Tony Jefferson, John Clarke, and Brian Roberts. 1978. *Policing the Crisis: Mugging, the State, and Law and Order*. London: Palgrave Macmillan.

Hallin, Daniel. 1986. *The Uncensored War: The Media and Vietnam*. Berkeley and Los Angeles: University of California Press.

Hamilton, James T. 2006. *All the News That's Fit to Sell: How the Market Transforms Information into News*. Princeton: Princeton University Press.

Hamilton, John Maxwell. 2009. *Journalism's Roving Eye: A History of American Foreign Reporting*. Baton Rouge: Louisiana State University Press.

Hamilton, John Maxwell, and Eric Jenner. 2004. "Redefining Foreign Correspondence." *Journalism* 5 (3): 301–321.

Hammer, Joshua. 2014, December 11. "As Legacy News Outlets Retreat, Who Will Be There to Report on the World?" *Nieman Reports*. https://niemanreports.org/articles/as-legacy-news-outlets-retreat-who-will-be-there-to-report-on-the-world/

Hammond, Philip. 2004. "Humanizing War: The Balkins and Beyond." In *Reporting War: Journalism in Wartime*, edited by Stuart Allan and Barbie Zelizer, 174–189. London: Routledge.

Haraway, Donna J. 1988. "Situated Knowledges: The Science Question in Feminism and the Privilege of Partial Perspective." *Feminist Studies* 14 (3): 575–599.

———. 2016. *Staying with the Trouble: Making Kin in the Chthulucene*. Durham: Duke University Press.

Hearns-Branaman, Jesse. 2016. *Journalism and the Philosophy of Truth: Beyond Objectivity and Balance*. London: Routledge.

Hedges, Chris 2002. *War Is a Force That Gives Us Meaning*. New York: Anchor.

Hegel, Georg Wilhelm Friedrich. 1956. *The Philosophy of History*. New York: Dover.

Hehir, Aidan. 2012. *The Responsibility to Protect: Rhetoric, Reality, and the Future of Humanitarian Intervention*. New York: Palgrave Macmillan.

Hennessy-Fiske, Molly, and W. J. Hennigan. 2017, May 1. "U.S. Reconsiders Its Responsibility for Civilian Casualties in Iraq and Syria." *Los Angeles Times*. https://www.latimes.com/world/middleeast/la-fg-coalition-air strikes-2017-story.html

Hepp, Andreas, and Nick Couldry. 2009. "What Should Comparative Media Research Be Comparing? Towards a Transcultural Approach to 'Media Cultures.'" In *Internationalizing Media Studies*, edited by Daya Kishan Thussu, 32–47. London: Routledge.

Herman, Judith Lewis. 1992. *Trauma and Recovery: The Aftermath of Violence from Domestic Abuse to Political Terror*. New York: Basic Books.
Herr, Michael. 1977. *Dispatches*. New York: Alfred A. Knopf.
Hillman Foundation. 2018. "2018 Hillman Prize for Magazine Journalism." https://hillmanfoundation.org/hillman-prizes/2018-hillman-prize-magazine-journalism
Hinnebusch, Raymond. 2015. *The International Politics of the Middle East*. Manchester: Manchester University Press.
Hirschkind, Charles, and Saba Mahmood. 2002. "Feminism, the Taliban, and the Politics of Counter-Insurgency." *Anthropological Quarterly* 75 (2): 339–354.
Hollingdale, R. J., ed. 1997. *Nietzsche: Untimely Meditations*. Cambridge, UK: Cambridge University Press.
Hong, Nicole. 2016, March 9. "Jury Finds U.S. Veteran Guilty of Supporting Islamic State." *Wall Street Journal*. https://www.wsj.com/articles/jury-finds-u-s-veteran-guilty-of-supporting-islamic-state-1457554216?mod=Searchresults_pos1&page=1
Hopgood, Stephen. 2013. *The Endtimes of Human Rights*. Ithaca: Cornell University Press.
Hoy, David Couzens, and Thomas McCarthy. 1995. *Critical Theory*. Cambridge, MA: Blackwell.
Hubbard, Ben. 2016, January 4. "Shiite Cleric Gained in Status as a Rivalry Deepened." *New York Times*. https://www.nytimes.com/2016/01/05/world/middleeast/shiite-cleric-gained-in-status-as-a-rivalry-deepened.html
Hubbard, Ben, and Anne Barnard. 2014, January 2. "Deadly Bombing in Beirut Suburb, a Hezbollah Stronghold, Raises Tensions." *New York Times*. https://www.nytimes.com/2014/01/03/world/middleeast/Beirut-Hezbollah-explosion.html
Hubbard, Ben, and Hwaida Saad. 2013, August 15. "Deadly Blast Rocks a Hezbollah Stronghold in Lebanon." *New York Times*. https://www.nytimes.com/2013/08/16/world/middleeast/beirut-bombing.html
Hughes, Chris. 2013, October 4. "Taliban Talks to the Mirror: Chilling Face-to-Face Interview with Terror Commander Qari Nasrullah." *Mirror*. https://www.mirror.co.uk/news/world-news/taliban-chief-qari-nasrullah-interview-2336926
———. 2016, October 17. "ISIS Under Devastating Attack as 'Mother of All Battles' Begins in Iraq City of Mosul." *Mirror*. https://www.mirror.co.uk/news/world-news/isis-under-devastating-attack-mother-9064344
Hüppauf, Bernd. 1993. "Experiences of Modern Warfare and the Crisis of Representation." *New German Critique* 59: 41–76.
Hynes, Samuel. 1997. *The Soldiers' Tale: Bearing Witness to Modern War*. London: Penguin.
Ignatieff, Michael. 1998. *The Warrior's Honor: Ethnic War and the Modern Conscience*. London: Chatto and Windus.
Illich, Ivan. 1978. "Disabling Professions." *India International Center Quarterly* 5 (1): 23–32.

Inglis, Fred. 2002. *People's Witness: The Journalist in Modern Politics*. New Haven: Yale University Press.

Iriye, Akira, Petra Goedde, and William I. Hitchcock. 2012. *The Human Rights Revolution: An International History*. Oxford: Oxford University Press.

Itani, Frances. 1994, February 20. "Zagreb: Building a Wall of Despair." *Ottawa Citizen*. https://www.newspapers.com/newspage/464863991/

James, Larry. 1990, August 17. "In War-Torn Liberia, Orphan Survives Odds." *Washington Post*. https://www.washingtonpost.com/archive/politics/1990/08/17/in-war-torn-liberia-orphan-survives-odds/2266e91d-2879-41c3-a222-99892aac49ed/

Jameson, Fredric. 1979. "Reification and the Utopia in Mass Culture." *Social Text* 1 (1): 130–148.

———. 2013. *The Antinomies of Realism*. London: Verso.

Janssen, Bram, and Lee Keath. 2017, December 4. "Smothered by the Islamic State, an Iraqi Teen Dares to Dream." *Associated Press*. https://apnews.com/article/collapse-of-the-caliphate-islamic-state-group-ap-top-news-middle-east-international-news-245f63bc98a7418e94546284e23b2a1f

Jay, Martin. 1992. "Of Plots, Witnesses, and Judgments." In *Probing the Limits of Representation*, edited by Saul Friedlander, 97–107. Cambridge, MA: Harvard University Press.

Jurkowitz, Mark. 2014, March 26. "What the Digital News Boom Means for Consumers." *Pew Research Center*. https://www.journalism.org/2014/03/26/what-the-digital-news-boom-means-for-consumers/

Kafer, Alison. 2016. "Un/Safe Disclosures: Scenes of Disability and Trauma." *Journal of Literary & Cultural Disability Studies* 10 (2): 1–20.

Kahn, Joseph, and Alison Mitchell. 2015, October 6. "Getting to the Scene, No Matter Where, to Get the Story." *New York Times*. https://www.nytimes.com/2015/10/06/business/media/getting-to-the-scene-no-matter-where-to-get-the-story.html

Kaphle, Anup. 2015, March 2. "The Foreign Desk in Transition." *Columbia Journalism Review*. https://www.cjr.org/analysis/the_foreign_desk_in_transition.php

Kaplan, Fred. 2020. *The Bomb: Presidents, Generals, and the Secret History of Nuclear War*. New York: Simon & Schuster.

Katovsky, Bill, and Timothy Carlson. 2003. *Embedded: The Media at War in Iraq*. Guilford: Lyons Press.

Khan, Azmat. 2022, April 6. "Hidden Pentagon Records Reveal Patterns of Failure in Deadly Airstrikes." *New York Times*. https://www.nytimes.com/spotlight/the-civilian-casualty-files-pentagon-reports?name=styln-civilian-casualties&region=TOP_BANNER&block=storyline_menu_recirc&action=click&pgtype=Article&variant=0_Control

"Kill and Burn." 1902, November 22. *The Great Round World* XX (315): 499–500.

Kingsley, Patrick. 2023, October 25. "Israel's Strikes on Gaza Are Some of the

Most Intense This Century." *New York Times*. https://www.nytimes.com/2023/10/25/world/middleeast/israel-gaza-airstrikes.html

Knightly, Philip. 2013. *The First Casualty: The War Correspondent as Hero and Myth-Maker from Crimea to Iraq*. Baltimore: Johns Hopkins University Press.

Kotišová, Johana. 2023. "The Epistemic Injustice in Conflict Reporting: Reporters and 'Fixers' Covering Ukraine, Israel, and Palestine." *Journalism*. https://doi.org/10.1177/14648849231171019

Kozol, Wendy. 2014. *Distant Wars Visible: The Ambivalence of Witnessing*. Minneapolis: University of Minnesota Press.

Kristeva, Julia. 1982. *Powers of Horror: An Essay on Abjection*. New York: Columbia University Press.

Kumar, Deepa. 2012. *Islamophobia and the Politics of Empire*. Chicago: Haymarket Books.

Kurtz, Howard. 2001, October 31. "CNN Chief Orders 'Balance' in War New." *Washington Post*. https://www.washingtonpost.com/archive/lifestyle/2001/10/31/cnn-chief-orders-balance-in-war-news/0953cacf-77a4-4801-b99b-41a730e43ca7/

Lacey, Marc. 2010, January 30. "In Haiti, a Puzzling Drought of Tears." *New York Times*. https://www.nytimes.com/2010/01/31/weekinreview/31lacey.html

Laclau, Ernesto. 1990. *New Reflections on the Revolution of Our Time*. London: Verso.

Laclau, Ernesto, and Chantal Mouffe. 1985. *Hegemony and Socialist Strategy*. London: Verso.

Landman, Todd, and Anita Gohdres. 2013. "A Matter of Convenience: Challenges of Non-Random Data in Analyzing Human Rights Violations During Conflicts in Peru and Sierra Leone." In *Counting Civilian Casualties: An Introduction to Recording and Estimating Nonmilitary Deaths in Conflict*, edited by Taylor B. Seybolt, Jay D. Aronson, and Baruch Fischhoff, 77–96. Oxford: Oxford University Press.

Leach, Edmund. 1966. "Ritualization in Man in Relation to Conceptual and Social Development." *Philosophical Transactions of the Royal Society* 251 (772): 247–526.

Leonhardt, David. 2020, May 3. "The Morning." *New York Times*. https://messaging-custom-newsletters.nytimes.com/dynamic/render?campaign_id=9&emc=edit_nn_20200503&instance_id=18192&nl=the-morning&productCode=NN&regi_id=63917580&segment_id=26529&te=1&uri=nyt%3A%2F%2Fnewsletter%2F0f6ec8c2-2528-4745-be7d-9e81c656286c&user_id=6087af793751ef0f665e6517c334e8b8

Lepore, Jill. 2019, January 28. "Does Journalism Have a Future?" *New Yorker*. https://www.newyorker.com/magazine/2019/01/28/does-journalism-have-a-future

Lobe, Jim. 2022, April 8. "Networks Covered the War in Ukraine More Than the US Invasion of Iraq." *Responsible Statecraft*. https://responsiblestatecraft

.org/2022/04/08/networks-covered-the-war-in-ukraine-more-than-the-us-invasion-of-iraq/

Loyd, Anthony. 2001. *My War Gone By, I Miss It So*. New York: Penguin.

Lugo-Ocando, Jairo, and An Nguyen. 2017. *Developing News: Global Journalism and the Coverage of "Third World" Development*. London: Routledge.

Luhmann, Niklas. 2000. *The Reality of Mass Media*. Stanford: Stanford University Press.

Lukács, György. 1971. *History and Class Consciousness: Studies in Marxist Dialectics*. London: Merlin Press.

Lynch, Marc. 2005. *Voices of the New Arab Public: Iraq, Al-Jazeera, and Middle East Politics Today*. New York: Columbia University Press

Mabweazara, Hayes Mawindi, ed. 2018. *Newsmaking Cultures in Africa: Normative Trends in the Dynamics of Socio-Political & Economic Struggles*. New York: Palgrave Macmillan.

Mageo, Jeannette Marie. 2003. "Theorizing Dreaming and the Self." In *Dreaming and the Self: New Perspectives on Subjectivity, Identity, and Emotion*, edited by Jeannette Marie Mageo, 3–22. Albany: State University of New York Press.

Mamdani, Mahmood. 2010. "Responsibility to Protect or Right to Punish?" *Journal of Intervention and Statebuilding* 4 (1): 53–67.

Mannoni, Octave. 1969. *Clefs pour L'Imaginaire ou L'Autre Scène*. Paris: Éditions du Seuil.

Marson, James, and Noam Raydan. 2016, November 2. "Russia Says Aleppo Airstrikes to Be Paused Friday to Allow People Out." *Wall Street Journal*. https://www.wsj.com/articles/russia-says-aleppo-airstrikes-to-be-paused-friday-to-allow-people-out-1478080050

Marx, Karl. 1976. *Capital: Volume 1*. London: Penguin.

Masco, Joseph. 2014. *The Theater of Operations: National Security Affect from the Cold War to the War on Terror*. Durham: Duke University Press.

Mattelart, Tristan. 2009. "Globalization Theories and Media Internationalization: A Critical Appraisal." In *Internationalizing Media Studies*, edited by Daya Kishan Thussu, 48–60. London: Routledge.

McAlister, Melani. 2005. *Epic Encounters: Culture, Media, and U.S. Interests in the Middle East Since 1945, updated edition*. Berkeley and Los Angeles: University of California Press.

McComb, Maxwell. 2004. *Setting the Agenda: The Mass Media and Public Opinion*. Cambridge, UK: Polity Press.

McDonell, Nick. 2018. *The Bodies in Person: An Account of Civilian Casualties in American Wars*. New York: Blue Rider Press.

McLaughlin, Greg. 2016. *The War Correspondent*. London: Pluto Press.

Meister, Robert. 2011. *After Evil: The Politics of Human Rights*. New York: Columbia University Press.

———. 2015. "What Comes After Evil?: Beneficiaries as Saviors in a Hu-

manitarian Age." Presentation at the American University of Beirut, December 4, 2015, Beirut, Lebanon.
Merrin, William. 2018. *Digital War: A Critical Introduction*. London: Routledge.
Merry, Sally Engle. 2016. *The Seductions of Quantification: Measuring Human Rights, Gender Violence, and Sex Trafficking*. Princeton: Princeton University Press.
Millar, Alan. 2011. "How Visual Perception Yields Reasons for Belief." *Philosophical Issues* 21 (1): 332–351.
Mittermaier, Amira. 2015. "How to Do Things with Examples: Sufis, Dreams, and Anthropology." *Journal of the Royal Anthropological Institute* 21 (S1): 129–143.
Moaveni, Azadeh. 2015, November 1. "ISIS Women and Enforcers in Syria Recount Collaboration, Anguish and Escape." *New York Times*. https://www.nytimes.com/2015/11/22/world/middleeast/isis-wives-and-enforcers-in-syria-recount-collaboration-anguish-and-escape.html
Morris, Loveday. 2014, June 20. "Iraqi Army Increasingly Bolstered by Shiite Militias as ISIS Advances." *Washington Post*. https://www.washingtonpost.com/world/middle_east/iraqi-army-increasingly-bolstered-by-shiite-militias-as-isis-advances/2014/06/20/0eabaf3a-f8b5-11e3-a606-946fd632f9f1_story.html
Moyn, Samuel. 2010. *The Last Utopia: Human Rights in History*. Cambridge, MA: Harvard University Press.
———. 2021. *Humane: How the United States Abandoned Peace and Reinvented War*. New York: Macmillan.
Muhlmann, Géraldine. 2008. *A Political History of Journalism*. Cambridge, UK: Polity Press.
Murrell, Colleen. 2010. "Baghdad Bureau: An Exploration of the Interconnected World of Fixers and Correspondents at the BBC and CNN." *Media, War & Conflict* 3 (2): 125–137.
———. 2015. *Foreign Correspondents and International Newsgathering: The Role of Fixers*. New York: Routledge.
———. 2018. "The Global Television News Agencies and Their Handling of User Generated Content Video in Syria." *Media, War & Conflict* 11 (3): 289–308.
Myers, Steve. 2011, May 18. "What News Organizations Owe the Fixers They Rely On, Leave Behind in Foreign Countries." *Poynter*. https://www.poynter.org/reporting-editing/2011/what-news-organizations-owe-the-fixers-they-rely-on-leave-behind-in-foreign-countries
Nakhoul, Samia, Michael Georgy, and Stephen Kalin. 2016, October 24. "Battle for Mosul Can Shape or Break Iraq Further." *Reuters*. https://www.reuters.com/article/us-mideast-crisis-iraq-mosul-insight-idUSKCN12N0QL/
Navaro-Yashin, Yael. 2002. *Faces of the State: Secularism and Public Life in Turkey*. Princeton: Princeton University Press.
Nettelfield, Lara J. 2010. *Courting Democracy in Bosnia and Herzegovina:*

The Hague Tribunal's Impact in a Postwar State. Cambridge, UK: Cambridge University Press.

Nixon, Rob. 2011. *Slow Violence and the Environmentalism of the Poor.* Cambridge, MA: Harvard University Press.

Nordland, Rod. 2016, October 16. "Iraqi Forces Attack Mosul, a Beleaguered Stronghold for ISIS." *New York Times.* https://www.nytimes.com/2016/10/17/world/middleeast/in-isis-held-mosul-beheadings-and-hints-of-resistance-as-battle-nears.html

Nyiri, Pál. 2017. *Reporting for China: How Chinese Correspondents Work with the World.* Seattle: University of Washington Press.

Obama, Barack. 2004. *Dreams from My Father: A Story of Race and Inheritance.* New York: Random House.

Obeyesekere, Gananath. 1990. *The Work of Culture: Symbolic Transformation in Psychoanalysis and Anthropology.* Chicago: University of Chicago Press.

Orford, Anne. 2019. "The Passions of Protection: Sovereign Authority and Humanitarian War." In *Militarization: A Reader,* edited by Roberto Gonzales, Hugh Gusterson, and Gustaaf Houtman, 208–211. Durham: Duke University Press.

Otto, Florian, and Christopher O. Meyer. 2012. "Missing the Story? Changes in Foreign News Reporting and Their Implications for Conflict Prevention." *Media, War & Conflict* 5 (3): 205–221.

Owczarski, Wojciech. 2020. "Dreaming 'the Unspeakable'? How Auschwitz Concentration Camp Prisoners Experienced and Understood Their Dreams." *Anthropology of Consciousness* 31 (2): 128–152.

Palmer, Lindsay. 2012. "'iReporting' an Uprising: CNN and Citizen Journalism in Network Culture." *Television & New Media* 14 (5): 367–385.

———. 2018a. *Becoming the Story: War Correspondents Since 9/11.* Champaign: University of Illinois Press.

———. 2018b. ' "Being the Bridge': News Fixers' Perspectives on Cultural Difference in Reporting the 'War on Terror."' *Journalism* 19 (3): 314–332.

Palmer, Lindsay, and Jad Melki. 2018. "Shape Shifting in the Conflict Zone: The Strategic Performance of Gender in War Reporting." *Journalism Studies* 19 (1): 126–142.

Pandolfo, Stefania. 2018. *Knot of the Soul: Madness, Psychoanalysis, Islam.* Chicago: University of Chicago Press.

Parkinson, Joe. 2014, August 18. "'Iraq Crisis" Kurds Push to Take Mosul Dam as U.S. Gains Controversial Guerrilla Ally." *Wall Street Journal.* https://www.wsj.com/articles/kurds-with-u-s-aid-push-to-take-mosul-dam-1408322338?mod=Searchresults_pos8&page=1

Pearl, Daniel, and Robert Block. 2001, November 27. "Despite Tales, the War in Kosovo Was Savage, but It Wasn't Genocide." *Wall Street Journal.* https://www.wsj.com/public/resources/documents/pearl123199.htm

Pedelty, Mark. 1995. *War Stories: The Culture of Foreign Correspondents.* New York: Routledge.

Pendry, Richard. 2015. "Reporter Power: News Organisations, Duty of Care and the Use of Locally-Hired News Gatherers in Syria." *Ethical Space* 12 (2): 4–13.

Perdomo, Gabriela, and Philippe Rodrigues-Rouleau. 2021, February 27. "Transparency as Metajournalistic Performance: *The New York Times*' *Caliphate* Podcast and New Ways to Claim Journalistic Authority." *Journalism*. https://journals.sagepub.com/doi/full/10.1177/1464884921997312

Peterson, Mark Allen. 2001. "Getting the Story: Unwriteable Discourse and Interpretive Practice in American Journalism." *Anthropological Quarterly* 74 (4): 201–211.

Pettegree, Andrew. 2014. *The Invention of News: How the World Came to Know About Itself.* Princeton: Princeton University Press.

Philipps, Dave, and Eric Schmitt. 2021, November 15. "How the U.S. Hid an Airstrike That Killed Dozens of Civilians in Syria." *New York Times.* www.nytimes.com/2021/11/13/us/us-airstrikes-civilian-deaths.html

Phillips, Christopher. 2016. *The Battle for Syria: International Rivalry in the New Middle East.* New Haven: Yale University Press.

Plaut, Shayna, and Peter Klein. 2019. "'Fixing' the Journalist-Fixer Relationship: A Critical Look Towards Developing Best Practices in Global Reporting." *Journalism Studies* 20 (12): 1696–1713.

Poitras, Laura. 2016. *Astro Noise: A Survival Guide for Living Under Total Surveillance.* New York: Whitney Museum of American Art.

Porter, Theodore. 1996. *Trust in Numbers: The Pursuit of Objectivity in Science and Public Life.* Princeton: Princeton University Press.

Puar, Jasbir. 2017. *Terrorist Assemblages: Homonationalism in Queer Times.* Durham: Duke University Press.

Pufahl, Shannon. 2020, April 21. "Numbering the Dead." *New York Review of Books.* https://www.nybooks.com/daily/2020/04/21/numbering-the-dead/

Rabinow, Paul. 1996. *Essays on the Anthropology of Reason.* Princeton: Princeton University Press.

Rajan, V. G. Julie. 2012. *Women Suicide Bombers: Narratives of Violence.* New Brunswick: Routledge.

Ray, Larry. 2020. "Social Theory, Photography and the Visual Aesthetic of Cultural Modernity." *Cultural Sociology* 14 (2): 139–159.

Rentschler, Carrie A. 2009. "Trauma Training and the Reparative Work of Journalism." *Cultural Studies* 24 (4): 447–477.

Reuters. 2022, September 5. "Putin Approves New Foreign Policy Doctrine Based on 'Russian World.'" https://www.reuters.com/world/putin-approves-new-foreign-policy-doctrine-based-russian-world-2022-09-05/

Revkin, Mara Redlich. 2020. "Competitive Governance and Displacement Decisions Under Rebel Rule: Evidence from the Islamic State in Iraq." *Journal of Conflict Resolution* 65 (1): 46–80.

Richardson, Allissa V. 2020. *Bearing Witness While Black: African Americans, Smartphones, and the New Protest #Journalism.* Oxford: Oxford University Press.

Richman, Jackson. 2022, May 11. "Pentagon Spokesman Praises NYT for Pulitzer Win on Coverage of U.S. Military Airstrikes Killing Civilians." *Mediaite*. https://www.mediaite.com/news/pentagon-spokesman-praises-nyt-for-pulitzer-win-on-coverage-of-u-s-military-airstrikes-killing-civilians/

Ritchie, Donald. 2006. *Reporting from Washington: The History of the Washington Press Corps*. Oxford: Oxford University Press.

Robben, Antonius. 1996. "Ethnographic Seduction, Transference, and Resistance in Dialogues About Terror and Violence in Argentina." *Ethos* 24 (1): 71–106.

Robinson, Piers. 2002. *The CNN Effect: The Myth of News, Foreign Policy and Intervention*. London: Routledge.

Robinson, Piers, Peter Goddard, Katy Parry, Craig Murray, and Philip Taylor. 2010. *Pockets of Resistance: British News Media, War, and Theory in the 2003 Invasion of Iraq*. Manchester: Manchester University Press.

Rodgers, James. 2012. *Reporting Conflict*. London: Red Globe Press.

Rogin, Michael. 1987. *Ronald Reagan: The Movie, and Other Episodes in Political Demonology*. Berkeley: University of California Press.

Roper, Caitlin. 2016, August 3. "How One Journalist Uses Social Media to Get Inside the Minds of ISIS." *Wired*. https://www.wired.com/2016/08/rukmini-callimachi-new-york-times-isis/

Ross, John. 2016. *Rebel Reporting*. New York: Hamilton Books.

Rotberg, Robert I., and Thomas G. Weiss, eds. 1996. *From Massacres to Genocide: The Media, Public Policy, and Humanitarian Crisis*. Washington, DC: Brookings Institution Press.

Rothberg, Michael. 2000. *Traumatic Realism: The Demands of Holocaust Representation*. Minneapolis: University of Minnesota Press.

Rubaii, Kali. 2020, February 13. "The Incredible Simplicity of Anti-Imperialism." *Public Anthropologies*. http://www.americananthropologist.org/2020/02/13/the-incredible-simplicity-of-anti-imperialism

Rudoren, Jodi. 2016, July 25. "2 Weeks, 8 Terror Attacks, 247 Victims: How We Learned Their Stories." *New York Times*. https://www.nytimes.com/2016/07/27/insider/terror-attacks-victims-reporting.html

Ruiz, Michelle. 2022, April 26. "How Female Correspondents Are Defining War Coverage in Ukraine." *Vogue*. https://www.vogue.com/article/female-correspondents-war-coverage-ukraine

Rutherford, Danilyn. 2009. "Sympathy, State Building, and the Experience of Empire." *Cultural Anthropology* 24 (1): 1–32.

Said, Edward. 1978. *Orientalism*. New York: Pantheon.

———. 1981. *Covering Islam: How the Media and the Experts Determine How We See the Rest of the World*. New York: Random House.

Santner, Eric L. 1990. *Stranded Objects: Mourning, Memory, and Film in Postwar Germany*. Ithaca: Cornell University Press.

Scales, Robert H. 2006, July. "Clausewitz and World War IV." *Armed Forces Journal*. http://armedforcesjournal.com/clausewitz-and-world-war-iv/

Schechter, Danny. 2003. *Embedded: Weapons of Mass Deception: How the Media Failed to Cover the War in Iraq.* New York: News Dissector.
Schelling, Thomas C. 1961. "Dispersal, Deterrence, and Damage." *Operations Research* 9 (3): 363–370.
Schielke, Samuli, and Mukhtar Saad Shehata. 2021. *Shared Margins: An Ethnography with Writers in Alexandria After the Revolution.* Berlin: De Gruyter.
Schmitt, Carl. [1934] 1985. *Political Theology: Four Chapters on the Concept of Sovereignty.* Chicago: University of Chicago Press.
Scott, James Brown, ed. 1920. *The Proceedings of the Hague Peace Conferences: Translation of the Original Texts.* New York: Oxford University Press.
Scott, James C. 1998. *Seeing Like a State: How Certain Schemes to Improve the Human Condition Have Failed.* New Haven: Yale University Press.
Scott, Wilbur J. 1990. "PTSD in DSM-III: A Case in the Politics of Diagnosis and Disease." *Social Problems* 37 (3): 294–310.
Scranton, Roy. 2015, January 25. "The Trauma Hero: From Wilfred Owen to 'Redevelopment' and 'American Sniper.'" *Los Angeles Review of Books.* https://lareviewofbooks.org/article/trauma-hero-wilfred-owen-redeployment-american-sniper
Searle, Thomas R. 2002. " 'It Made a Lot of Sense to Kill Skilled Workers': The Firebombing of Tokyo in March 1945." *Journal of Military History* 66 (1): 103–133.
Seaton, Jean. 2003. "Understanding not Empathy." In *War and the Media: Reporting Conflict 24/7*, edited by Daya Kishan Thussu and Des Freeman, 45–54. London: SAGE.
Segarra, Lisa Marie. 2017, August 15. "Read the Transcript of President Trump's 'Blame on Both Sides' Comments on Charlottesville." *Time.* https://time.com/4902144/donald-trump-charlottesville-blame-both-sides-kkk-nazi/
Seib, Philip M. 2004. *Beyond the Front Lines: How the News Media Cover a World Shaped by War.* New York: Palgrave Macmillan.
Selden, Mark. 2007. "A Forgotten Holocaust: US Bombing Strategy, the Destruction of Japanese Cities & the American Way of War from World War II to Iraq." *Asia-Pacific Journal* 5 (5). https://apjjf.org/-Mark-Selden/2414/article.html
Seybolt, Taylor B., Jay D. Aronson, and Baruch Fischhoff. 2013. "Introduction." In *Counting Civilian Casualties: An Introduction to Recording and Estimating Nonmilitary Deaths in Conflict*, edited by Taylor B. Seybolt, Jay D. Aronson, and Baruch Fischhoff, 3–14. Oxford: Oxford University Press.
Shadid, Anthony. 2009, December 24. "In Thuluyah, Reverberations of a U.S. Raid 2003 Foray Set Off a Series of Unfortunate Events that Still Haunt Iraq Town." *Washington Post.* Available at https://www.pulitzer.org/winners/anthony-shadid-0
Shaw, Martin. 1996. *Civil Society and Media in Global Crisis: Representing Distant Violence.* London: Pinter.

Shklar, Judith. 1984. *Ordinary Vices*. Cambridge, MA: Harvard University Press.

Siegal, Allan M., and William G. Connolly. 2015. *The New York Times Manual of Style and Usage*, revised and expanded edition. New York: Three Rivers Press.

Sigal, Leon V. 1973. *Reporters and Officials: The Organization and Politics of Newsmaking*. New York: DC Heath.

Silverstein, Michael, and Greg Urban. 1996. *Natural Histories of Discourse*. Chicago: University of Chicago Press.

Sirri, Omar. 2021. "Destructive Creations: Social-Spatial Transformations in Contemporary Baghdad." *LSE Middle East Centre Paper Series* 45 (February): 1–32.

Slaughter, Joseph. 2007. *Human Rights, Inc.: The World Novel, Narrative Form, and International Law*. New York: Fordham University Press.

Sloboda, John J., John Dougherty, and Hamit Dardagan. 2013. "How Accurate Is IBC?" In *Iraq Body Count: The State of Knowledge on Civilian Casualties in Iraq: Counts, Estimates, and Government Responsibility*. Presentation at the United States Institute of Peace, January 10, 2007, Washington, DC. https://www.iraqbodycount.org/analysis/beyond/state-of-knowledge/7

Solomon, Ben C. 2017, June 20. "Journalist's Notebook: Into the Battle of Mosul, Armed with a Camera." *New York Times*. https://www.nytimes.com/2017/06/20/insider/journalists-notebook-into-the-battle-of-mosul-armed-with-a-camera.html

Solomon, Erika, and Asser Khattab. 2018, February 2. "Ambulances Roam Eastern Ghouta for the Next Victims in Syrian War." *Financial Times*. https://www.ft.com/content/482c20f8-17c6-11e8-9e9c-25c814761640

Spagat, Michael, Andrew Mack, Tara Cooper, and Joakim Kreutz. 2009. "Estimating War Deaths: An Arena of Contestation." *Journal of Conflict Resolution* 53 (6): 934–950.

Spurr, David. 1993. *The Rhetoric of Empire: Colonial Discourse in Journalism, Travel Writing, and Imperial Administration*. Durham: Duke University Press.

Stam, Robert. 1992. "Mobilizing Fictions: The Gulf War, the Media, and the Recruitment of the Spectator." *Public Culture* 4 (2): 101–126.

Stewart, Kathleen. 1996. *A Space on the Side of the Road*. Princeton: Princeton University Press.

Stone, Nomi. 2018. "Imperial Mimesis: Enacting and Policing Empathy in US Military Training." *American Ethnologist* 45 (4): 533–545.

Streit, Clarence K. 1937. "The Problem of False News." In *Interpretations of Journalism: A Book of Readings*, edited by Frank Luther Mott and Ralph D. Casey, 65–87. New York: F. S. Crofts and Co.

Tabeau, Ewa, and Jakub Bijak. 2005. "War-Related Deaths in the 1992–1995 Armed Conflicts in Bosnia and Herzegovina: A Critique of Previous Estimates and Recent Results." *European Journal of Population* 21 (2/3): 187–215.

Tanaka, Yuki. 2009. "Introduction." In *Bombing Civilians: A Twentieth-Century History*, edited by Yuki Tanaka and Marilyn B. Young, 1–7. New York: W.W. Norton.

Taussig, Michael. 1992. *The Nervous System*. New York: Routledge.

———. 1993. *Mimesis and Alterity: A Particular History of the Senses*. London: Routledge.

Tedlock, Barbara. 1992. "Dreaming and Dream Research." In *Dreaming: Anthropological and Psychological Interpretations.*, edited by Barbara Tedlock, 1–30. Santa Fe: School of American Research Press.

Thépaut, Charles. 2022. *A Vanishing West in the Middle East: The Recent History of U.S.–Europe Cooperation in the Region*. London: Bloomsbury Academic.

Thompson, John B. 1995. *The Media and Modernity: A Social Theory of the Media*. Cambridge, UK: Polity Press.

Tifft, Susan E., and Alex S. Jones. 2000. *The Trust: The Private and Powerful Family Behind The New York Times*. New York: Back Bay Books.

Torfing, Jacob. 1998. *New Theories of Discourse: Laclau, Mouffe, and Zizek*. Cambridge, MA: Blackwell.

Townsend, Stephen J. 2017a. "Department of Defense Briefing by Gen. Townsend via Telephone from Baghdad, Iraq." *US Department of Defense*. https://www.defense.gov/News/Transcripts/Transcript/Article/1133033/department-of-defense-briefing-by-gen-townsend-via-telephone-from-baghdad-iraq/

———. 2017b, September 15. "Reports of Civilian Casualties in the War Against ISIS Are Vastly Inflated." *Foreign Policy*. https://foreignpolicy.com/2017/09/15/reports-of-civilian-casualties-from-coalition-strikes-on-isis-are-vastly-inflated-lt-gen-townsend-cjtf-oir/

Traboulsi, Fawwaz. 2012. *A History of Modern Lebanon*. London: Pluto Press.

Tumber, Howard, and Jerry Palmer. 2004. *The Media at War: The Iraq Crisis*. London: SAGE.

Tumber, Howard, and Frank Webster. 2006. *Journalists Under Fire: Information War and Journalistic Practices*. London: SAGE.

Turse, Nick. 2013. *Kill Anything That Moves: The Real American War in Vietnam*. New York: Picador.

US Air Force. 2006. "Targeting: Air Force Doctrine Document 2–1.9." Washington, DC: Secretary of the US Air Force. https://apps.dtic.mil/sti/citations/ADA454614

US Department of Defense. 2005, March. "The National Defense Strategy of the United States of America." Washington, DC: Secretary of the Department of Defense. https://www.hsdl.org/c/view?docid=452255

———. 2016. "Department of Defense Law of War Manual." Washington, DC:

Office of General Counsel of Department of Defense. https://dod.defense.gov/Portals/1/Documents/pubs/DoD%20Law%20of%20War%20Manual%20-%20June%202015%20Updated%20Dec%202016.pdf

———. 2020, May 1. "Annual Report on Civilian Casualties in Connection with United States Military Operations in 2019." Washington, DC: US Department of Defense. https://media.defense.gov/2020/May/06/2002295555/-1/-1/1/sec-1057-civilian-casualties-may-1-2020.PDF

Van Dijk, Tuen. 1988. *News as Discourse*. London: Routledge.

Van Hout, Tom, and Geert Jacobs. 2008. "News Production Theory and Practice: Fieldwork Notes on Power, Interaction and Agency." *Pragmatics* 18 (1): 59–85.

Varma, Anita. 2020. "Evoking Empathy or Enacting Solidarity with Marginalized Communities? A Case Study of Journalistic Humanizing Techniques in the *San Francisco Homeless Project*." *Journalism Studies* 21 (12): 1705–1723.

Vázquez, Rolando. 2011. "Translation as Erasure: Thoughts on Modernity's Epistemic Violence." *Journal of Historical Sociology* 24 (1): 27–44.

Verini, James. 2017, July 19. "The Living and the Dead." *New York Times Magazine*. https://www.nytimes.com/interactive/2017/07/19/magazine/mosul-battle-against-isis.html

Virilio, Paul. 2002. *Desert Screen*. London: Continuum.

Vitoria, Francisco de. 1991. *Political Writings*. Cambridge, UK: Cambridge University Press.

Von der Lippe, Berit, and Rune Ottosen. 2016. *Gendering War and Peace Reporting: Some Insights, Some Missing Links*. Gothenburg: Nordicom.

Wahl, Paul, and Don Toppel. 1971. *The Gatling Gun*. New York: Arco.

Waisbord, Silvio. 2013. *Reinventing Professionalism: Journalism and News in Global Perspective*. Cambridge, UK: Polity Press.

Warner, Michael. 2002. *Publics and Counterpublics*. New York: Zone Books.

Weber, Max. 1949. *The Methodology of the Social Sciences*. New York: Free Press.

———. [1930] 2013. *The Protestant Ethic and the Spirit of Capitalism*. New York: Routledge.

Wedeman, Ben. 2016, August 25. "Will ISIS Be Pushed Easily from Mosul After 'Mother of All Battles'?" *CNN*. https://www.cnn.com/2016/07/11/middleeast/iraq-mosul-isis-conflict-explainer/index.html

Weizman, Eyal. 2011. *The Least of All Possible Evils: Humanitarian Violence from Arendt to Gaza*. London: Verso.

Wheeler, Nicholas J. 2000. *Saving Strangers: Humanitarian Intervention in International Society*. Oxford: Oxford University Press.

White, Hayden. 1978. *Tropics of Discourse: Essays in Cultural Criticism*. Baltimore: Johns Hopkins University Press.

———. 1980. "The Value of Narrativity in the Representation of Reality." *Critical Inquiry* 7 (1): 5–27.

———. 1987. *The Content of the Form: Narrative Discourse and Historical Representation*. Baltimore: Johns Hopkins University Press.

———. 1990. *The Content of the Form*. Baltimore: Johns Hopkins University Press.

———. 1999. *Figural Realism: Studies in the Mimesis Effect*. Baltimore: Johns Hopkins University Press.

———. 2009. "The Aim of Interpretation Is to Create Perplexity in the Face of the Real: Hayden White in Conversation with Erlend Rogne." *History and Theory* 48 (1): 63–75.

Whitman, Walt. [1855] 1995. *Specimen Days*. New York: Dover.

Wieviorka, Annette. 2006. *The Era of the Witness*. Ithaca: Cornell University Press.

Wiggins, Chris, and Matthew L. Jones. 2023. *How Data Happened: A History from the Age of Reason to the Age of Algorithms*. New York: W.W. Norton.

Williams, Raymond. 1974. *Television: Technology and Cultural Form*. London: Fontana.

Winston, Brian, and Matthew Winston. 2021. *The Roots of Fake News: Objecting to Objective Journalism*. New York: Routledge.

Wright, Katie, Martin Scott, and Mel Bruce. 2020. "Soft Power, Hard News: How Journalists at State-Funded Transnational Media Legitimize Their Work." *International Journal of Press/Politics* 25 (4): 607–631.

Zaller, John, and Dennis Chiu. 1996. "Government's Little Helper: U.S. Press Coverage of Foreign Policy Crises, 1945–1991." *Political Communication* 13: 385–405.

Zelizer, Barbie. 1990. "Where Is the Author in American TV News? On the Construction and Presentation of Proximity, Authorship, and Journalistic Authority." *Semiotica* 80 (1–2): 37–48.

———. 2004. *Taking Journalism Seriously: News and the Academy*. New York: SAGE.

———. 2007. "On 'Having Been There': 'Eyewitnessing' as a Journalistic Key Word." *Critical Studies in Media Communication* 24 (5): 408–428.

———. 2018. "Cold War Redux and the News: Islamic State and the US Through Each Other's Eyes." *Critical Studies in Media Communication* 35 (1): 8–23.

Zhang, Shixin Ivy. 2016. *Chinese War Correspondents: Covering Wars and Conflicts in the Twenty-First Century*. New York: Palgrave Macmillan.

Zucchino, David. 2017, February 14. "In Eastern Mosul, Liberated From ISIS, Battle Rages 'Day and Night.'" *New York Times*. https://www.nytimes.com/2017/02/14/world/middleeast/isis-battle-for-mosul.html

INDEX

abjection, 161, 196, 197, 207–8
Abu El-Haj, Nadia, 274–75n14
Abu Ghraib prison, 211
access to sources, 192–93
Adorno, Theodor, 227
advertising, 139, 140
Afghanistan, xii, 8, 52, 63, 66, 137, 234
air war, 109, 110, 137, 174, 177
Airwars, 66
Aleppo, Syria, x, 69, 145, 177, 178
Al Jazeera, 236, 266n25
Allan, Stuart, 202–3
Alloula, Malek, 276n22
al-Qaeda, 53, 104
Althusser, Louis, 15, 86
Amal (Shia political party), 54
Ananny, Mike, 260–61n5
Anglo-Zulu War (1879), 125
Ankawa (neighborhood), 135
Aqrab ("Scorpion") checkpoint, 101, 102
Arab Spring, 25
Arkady, Ali, 38–44, 229
Asad, Talal, 98, 121
Assad, Bashar al-, 145

Associated Press, 97, 106–7, 121
Auerbach, Erich, 34
Augustine of Hippo, Saint, 121
Austin, J. L., 36, 195
Austin, Lloyd, 238
Australia, 11

Baath Party, 135
Baghdad, x–xi, 57
Baghdadi, Abu Bakr al-, 128
Baghuz, Syria, 208–12
Bargu, Banu, 50, 190
Barnard, Anne, 262–63n12
Barthes, Roland, 278n8
Baudelaire, Charles, 120
Baudrillard, Jean, 2–3
Bauman, Zygmunt, 47–48, 49
bearing witness, 202–7
Beirut, 18, 32, 53–54, 56–57
Belgium, 11
Benjamin, Walter, 7, 52, 157, 224–25, 273–74n9
Benveniste, Émile, 75
Bersani, Leo, 33
Biden, Joe, 52, 238
"blank stare," 193–96, 200–201, 229

307

Index

Borges, Jorge Luis, 208
Boshin War (1868–69), 125
Bosnia, 72, 255n7
Boyd-Barrett, Oliver, 269n8
Briggs, Charles, 186, 189, 251n5, 271n18
Brokaw, Tom, 184
Browning, Christopher, 203
Burke, Edmund, 141
Bush, George W., 114
Butler, Judith, 225
bylines, 18–19, 32, 73–78, 83–85, 170

Caillois, Roger, 228
Calhoun, Craig, 122
Canada, 11
Carey, James, 94, 141, 142
Carruthers, Susan, 269n6
casualty counts, 18, 32, 60–72, 151, 165, 182
Certeau, Michel de, 144
checkpoints, 101–2
chemical warfare, 94, 173
China, 230
Chomsky, Noam, 178
Christianity, 121
Churchill, Winston, 278–79n11
Civil War, US, 125, 254n3
Clark, Wesley, 29, 52
Classy Hotel (Erbil), 1–4, 21, 22–23
Clifford, James, 227, 233
Cmiel, Kenneth, 130
"CNN effect," 122–23, 247n5
Cobley, Evelyn, 31, 113
Cohn, Carol, 48
colonialism, 122
Colvin, Marie, 169, 201, 216, 255–56n8
Committee to Protect Journalists, 66
commodity fetishism, 162
confirmation bias, 203
Conrad, Joseph, 113
Corbett, Philip B., 253n13
counterinsurgency, 48
Crimean War, 172

Crozier, William, 268n4
Crusades, 121
cyber warfare, 230

Dahiyeh (Beirut suburb), 53–59
Damon, Arwa, 247n5
datelines, 76–78
death tolls, 18, 32, 66–70, 72
de Man, Paul, 195
Denmark, 11
Diagnostic and Statistical Manual of Mental Disorders (DSM-III, 1980), 173
di Giovanni, Janine, 126–27
disinformation, 12, 14, 15, 16, 181, 227
Dolar, Mladen, 181
Douzinas, Costas, 98
dreams, 157–58, 160, 177–78, 182–83, 229
Dresden, 110
drones, 52, 94, 124, 137, 230–31

East Aleppo, Syria, 145, 177
Edward, Herman, 178
Eliot, George, 270n10
embedding, 192
Emergency Response Division (ERD), 38–40, 43
empathy, 129–33
enemy combatants, 50
epigenetics, 198
Erbil, Iraq, x–xii, 90
estimation, of war deaths, 66, 67
event data, 66

fact checking, 227
Fadel, Leila, 259–60n2
"fake news," 12, 14, 15, 16, 181, 227
fantasy, 181–83
Fassin, Didier, 96, 98, 173, 175, 198
Fattal, Alex, 275n18
Feldman, Allen, 47, 167, 168, 178, 228
Ferge, Zsuzsa, 259–60n2

Festa, Lynn, 131
First World War, 172
fixers, 18–19, 78–85, 126, 229
Foley, James, 104, 169, 201
foreign bureaus, 13
foreign correspondents, 13, 14, 33
Foucault, Michel, 29, 31, 32, 58, 73, 74, 87
France, 11, 69
Franken, Al, 190
Freedom of Information Act (FOIA, 1967), 119, 213
freelancers, 9, 14, 101, 206
Free Syrian Army, 11
Freud, Sigmund, 159–60, 166, 168
frontlines, 191–92, 237
Fussell, Paul, 172

Gatling, Richard, 125
Gatling gun, 125
Gaza, xii, 57, 270n13
Geneva Conventions, 50
genocide, 46, 48, 65, 234
Germany, 11
Ghouta, Syria, 145, 177
Gitlin, Todd, 36
giving voice, 197–202
Goethe, Johann von, 1
Gould, Ruth, 251–52n8
Gramsci, Antonio, 15, 29–30
Great Britain, 69
Greenburg, Jennifer, 269n8
Grusin, Richard, 260–61n5
Guilhot, Nicolas, 131, 205
Gulf War (1991), 52, 234
Gutenberg, Johannes, 254n1

Haditha massacre (2005), 206
Halilovic, Sefer, 255n7
Hall, Stuart, 15, 59, 110, 158, 166, 172, 185; closures viewed by, 86, 224; common sense viewed by, 30; journalism viewed by, 6, 32, 44–45, 142, 148, 150
Hallin, Daniel, 140, 141

Hama, Syria, x
Hamas, 54
Haraway, Donna, 83, 160
Hearns-Branaman, Jesse, 132
Heart of Darkness (Conrad), 113
Hedges, Chris, 94
Hegel, Georg Wilhelm Friedrich, 140–41, 180
Hellfire missile, 124
Herr, Michael, 159
Hezbollah, 18, 53–56
Holbrooke, Richard, 255n7
Holocaust, 173, 203, 254–55n5, 275n15
Homs, Syria, x
Hopgood, Stephen, 96, 97
human interest stories, 143
humanism, 121
human rights, 38, 43, 97, 186
Hüppauf, Bernd, 278n10
Hurley, Frank, 278n10
Hussein, Saddam, 37, 234
Hynes, Samuel, 275n15

Idlib, Syria, 145
Illich, Ivan, 148
incident reporting, 66–67
Independent (newspaper), 49–50
insurgency, 48, 49
International Commission on Intervention and State Sovereignty, 100
International Criminal Court (ICC), 234
International Crisis Group, 66
international law, 50
International Peace Research Institute, 66
interviews, 185–91
Iran, x, 11
Iraq, 8, 19; casualty counts in, 61–62, 66, 67, 72, 151; US invasion of, x–xi, 11, 12, 67, 116, 122. *See also* Islamic State (ISIS); Mosul, Iraq

Iraq Family Health Survey, 67
Iraqi Special Operations Forces (ISOF), 40, 43
Islamic State (ISIS), x–xi, xii, 2, 43, 45–46, 50, 116–17, 119, 135–36; in battle for Mosul, 38–39, 97, 113, 114, 138, 208; Dahiyeh targeted by, 54; Mosulawis' links to, 115; rise of, 11–12, 122
Israel, xii, 53, 54, 199, 230, 270n13
Italy, 11
Izetbegivic, Alija, 255n7

Jabhat al-Nusra, 11
Jackson, Andrew, 264n19
Jameson, Fredric, 35, 167, 275–76n20
Jay, Martin, 203
Jordan, 11
journalistic realism, 32, 33–38
journalistic unconscious, 159, 161–62, 172, 188
Junger, Sebastian, 24

Kasaabeh, Muath al-, 104
Kirby, John, 267n35
knowledge stock, 150
Kobani, Syria, 145
Kosovo War, 52, 63, 110, 116, 123, 252n9, 269n8
Kozol, Wendy, 269n8, 269–70n9
Kristeva, Julia, 161, 196
Kurds, 11, 40, 135, 208

Lacan, Jacques, 182
Laclau, Ernesto, 220
Lea, Thomas, 277n6
Leach, Edmund, 60, 86
Lebanon, 8, 11, 12, 46–47, 208
legibility, 32–33, 35, 82, 84
Lepore, Jill, 139
"liberation," 106, 178
Libya, 110, 116
Luhmann, Niklas, 15
Lukács, György, 88

Mamdani, Mahmoud, 46, 48, 100
Mannoni, Octave, 275n17
martyrdom, 189–90
Marx, Karl, 162
Masco, Joseph, 132, 261n7
McAlister, Melani, 17, 260n3
McComb, Maxwell, 261n8
Meister, Robert, 97, 98
Merrin, William, 63, 268–69n5
militarized humanitarianism, 97, 139, 143, 150, 225, 236; as doctrine for the powerful, 100, 112; liberal worldview linked to, 96; rationale for, 108, 120, 133, 136, 144; war reporting shaped by, 100–101, 132, 230
militias, 49, 69
Milley, Mark, 272n24
Milošević, Slobodan, 234, 265n22
Mimesis (Auerbach), 34
Mouffe, Chantal, 220
Morocco, 11
Mosul, Iraq, x, 11, 19; battle for, 38–39, 44, 93–95, 97, 101–14, 116, 118, 121, 137–38, 145, 146, 147, 151, 170–71, 177, 178; civilian deaths in, 42, 106–20, 137–38; civilians displaced from, 126–27, 135
Moyn, Samuel, 96, 123
Muhlmann, Géraldine, 146, 191
Muir, Jim, 216
My Lai massacre (1968), 211

naming, 44–52, 230, 234; of military operations, 262n11
NATO (North Atlantic Treaty Organization), 110, 230
Navaro-Yashin, Yael, 179
Netherlands, 11
New York Times, 53, 55, 117–18, 188–89; awards to, 97, 109, 260n4, 267n33, 282n6; datelines of, 77; Gaza coverage by, 245–46n3; as paper of record, 15;

stylistic conventions of, 29, 86, 87, 104, 190, 277n4, 256n12;
Ukraine coverage of, 237, 238
New Zealand, 11
Nietzsche, Friedrich, 121
9/11 attacks, 55
non-combatant casualty cutoff value (NCCV, NCV), 136–37
Noriega, Manuel, 234
notepads, 187–88, 229
nuclear weapons, 235, 264n20, 269n6

Obama, Barack, 11, 114, 124, 197
Obeyesekere, Gananath, 160
objectivity, x, 4, 19, 60–61, 74, 88, 114, 139–47, 163
Operation Rolling Thunder, 110
Operation Speedy Express, 110
Orford, Anne, 100
Ottoman Empire, 61
Owczarski, Wojciech, 160
Owen, Wilfred, 223

Palestine, 199
Pandolfi, Mariella, 98
Pandolfo, Stefania, 272–73n3
Pauly, John, 177–78
Pedelty, Mark, 164
Perdomo, Gabriela, 280n2
Peshmerga, 40
Peterson, Mark Alan, 276n21
Pettegree, Andrew, 61, 257n15
proportionality, 68, 108, 112, 117–18, 137
psychoanalysis, 161, 170–76
PTSD (post-traumatic stress disorder), 172
Pufahl, Shannon, 254n3
Pulitzer Prize, 97
Putin, Vladimir, 234, 238

Qaddafi, Muammar, 234, 265n22

R9X weapon, 125
Rabinow, Paul, 182

Raqqa, Syria, x, 145, 146, 208
Rechtman, Richard, 173, 175, 198
reflexive turn, in anthropology, 163
refugees, 200
responsibility to protect (R2P), 100, 235
Reuters, 102
Richardson, Allissa, 279n13
Rilke, Rainer Maria, 195
Rodgers, James, 192
Rodrigues-Rouleau, Philippe, 280n2
Rothberg, Michael, 227
Rumsfeld, Donald, 254n2, 264n19
Rusell, William Howard, 274n12
Russia, 11, 69, 145, 233–39

Said, Edward, 8, 10, 17
sanctions, 52
Santner, Eric, 194, 195
Saudi Arabia, 11
Scales, Robert, 131
Schelling, Thomas, 265–66n24
Schmitt, Carl, 112
science, 142
Scoop (Waugh), 25
"Scorpion" (Aqrab) checkpoint, 101
Scott, Joan, 225
Scott, Wilbur, 274n13
Scranton, Roy, 172–73
Scrocca, Joseph, 107
search engine optimization (SEO), 252–53n11
Second World War, x, 110
sectarianism, 11, 39, 43, 53–55, 56, 58
September 11 attacks, 55
Shadid, Anthony, 79, 187, 280n3
Shakespeare, William, 233
Shia, 39, 53
sieges, 145–47, 151
Silajdzic, Haris, 255n7
situated knowledge, 83
Smith, Adam, 270n10
Spain, 11
Stam, Robert, 246n3, 259n24

standardization, of language, 30
statehood, 50
Stewart, Kathleen, 167
"strongholds," 18, 32, 53–59
style manuals, 18, 29, 30, 49, 86–87
suicide bombings, 94, 134, 170, 190
Sullivan, Jake, xii, 264n18
Sunnis, 11, 39, 105
surveillance, 137, 231
Sylvia, Brett, 38–39
Syria, x–xi, 8, 11–12, 13, 127–28; civil war in, 19, 52, 53, 55, 64, 170, 177, 208; death toll in, 18, 32, 66, 68–70, 72; sieges by, 145
Syrian Human Rights Committee, 70
Syrian Network for Human Rights, 66
Syrian Observatory for Human Rights (SOHR), 69–72

Taliban, 52, 63, 66
Talon Anvil (special operations force), 210
Tao Yuanming, ix
Taussig, Michael, 159, 225
Teachers Club (restaurant), 133–35
technology, in news coverage, 12–13
terminology, 44–52, 230, 234; for military operations, 262n11
terrorism, 49–51, 56; War on, xi, xii, 43, 50, 51, 110, 115, 123, 234, 239
third-person narrative, 73, 75
Thirty Years War, 61
Thompson, John B., 261n8
"thousand-yard stare," 175, 277n6
Tice, Austin, 255–56n8
Tokyo, 110, 116
torture, 38–39, 40, 44, 123
Townsend, Stephen, 107–8
trauma, 170–76, 196–200, 205, 230
Truman, Harry, 264n20
Trump, Donald, 51
Turkey, 11
Twitter, 12

Ukraine, xii, 8, 21, 233–38
United Arab Emirates, 11
United Kingdom, 11
United Nations High Commissioner for Human Rights (UNHCR), 66, 68–69

Valéry, Paul, 93
Van Dijk, Tuen, 75, 77, 150
Veale, Thomas, 111–12
victimhood, 65, 113, 129, 130–31, 139
Vietnam War, 39, 109, 110, 116, 121, 146, 172, 275n19
Violations Documentation Center, 70
Virilio, Paul, 3, 8
Vitoria, Francisco de, 265n23
voice-giving, 197–202

Wall Street Journal, 145, 190, 276–77nn3–5
War (Junger), 24
war crimes, 52, 110, 112, 210–11, 234
War on Terror, xi, xii, 43, 50, 51, 110, 115, 123, 234, 239
Washington Post, 67, 190, 209
Waugh, Evelyn, 25
Weber, Max, 261n8, 271n18
Weizman, Eyal, 99, 137
White, Hayden, 5, 140, 180, 204; historiography viewed by, 87; interpretation viewed by, 226; on moral authority of narrative, 7, 149, 180; story form viewed by, 179, 203; war reportage and realism linked by, 34, 88, 151–52
Whitman, Walt, 159
Wieviorka, Annette, 279n14
Williams, Raymond, 13
witnessing, 202–7
World Health Organization, 66

Yazidis, 157–58
yellow journalism, 139–41, 144, 229
Young, S. B. M., 264n17
Yugoslavia, 110

Zelensky, Volodymyr, 237
Zelizer, Barbie, 13, 77, 202–3, 262–63n12
Zhang, Shixin Ivy, 248n10

Printed in the USA
CPSIA information can be obtained
at www.ICGtesting.com
JSHW022333110524
62910JS00002B/4

9 781503 639447